THIS LAND IS HERLAND

Women and the American West

RENÉE M. LAEGREID, Series Editor

This Land Is Herland: Gendered Activism in Oklahoma from the 1870s to the 2010s centers Indigenous, Black, and white women whose activism shaped Oklahoma geographically, culturally, politically, and economically and whose activism was shaped in the context of Oklahoma's settler colonial history.

We recognize that the state of Oklahoma exists as a direct result of the systematic dispossession of Indigenous homelands. The Wichitas and Caddos, and then the Apaches, Comanches, Kiowas, and Osages, called this land home long before the arrival of Europeans. Dozens of other tribal nations—forcibly removed from their ancestral homelands on "trails of tears" as part of the United States' devastating Indian Removal Act—rebuilt their nations in this place, the newly designated "Indian Territory."

Today, 39 tribal nations persist as distinct political and cultural entities in what is now Oklahoma, and their identities and cultures are inextricably linked to this land.

We acknowledge the role of settler colonial dispossession in the history of Oklahoma, and we honor the contributions and cultures of the original Indigenous nations of this land and the Indigenous nations who came to this land through forced removal, and we recognize and honor their status as sovereigns today and support their continued exercise of tribal sovereignty.

THIS LAND IS HERLAND
Gendered Activism in Oklahoma
from the 1870s to the 2010s

Edited by
SARAH EPPLER JANDA and PATRICIA LOUGHLIN

Foreword by RENÉE M. LAEGREID

UNIVERSITY OF OKLAHOMA PRESS : NORMAN

This book is published with the generous assistance of the Oklahoma Historical Society, the Cherokee Strip Regional Heritage Center, Oklahoma Humanities, the National Endowment for the Humanities, and the Wallace C. Thompson Fund of the University of Oklahoma Foundation.

Portions of the following chapters were previously published in a form since revised. Chapter 7: Cheryl Elizabeth Brown Wattley, *A Step toward* Brown v. Board of Education*: Ada Lois Sipuel Fisher and Her Fight to End Segregation* (Norman: University of Oklahoma Press, 2014). Chapter 8: Rachel E. Watson, "An Unflinching Call for Freedom: Clara Luper's Pedagogy at the Center of Sit-Ins," *Chronicles of Oklahoma* 97, no. 3 (Fall 2019): 278–95. Chapter 10: Amanda Cobb-Greetham, "Powerful Medicine: The Rhetoric of Comanche Activist LaDonna Harris," *Studies in American Indian Literatures*, ser. 2, 18, no. 4 (Winter 2006): 63–87.

Library of Congress Cataloging-in-Publication Data

Names: Janda, Sarah Eppler, editor. | Loughlin, Patricia, 1971– editor. |
    Laegreid, Renee M., writer of foreword.
Title: This land is herland : gendered activism in Oklahoma, 1870–2010 / edited by
    Sarah Eppler Janda and Patricia Loughlin, foreword by Renée M. Laegreid.
Other titles: Women and the American West ; Volume 1.
Description: Norman : University of Oklahoma Press, [2021] | Series: Women and
    the American West ; Volume 1 | Includes bibliographical references and index. |
    Summary: "Contributed volume explores women's activism in Oklahoma from
    the 1870s to 2010s and evaluates Indigenous concepts of equality, sovereignty,
    and the impact of conservative politics in shaping women's rights in the American
    West through biographical essays"—Provided by publisher.
Identifiers: LCCN 2021003617 | ISBN 978-0-8061-6926-2 (paperback)
Subjects: LCSH: Women social reformers—Oklahoma—Biography. |
    Women's rights—Oklahoma—History. | Oklahoma—History.
Classification: LCC HQ1236.5.U6 T456 2021 | DDC 305.4209766—dc23
LC record available at https://lccn.loc.gov/2021003617

This Land Is Herland: Gendered Activism in Oklahoma from the 1870s to the 2010s is Volume 1 in the Women and the American West series.

The paper in this book meets the guidelines for permanence and durability of the Committee on Production Guidelines for Book Longevity of the Council on Library Resources, Inc. ∞

Copyright © 2021 by the University of Oklahoma Press, Norman, Publishing Division of the University. Manufactured in the U.S.A.

All rights reserved. No part of this publication may be reproduced, stored in a retrieval system, or transmitted, in any form or by any means, electronic, mechanical, photocopying, recording, or otherwise—except as permitted under Section 107 or 108 of the United States Copyright Act—without the prior written permission of the University of Oklahoma Press. To request permission to reproduce selections from this book, write to Permissions, University of Oklahoma Press, 2800 Venture Drive, Norman OK 73069, or email rights.oupress@ou.edu.

To Linda Williams Reese, our mentor and friend, author of *Women in Oklahoma, 1890–1920*; *Trail Sisters: Freedwomen in Indian Territory, 1850–1890*; and coeditor of *Main Street Oklahoma: Stories of Twentieth-Century America*, whose commitment to the scholarship of western women's history in its broadest sense inspires us all

CONTENTS

Foreword • ix
Renée M. Laegreid

Acknowledgments • xiii

Introduction • 1

PART ONE. THE FLUIDITY OF POWER • 7

1. Lilah Lindsey: Mvskoke Creek Educator and Civic Reformer • 11
   Rowan Faye Steineker

2. "My Heart Had Been Burdened for the Orphaned and Homeless Children": Religious Imperative and Maternalism in the Work of Mattie Mallory • 32
   Heather Clemmer

3. "Give Me a Nation of Great Mothers": Alice Robertson's Conservative Maternalism • 53
   Amy L. Scott

4. "Intrepid Pioneer Leader": The A-suffrage Gendered Activism of Kate Barnard • 75
   Sunu Kodumthara

5. "Loyal Countrywoman": Rachel Caroline Eaton, Alumna of the Cherokee National Female Seminary • 99
   Farina King

PART TWO. THE GENDERED POLITICS OF CIVIL RIGHTS • 121

6. Freedom on Her Own Terms: California M. Taylor and Black Womanhood in Boley, Oklahoma • 125
   Melissa N. Stuckey

7. Making History as an NAACP Plaintiff: Ada Lois Sipuel Fisher • 145
   Cheryl Elizabeth Brown Wattley

8. Beyond the Walls: From Sit-Ins to Integration in the Activism of Clara Luper • 166
   Rachel E. Watson

9. "To Speak So Forthrightly as to Offend": The Civil Rights Activism and Confinement of Rosalyn "Rosie" Coleman Gilchrist • 183
   Sarah Eppler Janda

PART THREE. CONTESTED NOTIONS OF EQUALITY • 203

10. LaDonna Harris: Comanche Leader, Activist, Matriarch • 207
    Amanda Cobb-Greetham

11. "Until We Organized": Wanda Jo Peltier Stapleton and the Equal Rights Amendment Debate in Oklahoma, 1972–1982 • 228
    Chelsea Ball

12. Barbara "Wahru" Cleveland and Herland Sister Resources • 246
    Lindsey Churchill

13. "My Children Are More Important to Me than Any Office I Might Hold": Mary Fallin's Use of Motherhood as a Conservative Political Strategy • 262
    Patricia Loughlin

Conclusion • 278

Selected Bibliography • 281

Contributors • 287

Index • 293

RENÉE M. LAEGREID

■
FOREWORD

Oklahoma. The name evokes images of a western place, one of austere beauty and a deep sense of history connecting people to the land across time and its wide-open spaces. Most people who consider Oklahoma, I would imagine, focus on versions of its nineteenth-century past: the creation of Indian Territory as a forced resettlement place for Native people who were inconveniencing white settlement or the chaotic competition for "free land" when the federal government opened Indian Territory to whites. The high-spirited musical *Oklahoma* connects white settlement on Indian lands with the story of a farmer's daughter being courted by two cowboys, the stereotypical cast of characters reinforcing its image of a nineteenth-century frontier—vast, open, rural, and western.

But behind the popular culture story is one much more complex and interesting. In addition to acknowledging the influence of the South, including demographic and racial attitudes in what is now considered a solidly western state, it also comprises urban as well as rural histories and, more important, not just acknowledges but emphasizes the role of women as actors in shaping Oklahoma from its earliest days into the twenty-first century. Sarah Eppler Janda and Patricia Loughlin's anthology, *This Land Is Herland: Gendered Activism in Oklahoma from the 1870s to the 2010s*, the first book in the Women and the American West series at the University of Oklahoma Press, does just that, bringing to light the too-often-overlooked roles of women in Oklahoma's history. These meticulously researched biographies of Native, African American, and white women chronicle the lives of women who engaged in the challenges of their day and chose to make a difference for their tribes, their communities, and their state.

The stories of activist women in this anthology focus on their work in Oklahoma. Importantly, though, their stories situate Oklahoma within larger reform efforts at regional and national levels. Reform movements such as Native rights, suffrage, child welfare, and civil rights have inspired, provided guidance, and in some cases paved the way for acceptance for the women's work by tapping into the driving social and political ideas of the day. And yet just as the places they lived were full of complexities, reformers often had complicated and contradictory ideas of how to achieve their goals. For example, both suffragists and anti-suffragists fought hard to protect women's status in Oklahoma—either by promoting the political right to vote or by protecting women from what activists considered would be the harmful consequences of enfranchisement. Or consider the nineteenth-century acceptance of maternalism, which allowed women to be involved in activities that were beneficial to society but only so long as the activities remained within the parameters of women's gendered responsibilities related to motherhood. This often required reformers to navigate a delicate balance between achieving their goals and maintaining community support for those goals. While the activist highlighted in each chapter had her own motivations, taken together these stories reveal contested notions about Oklahoma: to whom it belongs and who should guide its future.

The chapters in *This Land Is Herland* reveal the importance of looking at Oklahoma history across time and space through the lens of women: their relationships to the South and the West, the land, the opportunities and challenges it offered, and the ideas that filtered in from outside the region. The biographies build on one another to inform, enlighten, and enrich our understanding of how activist women shaped Oklahoma for more than two centuries. In the end, this book's editors seek to reveal a "place shaped by the gendered activism of women," and they succeed beautifully.

University of Wyoming

ACKNOWLEDGMENTS

We would first and foremost like to thank the eleven women scholars who joined us in writing chapters for *This Land Is Herland*: Chelsea Ball, Lindsey Churchill, Heather Clemmer, Amanda Cobb-Greetham, Farina King, Sunu Kodumthara, Amy Scott, Rowan Steineker, Melissa Stuckey, Rachel Watson, and Cheryl Wattley. It has been a great pleasure to work with each of these talented scholars. We are grateful to Natalie Panther at the Helmerich Center for American Research at the Gilcrease Museum and Bob Blackburn at the Oklahoma Historical Society's Oklahoma History Center for allowing us use of facilities to conduct author workshops. The workshops provided wonderful opportunities for discussion and the exchange of ideas as the chapters on women's activism in Oklahoma began taking shape.

We are deeply indebted to Kathy Dickson and Elizabeth Bass at the Oklahoma Historical Society and Jake Krumwiede at the Cherokee Strip Regional Heritage Center for their support and sponsorship of the public programming panel series "This Land Is Herland" as part of the "OK Women 100: A Century of Women's Suffrage" commemoration. We are grateful as well to the Oklahoma Historical Society, Oklahoma Humanities, and the National Endowment for the Humanities for the grant that made possible the public programming and a publication subvention to the University of Oklahoma Press.

We would also like to thank several people and organizations for their support and feedback in the process. We appreciate Kathleen Kelly's enthusiasm for the project in its early stages. We wish to thank Kent Calder and Steven Baker at the University of Oklahoma Press for their support of the project and Women and the American West series editor Renée M. Laegreid for her encouragement. We appreciate the helpful, insightful feedback offered by Cathleen Cahill and Nancy Baker Jones. And we thank the Coalition for Western Women's History for providing a network of scholars who have been vital to our collaborative work. We are also grateful to our copy editor, Abby Graves, for her keen eye and close editing.

Finally, we would like to thank our families. Our spouses, Mike Logan and Lance Janda, and our children, Bryce Logan, Owen Logan, and Sydney Janda, have been great sources of support throughout the project's development and publication.

Sarah Eppler Janda and Patricia Loughlin

SARAH EPPLER JANDA AND PATRICIA LOUGHLIN

■
INTRODUCTION

In 1915, when Charlotte Perkins Gilman published *Herland*, a novel about a utopian feminist society, it seemed unlikely that she had in mind the state of Oklahoma, established just eight years earlier. The geographical space that makes up Oklahoma has meant different things to different groups of inhabitants over the course of the past several hundred years. For the Wichitas, the Indigenous people who once occupied all of present-day Oklahoma and beyond, the land provided a largely unchallenged home for centuries. For tribes such as the Comanches and Osages, Oklahoma became an adopted home through migratory choices, but other nations, such as the Cherokees, Chickasaws, and Creeks, came to Oklahoma through forced removal by the United States government. Some African Americans came to Oklahoma in forced bondage, enslaved by removed tribes, while others migrated to Oklahoma after the Civil War in hopes of owning land and establishing new communities in a space that, prior

1

to statehood, held significant promise for greater racial equality than existed elsewhere in the nation. Whites came to Oklahoma for varied reasons as well. Some came to proselytize, exploit, or educate Native Americans or carry out some combination of the three. Others came to escape poverty and pursue western opportunities that had been romanticized by frontier mythology. Whatever the case, contested notions about the space of Oklahoma—whose space it was and what sort of space it should be—underpin the history of the state and have proven central to understanding how Oklahoma became not a feminist utopia, certainly, but a place shaped by the gendered activism of women.

The symbolic marriage of "Miss Indian Territory" to "Mr. Oklahoma Territory" on November 16, 1907, as part of the statehood celebration foreshadowed the comingling of race, gender, subjugation, and opportunity that defined the backdrop of women's activism in Oklahoma over the course of the next century. By the start of the twenty-first century, Oklahoma fit firmly within the category of most conservative states in the country, but such a characterization misses the long history of activism and radical politics—both far left and far right— that have defined the state. The state's rich racial and ethnic diversity as well as the simultaneous prevalence of promise and poverty, hope and desperation, sovereignty and exploitation made Oklahoma a fertile environment for radical politics.

For example, on the eve of World War I, Oklahoma boasted the largest per capita population of Socialist Party members in the entire country. So opposed were the state's Socialist tenant farmers to the draft that a vast majority refused to register for it, instead engaging in multiple conspiracies to obstruct the process. The best-known of these—dubbed the Green Corn Rebellion because of the participants' plan to eat green corn as they marched from Oklahoma to Washington, DC, to demand that President Woodrow Wilson end the war—came to an abrupt end with the arrest of more than four hundred Native American, African American, and white men. Men dominated planning for the Green Corn Rebellion, but women were central to another, more sinister plot to obstruct the draft.[1] Court records from what came to be known as the Jones family conspiracy trial reveal that the wives of poor tenant farmers not only planned to hide draft-age men from federal agents, they also intended to lure the agents into their homes and offer them food laced with strychnine.[2] Following the conviction and sentencing of more than 150 men who participated in the Green Corn Rebellion and 8 men in the Jones family conspiracy (though no women were prosecuted), most Oklahomans quickly traded in their suspicion of the government and anti-draft sentiments for an ideology rooted in fear-based hyperpatriotism. By the fall of 1917, many an Oklahoman openly denounced "slackers," Socialists, union members, and others vaguely identified as un-American in their appearance, beliefs, and political leanings. The protection of family, property, and Oklahoma womanhood were central to this hyper-Americanism that transitioned Oklahoma from a state with a large number of Socialist Party members in the 1910s to one dominated by the Ku Klux Klan by the end of the next decade. Among its other goals for society, the KKK claimed protection of female virtue and warned against such dangers as "promiscuous joyrides after dark."[3]

While World War I largely ended Oklahoma's romance with Socialism, the anti-establishment suspiciousness that inadvertently fueled both activism and backlashes against activism persisted in the state. The intense suffering of the Great Depression gave rise to such homegrown radicals as Woody Guthrie, whose folk music captured well the desperation of many down-and-out Oklahomans.[4] Yet Depression-era Oklahoma further marginalized women and people of color, as historian Roxanne Dunbar-Ortiz's memoir *Red Dirt: Growing Up Okie* (1997) reveals.[5] Similarly, Agnes "Sis" Cunningham described her leftist politics as the logical outgrowth of growing up in intense poverty in Oklahoma during the Depression. Dunbar-Ortiz became a nationally renowned activist for Indigenous and women's rights, and Cunningham survived the scrutiny of Senator Joseph McCarthy when he attacked her "un-American" publication of the left-leaning magazine *Broadside*.[6] The social justice work of Dunbar-Ortiz and the Socialist advocacy of Cunningham reveal the continuity of radical politics and activism in Oklahoma that surfaced in particularly difficult periods.

Oklahoma has also been home to radical conservative politics. By the mid-1950s, Tulsa, Oklahoma, lay at the epicenter of the emerging Religious Right movement with Billy James Hargis's Christian Crusade.[7] Hargis's rabid warnings about communist threats lurking in nearly every shadow contributed to the growth of a more conservative but no less suspicious Oklahoma. Growing up in Tulsa in the 1950s, Anita Bryant no doubt honed her fear of liberalism while listening to Hargis's jeremiads. In addition to being a beauty queen and singer, Bryant became one of the best-known and most outspoken anti-gay activists in the country. By the 1960s, most Oklahomans no longer recalled the normalcy of radical leftist activism that had once existed in the state, nor did they have any appetite for it. The anti-gay rhetoric of Bryant offered greater comfort than did the Socialist critique of individual wealth and corporate power. That said, women's activism is central to understanding Oklahoma not only through the shifting ideologies of liberalism and conservatism but also in the context of both western and southern influences.

This land is herland. From the backdrop of the subjugation and exploitation of women apparent in the 1870s there emerged a fluid environment that allowed for gendered change and activism. Indigenous women used education and the women's club movement to facilitate new opportunities. White and Black women created their own notions of Oklahoma womanhood. By the mid-twentieth century, women were effecting change within the civil rights movement. They were at the forefront of fighting both for and against the Equal Rights Amendment. And Native women—none more so than LaDonna Harris and Wilma Mankiller—stood at the forefront of reasserting tribal sovereignty in the American West and beyond.

However, this is not a story of state or gender exceptionalism. Rather, it is an effort to understand how the peculiarities of Oklahoma—the juxtaposition of southern and western influences that converged in shared space with a rich Indigenous history—served to create a gendered activist space across three centuries. This book's biographical examination of thirteen individual women's activism creates a lens through which to better understand how race, ethnicity, gender, education, property ownership, and political power shaped—and were shaped by—the women's efforts to improve their communities, both locally and nationally.[8]

To that end, Part One explores the fluidity of power with which women took advantage of a society in flux by fashioning their own communities and identities. The women examined here vary—some earned advanced degrees, some developed real estate, some held elected office, and some ran orphanages—but each one constructed a gendered concept of activism that legitimized her particular work by framing it in terms of Indigenous tradition, maternalist politics, or religious imperative. Part Two focuses on the gendered politics of segregation through an examination of three African American women who interacted in and ultimately challenged segregated spaces and one white woman whose civil rights advocacy landed her in a state mental institution. An examination of these four women reveals the intersectionality of race and gender not only in their activism but also in the public reaction to that activism. In Part Three the authors tackle contested notions of equality in the late twentieth and early twenty-first centuries through such topics as Indigenous rights and sovereignty, the Equal Rights Amendment, LGBTQ+ rights, and the conservative politics of motherhood. The women studied in this section have in common a willingness to challenge accepted notions, and each in her own way sought to redefine and then normalize her particular concept of women's equality and the legitimacy of her gendered activism.

Each part offers a brief introduction that frames its central themes, and each of the biographical chapters is written by a different woman who is a scholar of Oklahoma women and western women's history. The title of the book and the chapters within represent a twofold meaning in the writing about Oklahoma women's activism. These women created their own "herland," and the featured scholars work to gender the scholarly landscape by highlighting women in Oklahoma and the ways in which their work and legacies connect to larger themes including intersectionality, suffrage, politics, maternalism, and civil rights in the American West and the nation. This is by no means a complete history of women's activism in Oklahoma. Instead, it is an exploration of the lives of individual women as vehicles through which to understand broader themes of advocacy and change. The pages that follow represent an effort to better understand how women fashioned palatable justifications for creating, shaping, and sometimes redefining the spaces in which they lived.

NOTES

1. See W. David Baird and Danney Goble, *Oklahoma: A History* (Norman: University of Oklahoma Press, 2008), 182–83; Garin Burbank, *When Farmers Voted Red: The Gospel of Socialism in the Oklahoma Countryside, 1910–1924* (Westport, CT: Greenwood, 1976), 5, 133–35.

2. *USA v. Clure Isenhour et al.*, US District Court, Western District of Oklahoma, No. 1553 (1917), trial transcript, National Archives–Fort Worth. See also Michael Morton, "No Time to Quibble: The Jones Family Conspiracy Trial of 1917," *Chronicles of Oklahoma* 59 (1982): 224–36.

3. "'Promiscuous Joy Rides after Dark': A Klan Manifesto," in W. David Baird and Danney Goble, *The Story of Oklahoma*, 2nd ed. (Norman: University of Oklahoma Press, 2007), 296.

4. Woody Guthrie's "This Land Is Your Land," written in 1940, offers a satirical response to "God Bless America." Living in Oklahoma during the Great Depression gave Guthrie keen insight into suffering and loss as he witnessed many people lose their homes and farms.

5. Roxanne Dunbar-Ortiz, *Red Dirt: Growing Up Okie* (Norman: University of Oklahoma Press, 2006).

6. See Agnes "Sis" Cunningham and Gordon Friesen, *Red Dirt and Broadsides: A Joint Autobiography*, ed. Ronald D. Cohen (Amherst: University of Massachusetts Press, 1999).

7. See Heather Hendershot, *What's Fair on the Air? Cold War Right-Wing Broadcasting and the Public Interest* (Chicago: University of Chicago Press, 2011), 188.

8. The term "activist" is used throughout this book to signify someone who actively engaged in efforts to promote change. Those studied here are politically, ethnically, and racially diverse women whose varied lives span three centuries.

PART ONE

THE FLUIDITY OF POWER

Part One explores the unique juxtaposition of Oklahoma's southern influence and western promise—where the American South blurs into the American West, to paraphrase Tiya Miles—in an examination of how both shaped the opportunities and activism of women in the critical years surrounding statehood in 1907.[1] This time period reveals the fluidity of regional political and decision-making power as Indian Territory and Oklahoma Territory became the state of Oklahoma. Such fluidity fostered opportunities for women in education, business, and politics and caused national reformers to laud Oklahoma's constitution as one of the most Progressive documents (and one of the longest state constitutions, numbering about 50,000 words) in the country. However, the state constitution privileged white men while continuing to disenfranchise white women, and violence against people of color was written into the document.

At the same time, women played critical roles in the development of educational institutions and orphanages in early Oklahoma. As the chapter by Rowan

Faye Steineker argues, Lilah Denton Lindsey, who in 1883 became the first Mvskoke Creek woman to earn a college degree, dedicated herself to numerous Progressive reform efforts, including temperance, women's suffrage, and orphan welfare. While Tulsa was emerging as an oil boomtown during the 1910s and 1920s, Lindsey founded a home for orphaned and neglected girls, and she remained active in local and national organizations such as the Tulsa Indian Women's Club and the Woman's Christian Temperance Union.

Similarly, Heather Clemmer examines Mattie Mallory, an educator, entrepreneur, and member of the Holiness movement, an offshoot of the Social Gospel movement, who founded institutions for orphans in Oklahoma City in order to address their spiritual, educational, and vocational needs. In addition, Mallory purchased property and expanded her mission in the new town of Bethany, located about ten miles west of Oklahoma City, in order to create city ordinances that adhered to Nazarene religious principles and thus exercise social and political control within the community.

Lindsey's ardent support for women's suffrage was far from universally shared by women, nationally or in Oklahoma. And yet, once Oklahoma extended the vote to women in November 1918—again, an example of the fluidity of power as territories became states—Alice Mary Robertson, an anti-suffragist from Muskogee, decided to run for office. "The men have thrust the vote on us," Robertson said, "and now I am going to see whether they mean it." She became the first woman from Oklahoma elected to the United States Congress in 1920. Oklahoma would not elect another woman to Congress until Mary Fallin in 2006. As Amy L. Scott argues, Robertson struggled to find a balance between pursuing the Republican Party's agenda, advancing conservative maternalism, and representing her constituents in Oklahoma.

While Robertson actively opposed women's suffrage, Kate Barnard often proved silent on the issue. Sunu Kodumthara explains the complexities of Kate Barnard, who practiced a-suffragist activism, meaning that she privileged other causes over the vote for women despite being the first woman ever elected to statewide office in the United States in 1907, before women could vote in Oklahoma. During the constitutional convention she lobbied for three reform measures, the prohibition of child labor, compulsory education, and the establishment of the Office of Commissioner of Charities and Corrections. Unfazed by intimidation and other silencing tactics, Kate Barnard was an activist for women, children, and all working people.

Rachel Caroline Eaton, a descendant of Cherokee beloved woman Nanye'hi (or Nancy Ward), was a graduate of the Cherokee National Female Seminary in Tahlequah and the first Cherokee woman to earn a PhD in 1919. Farina King maintains that even as she published one of the first major tribal-specific histories on Cherokee nationalism in the biography *John Ross and the Cherokee Indians* (1914), she "sustained ties to Cherokee knowledge and heritage—foundations for Cherokee peoplehood and nationhood—as her predecessors." As an alumna of the Cherokee National Female Seminary, Eaton demonstrated through her life and career as an educator how seminarians used their educational training to serve the Cherokee Nation.

An examination of women's activism reveals Oklahoma's peculiar history, at once a contentious and forced blending of Indigenous nations and others vying for political power and Indigenous women's and non-Indigenous women's challenges and contributions to the formation and development of the state. Women served as leaders of civic organizations in the Twin Territories in the nineteenth century and then in the newly formed state of Oklahoma beginning in 1907. The chapters that follow explore themes of Progressive reform networks, civic participation, leadership roles, institution building, and maternalist politics, revealing much about the fluidity of power.

NOTE

1. Tiya Miles, "The Long Arm of the South?" *Western Historical Quarterly* 43 (Fall 2012): 274–81.

LILAH LINDSEY

Mvskoke Creek Educator and Civic Reformer

A photograph of eighty-two-year-old Lilah Denton Lindsey seated in a rocking chair, weighed down with a large pile of cards and letters in her lap, appeared in a 1942 issue of the *Tulsa Tribune*. The image of the woman in her dotage belies her thriving presence. As one description noted, "Frank about her age, Mrs. Lindsey does not rely on it to secure favors. Her personality is neither wrapped in gray shawls nor hunched in sweet resignation by the fire-place." The paper profiled "Tulsa's first and most beloved school-teacher" as she read the "hundreds of letters of appreciation she has received through the 50 years she has lived in Tulsa."[1] By no means was this the first time that Lindsey had caught the media's attention. Newspapers and magazines had frequently featured her as a public figure well respected for her long teaching career and community contributions.

Native women like Lilah left an indelible impression on the history of Indian Territory and early Oklahoma. Rather than simply vanishing after Oklahoma entered the union, women of the Five Tribes worked to preserve what remained of their diverse cultures and dynamic civic institutions. Simultaneously, they continued to embrace Progressivism and demand reforms amid the turbulent political and social upheaval of the late nineteenth and early twentieth centuries. The federal government had promised Creeks that they would remain for "as long as the grass grows or the water runs," and so they did, forging a continuity during the transition to Oklahoma statehood.[2]

Lilah Denton Lindsey's career as an educator and civic reformer embodies both the advancement of a Progressive Creek Nation and the continuity between the territorial and statehood periods. A "short resume" of her work lauded, "With a real vision of high endeavor she has worked unstintedly [sic] toward the development and achievement of almost every phase of activity interesting to women, as well as to the community, whether it be educational, civic, legislative, political, cultural, or patriotic."[3] A careful examination of her life sheds light on the significant contributions of Indigenous women activists like her in the history of Indian Territory and early Oklahoma and, more broadly, the history of Progressivism in the American West from the 1870s through the 1920s.

Born in 1860, on the eve of the American Civil War, Lilah was no stranger to tragedy in her early life. Her father, a Cherokee named John Denton, and her mother, a Creek named Susan McKellop, emigrated as young children from Alabama to Indian Territory during the Indian removals of the 1830s. After marrying, the young couple settled near Blue Springs in the Coweta Creek District in accordance with matrilocal customs. Of their six children, four died in infancy and one during childhood, leaving Lilah as the only surviving child. When the Creek Nation became entangled in the American Civil War, the family suffered yet another loss: John Denton died from pneumonia, leaving behind his widow and three-year-old daughter.[4]

Susan McKellop Denton left two long-lasting impressions on her daughter. First, Susan, a gifted healer, often allowed young Lilah to accompany her as she tended to the sick and wounded. Witnessing the way her mother "devoted her life to her fellow man" proved formative for Lilah, who similarly wished to live her life in service to her people.[5] Second, as an educated Creek woman who had attended Tullahassee Manual Labor School in her youth, Susan inspired her daughter to value education, a passion that shaped Lilah's entire adult life. Susan registered Lilah at her alma mater when the girl turned twelve, and she went on to study "algebra, geometry, English grammar, natural philosophy, composition, and declamation" as well as history, music, geography, Latin, and Greek.[6]

Both Susan and Lilah attended Tullahassee during a period of significant educational reform in the Creek Nation during which "equal school privileges" for all Creeks became a priority. Nevertheless, male leaders' embrace of patriarchy pigeonholed Creek women into marginalized roles; they argued that Creek women should be educated so they would be "useful" to their sons and husbands and, by extension, to their nation. Unlike her male classmates at Tullahassee who had gone on to fill government positions, Susan McKellop had served her people as a wife, mother, and healer in her community. The different tracks for male and female students persisted when Lilah attended the school. In 1875, Principal Chief Lochar Harjo called for universal education, but he reinforced the different objectives for male and female students. He stated, "Educate the youth of both sexes to honesty industry and economy that the men may be good useful and prosperous citizens, the women that they may take their places in the household and culinary Departments and be helpmate for man."[7] Thus, the Creek government designed women's education to prepare them to serve as wives and mothers or as teachers in the national schools.[8]

In many ways, Lilah's education mirrored the experiences of young women at academies throughout the South. Southern women received the same rigorous academic training as their male counterparts, but their teachers were "intent on creating pious Christian women noted for their benevolent activities within the domestic sphere."[9] Despite the clear overlap in curriculum and expectations for both southern white women and female Creek students like Lilah, their schooling reveals divergent trajectories for women's roles in Creek and US society during the 1800s. Women's education in both the South and the North during the nineteenth century increasingly allowed women to create a wedge in society and enter the public sphere as teachers, writers, and reformers. Creek female schooling, however, marked an alternative trend: women's diminishing political and economic power in Creek society.[10]

While at Tullahassee, Lilah studied under the direction of Presbyterian missionary William Robertson and his wife, Ann Eliza Worcester, who was the daughter of longtime Cherokee missionary Samuel Worcester. Lilah, a lonely young girl, formed "a big happy family" with the couple along with their four children, her teacher Eliza Baldwin, and her fellow schoolmates, and they "enjoyed life together."[11] Nevertheless, when Lilah's mother, who had long battled tuberculosis, took a turn for the worse in 1878, Lilah left Tullahassee to care for her. Sadly, Susan died that year, leaving Lilah "alone in this cold world

Lilah Denton Lindsey in 1887, early in her teaching career. Courtesy of Beryl Ford Collection, Rotary Club of Tulsa, Tulsa City-County Library and Tulsa Historical Society & Museum.

without a near relative."[12] Despite the loss, Lilah did have an extensive network of matrilineal kin and community support to help guide her.

Over the course of the next year, Lilah lived as a guest in the homes of influential Creek families. She stayed first in the home of her maternal first cousin David Hodge, a Creek diplomat and delegate to Washington, DC. When Hodge departed once again for the East, she moved to the ranch of Pleasant Porter, another member of the Washington delegation. All the while, "the lonely little orphaned girl Lilah Denton," as she described herself, harbored the hope that she would have another opportunity to continue her education. While she lived with the Porters, a carpenter named Lee W. Lindsey, who worked at the ranch, developed an affection for Lilah and proposed marriage. She rejected him, audaciously claiming, "I have no idea of marrying you or anyone else now. I am planning to get a finished education and teach school. That is my ambition and I am not going to be derailed from my plan. I am going 'off to the states' to get an education and do missionary work among my people."[13] Despite her bold design, Lilah had no immediate avenue to a college education.

A fortuitous opportunity arose when she received a letter from Ann Eliza Worcester Robertson informing her of a vacancy for a "Creek Indian girl" at the Synodical Female College in Fulton, Missouri. Luckily, the cost of tuition did not pose an obstacle. During the 1870s, members of the Creek Council recognized the lack of local institutions of higher learning, so they designed Youth-in-the-States, a nationally subsidized college scholarship program specifically designed to send the nation's best and brightest to American universities.[14] Council members hoped that college attendees would return home and apply their education in service to their nation. The program fit perfectly with Lilah's "haunting desire for a finished education" and her aspirations to serve as an educator in the Creek schools.[15] In early March 1879 she departed for Missouri to begin her college career.

Although Lilah had not left Indian Territory before, her recent experience moving from household to household helped her adapt easily to her new surroundings. If she had difficulty adjusting to her academic or social life at the Synodical Female College, her memoirs do not reflect it. Instead, she recorded that from the day of her arrival, "my school work moved as all college work does, and I soon adjusted myself to my new environment, the girls all received me kindly and I had a very happy school life."[16] She also devoted herself to intellectual improvement not just in the classroom but also in her free time, during which she would take "advantage of the school library at all times."[17] Despite her seemingly smooth transition to college life, Lilah never abandoned her identity as a Creek woman. She described herself as "an Indian maid gathering her pale faced sisters about her" and made it clear she strove to make herself "fit for work among her own people."[18] She remained at the institution only until June 1880, when her former teacher and de facto guardian, Eliza Baldwin, arranged for her to transfer to Highland Institute in Hillsboro, Ohio, so she would be nearer to Baldwin's own home in Chillicothe. At Highland, a school that prepared female students to be teachers and missionaries, Lilah remained dedicated to pursuing a career as an educator.

Creek students often had to counteract misconceptions of Indigenous people in white-dominated social settings. Despite the fact that Youth-in-the-States students tended to excel in their college studies, they still had to challenge beliefs about Native American intellectual inferiority. Lilah was no exception. She earned "best in scholarship" in all her classes at Highland Institute.[19] Nonetheless, white audiences typically expected Native American students to perform the stereotypes they assumed of "real" Indians, ahistorical relics that reinforced beliefs in white superiority and justified colonial policies. Lilah learned this firsthand when a teacher assigned her to write a paper on Indian Territory and sing an "Indian song." She "protested to no avail" and offered to sing a Christian hymn in Mvskoke. Her teacher refused, saying, "Don't you know any songs that are real Indian not connected with the English language at all?" Lilah reluctantly selected a Mvskoke medicine song to present. For a costume she wrote home to friends to request that they send her a pair of moccasins and large hoop earrings, which she paired with a beaded headband and blanket. Her performance was such a hit that her teacher asked her to repeat it for local audiences.[20] Expectations of Indigenous behavior such as these often made students uncomfortable since they considered themselves to be "real" Indians even if their dress and performance didn't reflect others' ideas of Indianness.[21] Lilah understood herself to be a representative of her race and nation and worked to dismantle the stereotypes projected on her by white classmates, teachers, and policy makers.

One way she did so was by contributing to local reform efforts while at Highland Institute. Shortly after her arrival, her peers elected her as president of the Students' Missionary Society, which supported the National Women's Missionary Society of Presbyterians as well as other local aid organizations. It was in this capacity that Lilah first became interested in the temperance movement, which had deep roots in the area. A decade prior, a local woman named Eliza

"Mother" Thompson had organized approximately seventy-five women who marched on the local saloons and demanded they stop enticing "the youth and drunken husbands" who were "robbing the mothers and children of bread, milk, and the home comforts."[22] In Hillsboro, Lilah became well acquainted with Thompson and her daughter, and she continued to nurture these relationships as she became increasingly involved in the Woman's Christian Temperance Union in the decades that followed.

Lilah and other Youth-in-the-States students pursued degrees in higher education at a critical moment when the future of the Creek Nation seemed more uncertain than ever. During the 1880s and 1890s, so-called Friends of the Indians and federal officials had launched a multipronged Native American assimilation campaign. Assimilation advocates envisioned education, particularly forms that removed Native students away from their homes and families, as a tool to forcibly erase their Indigenous identity.[23] US officials also maintained that successfully "civilized" Indigenous people should willingly surrender sovereignty and communal landholdings. Subsequently, they hoped to strong-arm the Creek government to divide their land into private lots and open the "surplus" for settlement. Creek students in American colleges defied assimilationist ideology at every turn. Their time away in the states did not cause them to relinquish their identity as citizens of a sovereign tribal nation, nor did it make them embrace proposed allotment policies. Instead, they became even more determined to use their education to serve and protect their people against the unfolding colonization of their nation.[24]

Returning male and female students followed different paths in serving the Creek Nation during this period of uncertainty. Male students often sought careers in public service, filling positions as legislators, judges, interpreters, and diplomats. For instance, Lilah's maternal cousin Albert Pike ("A. P.") McKellop graduated from the College of Wooster and consistently expressed a desire to aid his nation. Upon returning, he wrote his former teacher: "I have decided to spend my life as a politician and statesman defending the sacred right of our people.'"[25] Over the next two decades, he served as a member of the Board of Examiners of Public Instruction, as an elected representative in the Creek legislature, and as a delegate to Washington, DC.[26]

Because the Creek government excluded women from participating in formal politics, Lilah could not follow the same path as McKellop, no matter what level of education she attained.[27] Nevertheless, she recognized that teaching offered a viable alternative to women who wished to serve their nation in a more formal role.[28] In an autobiographical sketch that Lilah sent to her mentor Eliza Baldwin, she wrote, "Her one and great desire was to graduate with honors and return to her native people as a teacher, having this high ambition for her motive she worked diligently to that end accomplishing all her desires."[29]

In 1883, Lilah became the first Creek woman to receive a college degree, an accomplishment that earned her lifelong recognition. Because so few women received college degrees during this period, she often joked that hers read "Mistress of Liberal Arts" instead of "Bachelors" like the degrees awarded to male graduates.[30] Lilah bade Eliza Baldwin goodbye, which, she said, "felt like losing another mother." She then departed on the train for Indian Territory, "being whirled away from all that had been dear" in Ohio.[31] New opportunities awaited Lilah back in the Creek Nation, including a teaching position.

With the assistance of Eliza Baldwin and the Robertsons, Lilah secured an appointment through the Presbyterian Board of Foreign Missions to work at Wealaka, a newly opened school. Although teaching had always been her ambition, she expressed apprehension about taking charge of a class of forty girls, including some who had been her former schoolmates at Tullahassee. She also suffered from an undisclosed ongoing illness that made her frail and regularly tired. As a "natural born teacher," however, she developed a gentle but firm approach. In addition to being qualified to teach the various academic subjects to her students, she also "taught them to depend on their conscience to know right from wrong and to obey it." Lilah employed pedagogical methods designed to actively engage her students in the material, including competitive spelling bees and storytelling. Her work during her first year earned praise from her superiors, who called her "a most successful teacher."[32]

Lilah soon found more than just professional fulfillment at Wealaka when Lee W. Lindsey, her spurned suitor, accepted a contract to complete repair work at the school. Lilah maintained, "I did not allow his presence to interfere in the least with my work as a teacher for I was very conscientious and loved my work."[33] Despite her obstinance, Lee Lindsey doggedly insisted they marry. Lilah resigned her position at Wealaka because of her ill health at the close of her first year in June 1884 and returned to the home of Pleasant Porter. Lindsey continued his courtship. Five years after they had initially met at the Porter ranch, Lilah "gave in and prepared for the wedding." The couple wed on September 17, 1884, at Wealaka Mission and then settled in Okmulgee.[34] For many female teachers in the late nineteenth century, marriage marked the ends of their careers. In Lilah's case, however, her long stint as an educator and activist had only begun.

Less than a year into her marriage, in the spring of 1885, Lilah had the urge to return to work. She first substituted at an Okmulgee school and then accepted a job offer at a Presbyterian mission school in Tulsa in 1886. Reverend W. P. Hayworth, a representative of the New York Board of Home Missions, had solicited her after he had "several requests from the parents of Indian children" who insisted he offer her a position.[35] At the time Tulsa, or "Tulsey Town," was a small settlement with approximately 125 residents and only one school. After her coteacher left in the middle of the term, Lilah singlehandedly led a class of sixty-five students. She soon learned that "a teacher in a mission school had to be resourceful in many respects and competent to respond to any call," which often meant lending assistance to students and community members outside the classroom.[36] Lilah described how, in addition to teaching, she found herself "visiting the Indian children in their homes, sitting up with and nursing the sick, and assisting in burying the dead."[37] Despite the unanticipated duties, she remained dedicated to "laying out the educational and spiritual foundations for the future citizenship of the community."[38]

Teaching remained Lindsey's main vocation for several years. Her status as a college-educated woman and successful instructor provided her with a great deal of respect from parents, pupils, and education officials in the Creek Nation. The Creek government typically upheld strict standards for their instructors, requiring attendance at the Annual Teachers' Institute, an examination, and a certificate. When Lindsey requested that the National School Board examine her and issue her a certificate for a school, however, they readily granted the certificate but dispensed with the exam, explaining, "No, we are not going to examine you, you might turn the table on us and examine us."[39] This level of privilege essentially guaranteed she could teach where and when she chose. She remained at the Tulsa school for three years and then, at the "earnest request of the Broken Arrow Community," accepted a position in its day school, where forty students from the surrounding areas attended every day.

At times Lilah demonstrated a clear elitist attitude in her career, despite her oft-professed desire to serve her fellow citizens. For instance, she grew dissatisfied with the day school, proclaiming it "beneath my dignity." Instead, she returned to Tulsa, where, upon the persuasion of predominantly white "bankers and businessmen's wives," she opened a private school "because they did not want their small children mixing and mingling with undesirable children of all classes."[40] Lilah's white contemporaries among Progressive southern women "shared the class elitism and racial biases of the time and place."[41] In the Creek

Nation, social divisions along lines of socioeconomic class and race were also deeply entrenched. Lilah enjoyed the privileges associated with a prominent extended family, an advanced education, and a comfortable, middle-class lifestyle, which set her apart from poor rural Creeks.[42] Perhaps this episode when Lilah espoused overtly elitist views toward those of "undesirable" classes was iconoclastic, or perhaps her class and racial biases conflicted with her deeply held Creek communal values. For whatever reason, she taught at the private school for only one year and then returned to the Creek national schools for three additional years. By 1894 continued ill health led her to once again resign, but she had firmly cemented her legacy as "Tulsa's first and most beloved school teacher."[43] In the years that followed, she remained compelled to assist those in need through personal acts and organizational philanthropy.

After retiring from teaching, Lilah followed in her mother's footsteps by caring for the most vulnerable members of her society. After she and her husband permanently settled in Tulsa, they fostered several children, at one point even fashioning a bedroom out of a tent in the backyard to accommodate them. One young girl, Alice Perryman, arrived on her doorstep one day with baggage in hand and asked, "May I come and live with you?" George Perryman, the girl's father, who often traveled for work, came to an understanding with the Lindseys. As Lilah explained, "I told the father I would treat Alice as my own child and give her every advantage for an education and home culture I was able to provide," and he agreed to visit but not interfere. The couple raised Alice as their own, ensured that she attended school, and provided her with a stable family life. After struggling for many years with tuberculosis, Alice died as a young woman. Several other youths also found temporary guardianship with the Lindseys, much as Lilah had with the Hodges and the Porters after her mother died. Lilah later wrote, "It was my happy privilege to take into my home at various intervals about sixteen children and give them the first foundation of a Christian home and education."[44]

The Lindseys' practice of opening their household to children based on real and fictive kinship connections was an enduring custom in the Creek Nation as well as in the Five Tribes more broadly. Values of communalism and cooperation formed the backbone of southeastern Indian societies. Historian James Hochtritt argues that among the Five Tribes "social cohesion depended on the goodwill of community members. Amity fostered cooperation."[45] The practice of sending children to live with matrilineal clan members, family friends, and other community members to afford them better material, spiritual, and educational advantages was a long-standing practice among Creeks that persisted through the nineteenth century and into the twentieth. During the early nineteenth century parents sent their children to be adopted into white households and attend schools in hopes that the potential access, power, and knowledge would aid them against ongoing threats to Indigenous sovereignty.[46] After removal to Indian Territory, the governments of the Five Tribes established their own institutional forms of support, including national school systems and orphan asylums.[47] Nevertheless, the practice of "extended families, both in the household and community sense," complemented the newer institutional forms.[48]

Lilah also found new ways to serve Native people, particularly women and children. Returning to her earlier activism in the temperance movement, she rededicated herself to the cause in Indian Territory, where the Five Tribes had their own distinct histories of alcohol curtailment. During the 1880s and 1890s Native women began to organize local chapters of the Woman's Christian Temperance Union (WCTU), a massive international network dedicated to reforming all manner of social ills.[49] Lilah's earlier work with temperance activists in Ohio provided her with a strong familiarity with the organization's strategies in the "fight against liquor traffic, the home's worst enemy," and its larger reform agenda, including women's suffrage, labor reform, legal protections, and pay equity in Indian Territory.[50] She organized the local Tulsa WCTU chapter in 1902 and acted first as superintendent of the chapter's Loyal Temperance Legion, the children's division of the organization, and later as Tulsa WCTU chapter president. She also served as the president of the Indian Territory WCTU in 1907.[51]

The Five Tribes had a deeply rooted history of curbing alcohol abuse. Not only did federal intercourse acts prohibit traders from selling alcohol in Indian Territory, the nations themselves passed temperance laws. Nevertheless, non-Native intruders flooded into the region during the late nineteenth century, making enforcement of those laws nearly impossible. The resulting rise in alcohol-related crime contributed to Indian Territory's reputation as lawless and reinforced stereotypes of "drunken Indians." Such negative perceptions further jeopardized the sovereign status of the Five Tribes, which were already under pressure to forfeit treaty rights, dissolve tribal governments, and allot land into private shares. Historian Izumi Ishii argues, "Reformers found the stereotype of 'drunken Indians' to be a powerful weapon to promote their own cause because it illustrated the depravity that resulted from intemperance."[52] Lilah, though, was introduced at national conventions as a "representative of the Creek people," and an obviously sober one, in an effort correct the misperception.⁵³ She and other members of the Indian Territory WCTU worked to educate fellow temperance workers of the fact that American citizens, not Native people, perpetuated alcohol-related problems in Indian Territory.

Despite Lilah's zeal to protect Native sovereignty, white, middle-class social reformers, including those in the WCTU, and politicians hell-bent on imposing assimilation policies undermined her campaign. In 1887, Congress passed the Dawes Act, which allotted reservation lands into private parcels and made the surplus available for sale. The Five Tribes initially received an exemption after successfully arguing that they had well-established schools, churches, economies, and republican systems of government as well as full title in fee simple over their lands. It proved a temporary reprieve as Congress soon created the Dawes Commission to coerce the Five Tribes into allotment agreements despite their continued opposition. When the Dawes Commission failed in its mission, the 1898 Curtis Act mandated land allotment, granted United States citizenship to members who accepted allotments, and scheduled a final dissolution of the tribal governments. The unilateral legislation catered to the desires of white settlers and, as a result, annulled time-honored treaties and undercut Native sovereignty.⁵⁴

When Oklahoma entered the United States in 1907, reformers across the nation hailed its constitution as one of the most Progressive in the union, particularly for its sections on regulation, referendum, and the prohibition of alcohol. The assimilation policies that led to Oklahoma statehood might have been viewed as Progressive by white, middle-class reformers and policy makers of the time, but they proved devastating to the Native people they targeted. Lilah reflected on the loss resulting from allotment and statehood, writing, "We Indians had our Government, churches, schools well organized and well functioning toward the well-fare of the masses. . . . The change was a shock. . . . We realized, all that we held dear was slipping away."⁵⁵ Despite the so-called Progressive measures written into the state constitution, Oklahoma statehood was predicated upon abolishing the sovereignty, stealing the land, and erasing the cultures of the Native Americans.

Native-led organizations, including the Indian Territory WCTU, became additional casualties of Oklahoma statehood. Lilah, who served as the Indian Territory WCTU's final president from 1907 to 1908, presided over its disbandment and absorption into the new Oklahoma State WCTU.⁵⁶ For a brief time, the WCTU had allowed women in Indian Territory to effect social and political change through a distinctly Native-led organization. After statehood, such opportunities diminished. Lilah and other Native women, however, did not simply abandon their activism in early statehood. Instead, they continued to attain positions of leadership, influence their societies, and advocate for moral and political reform issues.[57]

Statehood solidified power structures that privileged white males and marginalized and violently oppressed people of color. Women especially held a precarious position in society since they remained politically disenfranchised in Oklahoma. Nevertheless, civic reform efforts provided individual Native women with opportunities to make their voices heard in the public sphere. Lilah, who enjoyed the advantages of a comfortable middle-class status, connections with politically influential men, and esteem from fellow citizens, decided to take a leading role in mobilizing women in civic organizations. The WCTU served as the jumping-off point for Lilah and other female reformers concerned with social problems in early Oklahoma. As she wrote in the foreword of the history of the WCTU in Indian Territory and Oklahoma, "The Woman's Christian Temperance Union was the pioneer organization of women both in Indian Territory and Oklahoma, and blazed the way for all other women's societies."[58] Lilah, in particular, paved the way for other female reformers in Oklahoma by serving as "a leader in civic affairs" and an "honored member of the many associations that have been formed . . . by progressive women."[59]

Lilah divided her time between a number of Progressive causes. Although teaching always remained her "first love," she declared her other "greatest interest" to be assisting poor and struggling people, especially women and children. Her work began locally in the growing town of Tulsa, where she aided "Tent-town," an area where needy people, including "deserted mothers and children, the sick, the dying," lived in makeshift shelters. Lilah first asked each store in the area to donate a small number of supplies, then combined them, and used them to stock a larder for the settlement. Members of the community soon pressed her to organize a Tulsa chapter of the Humane Society.[60] Although the modern American Humane association is best known for protecting animals, the organization, founded in 1877, also worked to prevent the "cruelty, abuse, neglect, and exploitation of children" in the early twentieth century.[61]

As Tulsa transformed from a small settlement to an oil boomtown during the 1910s and 1920s, Lilah took further steps to support needy women and children in the growing city. She helped establish the Francis E. Willard Home in Tulsa in 1917. Named after the famous temperance reformer and suffragist, the home provided shelter and security to orphaned and neglected girls. Recognizing law enforcement's failure to properly protect women, Lilah proposed that the Tulsa City Council create the position of police matron as a solution. A persuasive and shrewd negotiator, Lilah personally lobbied each council member and secured their support. Nevertheless, the all-male council members acknowledged "they knew nothing about the duties of such an officer nor whom to support" and turned the matter over to Lilah, allowing her to recruit the inaugural police matron. She later recalled that of all her instances of service to Tulsa, creating the Office of Police Matron was "the one I most cherished for the good work done."[62]

Lilah did not approach reform issues singlehandedly, however. Instead, she drew on an extensive network of women's clubs to improve the city and promote the welfare, protection, and political rights of the marginalized. For instance, as the founder and two-term president of the Women's Civic League of Tulsa, she led a number of citywide initiatives, including beautification campaigns and garbage collection. Lilah also spearheaded "one of the most outstanding activities of the Women's Civic League" by addressing the problem of food insecurity among the city's growing population.[63] The Lindseys, who enjoyed economic security thanks to Lee's business, donated $2,500 of their own funds to establish a community kitchen in 1921, and Lilah volunteered to oversee its day-to-day operations. It ran successfully for many years, "forming the basis for the first government operated welfare agency in the area."[64] In addition to the Women's Civic League and WCTU, she actively served as a member and leader in dozens of local and national organizations, including the Tulsa Indian Women's Club, the Rebekah Lodge of the Independent Order of Odd Fellows, and the Tulsa Women's Club among others throughout the decades. When several women's clubs organized under the General Federation of Women's Clubs, she assumed leadership, serving as the first Oklahoma state district chief and the second president of the Tulsa City Federation of Women's Clubs in 1928.[65] The wide-ranging network of women's organizations she helped build acted as a powerful vehicle for achieving reform.

The United States' entry in the First World War in 1917 spurred Lilah to expand her civic work to include wartime organizations. Similar to other middle- and upper-class women, Lilah could allocate both time and resources toward the war effort. An active member of the National Woman's Relief Corps, the auxiliary to the Grand Army of the Republic since 1898, she had long since supported the commemoration of military service in her community. Her role in this organization helped earn an appointment from Governor R. L. Williams as the only female member of the Tulsa County Council of Defense during the war. Not only did she serve as the secretary and treasurer of the council, but she also founded a Women's Division to better mobilize support for the war effort. She organized women in the area to "conduct intensive educational campaigns" and to collect food pledges and war savings stamp collections. Lilah proved adept at fundraising, in one drive leading the Women's Division to collect $1,216,000 worth of pledges. Her success garnered her considerable recognition from prominent male members of the Tulsa community, which in turn provided her with additional momentum for her civic leadership following the war.[66]

In some respects, Lilah's patriotic support of the US war effort may be surprising considering the federal government's various policies targeting the Creek Nation. Nonetheless, Lilah and other Native Americans showed an uncommonly high level of patriotism during the First World War, especially considering that many Natives did not have US citizenship rights.[67] On the home front, both male and female Native Americans actively contributed to the war cause. Support of the war effort provided Native communities with leverage to reject American Indian policies imposed by non-Natives and to demand reform. In some ways they achieved success, most notably the passage of the Indian Citizenship Act of 1924, which extended citizenship to those who had not previously acquired it. Lindsey's position as a Native woman in Oklahoma sheds light on the complicated nature of citizenship and voting rights in the state. Although many members of the Five Tribes had United States citizenship following allotment and prior to the Indian Citizenship Act, female citizens in Oklahoma like Lindsey were still precluded from the right to vote prior to 1918.[68]

Just as Native activists used their contributions to the First World War as leverage for democratic reforms, female activists also used the conflict as opportunity to demand expanded suffrage. For years, Lindsey had worked toward equal voting rights, especially through her activism with the WCTU. As early as 1906, an opportunity arose at the Oklahoma Constitutional Convention when delegates had proposed women's suffrage as a Progressive measure for the new state, but they had ultimately settled on granting women only the right to vote in school elections. Delegates had rejected wholesale women's suffrage for fear

Lilah Denton Lindsey, date unknown. Courtesy of Beryl Ford Collection, Rotary Club of Tulsa, Tulsa City-County Library and Tulsa Historical Society & Museum.

it would undermine patriarchy and white supremacy, particularly by extending the vote to African American women. Nevertheless, women's support for the Democratic Party in national elections and their patriotic contributions to the war effort persuaded male Democratic politicians to advocate for equal voting rights.[69] Lilah, who served as the WCTU state citizenship director, "helped largely in Tulsa and Tulsa County in securing Women Suffrage."[70] As "an indefatibable [sic] worker for suffrage," Lilah, who was not content with voting only in school elections, considered Oklahoma's ratification of an amendment granting women the right to vote on November 5, 1918, a substantial victory.[71]

Lilah recognized that granting women's suffrage on paper did not automatically guarantee the full inclusion and participation of women in Oklahoma politics. Still a teacher at heart, she launched a campaign to educate women on their new voting rights. First she organized "citizenship mass meetings" and invited speakers to instruct women on how and why they should vote. Lilah then addressed questions: "Since we now have the vote and know how to vote, what do we know about the Laws of Oklahoma?" To instruct recently enfranchised women, she compiled and published a book in 1924 titled *Study Course in Citizenship on Federal and Oklahoma Laws Pertaining to Women and Children*.[72] The volume helped inform the new voters so they could make decisions for themselves at the ballot box.

Even before she secured the right to vote, Lilah had relied on connections with prominent government officials, working across the aisle to bolster her various reform campaigns. Although she favored the Republican Party in the solidly Democratic state, she earned appointments from every Oklahoma state governor who served during her lifetime. For instance, Lilah's civic contributions caught the notice of the first governor of Oklahoma, Democrat Charles N. Haskell. He appointed her to represent the new state at the World's Tuberculosis Congress in Washington, DC, and then sent her as a delegate to the National Charities and Corrections Convention in Richmond, Virginia. She also enjoyed a close friendship with Kate Barnard, the pathbreaking reformer and first woman to hold an elected position in the state of Oklahoma as commissioner of the Department of Charities and Corrections. Lilah consulted with Barnard on various civic projects, and they also traveled together to national conventions on several occasions.[73]

Although they were widely acknowledged at the time, Native women reformers like Lilah Lindsey have since been marginalized in histories of Oklahoma as well as histories of the Progressive Era in the United States. After serving as an accomplished and respected teacher in the Creek Nation, she dedicated herself to several Progressive causes, including temperance, women's suffrage, and orphan welfare. Her early career reveals that female members of the Five Tribes influenced their nations through education and civic reform despite being excluded from formal politics. Their work did not end following statehood. Instead, Lilah and other Native women continued to advocate for and achieve

Progressive reforms in the new state. Lindsey's career showcases how Progressive Indigenous women used activism to make their voices heard before, during, and after the transition to Oklahoma statehood. Their legacy continues today.

NOTES

1. "An Early Day Teacher," series 6, box 1, folder 1, Lilah D. Lindsey Papers, McFarlin Library Special Collections, Tulsa, OK (hereafter MLSC); undated clipping, *Tulsa Tribune*, series 6, box 1, folder 1, Lilah D. Lindsey Papers, MLSC.

2. "From the President of the United States to the Creek Indians, through Colonel Cromwell," *Niles Weekly Register* 36 (March 23, 1929).

3. "A Short Resume of the Activities of Mrs. Lilah D. Lindsey," series 1, box 1, folder 10, Lilah D. Lindsey Papers, MLSC.

4. "A Sketch of My Life. To My Friend E. J. Baldwin," series 1, box 1, folder 1, MLSC.

5. J. O. Misch, "Lilah D. Lindsey," *Chronicles of Oklahoma* 33, no. 2 (1955): 200.

6. Althea Bass, *The Story of Tullahassee* (Oklahoma City: Semco, 1960), 53; "A Sketch of My Life."

7. "Message of Lochar Harjo, Principal Chief of the Creeks, to the Houses of Warriors and Kings, December 6, 1875 (typescript)," folder 1, Lochar Harjo Collection, Western History Collection, University of Oklahoma Libraries (hereafter WHC).

8. For more on schools among the Five Tribes during the same period, specifically Cherokee institutions, see Julie L. Reed, *Serving the Cherokee Nation: Cherokee Sovereignty and Social Welfare, 1800–1907* (Norman: University of Oklahoma Press, 2016); Devon Mihesuah, *Cultivating the Rosebuds: The Education of Women at the Cherokee Female Seminary, 1851–1909* (Champagne: University of Illinois Press, 1997).

9. Christie Anne Farnham, *The Education of the Southern Belle: Higher Education and Student Socialization in the Antebellum South* (New York: New York University Press, 1995), 4.

10. Rowan Faye Steinecker, "'Fully Equal to That of Any Children': Experimental Creek Education in the Antebellum Era," *History of Education Quarterly* 56, no. 2 (May 2016): 273–300.

11. "Memory [Lane] of Other Days, or November 12th, 1939," series 1, box 1, folder 8, Lilah D. Lindsey Papers, MLSC.

12. Lilah D. Lindsey, "Memories of Yesterday: My School Life in Indian Territory Mission Field," interview, 54:202, Indian-Pioneer Papers, WHC.

13. "Memory [Lane] of Other Days."

14. For a detailed examination of the Youth-in-the-States program, see Myra Alexandra-Starr, "Youth-in-the-States: The Mvskoke Indian Nation's Nineteenth Century Higher Education Program" (PhD diss., Ohio State University, 2000).

15. "Memory [Lane] of Other Days."

16. "Memory [Lane] of Other Days."

17. "Memory [Lane] of Other Days."

18. "A Sketch of My Life."

19. "A Sketch of My Life."
20. "Memory [Lane] of Other Days."
21. See Phillip J. Deloria, *Indians in Unexpected Places* (Lawrence: University Press of Kansas, 2004), 4–11, for more cultural expectations of Indigenous behavior.
22. "Memory [Lane] of Other Days."
23. See David Wallace Adams, *Education for Extinction: American Indians and the Boarding School Experience, 1875–1928* (Lawrence: University Press of Kansas, 1995).
24. Mvskoke scholar Myra Alexander-Starr demonstrates that many of the students, including the initial class of eighteen who attended the College of Wooster, returned to fill vital roles in the Creek national government and education bureaucracy. Some began in clerkships and administrative roles and then ascended to influential judicial and legislative positions while "many students were found somewhere in the developing educational programs of the Mvskokes. They were found as instructors, school trustees, and National Council educational committee members, and as school builders." Like Lilah Lindsey, fellow female student Tooka Butler also taught in the national schools. Alexandra-Starr, "Youth-in-the-States," 249–50.
25. Alexandra-Starr, 174.
26. Deposition of A. P. McKellop, Report of the Select Committee to Investigate Matters Connected with the Affairs in the Indian Territory, Senate Reports, 59th Congress, 2nd Session, 1904.
27. "Memory [Lane] of Other Days."
28. "Teachers of the Muskokee Nation, Term of 1875–1876," roll 47, slide 37384, Creek National Records, National Archives; "Life and Experiences of a Creek Indian Woman, Mrs. Mary Lewis Herrod," 1:312–16, Indian-Pioneer Papers, WHC; Mathilda Porter to Alice Robertson, 1870, series 2, box 9, folder 5, Alice Mary Robertson Collection, MLSC.
29. "A Sketch of My Life."
30. "A Sketch of My Life."
31. "Memory [Lane] of Other Days."
32. "Memory [Lane] of Other Days."
33. "Memory [Lane] of Other Days."
34. "Memory [Lane] of Other Days."
35. "Memory [Lane] of Other Days."
36. "Memory [Lane] of Other Days."
37. "A Sketch of My Life."
38. "Memory [Lane] of Other Days."
39. Lindsey, "Memories of Yesterday," 221.
40. Lindsey, 221.
41. Judith N. McArthur, *Creating the New Woman: The Rise of Southern Women's Progressive Culture in Texas, 1893–1918* (Urbana: University of Illinois Press, 1998), 6.
42. See David Chang, *The Color of Land: Race, Nation, and the Politics of Landownership in Oklahoma, 1832–1929* (Chapel Hill: University of North Carolina Press, 2010); Claudio Saunt, *Black, White, and Indian: Race and the Unmaking of an American Family* (New York: Oxford University Press, 2005).

43. Newspaper clipping, series 6, box 1, folder 1, Lilah D. Lindsey Papers, MLSC.

44. "Memory [Lane] of Other Days."

45. James Hochtritt, "Let Us Help You Help Yourselves: New Deal Economic Recovery Programs and the Five Tribes in Rural Oklahoma," in *Main Street Oklahoma: Stories of Twentieth Century America*, ed. Linda W. Reese and Patricia Loughlin (Norman: University of Oklahoma Press, 2013), 184.

46. For adoption practices among southeastern Indigenous nations, see Dawn Peterson, *Indians in the Family: Adoption and the Politics of Antebellum Expansion* (Cambridge, MA: Harvard University Press, 2017).

47. For more on welfare policies and institutions in the postremoval Cherokee Nation, see Julie L. Reed, *Serving the Cherokee Nation: Cherokee Sovereignty and Social Welfare, 1800–1907* (Norman: University of Oklahoma Press, 2016).

48. Hochtritt, "Let Us Let Us Help You Help Yourselves," 184.

49. Izumi Ishii, "Cherokee Women and the Woman's Christian Temperance Union," in *The Native South: New Histories and Enduring Legacies*, ed. Tim Alan Garrison and Greg O'Brien (Lincoln: University of Nebraska Press, 2017), 181–86. The temperance activism of Lindsey and other Native women in Indian Territory contributed to a large-scale international movement. The World's WCTU included members in forty nations and, at its peak in 1927, claimed to have more than a million followers, both white and nonwhite. Despite what historian Ian Tyrell argues was a complicated cultural imperial vision of the organization, nonwhite women such as Lindsey rose to positions of leadership. For more on the history of the WCTU in international contexts, see Ian Tyrell, *Woman's World, Woman's Empire: The Woman's Christian Temperance Union in International Perspective, 1880–1930* (Chapel Hill: University of North Carolina Press, 2010), 3–5.

50. Lilah D. Lindsey, "Foreword," in *History of the Woman's Christian Temperance Union of Indian Territory, Oklahoma Territory, State of Oklahoma*, ed. Abbie Hillerman (Sapulpa, OK: Jennings, 1925). This "do everything" approach advocated by WCTU's president Frances Willard provided an avenue for women to move into public life in an effort to achieve widespread social reform. For more on Willard and the reform agenda of the WCTU, see Ruth Bordin, *Frances Willard: A Biography* (Chapel Hill: University of North Carolina Press, 1986).

51. Lindsey, "Foreword," *History of the Woman's Christian Temperance Union*.

52. Ishii, "Cherokee Women and the Woman's Christian Temperance Union," 189.

53. "A Sketch of My Life."

54. Kent Carter, *Dawes Commission: And the Allotment of the Five Civilized Tribes, 1893–1914* (Orem, UT: Ancestry, 1999), 1–2; Adams, *Education for Extinction*, 21–23.

55. "How I Felt When Statehood Came," series 4, box 1, folder 15, Lilah D. Lindsey Papers, MLSC.

56. Lindsey, "Foreword," *History of the Woman's Christian Temperance Union*.

57. Ishii, "Cherokee Women and the Woman's Christian Temperance Union," 193–94.

58. Lindsey, "Foreword," *History of the Woman's Christian Temperance Union*.

59. "A Short Resume."

60. "A Sketch of My Life."

61. American Humane, "History," accessed May 21, 2019, https://www.americanhumane.org/about-us/history/.

62. "A Sketch of My Life."

63. "A Short Resume."

64. "Newspaper Clipping," series 6, box 1, folder 1, Lilah D. Lindsey Papers, MLSC, 5781.

65. "A Short Resume"; Misch, "Lilah D. Lindsey," 196; Lindsey, "Memories of Yesterday," 224.

66. "A Short Resume"; Misch, "Lilah D. Lindsey," 195–96; Lindsey, "Memories of Yesterday," 224.

67. Russel Lawrence Barsh, "American Indians in the Great War," *Ethnohistory* 38, no. 3 (Summer 1991): 277–82.

68. Although many members of the Five Tribes had United States citizenship following allotment, citizenship rights were not uniformly granted to Native Americans until the Indian Citizenship Act of 1924. For more on Native Americans in the World War I era, see Susan Applegate Krouse, *North American Indians in the Great War* (Lincoln: University of Nebraska Press, 2009).

69. Bill Corbett, "Suffrage Amendment," *The Encyclopedia of Oklahoma History and Culture*, Oklahoma Historical Society, https://www.okhistory.org/publications/enc/entry.php?entry=SU002.

70. "A Sketch of My Life."

71. "A Short Resume."

72. Lilah D. Lindsey, *Study Course in Citizenship on Federal and Oklahoma Laws Pertaining to Women and Children* (Muskogee, OK: Bowman, 1924).

73. Kate Barnard to Mrs. Lilah D. Lindsey, March 26, 1909, March 27, 1913, series 2, box 2, folder 8, Lilah D. Lindsey Papers, MLSC. For more on Kate Barnard, see chapter 4.

HEATHER CLEMMER

2

"MY HEART HAD BEEN BURDENED FOR THE ORPHANED AND HOMELESS CHILDREN"

Religious Imperative and Maternalism in the Work of Mattie Mallory

On March 5, 1938, Maranda "Mattie" Mallory Morgan, the founder of the Oklahoma Orphanage, succumbed to cancer. A resident of Oklahoma City for almost forty years, she had established one of the earliest and most resilient orphanages in the community. Relocated in 1909 to Bethany, a western suburb of Oklahoma City, the Oklahoma Orphanage had been the culmination of Mattie's lifelong vision to provide a home and educational opportunities to orphaned and homeless children. By the time of her death, Mattie had transferred operations of the orphanage to the Welfare League of Oklahoma, which paid for her funeral and burial in Oklahoma City's Fairlawn Cemetery. Mattie herself had buried orphans in that very same cemetery as early as 1901. Now the Welfare League purchased a modest headstone for Mattie, surrounded by the simple headstones of these children. Besides her name and life dates, the marker included only one word: "Mother." For the Welfare League, Mattie Mallory Morgan's legacy was defined by sacrificial motherhood, a product of feminine domesticity. This image undermines her significance to Oklahoma City history and to our understanding of opportunities for women in early twentieth-century Oklahoma. Mattie reflected her geographic and temporal placement at the confluence of women's activism, a spiritual awakening, and frontier development in Oklahoma City. Within that moment, she had the authority to craft her own narrative. In telling her own story of how she established and maintained an orphanage in Oklahoma Territory, Mattie combined elements of frontier individualism, Progressive communalism, and religious belief to elucidate her assumptions that women's spiritual equality could be transferred to public spaces. Mattie had come to Oklahoma City in 1898 with a vision to help children, bringing with her a printing press to publish that message. Within the pages of her newspaper, *The Guide*, Mattie constructed a public image as a woman willing to mother other people's children, but there is more to Mattie's story. Through *The Guide*, Mattie served as a religious tutor, using her own words and those of other women to address social and moral issues through the lens of the Holiness movement, which professed a belief in the equality of souls. Real estate records also reveal Mattie as a businesswoman, purchasing and selling property as part of her mission to create a self-sustaining orphanage. This mission led her to purchase enough property for an Oklahoma City addition and, subsequently, a suburb. However, after Mattie stopped publishing *The Guide* in 1903, she could no longer control her own story, and others elected to define her only as "Mother."

Maranda Mallory was born March 12, 1865, in Franklin County, Kansas. While she never wrote about her childhood in detail, the Kansas environment in which she was raised suggests a familial community where she learned the benefits of land ownership and the crucial role of education in pursuing individual progress. Mattie, the oldest of five children, grew up on her father's sixty acres, close to her maternal grandmother, an illiterate transplant from North Carolina who continued to hold her 160-acre homestead for more than forty years after her husband's death in 1865.[1] Mattie received a public-school education and then attended Baker University, a Methodist institution in Baldwin City, less than ten miles from the Mallory homestead. Upon her graduation in 1889, she completed another year of educational training in Emporia, Kansas. She then taught for two years in Ottawa, Kansas, before leaving the state in September 1893 for a teaching position at the Dawes Academy in Berwyn, Indian Territory. Established by the Baptist Home Missionary Society, the Dawes Academy served the orphans of freedmen and freedwomen of the Chickasaw tribe.[2] Mattie later rarely discussed her work with the Dawes Academy children.

She mentioned Dawes only when describing how God began to call her and her teaching colleagues Fannie Johnston and Laura Shaw to establish their own school. Fannie and Laura shared Mattie's "burden" for "homeless, and friendless children." With nothing more than their meager teaching salaries, Mattie later opined that all they could do, "being without money or any extended influence," was pray and wait for God's providence.[3]

Mattie believed that God provided for those who believed, followed scripture, and prayed fervently. While she and her friends could see no way to start their own school for orphans, a woman named Annie Douglas invited Mattie to work with her at the Mizpah Mission in Winnipeg, Manitoba, during the summer of 1898. For Mattie, the educational and spiritual goals of the Mizpah Mission far exceeded those of the Baptist orphanage and public schools in which she had previously taught. The Mizpah Mission provided a boarding school for the "care, training, education, and salvation" of the community's children. These children, along with the adults in charge of their care and education, were in turn expected to serve the community by spreading the Gospel. In September 1898, Mattie returned to Indian Territory but did not resume her duties at the Dawes Academy. Instead, she felt called by God to answer the request of Reuben E. and Anna Hershey to join them in their mission work in Oklahoma City. They had recently opened an orphanage and boarding residence for the children of missionary parents, and they were unable to care for all the children alone. They had already asked Reuben's younger sister Susan Hershey to join the household. The Hersheys' home on Reno Avenue sat in the epicenter of this rapidly growing city, and they wanted to expand educational opportunities with a teacher like Mattie. Laura Shaw and Fannie Johnston quickly joined her, believing God had answered their prayers to start a school.[4]

Once in Oklahoma City, Mattie's activities stemmed from the confluence of her religious beliefs and her teaching experience. On October 6, 1898, Mattie and Laura, as editor and assistant editor, began publication of *The Guide* in Oklahoma City. The women described *The Guide* as "A WEEKLY HOLINESS JOURNAL, for the teaching of a full Gospel, as laid down in the Scriptures." While this newspaper was new to Oklahoma City, Mattie and Laura had published forty-four previous issues of *The Guide* while they were working at the Dawes Academy in Berwyn and had brought the printing press with them. Throughout *The Guide*'s run in Oklahoma City, the paper never sold advertisements, and no one associated with the newspaper received wages for their articles or other publication work. The subscriptions they received from readers paid for the expenses of publication and distribution. At first, any profits made from subscriptions were "used in spreading the true Gospel."[5] Each week, Mattie promoted what she considered to be sound Biblical doctrine, infused with personal testimonies, sermons, and spiritual advice from men and women who were part of the era's Holiness movement. This movement was born out of the American revivalism of the early nineteenth century and sought to maintain spiritual intensity by emphasizing personal piety. Much of the movement's teachings came from Methodist founder John Wesley, who called for an outpouring of the Holy Spirit through love and compassion for others and the rejection of social norms that he believed caused people to sin.[6]

Like other newspapers associated with elements of the larger Holiness movement, Mattie used *The Guide* as a mouthpiece for her brand of Holiness and encouraged like-minded authors to write for her paper and subscribe to the weekly publication. Mattie believed that anyone could receive God's grace and be saved but that such salvation required worldly sacrifices. People should rebuke their constant striving for wealth, devote time to understanding and interpreting Biblical Scripture, and reject the popular trends in society that undermined personal health and well-being. In the sermons and Bible studies she personally wrote for *The Guide*, Mattie encouraged her readers to remember that riches on earth were fleeting; the real rewards awaited them in Heaven. "While God may give us poverty in this world," she wrote, "still we are not poor, we have the promise that God will supply all our needs."[7] One of the core tenets of Mattie's faith was her belief that God would provide for his people in their time of need. That meant that if God provided more to some than to others, those who were fortunate had a Christian duty to give freely. She believed that most people did not give as much as they should and used Biblical Scripture as evidence to prove that it was necessary to give in order to receive: "How can you expect God to prosper you, when you give nothing?" Mattie did not expect that everyone could give monetarily. She often encouraged her readers to give what they could to others, be it their time, their talent, or what they produced: "We are to give our substance, our increase, our raiment, our meat, ourselves, yea in truth OUR ALL."[8]

Mattie, in her own life and work, attempted to embody this desire to give all of oneself. This led her to express frustration in the pages of *The Guide* when others, particularly those who led established denominational churches, did not model such behavior. Mattie, who had attended a Methodist university and worked for the Baptist denomination in Berwyn, reflected the Holiness movement's rejection of sectarianism and the belief that the reunification of all Christians was possible.⁹ She believed that leaders in the modern church were failing people by not living according to Scripture and rebuked them for accepting and sometimes participating in what many in the Holiness community considered to be the sins of the flesh. In attending her first Oklahoma County Fair in 1898, Mattie was appalled to see a whole block of gambling houses and saloons near Broadway, a major thoroughfare. What incensed her more than the lascivious nature of these businesses were the church booths set up alongside these places "where they [churches] displayed their different work and trafficked [sic] in human souls." She did not see ministers attempting to bring souls to God or minister to those in need. Rather, they were "urging their people to take part in this soul-destroying affair."¹⁰ Mattie could not tolerate when churches refused to acknowledge the hypocrisy of their leaders. She reported in *The Guide* the acquittal of a Methodist minister in Kansas who had presumably engaged in an extramarital relationship and raged that this was another example of "the church conniving to the world." Although she did not explicitly report the sin he committed, she did call out the hypocrisy of a denomination that embraced its minister but left his "partner in the guilt . . . out in the world to receive the scorn and censure of a proud cold world."¹¹ By naming the male minister, but not the woman who had been rejected by the church for the sin they shared, Mattie made public her condemnation of the inequality often inherent in discussions of extramarital sex within denominations.

The Holiness movement did not recognize one gender as more likely to sin or be saved. In fact, many in the movement believed that if a person felt called to speak or write in God's name, their gender should not prevent them from doing so. *The Guide* was Mattie's manifestation of this spiritual equality. In the eight pages published weekly, Mattie collected Holiness material from those she trusted to provide theologically appropriate sermons and Bible studies along with reports from Holiness evangelists who were spreading the message in the region. In the November 17, 1898, edition, for example, page 1 continued an article from the previous week by Reuben Hershey about how people could spot Satan's work in their lives, and Mattie published her own sermon titled "Living in Canaan" on page 2. Page 5 included a Sunday school lesson from Dana A. Boles, a friend from Berwyn who was preaching in Jet, Oklahoma Territory, at the time. Page 8 was a theological study on "Holy Fire" by Ashley L. George, who was serving the Cherokees in Indian Territory.¹² In *The Guide*, women's voices did not dominate, but neither were they relegated to a ladies' page. Throughout the life of the newspaper, Mattie used *The Guide* as her mouthpiece, engaging in theological conversations about what it meant to be a member of the Holiness movement and to challenge the societal ills and denominational sins that she and others believed degraded their communities.

From the beginning, *The Guide* served as Mattie's platform for extolling the importance of a Christian education and her role as an advocate for equal access to education. What had drawn her to Oklahoma City had been the opportunity to begin a school that would serve the educational and spiritual needs of the community. Three weeks after arriving in Oklahoma City, Mattie and Fannie Johnston opened a school within the Hershey home on Reno Avenue, providing an education for orphans and the children of missionaries who were already living there. They also accepted any children whose parents wanted them to have teachers "who have had years of experience in graded and high school work and who are completely consecrated to God and filled with the Holy Ghost." Mattie, fresh off her experience working with Annie Douglas in Winnipeg, named it the Mizpah School. In an advertisement to the subscribers of *The Guide*, Mattie enumerated the reasons parents should send their children to the new school. She believed that it could provide a higher-quality education with more specialized courses than the territorial public schools, where children might also be unduly influenced by nonbelieving peers and teachers. Mattie also advertised that the "charges are low—considering the advantages of the school."[13] By Thanksgiving, two months after Mattie's arrival in Oklahoma City, there were sixteen enrolled students. However, most of the students were orphans and not tuition-paying students from the community. According to several later accounts, Mattie reflected that the growing number of orphans in the home caused her to reassess God's calling for her life. Instead of just operating a school, she now felt led to "open a refuge for orphan, homeless and friendless children."[14] Mattie expressed concern that the Hershey home would not be big enough to provide refuge to all the children in need if their numbers continued to increase. She urged her readers to pray that God would "speedily provide the means for a HOME—a building—separate from our other building where we may care for all whom God will send us."[15]

In a later narrative, Mattie never mentioned the Mizpah School by name. Rather, she declared that the school in the Hershey home had been a brief endeavor, based on her previous educational experiences, which led her to God's true calling for her life by exposing her to the needs of Oklahoma City's orphan population. She never spoke negatively of the work done at the Hershey home, nor did she mention in *The Guide* any problems with Mr. or Mrs. Hershey. However, after the January 5, 1899, edition, *The Guide* ceased publication for ten weeks. Upon its resumption on March 23, Mattie apologized for the disruption in service, explaining that "in the providence of God (for what he permits is as truly his providence as what he sends) it became necessary to move from the place where we were."[16] At the time, that was the only explanation she gave for the disruption in *The Guide*. This lack of explanation was likely due to the speed with which circumstances had drastically changed for Mattie, her fellow teachers, and the orphans in their care. Several years later, while reflecting on the chain of events, Mattie elucidated the story of why she and the other adult women took the orphans and left the Hershey home. In explaining the situation, she crafted a narrative in which spiritual equality had given her the right to serve as the head of a growing household and make decisions for that family construct. She claimed that she was thankful for the time in the Hershey home, but Reuben Hershey had failed to meet moral standards. Mattie did not explain the rift with Reuben, and given her beliefs that individuals should live a sanctified life, it is impossible to speculate what she deemed sinful in Reuben's actions or thoughts. Asserting their belief in the equality of souls, she and three other women in the home (including Reuben's sister Susan) had "repeatedly warned" Reuben that he was following "another spirit than the Spirit of the Lord." Reuben had insisted that those who questioned his beliefs "repent, or leave." This led Mattie and her friends in the home to begin a twenty-eight-day fast, with constant prayer and Biblical study, in search of God's will.

These women were empowered by the Holiness movement to seek divine inspiration and take action even when it usurped male authority. On day twenty-three of the fast, they read Ezekiel 12, which states, "Thou dwellest in the midst of a rebellious house," and they considered that warning to be the sign that they should not relent to Reuben's demands. On January 5, Mattie published *The Guide*, and as in the preceding few weekly editions, she made no mention of the spiritual war raging at home. Recounting the story later, Mattie wrote, "After 28 days of fasting, the Lord said, 'Move out.'" So, on the evening of January 7, the fast came to an end and "we (ladies) carried out our stuff." More than once over the years, Mattie recalled this female-led exodus: "We had four workers, sixteen children, five cents in money, two postage stamps, faith in God and a divine conviction that God was leading." By bedtime, however, they had secured a rental house on Fifth Street. The landlady allowed them to stay the night, but demanded the monthly rent of twenty dollars by the next day at three

P.M. The next morning they awoke with enough groceries for only one meal, a set of four dishes, and a sewing table. As the children rotated into the kitchen to eat breakfast at the sewing table in shifts of four, word of their sudden move traveled through town. By ten A.M., friends had provided thirty dollars, which they used to pay the rent and purchase wood, food, dishes, and a larger table. Other donations, including a stove, poured in throughout the day, "so the night of the 8th closed its curtains of darkness around a happy family."[17] For Mattie, this became the oft-repeated origin story for the Oklahoma Orphanage. Mattie's exodus narrative validated her maternal identity as the leader of a family she had created. Her ability to weave into the story elements of spiritual struggle, individual perseverance, and God's providence established a narrative thread that she could use to justify her authority as the head of her own orphanage.

The move to Fifth Street was not the end of their pilgrimage as the lodging proved temporary. In explaining the circumstances later, Mattie claimed the landlady, who lived next door, quickly came to regret her decision to rent to an orphanage with sixteen children. Instead of conceding that perhaps the noise associated with sixteen children in a home was the reason for the landlady's frustration, Mattie was sure the real problem was that "she was so disturbed by the Holy Spirit that she could rest neither day nor night." In any case, the "old lady" refused to take the next month's rent and demanded that they leave immediately. Mattie continued to emphasize the narrative of God's providence and the women's divine authority to act on behalf of "our little company of believers." In recalling this story, Mattie reiterated that her faith was rooted in a God who looked after the marginalized—the widowed, the fatherless, and the helpless. These prayers were not only for deliverance from their current situation but also for strength in their own faith journeys. If the landlady kicked them out the next day, they would go willingly, because "anywhere with Jesus will be home sweet home."

Mattie reported that their prayers were heard by God, who interceded to soften the landlady's heart. The next morning, instead of throwing them out, she told them they could stay at the house and pay rent until they found a new home. For two weeks, they searched for a new home on the northwestern edge of town. The women were not seeking to create a religious enclave separate from Oklahoma City but wished to avoid disturbing and angering neighbors in close quarters. Their search turned up a large brick building at the corner of Walker Avenue and Pottawatomie Street, but the rental agent feared the owner would not be interested in renting due to the large number of children. Just as she had done the night the landlady threatened to evict them, Mattie brought "our little circle" together in prayer. The next day Mattie went to see the agent and was disappointed to find that he had been unable to reach the owner and had no answer for her. As she got up to leave, the owner entered the office, and Mattie was able to advocate in person. He agreed, allowing her a one-year lease and giving her the keys on the spot. When she returned to the orphanage, the children were sitting around the table eating, "but as I waved the key in front of them knives forks and spoons were dropped and all of one accord praised God."[18] One month and one day after leaving the Hershey home, Mattie and her colleagues moved the children to their new home, where they remained for the next two years.

Settled into a more permanent residence, Mattie resumed *The Guide* on March 23. Through the paper, Mattie related to subscribers her new responsibilities as a mother and educator to the orphans and as the leader of a group of women who were actively involved in providing for this family. No sooner had they moved into their new home than Susan Hershey came down with the measles, which quickly spread to all the children. Mattie and the other healthy women living in the home provided all the care for the ailing residents as no one dared enter the home for risk of infection. Although Susan and most of the children made quick recoveries, a fourteen-year-old named George did not. George had come to the orphanage after they had moved to Fifth Street and, according to Mattie, had been "very wild and wicked." However, his heart had softened. Now, as he was sick with the measles, Mattie witnessed in George a desire to have a personal relationship with God. After a feverish night in which Mattie and others stayed up and prayed over George, he awoke and said, "Thank God he kept me from sin." George then began to improve and "many times testified to God's power to save." However, in the middle of the night on April 1, Mattie was called to George's room, where he appeared to be hemorrhaging. As she entered the room, Mattie said she caught "a smile of recognition as the spirit went out like a candle and George was with the angels safe beyond all temptation." She mourned for "our boy at rest" within the pages of *The Guide* and testified to feeling confident that she would see him again in Heaven.[19] Mattie later recalled George's story in greater detail, explaining his struggles with sin when he had entered their orphanage as well as the tender moments when she and others had sat with him through his medical travails and spiritual journey.[20] Despite his brief time in Mattie's care, his story elucidates in the pages of *The Guide* Mattie's maternal and spiritual role in the orphanage. George's narrative—

Miss Mattie Mallory and Children. In 2009, the City of Bethany commissioned artists to design murals throughout the downtown district to commemorate the hundredth anniversary of the city's founding. The artist used a 1909 photograph of Mattie Mallory, which depicted her alone and leaning against a tree. For the mural, her pose is exactly the same, but she is leaning on one of the pillars at the orphanage she constructed in Bethany in 1910. Another photograph shows children in front of that Bethany building, but it was taken after Mattie's death when the Oklahoma Orphanage became the Children's Convalescent Home. Photograph by Heather Clemmer.

from orphan to son—is an example of how Mattie created her own image as a maternal leader through a lens of domesticity that traditionalists could support. Yet, at the same time, Mattie was a spiritual leader to *The Guide*'s subscribers as she preached a sermon to them about the road from sin to redemption.

Although Mattie's spiritual and maternal leadership were extolled through *The Guide*, the publication made no mention of her emerging role as a businesswoman. On April 12, 1899, just two weeks after George's death, Mattie (signing as Maranda Mallory), Laura Shaw, and Fanny Johnston filed paperwork to incorporate the Oklahoma Orphanage as a domestic for-profit business corporation.[21] Mattie never published anything about the incorporation filing in her future stories about the founding of the orphanage—she merely began referring to herself as the superintendent of the orphanage—but this action was significant, for it established the legal origin of the Oklahoma Orphanage. She might not have believed anyone was interested in her business dealings, but the event also did not fit with the origin story she had in mind for the orphanage and her image as its mother. *The Guide* continued to be Mattie's spiritual platform, not a place to advertise secular transactions.

Mattie also did not use *The Guide* to discuss her emerging role as a preacher and activist on behalf of the orphanage and the Holiness movement. On June 1, 1899, she announced in her editorial, "God has told us to put our house in order for he has called us for a few days to labor in another field." She noted she would be gone to Fort Worth, Texas, "to hold a meeting" but did not explain for how long or the meeting's purpose. In retelling the story later, Mattie provided scant explanation, merely mentioning that she had received word, along with money for her train ticket, to join others at a Holiness camp meeting in Fort Worth. She never explained who else was in attendance, but she said they "opened fire on the enemies rank" with their religious services.[22] In early August, Mattie left the orphanage again, this time for a camp meeting in Lamont, Oklahoma Territory, with itinerant preacher George Henson. Upon her return from Lamont, Mattie wrote the August 17 editorial and then left for another camp meeting in Moonlight, Kansas.[23] She never described her role at these camps, but such meetings in the Holiness movement sometimes lasted for several weeks; a few planned days of sermons and prayer would turn into longer revivals as people camped locally. In Mattie's absence, Laura Shaw wrote *The Guide*'s editorial and apologized to subscribers for the lack of Mattie's spiritual message.[24]

Mattie's preaching schedule would not have been possible without her community of women, including Laura Shaw, Fannie Johnston, and Susan Hershey.

These were Mattie's spiritual sisters whom she trusted to care for the orphans just as she did. Mattie gave praise to "the Lord for the little band of consecrated workers he has given us to help us and hold up our hands." With the orphanage so close to Oklahoma City's railyards, Mattie could catch a train south to communities like Fort Worth or north to Kansas, spreading her influence and message, but without her trusted colleagues she would not have been able to leave the orphanage for these opportunities.[25] The fact that ministers and evangelists requested Mattie's participation at camp meetings and revivals speaks to the Holiness movement's openness to women as ministers of the Gospel, particularly in rural areas. As Mattie explained, "By being consecrated, sanctified, and baptized by fire, one is ready to lead others."[26] Just as she justified her sermons in *The Guide*, Mattie assumed a role as spiritual leader based on her conviction that anyone could be called to preach the word of God.

Mattie's travel schedule in August 1899 did not prevent her from promoting the sacred educational experience she envisioned for the orphans and Oklahoma City residents. Since their move in March, the number of orphans had grown to twenty-two. She announced that the school at the orphanage would open for the year on September 11 and that all children were welcome. She wrote to *The Guide* subscribers that the school was for anyone who wanted "to be educated for God and to escape the pollution that is in the world through sin." Mattie believed all children should receive academic training while being mentally and spiritually prepared to live in a sinful world. To bolster her argument for a private religious education, Mattie leaned on the writings of Methodist founder John Wesley. Despite the Holiness movement's condemnation of sectarianism, Mattie and others continued to support Wesley's theology, which included an emphasis on the power of human reasoning. Wesley argued that children must be educated, no matter their class or station, and that to send children to public schools was to raise them in "nurseries of all manner of wickedness." While Wesley's admonition encouraged people of his time to send their boys to private schools, Mattie included her own editorial comment, adding, "He might with equal truth [have] said girls." Mattie agreed with Wesley that education was invaluable, but she recognized that much had changed for women in the century since he had written those words. This equality in education was at the core of Mattie's theological beliefs. A Christian education could prepare children, regardless of gender, to intellectually combat sin in this world and prepare their souls for the coming of the Lord. Religious education was critical, in Mattie's mind, to the perpetuation of the Holiness movement: "It is an historical fact that any genuine religious movement has remained true to God little more than a generation."[27] Mattie could have a significant impact on the future of the Christian faith by providing a nonsectarian educational experience that emphasized outreach to the marginalized. She considered education to be vital to her orphans and the community. This meant hiring two new teachers for the spring 1900 term. It also pushed her to seek more land on which to grow her family and its educational opportunities.[28]

Mattie trusted that God would provide for her and the children in her care, but she needed a steady stream of resources in order to expand the care and educational opportunities she expected to offer through the Oklahoma Orphanage. Charity was a cornerstone of Holiness beliefs, and Mattie therefore used the editorial page in *The Guide* to report on the work of the orphanage and encourage readers to give, but that was not enough. The Oklahoma City *Daily Times-Journal* also took notice of Mattie's and her colleagues' work with orphans. In March 1900 it published several articles encouraging donations to the Oklahoma Orphanage. Mattie's newspaper had previously solicited within the confines of the Holiness community in the region, and in that context she could control the narrative through the lens of God's providential support and the spiritual benefits of giving. In the *Daily Times-Journal* she was unable to control the secular narrative, but it gave Mattie access to a wider audience, targeting the gentlemen and ladies of Oklahoma City society who sought to give back to their community. The results were articles devoid of the religious purpose of the Oklahoma Orphanage and Mattie's calling. An uncredited author for the *Daily Times-Journal* vouched for the worthiness of the institution and the women actively engaged in what they considered to be the noble work of caring for unwanted children. The author noted that the ladies wanted to expand their work, but "the extent of the work depends on the support that they receive."[29] In the article Mattie's work was characterized as charitable, but it was disconnected from her religious purpose. Mattie might not have liked the way her work was communicated, but the articles did lead city businessmen to begin a subscription drive that gave her the opportunity to redirect the narrative. She wrote a thank-you card that was published in the *Daily Times-Journal* in which Mattie thanked the local citizens for a "monthly offering" of $21.50. She called the friend who had notified the paper of the orphanage's need "God's agent" and reminded readers that neither she nor anyone at the orphanage was known to solicit or beg for donations. Instead, she said, "We go to Him with our needs and he so wonderfully moves on the hearts of the people to provide the things needful."[30] Mattie clearly wanted the people of Oklahoma City to know that the work of the orphanage was led by God and not dependent on society's charitable donations.

Over the next few years, businessmen and society ladies subscribed to fund the orphanage and collected contributions at their clubs and offices. While Mattie was thankful for these charitable contributions and those from Holiness adherents, she worried about long-term sustainability. She did not want to depend on the whims of wealthy urban residents or members of a Holiness movement who already showed signs of splitting into rival denominations. In *The Guide*, Mattie continued to profess the orphanage's reliance on God's providence while seeking a business solution to its financial needs. The booming real estate market in burgeoning Oklahoma City provided an answer to the need for revenue and space in which to grow. In June 1901, Mattie (signing as Maranda) purchased fifteen acres from William and Mamie Guernsey in the southeast quarter of Section 20 in Oklahoma Township (today it is at Western Avenue, just north of Twenty-Third Street). Mattie paid $500 for the property, and while there are accounts that claim she paid for the property up front, a mortgage book for the same date lists Mamie Guernsey as the holder of the mortgage.[31] When Mattie announced in *The Guide* that the orphans would be moving to the new property, she did not note who held the title or the mortgage to the property. Rather, she stated that the orphanage now had fifteen acres on which they hoped to build a home so that they could stop paying rent and which they hoped would "help the children feel like *they* have a home and encourage them to habits of industry."[32] Mattie's report on the orphanage to Holiness readers focused on how the property would benefit the children and their future development. By not publicly advertising her new role as a property owner and businesswoman, she was able to maintain the maternal narrative.

With the land purchased, Mattie sought public support for the funds needed to build a home. In September 1901, she (signing the warranty deed as president of the orphanage) sold five of the fifteen acres for $375.[33] She used the editorial page of *The Guide* to solicit from her Holiness subscribers personally, but she also decided to ask Oklahoma City residents for aid through a more traditional construct. In January 1902, Mattie asked a male associate, W. W. Storm, to request funding on the orphanage's behalf. In an article for the *Daily Oklahoman*, Storm articulated Mattie's goal of building a home and cultivating the surrounding land so that the orphanage could become "more self-sustaining and have more room for the ever increasing family of orphans." In vouching for

Mattie's character, Storm referred to her as "Mrs. Mallory" despite the fact that, having claimed to have first met Mattie upon her arrival in Oklahoma City, he must have been aware that she was a single woman. Whether the newspaper or Storm erred in her title, it further fostered the maternal narrative. Nowhere in the article did Storm mention the religious purposes for the orphanage and school, referring to it as a "noble, practical charity." He did not describe the success of the orphanage as God's providence but claimed it was the result of "excellent management." Storm's description of Mattie's work was secular and emphasized the domestic nature of her endeavor in providing the "best practical advantage of these destitute, homeless children."[34] The next day, the board of directors of the Commercial Club passed a motion recommending that the public contribute to the orphanage and to "Mrs. Mallory" so that they could build a "suitable home." They recommended that all the newspapers publish the Commercial Club's recommendation and that businessmen provide donation boxes at their stores and offices. One of those in attendance at the Commercial Club meeting was I. M. Putnam.[35] Putnam owned much of the property surrounding Mattie's ten acres, which he had already begun to develop into individual lots as part of what would be platted as the Military Park neighborhood and the Westbrook Addition.

There is no record of how much money local businessmen raised, but construction of the orphanage's new home was completed by the summer of 1902. Mattie paid off the mortgage in June 1902, and all costs associated with the construction of the home were paid as it was built.[36] By December 1902 there were thirty-two children with a nurse and several "aunties" providing care. Mattie's frequent travel led her to turn the school over to Susan Hershey and her new husband, Clarence Girton. Despite continued donor subscriptions, some building amenities remained unfinished: a cistern, a washroom, and a bake oven still needed to be installed. By the end of 1902 Mattie and the other caregivers worried that even with these amenities, they might have to stop taking in new children due to limited space.[37] No sooner had the orphanage made these ten acres its home than it exhausted the property's capacity. Mattie's goal of a self-sustaining orphanage required enough land for livestock, farmland, a home, a school, and an office for *The Guide*. As was the orphanage family's tradition, they prayed for guidance. Mabel Porter, the new office editor for *The Guide*, recalled several months later that God "gave Sister Mallory the message to 'Build houses.'" God's call perplexed them all since there was not enough room on their ten acres for more houses, but they "continued to trust and obey and wait on God."[38] Mattie and the rest of her staff surely considered it God's providence when I. M. Putnam offered the answer to the their prayers. Putnam, seeking to take advantage of the Oklahoma Railway Company's new trolley line on Western Avenue and consolidate his holdings, offered $3,000 for the orphanage's ten acres. In return, he agreed to sell the orphanage thirty acres just three-quarters of a mile to the northwest for $2,000. This new property stretched along the eastern side of Pennsylvania Avenue from Thirtieth Street to Thirty-Sixth Street. On February 3, 1903, Mattie sold her first piece of real estate for a profit and signed the deed for a second property, free of debt, which doubled her landholdings.[39]

The new property already had a small cottage and a few outbuildings, but Mattie and the rest of the staff felt God calling them to immediately prepare the land for farming and raising livestock before constructing a new home. I. M. Putnam did not require the orphanage's residents to immediately vacate the sold property and allowed them to reside in the old home while they developed the new property. With farmland that provided food for the orphanage as well as crops for market, the goal of self-sufficiency was more likely assured. Friend of the orphanage O. C. Woodrow donated the use of his own farm implements and brought them from Anvil, Oklahoma. Susan and Clarence Girton, along with the fourteen oldest boys, tilled the ground and prepared a farm on the site. They lived in the three-room cottage during the week and returned to the orphanage on weekends. A tree nursery in McLoud, Oklahoma, donated 130 fruit trees at the end of February, and another 500 trees arrived from various donors over the next several months. By April 1903, *The Guide* had moved its office into a small building on the farm, which proved to be the paper's last home. In the August edition of *The Guide*, Mattie announced that it would be ceasing production. She explained, "We feel the need of retrenching and feel after much prayer and consultation among the workers that, to discontinue the paper is the will of the Lord." She believed that by ending the paper, she and others would be able to put "all our strength and time in the bringing in, caring for and training the orphan children God may give us." The timing of Mattie's announcement coincided with the transport of a large brick house onto the new property. Mattie did not have time to mourn the loss of the newspaper she had worked diligently to produce for years, a paper that had provided her with the opportunity to preach, spread the theological studies of others, and communicate her goals for the orphanage and her charges. She would have only a few months to get the house ready for winter, construct school rooms, and make sure the orphanage's thirty-six children were comfortable before winter. Before finishing her last editorial, Mattie listed the name and age of every child in the orphanage along with the six women who served as full-time workers, placing her own name last on that list. She asked readers to pray for them and the work ahead.[40]

Through *The Guide*, Mattie established herself as a preacher and an advocate for orphans, but the newspaper ended before her extensive real estate deals and land development began. In April 1905, Mattie Mallory paid $12,000 for an entire quarter section, 160 acres, across the street diagonally from the orphanage's location, west of Pennsylvania Avenue and north of Thirty-Sixth Street. In March 1906, Mattie (this time noted as "a single woman") sold the western eighty acres of the quarter section to Kate Dunn for $9,000.[41] These transactions paved the way for her to establish a new Oklahoma City neighborhood on her remaining eighty acres. While Mattie had purchased the property, the survey plat filed with the city in May 1906, naming it the Beula Heights Addition, included the signatures of three men: J. B. McBride, G. W. Sawyer, and J. F. Page. Each was associated with Mattie and the orphanage, but none of their names are on the property deed. The plat appears to include some of what Mattie envisioned: one block for the orphanage and an adjacent block for a school. There were also ten acres on the southern end of the property for a rescue home for unwed mothers, a project Mattie had mentioned many times in *The Guide* but had never had the space to include. Instead of being used as farmland, the rest of the addition was prepared to be divided into lots, which would be sold to individuals interested in supporting the mission of this new community. The two major streets parallel to Pennsylvania Avenue were named Sawyer Avenue and Page Avenue.[42] Mattie's name, and her power as a property-owning woman, were thus diminished in the presence of men.

For a brief time during the frontier days of Oklahoma City, Maranda "Mattie" Mallory constructed a narrative through her own newspaper that expressed her personal spiritual beliefs and her vision for the organization that became the Oklahoma Orphanage. With the closing of *The Guide*, Mattie's public voice began to fade, though she continued to amass property across Oklahoma County, culminating in her role in the founding of Bethany, Oklahoma, and the move of the orphanage to that suburb. In 1912 Mattie married John Morgan, and despite her well-established business acumen, she was relegated to the second signatory on subsequent property transactions. Her role as a spiritual leader also waned as the Holiness movement fragmented, leaving women with less authority in

Mattie Mallory Morgan's second graveside memorial. This three-foot memorial to Mattie, located in Fairlawn Cemetery in Oklahoma City, is approximately six feet away from her original gravestone. The memorial emphasizes the geographic and religious connections the present-day Children's Center Rehabilitation Hospital draws between itself and Mattie Mallory Morgan. Photograph by Heather Clemmer.

the emerging denominations that followed. A year after Mattie's death in 1938, the Oklahoma Orphanage became the Children's Convalescent Center, which offered long-term medical care, and the orphans were relocated. Mattie's original vision of a self-sustaining orphanage was lost. After rebranding the Children's Convalescent Center as the Children's Center Rehabilitation Hospital in 2014, the organization decided to erect a new gravestone in Fairlawn Cemetery for its founder, Mattie M. Mallory Morgan. This monument says more about the Children's Center than it does Mattie's importance to the community. Three lines of the gravestone are in Mattie's words: "MY HEART HAD BEEN BURDENED FOR THE ORPHANED AND HOMELESS CHILDREN. GOD SAID, 'GO OPEN THE WORK AND TRUST ME.'" The monument makes no mention of her belief in the spiritual equality of all souls, nor does it acknowledge her real estate and business prowess. Rather, the marker stakes a claim to Mattie as a matron and provides eight lines of text relating the hospital's interpretation of her mission and reflecting its current work, not Mattie's true legacy. As others embraced Mattie's work and her mission to craft her own narrative, she became a stereotypical maternal woman who sacrificed a traditional domestic life in service of others. Her story and her importance to the history of Oklahoma City have been minimized to place her completely within the expectations of a gendered sphere.

NOTES

1. 1865 Kansas State Census, Ottawa, June 7, 8, 1865, Ancestry; 1870 US Federal Census, Franklin Township, Franklin County, Kansas, July 11, 1870, Ancestry.
2. "Home Mission Appointment," *Baptist Home Missionary Monthly* (October 1893): 350, https://babel.hathitrust.org/cgi/pt?id=wu.89077054773&view=1up&seq=368.
3. Mattie M. Mallory, "History of the Oklahoma Orphanage, 1st Chapter," *The Guide*, December 1902, 1.
4. Editorial, *The Guide*, October 6, 1898, 2; Mallory, "History of the Oklahoma Orphanage, 1st Chapter," 1.
5. *The Guide*, October 13, 1898, 4.
6. George M. Marsden, *Religion and American Culture* (San Diego, CA: Harcourt Brace Jovanovich, 1990), 153–55; Stan Ingersol, Harold E. Raser, and David P. Whitelaw, *Our Watchword and Song: The Centennial History of the Church of the Nazarene* (Kansas City, MO: Beacon Hill, 2009), 10.
7. Mattie M. Mallory, "Sons of God," *The Guide*, October 27, 1898, 2.
8. Mattie M. Mallory, "Christian Giving," *The Guide*, December 15, 1898, 2, 3, 8.
9. Ingersol et al., *Our Watchword and Song*, 53–56.
10. Editorial, *The Guide*, October 20, 1898, 4.
11. "An Acquittal," *The Guide*, March 30, 1899, 5.

12. *The Guide*, November 17, 1898.

13. "Our School," *The Guide*, October 20, 1898, 5; "The Mizpah School," *The Guide*, October 20, 1898, 8.

14. Mallory, "History of the Oklahoma Orphanage, 1st Chapter," 1; Sam Boles, "Woman's Pluck Plus Five Dollars Builds Home for Orphans on Virgin Spot," *Daily Oklahoman*, February 28, 1909, 8.

15. "The Editor," *The Guide*, December 15, 1898, 2.

16. Editorial, *The Guide*, March 23, 1899, 4.

17. Mattie M. Mallory, "History of the Work," *The Guide*, September 5, 1901, 4; Mallory, "History of the Oklahoma Orphanage, 1st Chapter," 1; Mallory, "History of the Oklahoma Orphanage, 1st Chapter Continued," *The Guide*, January 1903, 1.

18. Mallory, "History of the Oklahoma Orphanage, 1st Chapter Continued," 1.

19. "Our Boy at Rest," *The Guide*, April 6, 1899, 3.

20. Mallory, "History of the Oklahoma Orphanage, 1st Chapter Continued," 1–2; Mallory, "History of the Oklahoma Orphanage," *The Guide*, March 1903, 2; "Our Boy at Rest," 3.

21. Filing Number 1900003523, Oklahoma Secretary of State, Business Services Search, https://www.sos.ok.gov/corp/corpInformation.aspx?id=1900003523.

22. Editorial, *The Guide*, June 1, 1899, 5; Mattie M. Mallory, "History of the Oklahoma Orphanage," *The Guide*, April 1903, 1.

23. *The Guide*, August 10, 1899, 4, 8.

24. *The Guide*, August 24, 1899, 4.

25. "Noble," *Norman (OK) Democrat-Topic*, November 1, 1901, 2, https://gateway.okhistory.org/ark:/67531/metadc118983/m1/2/?q=mattie+mallory+norman+democrat+topic; "County News: Quincy," *Norman Democrat-Topic*, March 6, 1903, 4, https://gateway.okhistory.org/ark:/67531/metadc119098/m1/4/?q=mattie+mallory+norman+democrat+topic.

26. *The Guide*, July 20, 1899, 4.

27. *The Guide*, August 17, 1899, 4.

28. "Territorial Topics," *Daily Times-Journal* (Oklahoma City), March 10, 1900, 2, https://gateway.okhistory.org/ark:/67531/metadc95442/m1/2/?q=orphans.

29. "The Orphanage," *Daily Times-Journal*, March 20, 1900, 4, https://gateway.okhistory.org/ark:/67531/metadc95449/m1/3/.

30. Mattie M. Mallory, "A Card of Thanks," *Daily Times-Journal*, March 23, 1900, 3.

31. Warranty Deed Record Book No. 30, June 25, 1901, Oklahoma County Clerk Records, 347; Mortgage Record Book No. 16, June 25, 1901, Oklahoma County Clerk Records, 353. In Charles Edwin Jones's article, he says she used $300 from the sale of Kansas property but provides no evidence of this transaction; Charles Edwin Jones, "Miss Mallory's Children: The Oklahoma Orphanage and the Founding of Bethany," *Chronicles of Oklahoma* 71 (Winter 1993–94), 397.

32. Mattie M. Mallory, "The Work, What Is It?," *The Guide*, July 4, 1901, 2.

33. Warranty Deed Record Book No. 34, September 27, 1901, Oklahoma County Clerk Records, 79.

34. W. W. Storm, "To the Public," *Daily Oklahoman*, January 23, 1902, 3.

35. "Committeemen," *Daily Oklahoman*, January 25, 1902, 4.

36. Release of Mortgage Book No. 35, June 7, 1902, Oklahoma County Clerk Records, 524; Mattie M. Mallory, "Report of the Work," *The Guide*, June 20, 1901, 4; Mallory, "History of the Work," *The Guide*, September 5, 1901, 4.

37. M. M. Porter, "The Work," *The Guide*, December 1902, 2, 4.

38. Mabel Porter, "Orphanage to 'Build Houses,'" *The Guide*, April 1903, 2.

39. Warranty Deed Record Book No. 42, Oklahoma County Clerk Records, 571, 634.

40. *The Guide*, August 1, 1903, 4.

41. Warranty Deed Record Book No. 42, 571, 634.

42. Warranty Deed Record Book No. 42, 571, 634.

AMY L. SCOTT

3
"GIVE ME A NATION OF GREAT MOTHERS"
Alice Robertson's Conservative Maternalism

In 1916, Alice Robertson, the vice president of the Oklahoma Association Opposed to Woman Suffrage, made clear her position on voting rights for women: "I do not ever want to see a woman political candidate; I do not want the right to march around handing out cigars."[1] Just five years later, a photographer captured a playful Robertson, the first woman to preside over the United States House of Representatives, gleefully holding the gavel with which she had called Congress to order.[2] This chapter examines the shifting gendered ideologies that shaped the public life and political career of Alice M. Robertson, Oklahoma's first congresswoman. Her story became a national media sensation in November 1920, when she was elected on the Republican ticket out of Oklahoma's traditionally Democratic Second District. The sixty-six-year-old self-described "old maid" arrived in Washington, DC, reporting for duty as the sole woman to win a congressional race in the first national election after the Nineteenth

Amendment had enfranchised all white women with the vote, granting them the foundational right of full democratic citizenship.

Since her victory in 1920, Alice Robertson has been portrayed by contemporary writers and academic historians as puritanical, anti-suffragist, antifeminist, and even anti-woman.[3] Political historians have mostly overlooked Robertson, portraying her as a colorful Oklahoma pioneer who achieved some political "firsts" while dismissing her time in Congress as insignificant.[4] Most scholars who have studied Robertson are generally frustrated by the contradictions that at first glance seem to define her.[5] It is difficult, after all, to reconcile the congresswoman's essentialist understanding of gender and her conservative votes on gender equality issues with her educational accomplishments, her employment as a federal worker and political appointee, her election to Congress, and her decision to live her life independently as a single woman. More recent interdisciplinary studies of Robertson portray her as a transitional, hybrid figure. Her identity and political career, these scholars argue, were shaped by the Victorian-era "cult of true womanhood" gender ideology that dictated a separate, domestically oriented sphere of influence for women; yet Robertson also embraced elements of a more modernist new-womanhood ideology that encouraged education as well as the possibilities of economic independence and political autonomy for women.[6]

Robertson's story signifies more than a bridge between the gendered political formations of the cult of true womanhood and the new woman. Her words and the political philosophies she espoused are better understood when traced over a lifetime of educational and community development work, government service, and political activism. She was both a Republican Party loyalist and a "mother of conservatism."[7] She forged her political identity in the gendered and racialized world of the federal Bureau of Indian Affairs (BIA), a national network of Republican Party patronage, and local party building in Indian Territory and, eventually, in Oklahoma, where state and local politics had come to be defined by single-party Democratic rule.

Alice Robertson's political consciousness and conservative gendered identity appear less enigmatic when examined in the context of her formative working experiences as the daughter of Presbyterian missionaries in Indian Territory and as a bureaucrat in the expanding federal Bureau of Indian Affairs and when read through the lens of recent scholarship on gender and settler colonialism.[8] As a clerk, secretary, and teacher in the BIA, Robertson absorbed Republican free-labor ideology and participated in emerging conservative maternalist reform politics, a predominant gendered anti-statist movement that reached its pinnacle in the 1920s and 1930s.[9] In the years after World War I, conservative women like Alice Robertson feared that women's suffrage and Progressive reforms would lead to state interference in the patriarchal family structure. Organizing within the Republican Party and in women's clubs that operated independently of party politics, such women played an important role in articulating a conservative, often reactionary, agenda and a model for women's political leadership.[10] Their activism constrained Progressive reforms and liberal social welfare policies.[11] As a Republican congresswoman, Robertson struggled to find a balance between pursuing her party's agenda, advancing the conservative maternalism that animated women on the far right, and representing her constituents in Oklahoma. Robertson's story demonstrates that as politically active women moved along a spectrum of maternalist politics from the 1870s through the 1920s, their political arguments and strategies for advocacy were influenced by their urban and rural regional identities, by their attachment to a political party, and by the assumptions that they made about immigrants and people of color.

Alice Robertson was born on January 2, 1854, on the Tullahassee Mission in the Muscogee Creek Nation, Indian Territory.[12] Robertson's maternal grandfather, the Presbyterian minister Samuel Worcester, had utilized Sequoyah's syllabary to translate the Bible into Cherokee and assisted newspaper editor Elias Boudinot with the publication of the *Cherokee Phoenix*. Worcester gained notoriety when he sued the State of Georgia for unlawful imprisonment after violating a racist Georgia law intended to segregate whites from Cherokees.[13] When the United States military, under orders issued by Democratic president Andrew Jackson, forcibly exiled the Cherokees to Indian Territory, Worcester followed with his family. He continued his missionary work in Indian Territory, publishing the *Cherokee Messenger* and establishing a school at Park Hill near the Cherokee capital. Worcester's daughter Ann also dedicated herself to the work of converting and educating American Indians. She married Presbyterian missionary William Robertson. Together the young couple ran the Tullahassee Mission School in the Muscogee Nation.[14]

Alice was the second of seven Robertson children. Her letters, journals, and memoirs reveal a childhood in which gendered expectations for girls' and women's behavior existed in tension with daily life in Indian Territory. As Ann Robertson devoted her energies to translating the Bible into Mvskoke, Alice witnessed her mother's study of linguistics and translation, intellectual enterprises traditionally coded masculine. Her mother's devotion to scholarship influenced

Alice from a young age to believe that women's potentialities reached beyond the traditional roles of helpmate, mother, and caretaker that confined most women's ambitions to hearth and home. During the Civil War, the Robertsons' reputation as Union loyalists forced them to flee Indian Territory and abandon the Tullahassee Mission.[15] At Tullahassee, young Alice had already performed much of the family's domestic labor, but her refugee status interrupted her formal education and brought even harder forms of work. As her family crossed Confederate lines, traveling between Union camps en route from Indian Territory to Illinois, Wisconsin, and finally Kansas, Alice witnessed the torment that war wrought on Americans in every region. At each campsite, twelve-year-old Alice rose at 4:30 A.M., built a fire, and prepared biscuits, bacon, and coffee for her family.[16] Resenting the Democratic Party over Indian removal was already a Worcester-Robertson family tradition. Civil War hardships turned Alice into a lifelong Republican.[17]

When the Robertsons returned to Indian Territory after the Civil War, they found the Tullahassee Mission in ruins.[18] As the family rebuilt, household chores and farmwork usually assigned to boys and men fell to young Alice. Her bilingualism also pulled her into the cultural exchanges that accompanied Anglo colonization of the Muscogee Nation. She served as an interpreter between Muscogee people and white squatters who moved illegally into Indian Territory after the Civil War.[19] After the war, the Robertsons toiled with the support of the Muscogee Tribal Council and the Presbyterian Church Board of Home Missions to rescue the Tullahassee Mission from ruin. Once financially stable, the Robertsons sent seventeen-year-old Alice to Elmira College in New York. She excelled in her studies but found transitioning from Indian Territory to eastern society challenging. In letters home to family, she reported her aversion to joining social clubs.[20] Instead, the dedicated civics major looked forward to the school's annual trip to Washington, DC. Field trips to the nation's capital heightened her awareness that educated women held the potential, even the obligation, to break gender barriers by moving into occupational fields and public spaces dominated by men. "I have ever been much interested in the subject of woman's work in her various spheres," she wrote. "Wherever I go I try to see all that I can of what she is doing." Robertson also observed that overcoming gender barriers required the individual fortitude to withstand the criticism and public scrutiny that shadowed women who entered public space and participated in political discourse: "At the capitol I saw that severely criticized specimen of woman's work—Vinnie Ream's statue of Lincoln.... It seemed to tell how obstacles may be overcome and prejudices removed by perseverance."[21]

Elmira's expedition courses presented Alice with opportunities to network in Washington, DC. In addition to visiting the White House, occupied by President Ulysses S. Grant, Robertson met with several senators and Muscogee leaders, including Civil War veteran Pleasant Porter. With the support of influential Republican friends, she parlayed her family's reputation as "friends of the Indian" into her first paid government post at the Bureau of Indian Affairs in the Department of the Interior. Although she left Elmira at the age of nineteen without a degree, Robertson secured a leadership position as the first woman clerk at Indian Affairs. She mastered the professional skills and educational pedagogies required of a bureaucrat engaged in the work of assimilating Indigenous people. She taught herself shorthand and typing, both skills she would use later as a court reporter in Indian Territory and in her work as an interpreter for the Dawes Commission. She read avidly in the emerging literature on domestic science, social welfare work, and federal Indian policy.[22]

Robertson's Indian Affairs appointment exposed her to political philosophies with which she would reckon for the rest of her long career. There she first encountered maternalism being practiced as state policy. Maternalism was a gendered political ideology held by mostly middle-class white women who adopted it to justify their political organizing and community reform work.[23] Maternalists believed that their feminine qualities—defined by their biological roles as mothers, caregivers, and pure moral arbiters of home and family—naturally equipped middle-class white women for "social housekeeping" and public reform work and especially prepared them to set social standards and policies for working-class women and all people of color in need of uplift or "rescue." The growing Bureau of Indian Affairs pulled thousands of women workers into its ranks, many as teachers and secretaries in the field. Historians Cathleen Cahill and Margaret Jacobs argue that women's political culture, increasingly defined by maternalist reform politics, became critical to the federal government's mission of assimilating Indigenous people who had been defeated in war.[24] The US government intended for such policies to destroy tribal identity and sovereignty and to turn Native people into individualist-minded Americans.[25] In addition to transferring Native lands to white settlers, supporters of assimilationist policies believed that they would solve the "Indian problem" by ending the "dependency" of Native American people on the federal government. A post with Indian Affairs was Robertson's most promising path toward a professional career. She witnessed firsthand and participated in the building of a system in which free-labor ideology and maternalism would be deployed by the US government to dramatically alter the lives of Native American people. Her experiences informed her eventual shift toward a more conservative anti-statist politics.

In 1880 Indian Affairs assigned Robertson to serve as secretary to Captain Richard Henry Pratt, superintendent of the infamously militaristic Carlisle Indian School in Pennsylvania.[26] Pratt's self-described approach to assimilation was to "kill the Indian and save the man." His strategy for cultural genocide began with the severing of Native children's ties to tribal identity and land and progressed to militaristic education toward a life of servitude and manual labor defined by Westernized gender roles. Few records from Robertson's employment at Carlisle exist, but her unpublished manuscripts include sorrowful notes about Indian children who died at the school while separated from the love of family and comforts of home. In later years, Robertson ceased her recruitment of Muscogee children for Carlisle. Believing that young children should attend the Creek Nation's day or boarding schools, she encouraged advanced students to apply to distant boarding schools, such as Carlisle, only of their own free will.[27]

While stationed at Carlisle, Robertson received doubly devastating news from home: the Tullahassee Mission had burned to the ground and her father had died. Left destitute by the fire, Alice's grieving mother could not rebuild alone. Familial duty prompted Alice's request for reassignment to Indian Territory. Her homecoming revealed that the Muscogees were managing both postwar economic recovery and intense political factionalism surrounding the adoption of a new constitution. In 1882, the Green Peach War broke out when traditionalist leader Isparhecher led the Nuyaka faction in establishing a rival government and taking up arms against elected principal chief Samuel Checote.[28] Before fleeing to Kansas, the Nuyaka faction established a military camp near the ruins of the Tullahassee Mission and consumed the Robertsons' stock of winter fuel. In response, Alice located her mother's axe and readied a team of horses. After hours of chopping and loading, she returned, chilled to the bone but with a fresh supply of wood.

Economic survival also required Robertson to embrace mobility, moving around the Muscogee Nation as a roustabout teacher and administrator. After the Muscogee Council converted the Tullahassee Mission into a school for Creek freedmen, Alice began teaching at Nuyaka, a newly established Presbyterian mission and school near Okmulgee, the Muscogee capital.[29] In 1885, Robertson relocated once again within the Muscogee Nation when the Presbyterian Home Mission Board hired her to oversee the fledgling Minerva Boarding School for girls from the Five Tribes. Robertson wasted no time in working her political connections. Making several trips east, she convinced several wealthy industrialists and their wives to contribute to the expansion of Minerva School.

Robertson also oversaw the development of Minerva's curriculum. Reflecting the social-evolutionist theories of the day, which situated Anglo-American gendered labor divisions as a primary marker of civilization, Minerva's curriculum emphasized domestic science education.[30] Minerva School's mission partly reflected the assimilationist goal of socializing Indian women into the essentialized femininity required by the dominant Anglo-American culture; it also reflected Robertson's conservative maternalism, which held that the nuclear, patriarchal family was the building block of the nation. Women were the primary protectors of home and family; men's roles in domestic affairs were merely formulary. "Give me a nation of great mothers," Robertson pronounced, "and I care not who the husbands be."[31] In a departure from the Carlisle model of Indian education, and likely influenced by the curricula of the well-established Muscogee day school and Alice's studies at Elmira, Minerva students also studied language, literature, and the arts. In 1894, the Presbyterian Board of Home Missions began operating Minerva School as Henry Kendall College; eventually, Kendall College was moved to Tulsa and chartered as the University of Tulsa, where Robertson served on the history faculty.[32]

As she built Minerva School into a reputable educational institution, Robertson continued to cultivate eastern political connections and positioned herself as a national expert on Indian education. In 1891, she lectured at the prestigious Lake Mohonk Friends of the Indian Conference. Theodore Roosevelt, an employee of the US Civil Service Commission, attended Robertson's talk and afterward introduced himself.[33] The rapport established between the two Republicans at Lake Mohonk signaled the beginning of a long, mutually beneficial friendship. During the Spanish-American-Cuban-Filipino War, Robertson personally recruited boys and men from Indian Territory boarding schools to join Roosevelt's Rough Riders.[34] Her hawkish collaboration with Roosevelt, while a common strategy of upward mobility for politically ambitious men, appeared novel as a path to leadership for a woman.

During the 1890s, Robertson also built up political capital with Republican Party leaders by serving as a translator during negotiations between the

Muscogee government and the federal Dawes Commission. The commission had been appointed to end tribal ownership of land in Indian Territory by forcing allotment on the Five Tribes. In 1898, the Curtis Act stripped tribal governments in Indian Territory of their power by dissolving tribal courts, declaring federal jurisdiction over all residents, and permitting the establishment of public schools in Indian Territory.[35] With the federal government asserting authority over Indian Territory and her old friend Theodore Roosevelt occupying the White House, Robertson saw an opportunity to move from her position as a professor of history at Kendall College into a political appointment. Having garnered favor with Roosevelt by recruiting for the Rough Riders, Robertson wrote to him, requesting his support for her appointment as supervisor of Creek schools. She carefully avoided the appearance of party patronage by pointing to her merits. "I want that appointment," she insisted, "because I believe that I am better fitted by training and experience to perform its duties than anyone else. I know I am capable and competent."[36] Robertson addressed directly the question of "whether any woman could discharge properly the responsibilities of that position." She knew she was qualified; she also recognized that securing the position required raising the president's consciousness on gender discrimination while also assuring him that teaching required feminine qualities. "The only objection which can logically be raised—my being a woman[—]can surely be met," wrote Robertson.[37] Using gender-essentialist arguments to advance her candidacy, she argued that her innate feminine values left her immune to political corruption and would allow her to "eliminate party politics wholly in the interest of Muskogee county schools."[38] Robertson's letter-writing campaign secured her the position of US supervisor of Creek schools. For the next five years, she traversed Indian Territory by horse and buggy to visit and report upon the operations of day schools, boarding schools, and freedmen's schools in the Muscogee Nation.[39]

Robertson served as supervisor of Creek schools until December 1904, when President Roosevelt appointed her postmaster for the booming city of Muskogee, Indian Territory.[40] Assured of a monthly income by her federal salary, in 1910 Alice purchased fifty-five acres of land near Muskogee and built a home.[41] Her property, which she called Sawokla, included pastures for livestock and chickens, and she hired workers to plant orchards and vegetable gardens. She settled into life in Muskogee, stepping away from her roles as educator, civil servant, and political appointee to become a farmer, restaurateur, and civic leader.

Having invested most of her savings in real estate, Robertson used Sawokla as collateral to bankroll her next venture. "I have decided," she wrote in a letter to her sister, "to make the farm my bank."[42] She opened the Sawokla Cafeteria in downtown Muskogee as an outlet from which she could retail her surplus farm goods. From its origins, the café also had a social mission that demonstrated Robertson's gender consciousness. She advertised Sawokla Cafe as a space for women workers. For a small membership fee, women could use the reading room, lockers, showers, and restrooms and gather in the communal dining room. It soon became obvious that a communitarian business catering only to Muskogee's working-class women would not pay, especially when the majority of workers in the city's primary industries of lumber, petroleum, and railroads were men. To keep Sawokla Cafe open, Robertson began advertising to a broader clientele, eventually turning her restaurant into one of the most popular dining spots in Muskogee. By age fifty, Alice Robertson was one of Muskogee's most successful entrepreneurs, regardless of gender.

In all of her public roles, whether missionary, teacher, educational administrator, entrepreneur, or congresswoman, Robertson legitimated her work by claiming the moral responsibilities of feminine caretaker and protector. Her Red Cross work during World War I demonstrated that her brand of conservative maternalism—entering public discourse and gaining influence through activities that were gendered feminine through their association with mothering, caretaking, and protecting—was well established by 1917. During World War I, she gained notoriety by feeding more than five thousand American soldiers who passed through Muskogee. "Her cafeteria was the soldiers resting place," reporters wrote of Sawokla Cafe. "No boy in khaki ever went through Muskogee hungry."[43] Her ability to speak the language of conservative maternalism even as she strode toward greater leadership opportunities, violating gender norms as she gained prominence, proved critical to Robertson's advancement in Republican politics.

In September 1920, shortly after the adoption of the Nineteenth Amendment, Oklahoma Republican Party leaders invited Robertson to run on the Republican ticket. By 1920, she boasted a forty-seven-year work history featuring multiple political appointments. She had proven herself to be a capable leader, and at the age of sixty-six, Robertson still craved adventure and an intellectual challenge. She was well positioned to run for political office, and she embraced the opportunity.

As the 1920 congressional race heated up in the Second District, both of Muskogee's daily newspapers supported three-term incumbent Democrat W. W. Hastings, and the editors of Robertson's hometown papers chose not to run her political advertisements. In a clever response, she utilized the newspapers' classified sections, printing her campaign messages as well as folksy reminiscences about growing up in Indian Territory alongside daily advertisements for Sawokla Cafe. In the advertisements, Robertson touted her conservative beliefs about home and family. Her "kitchen campaign" proved that she could simultaneously serve up home cooking and put forward a conservative political agenda. Muskogee voters were intrigued, and according to postelection news reports, "It was known weeks before her election that persons were turning to the classified pages to read what the woman candidate had to say."[44] In addition to the classified newspaper advertisements, Robertson's kitchen campaign targeted every voter who dined at Sawokla Cafe. Campaign cards distributed at the restaurant encouraged voters to embrace Robertson's gender identity as a strength that would allow her to serve the needs of all citizens in the district and to represent them effectively in Congress.

Robertson's campaign also needed to explain a glaring inconsistency between her history of conservative activism and her ambitions for elected office: her congressional race followed upon her long-established record of anti-suffragism, including a term as vice president of the Oklahoma Association Opposed to Woman Suffrage.[45] Anti-suffragists believed that women's most assured path to economic security lay in marriage and that women had the right to expect economic support from their husbands. Accordingly, anti-suffragists argued that voting rights for women threatened the patriarchal family model by destroying women's elevated position within the family and burdening them with additional political responsibilities. Robertson also feared that by demanding voting rights, women risked alienating men. In Robertson's assessment, women imperiled economic security for themselves and their children in exchange for a right to the ballot box, a right which held no promise of immediate economic returns. She explained that her anti-suffragism had been informed by her lifelong dance with poverty. Most women and children, Robertson believed, would be better off if women did not have to compete with men in the labor market or do "men's work." Robertson's anti-suffrage position acknowledged that most women's lives were determined by a gendered class structure that limited their educational and work opportunities and made them dependent on men. She understood from personal experience that living as an independent woman carried risks of economic hardship. She explained, "I've always done a man's work, carried a man's burden and have had to pay the bills. I believe that's why I never wanted to see suffrage for women."[46]

Finally, Robertson relied on conservative maternalism to explain her opposition to voting rights for American women. Consistent with the arguments of anti-suffragists, she contended that men were obligated to protect and support women while domestic matters rested within women's domain. "I was opposed to suffrage," she explained, "because I loved my home life and I think that is a woman's sphere."[47] The question of how Robertson could have been anti-suffragist and then proceeded to pour her energies into a run for Congress in 1920 has vexed historians more than it did Alice Robertson or Oklahoma voters in 1920. Involved in political and community work for most of her adult life, Robertson understood that women's political participation was changing. Ever the pragmatist, she was willing to reevaluate some of her long-held beliefs about gender identity in relation to political power in order to seize new opportunities. While she had never advocated for greater citizenship rights for women, her ambition prompted her to embrace her new citizenship responsibilities and move into a new phase of her career as a Republican Party woman. "The men have thrust the vote on us," Robertson told the press repeatedly, "and now I am going to see whether they meant it."[48]

In addition to addressing her history of anti-suffragist activism, Robertson's campaign also worked to downplay her personal ambition. She assured voters that she had no intention of taking unorthodox positions in favor of gender equality. In a campaign speech, Robertson advocated for proper political behavior by women voters that included assuming their new duties in electoral politics "without strife or unwomanly aggressiveness." "Our first lesson," Robertson told Muskogee voters, "is to learn thoroughly to think of ourselves as citizens and to avoid attempted sex dominance. Women's parties, as such, should be thrown into the discard and as men and women together make the home, so in national affairs they must work side by side for the upholding and perpetuation of the highest ideals of government."[49]

Pledging to be more of a political helpmate to the men in power than their equal, Robertson signaled to voters that she understood her subordinate status in relation to men as "natural." Robertson assured voters that she herself was no radical despite her status as an unwed, childless woman who lived independently of men and found community primarily with other women.[50] She contrasted herself to the famously wealthy Wall Street investor Henrietta "Hetty" Green.

The pathbreaking financier, commonly derided in the press as the "Witch of Wall Street," was known to have negotiated a prenuptial agreement with her husband and had declared, "I live as I like and I always shall."[51] During her campaign and in interviews with the national press, Robertson described Hetty Green as the only woman she knew of "who ever handled her financial affairs without male assistance"; Green, said Robertson with a proverbial wink and a nod, "was not a woman. She was a freak."[52] In calling out Green by name and positioning the independent business woman as unnatural and unwomanly and as an abject other to be ridiculed and not emulated, Robertson assured her constituents and her new colleagues in Congress that her political ambition and independence would never challenge men's patriarchal prerogatives.

Robertson's kitchen campaign worked. She earned the majority of Republican votes cast in the primary and won the general election by nearly three hundred votes. Women, who were voting for the first time in a national election, represented her margin of victory. While Robertson ran a creative and victorious campaign, historians stress that her victory was not a mandate for gender equality or even a great show of support for Robertson's platform. More likely, Robertson came in on the coattails of Warren G. Harding's landslide as well as Muskogee voters' short-lived rejection of the Democratic Party.[53] Robertson's election might have been an anomaly, but it was also momentous. She was Oklahoma's first congresswoman, the first congresswoman elected after the passage of the Nineteenth Amendment, and only the second congresswoman in the history of the nation. Out of 27 million American women, eighteen ran for Congress in 1920. Alice Robertson alone emerged victorious.[54]

Congresswoman-elect Robertson immediately attracted the attention of the national press as journalists hustled to learn more about the sixty-six-year-old former anti-suffragist from Oklahoma. Early biographers portrayed postcampaign newspaper coverage of Robertson as positive. Closer analysis reveals that the coverage was hardly favorable. Media representations of Robertson reflect sexist stereotypes of the time, often echoing gendered language that Robertson used to describe herself. Americans were steeped in aspirational media representations of the modern new woman, yet most facets of Robertson's identity—her age, her conservative politics and loyalty to the Republican Party, even her fashion sense—stood in stark relief to that image. Journalists focused initially on Robertson's personality, which they characterized as folksy, witty, and direct. Eastern writers described her as a relic of pioneering days with roots in Indian Territory and Oklahoma, and the *New York Times* inaccurately reported that

On June 21, 1921, Alice Robertson became the first congresswoman to call the US House of Representatives to order and preside over a short session. She is pictured here, with a gavel, next to Speaker Pro Tempore Joseph Walsh of Massachusetts, as the representative of the Second District of Oklahoma. Courtesy of McFarlin Library, Department of Special Collections and University Archives, University of Tulsa.

she had arrived in Oklahoma on a "prairie schooner." Journalists took pains to explain her single status, with one reporter describing her as a missionary "daughter who sacrificed the best years of her life for the Indians."[55] Another headline foregrounded Robertson's age *and* her marital status while seemingly assuring readers that she was not a feminist or, even worse, a lesbian: "Old Maid Elected to Congress Is Not a 'Man-Hater.'"[56]

Robertson's congressional committee assignments included Indian Affairs and expenditures in the Department of the Interior, work for which her federal appointments had prepared her. Ironically, Robertson also garnered a seat on the Committee on Woman Suffrage. Almost immediately, she dashed expectations from Progressive women's organizations that the only woman in Congress could be relied upon to advance the cause of greater political power for women. Prior to 1920, women as a group had little experience holding national political office. Robertson's story illuminates some of the challenges that newly enfranchised women faced as they attempted to share political power with men. She had a running battle with the Progressive women, represented by the National League of Women Voters, the National Woman's Party, the Women's Joint Congressional Committee, and other groups commonly referred to by politicians and the press as the "women's lobby." These contentious relationships illustrate the competing visions of women's political participation that were emerging after 1920. Progressive women intended to translate voting rights into political power by lobbying for legislation that addressed the needs of women and children; they would not be guided or constrained by party loyalty. In 1920, the Sheppard-Towner Maternity and Infancy Act was the legislative priority for Progressive women.

Alice Robertson was a party woman and an institutionalist. Her political strategy contrasted starkly to that of Progressive women whom she accused of "bullying men."[57] Because she subscribed to the dominant American narratives of meritocracy and individualism, she did not acknowledge that an individual's social position and political rights could be influenced or determined by social identity. Consequently, she rejected movement organizing based primarily on gender identity. Deriding separate women's groups as dangerous examples of "class selfishness," she pronounced, "I therefore oppose all organizations of women as women voters, instead of American citizens—such organizations tending to the most dangerous class of legislation, that of sex."[58] Adopting a position that was not surprising for someone who had benefited from her association with the Republican Party, Robertson argued that women were most likely to effect change by creating coalitions within the existing party structure. Furthermore, she believed, effective alliances could not and should not be created without men. Robertson maintained that prioritizing feminist legislation would only "antagonize men" and was "the silliest kind of weakness."[59]

Congresswoman Robertson went beyond a structural critique of women-centered political organizing, engaging in what many interpreted as character attacks. She implied that the character deficits of weakness, selfishness, entitlement, and even laziness plagued women who organized into separate political groups. "Don't be beguiled away from your work or from your place in the party ranks because you think politics isn't nice," she admonished. "Get out and work for your party, and, if conditions aren't right, change them."[60] She accused women who organized outside the party structure of trying to gain something for nothing: "To me, it is simply plain laziness. It is the way of those who are not willing to work up from the bottom."[61] Robertson chastised clubwomen on both the left and right because she had never believed that women's attention should be fixed entirely on domestic tasks or socializing solely in gender-segregated spaces. She was critical of women who did not take an interest in government or whose organizing appeared to keep them on the margins of political discourse and who concerned themselves more with appearances than with policy.[62] Echoing the paranoid climate that characterized the Red Scare, Robertson reserved special ire for Progressive women, referring to them as "agitators."

Robertson's folksy and direct pronouncements and her disavowal of solidarity on gender legislation greatly upset women who understood that they had won voting rights by organizing outside and challenging political parties on questions of citizenship rights for women. Robertson's determination to never waiver from her political philosophy—to be a "standpatter" for conservatism—led to epic showdowns, pitting her against Progressive women during congressional debates over the Sheppard-Towner Act and spoiling her support among veterans when she opposed the Bonus Bill.

The Sheppard-Towner Maternity and Infancy Act, also called the Maternity Bill, was the first major welfare measure aimed at educating rural and urban mothers about prenatal care, childbirth, and infant care.[63] Robertson's opposition to Sheppard-Towner took shape within the context of the Red Scare and the rise of an anti-statist conservative movement that positioned women as the protectors of home and family from an encroaching paternalistic federal government. Patriotic women's groups took the lead in anti-communist attacks against reformers and welfare legislation in the 1910s and 1920s. Their goal was to immobilize the agenda of Progressive women.[64] Robertson had accepted considerable financial support from leading conservative activist Elizabeth Putnam Lowell. The Congresswoman's opposition to Sheppard-Towner demonstrates the influence that her benefactor as well as the increasingly popular conservative women's clubs held over Congresswoman Robertson. She went before Congress six times to explain her opposition. Each time she argued that the law represented a radical departure from the traditional relationship between the nation-state and the American family structure. Describing Sheppard-Towner as paternalistic and socialistic, Robertson argued that the bureaucratization of childbirth and motherhood would supplant the autonomy of the American family with an intrusive government presence. She warned that the purpose of Sheppard-Towner was to "loot the treasury" and unleash on the American heartland "spinster fieldworkers" who were empowered as federal agents to "investigate, advise, and frighten expectant mothers with political propaganda."[65]

Additionally, Robertson raised basic questions that conservatives have always tended to ask about federal social programs: How much will this program cost taxpayers in comparison to expected returns? Who are the experts on this issue? Will the measure decrease local control and increase the power of the federal government to influence social relations? More specifically, she argued that the bill did not contain effective implementation mechanisms; it was unclear how programs would be set up and how federal funds would be spent. "I am against every appropriation that we can do without," Robertson concluded. Although President Harding supported Sheppard-Towner and the measure passed with Republican support, Robertson's fiscal conservatism on the matter remained in line with her party's platform.

Scholars have argued that Robertson opposed all gender-based legislation.[66] More accurately, she advanced conservative gender-based politics by opposing legislation that she viewed as altering men's and women's roles within the family and thereby threatening domestic patriarchy. To that end, she opposed legislation that would soften expectations of men as family breadwinners or mitigate economic hardships for men. Press accounts of the day emphasized Robertson's conservative positions on maternalism concerning women's role in the family and American society. She also took positions that situated culturally dominant expressions of masculinity as the standard for the only acceptable relationship between American men and the state. These views were reflected in her vote against providing federal pensions to veterans. Despite campaigning as a "friend of the soldier boy," Robertson voted against the soldiers' Bonus Bill. Supported by veterans' groups like the American Legion, it was crafted to compensate veterans for economic losses incurred while serving in the military. Veterans in need of medical care, Robertson pronounced, could seek assistance at the Soldiers' Memorial Hospital in Muskogee, a federal institution for which Robertson had helped to procure funding; however, she opposed direct federal payments to "able bodied men" and described the Bonus Bill pejoratively as "putting a dollar sign on patriotism."[67]

Alice Robertson's positions on Sheppard-Towner and the soldiers' Bonus Bill were consistent with her conservative maternalist politics in ways that have been overlooked by historians. She acknowledged that mothering and soldiering constituted valuable work, but she saw both tasks as obligations—work that women and men did out of duty to family and the nation. Such duty-bound work, she believed, should not be compensated by the federal treasury, nor should it be shaped by either social provisions or social programs of the state.

Almost without exception, Robertson fought against any legislation that had the potential to expand the role of government into private life.

Congresswoman Robertson exhibited an abiding loyalty to the Republican Party and tended to support President Harding's agenda. She voted mostly along party lines, and she used the language of individualism and meritocracy to justify her votes. She believed that women should attempt to enter politics on the same terms as men, yet her strategy ignored historical gender inequalities and did not recognize that political rights would not easily translate into social justice for women. Her commitment to the narrative of individual meritocracy could not admit any historical usurpations by men of women's freedoms or rights. To her last day in Congress, Robertson employed maternalist arguments and analogies that illuminate her understanding of her own gendered identity in relation to political power: "If you asked a housekeeper what she accomplished, what do you think she would say? I've been busy keeping house for the nation just like a woman would her own home—busy, busy, every day, in every way, without any outstanding thing to show for it."[68]

Always one to spin an entertaining yarn, Robertson frequently compared her rise to power with the fairy tale "Cinderella": "I've been Cinderella at 69, but now, the pumpkin is round the corner, waiting to whisk me back."[69] Robertson was too pragmatic to hold out for a fairy-tale ending, and she was not to have one. Not long after she returned to Oklahoma, her business went bankrupt and her home burned to the ground.[70] Once again, Robertson faced the precarity that accompanied her status as an economically independent aging woman. Neither her reputation nor her achievements nor her long and storied career prevented her slide back into poverty. Destitute in her final years, she survived on the goodwill of friends, some of whom sent her a monthly allowance. Succumbing to a debilitating and painful cancer of the jaw, Alice Robertson died on July 31, 1931, at Veterans' Memorial Hospital in Muskogee at the age of seventy-seven.[71]

Robertson's remarkable public life unfolded over five decades. In all her endeavors, her unique, multifaceted intersectional identity informed her standpoint. If Alice Robertson appears to the modern student of history to be a case study in contradictions, it is because some facets of her identity positioned her in proximity to power while others forced her into the role of the abject other. She was a white female but also a bilingual native of Indian Territory and the third generation of a family that chose to live among the people of the Cherokee and Muscogee Nations. She was a university-educated woman from a prominent family of missionary intellectuals, yet she occupied a position of economic precarity for most of her life. She was a lifelong Republican in a state dominated by the Democratic Party. The first woman to serve as a clerk in the federal Bureau of Indian Affairs, she considered herself a "friend" and "mother" to Indian girls even as she worked to assimilate Indigenous people into what she considered to be a superior white national culture. A prominent anti-suffragist prior to the passage of the Nineteenth Amendment, she was elected to Congress in 1920, with her margin of victory attributed to first-time women voters. She was a devoted wartime Red Cross volunteer who, once elected to Congress, voted against federal payments to veterans. Robertson's family lineage, religion, race, class, and educational status meant that she had the power to determine educational opportunities and family structures for some American Indian people. Simultaneously, her determination to break gender barriers by pursuing a political career with a direct, folksy, populist style and mannerisms that were generally admired in ambitious men but scorned when adopted by women also left her marginalized. She tried to straddle obstacles to achieve full participation in politics, first by adopting maternalist language, then by disavowing solidarity with women on the emerging feminist politics of the day in favor of Republican Party loyalty and a sincere desire to represent her district. Despite Alice Robertson's election to one term as congresswoman, none of these strategies resulted in sustained political power or economic stability or even acceptance and respect from those she considered her peers.

Robertson deserves more than historical obscurity. Understanding her story helps us to remedy deficiencies in the narrative of Oklahoma history and deepens our understanding of how gendered ideologies have shaped the political history of the nation. Robertson never presented herself as a pioneer for women's equality. She believed that advocacy for gender equality was politically divisive in that it antagonized men, created separate political classes, and threatened the social order. Instead, she regularly referred to herself as an "old maid" and held herself as "a warning, not an example," to other women. Contradictions notwithstanding, it is neither fair nor accurate to judge Alice Robertson for her refusal to stand in solidarity with other women who advocated for greater gender equality. Judging her in this manner overlooks the rising conservative anti-feminism of the Progressive Era and ignores the emergence of different understandings of women's political leadership and modes of participation in American politics. Finally, although Alice Robertson understood the world through a lens of gender essentialism, she never underestimated women's potential or limited her own aspirations for leadership. She took risks that required incredible personal fortitude and strength. Congresswoman Robertson's story continues to inspire as an example of what might be accomplished when women of any political persuasion defy social expectations and challenge unfair limits.

NOTES

1. *Muskogee Phoenix*, July 25, 1916, Personal Papers, Papers of the Robertson and Worcester families, 1815–1932, McFarlin Library, Department of Special Collections and University Archives, University of Tulsa.

2. "Woman Presides in Congress; Precedent Broken amid Cheers," *Washington Post*, June 21, 1921, 1.

3. Louise B. James, "Alice Mary Robertson—Anti-feminist Congresswoman," *Chronicles of Oklahoma* 55 (Winter 1977–78): 454–62.

4. W. David Baird and Danney Goble, *Oklahoma: A History* (Norman: University of Oklahoma Press, 2008); James R. Scales and Danney Goble, *Oklahoma Politics: A History* (Norman: University of Oklahoma Press, 1982); Ruth Stanley Moore, "Alice M. Robertson, Oklahoma's First Congresswoman," *Chronicles of Oklahoma* 45 (Fall 1967): 259–89.

5. Reba Neighbors Collins and Bob Burke, *Alice Robertson: Congresswoman from Oklahoma* (Edmond: University of Central Oklahoma Press, 2001); Joe Powell Spaulding, "The Life of Alice Mary Robertson," (PhD diss., University of Oklahoma, 1959); Bessie Allan Miller, "The Political Life of Alice M. Robertson" (MA thesis, University of Tulsa, 1946); Maitreyi Muzumdar, "Alice's Restaurant: Expanding a Woman's Sphere," *Chronicles of Oklahoma* 70 (Fall 1992): 302–25.

6. Emily E. Ruggs, "'A Man's Job': Congresswoman Alice Robertson Cleans House" (MA thesis, University of Tulsa, 2009); Deah Caldwell, "A True, New Woman: Alice Mary Robertson during First-Wave Feminism, 1854–1931" (MA thesis, University of Central Oklahoma, 2010); Suzanne H. Schrems, *Across the Political Spectrum: Oklahoma Women in Politics in the Early Twentieth Century, 1900–1930* (San Jose, CA: Writer's Club, 2001).

7. Michelle M. Nickerson, *Mothers of Conservatism: Women and the Postwar Right* (Princeton, NJ: Princeton University Press, 2012).

8. John M. Rhea, *A Field of Their Own: Women and American Indian History, 1830–1941* (Norman: University of Oklahoma Press, 2016); Cathleen D. Cahill, *Federal Fathers and Mothers: A Social History of the United States Indian Service, 1869–1933* (Chapel Hill: University of North Carolina Press, 2011); Margaret D. Jacobs, *White Mother to a Dark Race: Settler Colonialism, Maternalism, and the Removal of Indigenous Children in the American West and Australia, 1880–1940* (Lincoln: University of Nebraska Press, 2009); Louise Michele Newman, *White Women's Rights the Radical Origins of Feminism in the United States* (New York: Oxford University Press, 1999).

9. Kim E. Nielsen, *Un-American Womanhood: Antiradicalism, Antifeminism, and the First Red Scare* (Columbus: Ohio State University Press, 2001), 51–53, 109–10.

10. Catherine E. Rymph, *Republican Women: Feminism and Conservatism* (Chapel Hill: University of North Carolina Press, 2006), 41–45.

11. Nickerson, *Mothers of Conservatism*, 13.
12. "Alice Mary Robertson," History, Art & Archives, US House of Representatives, accessed January 12, 2019, https://history.house.gov/People/Listing/R/ROBERTSON,-Alice-Mary-(R000318)/.
13. Worcester v. Georgia, 31 US 515, 8 L. Ed. 483, 1832 US LEXIS 489 (1832).
14. Collins and Burke, *Alice Robertson*, 7–8; Dianna Everett, "Robertson, Ann Eliza Worcester (1826–1905)," *The Encyclopedia of Oklahoma History and Culture*, Oklahoma Historical Society, accessed January 21, 2020, https://www.okhistory.org/publications/enc/entry.php?entry=RO040.
15. Collins and Burke, *Alice Robertson*, 16.
16. Collins and Burke, *Alice Robertson*, 24.
17. Collins and Burke, *Alice Robertson*, 13.
18. Collins and Burke, *Alice Robertson*, 25.
19. Mazumdar, "Alice's Restaurant," 308.
20. Collins and Burke, *Alice Robertson*, 32.
21. Caldwell, "A True, New Woman," 34.
22. Collins and Burke, *Alice Robertson*, 35–36.
23. Seth Koven and Sonya Michel, *Mothers of a New World: Maternalist Politics and the Origins of Welfare States* (New York: Routledge, 2016), 1–43; Molly Ladd-Taylor, *Mother-Work: Women, Child Welfare, and the State, 1890–1930* (Urbana: University of Illinois Press, 1995), 3.
24. Jacobs, *White Mother to a Dark Race*; Cahill, *Federal Fathers and Mothers*.
25. Cahill, *Federal Fathers and Mothers*, 26–33.
26. Schrems, *Across the Political Spectrum*, 85.
27. Schrems, *Across the Political Spectrum*, 87.
28. Baird and Goble, *Oklahoma*, 116.
29. Collins and Burke, *Alice Robertson*, 39–40; "Creek (Mvskoke) Schools," *The Encyclopedia of Oklahoma History and Culture*, Oklahoma Historical Society, accessed January 21, 2020, https://www.okhistory.org/publications/enc/entry.php?entry=CR009.
30. Newman, *White Women's Rights*, 36, 51–54.
31. *Oakland News*, June 7, 1921, Alice Robertson Collection, Oklahoma Historical Society, quoted in Joe Powell Spaulding, "The Life of Alice Mary Robertson" (PhD diss., University of Oklahoma, 1959), 57.
32. Marc Carlson, "Early University History, Part 2. Henry Kendall College, Muskogee, I. T.," *From McFarlin Tower* (blog), University of Tulsa Department of Special Collections and University Archives, March 18, 2016, http://orgs.utulsa.edu/spcol/?p=1818.
33. Collins and Burke, *Alice Robertson*, 42.
34. Schrems, *Across the Political Spectrum*, 88.
35. M. Kaye Tatro, "Curtis Act (1898)," *The Encyclopedia of Oklahoma History and Culture*, Oklahoma Historical Society, accessed January 15, 2020, https://www.okhistory.org/publications/enc/entry.php?entry=CU006.
36. Alice M. Robertson, "I Want the Job: A Letter to President Theodore Roosevelt, December 24, 1901," in Collins and Burke, *Alice Robertson*, 85.

37. Ruggs, "A Man's Job," 34.

38. Mazumdar, "Alice's Restaurant," 312.

39. Collins and Burke, *Alice Robertson*, 47–48; Schrems, *Across the Political Spectrum*, 88–89.

40. Schrems, 90.

41. Alice M. Robertson, "Memories of Sawokla: In the *Muskogee Daily Phoenix*, August 24, 1930," in Collins and Burke, *Alice Robertson*, 151.

42. Mazumdar, "Alice's Restaurant," 313.

43. "Local Popularity and Campaign of Want Ads Sends Woman to Congress," *Evening Star* (Washington, DC), November 14, 1920, Chronicling America, Library of Congress, accessed November 18, 2020, https://chroniclingamerica.loc.gov/lccn/sn83045462/1920-11-14/ed-1/seq-77/.

44. "Local Popularity and Campaign of Want Ads Sends Woman to Congress."

45. Tally Fugate, "Where Angels Belong: The Oklahoma Antisuffrage Movement," *Chronicles of Oklahoma* 82 (Summer 2004): 210.

46. "Old Maid Sent to Congress Is Not 'Man Hater,'" undated newspaper clipping, Personal Papers, Papers of the Robertson and Worcester families, 1815–1932, McFarlin Library, Department of Special Collections and University Archives, University of Tulsa.

47. Mazumdar, "Alice's Restaurant," 316.

48. "Local Popularity and Campaign of Want Ads Sends Woman to Congress."

49. Alice M. Robertson, "The Danger of Class Selfishness: Campaign Speech, November, 1920," in Collins and Burke, *Alice Robertson*, 112.

50. Kat Eschner, "The Peculiar Story of the Witch of Wall Street," *Smithsonian Magazine*, November 21, 2017, accessed August 31, 2020, https://www.smithsonianmag.com/smart-news/peculiar-story-hetty-green-aka-witch-wall-street-180967258/.

51. "Local Popularity and Campaign of Want Ads Sends Woman to Congress."

52. Mabel Potter Daggett, "Hetty Green: Mistress of Finance," *Maclean's* 15, no. 4 (February 1908): 116, Maclean's: The Complete Archive, accessed August 31, 2020, https://archive.macleans.ca/article/1908/2/1/hetty-green-mistress-of-finance.

53. Baird and Goble, *Oklahoma*, 184.

54. Caldwell, "A True, New Woman," 55.

55. "Local Popularity and Campaign of Want Ads Sends Woman to Congress."

56. "Opposed to 'Bullying' Men: Women Voters Shouldn't Try to Force Issues, Ms. Robertson Says," newspaper clipping, February, 10, 1921, Personal Papers, Papers of the Robertson and Worcester families, 1815–1932, McFarlin Library, Department of Special Collections and University Archives, University of Tulsa.

57. "Old Maid Sent to Congress Is Not 'Man Hater.'"

58. Collins and Burke, *Alice Robertson*, 58; "Opposes Women Voters' League," *New York Times*, February 25, 1921.

59. Mazumdar, "Alice's Restaurant," 319. Fear of sex antagonism and abandonment by men had also informed anti-suffragist arguments; Susan E. Marshall, *Splintered Sisterhood: Gender and Class in the Campaign Against Woman Suffrage* (Madison: University of Wisconsin Press, 1997), 226.

60. "Woman M. C. Fights 'Bonus Patriotism,'" *New York Times*, February 14, 1922; "Miss Alice Wants to Go Back to Show Up Women Who Want to Boss Her," *Daily Oklahoman*, August 6, 1922.

61. Mazumdar, "Alice's Restaurant," 319.

62. Caldwell, "A True, New Woman," 82.

63. Ladd-Taylor, *Mother-Work*, 2.

64. Nickerson, *Mothers of Conservatism*, xv, 8.

65. Alice M. Robertson, "A Bill to Loot the Treasury: In the House of Representatives, August 24, 1921," in Collins and Burke, *Alice Robertson*, 114, 119.

66. Caldwell, "A True, New Woman," 58.

67. Schrems, *Across the Political Spectrum*, 99.

68. Mazumdar, "Alice's Restaurant," 323.

69. Undated clipping, Alice Robertson Collection, Oklahoma Historical Society, quoted in Mazumdar, "Alice's Restaurant," 321, 325.

70. Collins and Burke, *Alice Robertson*, 66.

71. Bob Burke, "Robertson, Alice Mary (1853–1931)," *The Encyclopedia of Oklahoma History and Culture*, Oklahoma Historical Society, https://www.okhistory.org/publications/enc/entry.php?entry=RO004.

SUNU KODUMTHARA

4

"INTREPID PIONEER LEADER"
The A-suffrage Gendered Activism of Kate Barnard

Reflecting on an extraordinary life and career, Kate Barnard reminisced, "What a privilege for [a] woman to use her gift of finesse and strategy in the Greatest Game of Life, reducing the load of toil from the back of Labor and increasing Human Happiness on her pathway to Eternity."[1] Like many white women during the Progressive Era, Barnard considered herself duty bound to rescue those who had been marginalized by larger society. She was a social and political activist, serving in leadership roles for charitable organizations, and eleven years before women were granted the right to vote, she was the first woman ever elected to serve in public office in Oklahoma. Yet, because she refused to identify herself as a suffragist, historians have unfairly described her as either anti-suffragist or anti-equality. Indeed, in examining Barnard's life, choices, and political career, historians are forced to reexamine how to define women's political activism. She consciously defied political and social labels in order to fight for a broad range of causes from workers' rights to the rights of Indian orphans. In purposely choosing her own path of advocacy, Kate Barnard also demonstrated that political activism need not be confined to the acceptable gendered categories of the time.

As Barnard's life demonstrates, the study of suffrage is far more complex than the simple categorization of suffragist or anti-suffragist. Instead, Barnard was an "a-suffragist." Neither for it nor against it, she prioritized other causes and issues over suffrage. While a-suffragists believed women were fully capable of political activity, they did not consider suffrage the most important issue. As Suzanne Crawford and Lynne Musslewhite remind us, "While Barnard for much of her career attached little significance to woman suffrage, she firmly believed that women as officeholders and private citizens had important contributions to make in politics and reform."[2] Examining her entire life and career would provide the most complete understanding of her motivations and ideologies, but this chapter focuses on the highlights of her time as a delegate to the Oklahoma Constitutional Convention—where she presented the three planks that would provide the foundation of her office, the Department of Charities and Corrections—and her time in office. In these eventful years she befriended leaders in the Farmers' Union,[3] challenged existing power structures, and confronted powerful, misogynistic men such as Charles Haskell and William H. "Alfalfa Bill" Murray. Even in these select few instances, Barnard's choices explain her value system: women could and should be leaders, but suffrage was not the only way for women to prove themselves.

Kate Barnard was born in 1875 in Geneva, Nebraska, and shortly after, her family moved to Kansas. After her mother died in 1877, when Kate was only two years old, she was left in the care of her father, John P. Barnard. By the time she was sixteen years old, the two of them had moved to Newalla, Oklahoma, where her father had staked a claim in the Oklahoma land run of 1889. John Barnard worked in Newalla as a surveyor, then as a lawyer, and eventually as a judge. Over the course of his career, he also made a name for himself in Oklahoma territorial politics. His daughter, meanwhile, grew up on the homestead and later moved to Oklahoma City.

Kate Barnard earned her teacher's certificate and went on to teach in one-room schoolhouses throughout the Oklahoma City area. After teaching for a few years, Barnard changed careers and attended secretarial classes at a local business school, and when she completed her coursework, she was retained as the secretary for the Oklahoma territorial legislature. In 1904, Barnard was selected to serve as "territorial hostess" for the St. Louis World's Fair, which ended up being a life-changing experience for her. While in Saint Louis, Barnard saw the depths of poverty and was shocked by the destitution. But she also met social scientists and encountered modern ideas about how to confront the adversities of poverty. Barnard began to rethink her life's work once again. She shifted her attention from secretarial tasks to philanthropy, and she brought her new ideas and passion to Oklahoma City.

Barnard's charity career began in October 1905, when she was chosen to serve as the president of the Provident Association in Oklahoma City. She wrote articles for the *Daily Oklahoman*, Oklahoma's primary state newspaper, about poverty in Oklahoma City, embarking on what was to become a lifelong relationship with the media that she would learn to use to her political advantage.

In her opinion pieces, Barnard educated her readers about the problems of poverty and insisted that everyday Oklahomans had a moral responsibility to aid the poor. Like other Progressive women throughout the American West, she presented herself as an advocate for working-class people. Just as historian Peggy Pascoe wrote in her seminal work *Relations of Rescue*, middle-class white women "made themselves arbiters of a morality that provided a positive counterpoint to the 'immoral' conditions surrounding them." Barnard stressed the Christian duty of citizens to care for the disadvantaged around them. But her work was not limited to charitable organizations that called for regular donations from the community.

Barnard's new work introduced her to the lives and conditions of working-class families. "Working for years among miners, ditch diggers, scavengers, murderers, stickup-men, politicians, riff raff and what not," she later wrote, "I enjoyed universal respect."[4] Her experiences taught her that poverty and low wages were directly linked. In addition, dangerous working conditions, especially for miners, meant that workers were not only impoverished; they were risking their lives each day as well, and it had been that way for years. In January 1892, a massive mine explosion had left nearly a hundred miners dead and another hundred injured. While an explosion of that magnitude had not happened again, very little had been done to improve working conditions in the mines. Barnard fought for women workers also—she served in leadership positions in unions for women workers in Oklahoma. She did not fear confrontation, and she boldly took on corporate owners. This courage would become a much-needed asset for her later career as a politician.

In order to bolster her activism for workers, children, and the poor, Barnard studied the practices of other reformers across the country. She traveled to Saint

Louis, Chicago, and Denver to learn about poverty in larger urban areas, but more important, to learn about Progressive experiments underway to resolve these issues. While in Denver, she met with Ben Lindsey, a Progressive judge who was implementing unique solutions to confront juvenile delinquency. As the author of the Colorado Adult Delinquency Act of 1903, which held adults criminally responsible for contributing to juvenile delinquency, Lindsey was considered an authority whose policies and leadership of the juvenile court system were applauded nationwide. Other state legislatures adopted the Adult Delinquency Act, and the juvenile court was an example to legislatures around the country of how to deal with children who failed to attend school or were involved in crimes. In Denver, Barnard also learned about housing codes, sanitation ordinances, and special courts. Her travels helped her gain a reputation among Oklahomans as a reformer. But, more pointedly, Barnard came to believe that government assistance was necessary to make reform most effective.

In many ways, Barnard's Progressive ideals were reflective of her time. Progressives of her day shared her commitment to social justice, and her devotion to Progressive reforms was founded in her Christian faith, as she reminded *Daily Oklahoman* readers. She believed that Christians had a moral and religious responsibility to address human suffering and eliminate its causes as best as possible. Additionally, Barnard used scientific research and data to create solutions for her community's many problems, ranging from help for the mentally ill to criminal justice reforms.

Barnard's approach to reform serves as a window into Oklahoma's political climate in the early 1900s. It is a factor that many of Barnard's biographers have not addressed in writing about her political career. Her close alliance with Oklahoma's working class was much deeper than simply providing help for the helpless. In fact, she joined an ongoing movement of political and economic activism as Oklahoma farmers and workers grew tired of Democratic and Republican economic policies. Historian Jim Bissett argues, "The twin evils of low crop prices and high credit costs consigned most Oklahoma farmers to a life of poverty and indebtedness, and many responded to this plight by turning to the Socialist Party."[5]

While she never professed to be a member of any party, Barnard demonstrated an admiration for notable Socialists and anarchists and their commitment to fight for the people. Patrick Nagle, who became one of the organizers of the Oklahoma Socialist Party, worked closely with Barnard during her early years in Oklahoma politics. After describing him as a "Socialist," Barnard wrote that

Kate Barnard, date unknown. Photograph by Frederick S. Barde. Courtesy of the Research Division, Oklahoma Historical Society.

he was a "statesman" possessing "one of the best Legal minds" and that he "spent years trying to perfect his own Party." After initially working as a Democrat, he felt betrayed, she claimed, by those in the party "who promised to fulfill part of his dream for humanity." According to Barnard, Nagle "died of a broken heart at [the] failure of his dream."[6] Barnard did not explain what Nagle's dream or great disappointment was, but her political career certainly paralleled his. She, too, felt betrayed by her party despite her efforts to lead and better her state. She also wrote highly of noted anarchist and non-suffragist, Emma Goldman, whom she described as an "independent thinker" who accepted "almost sure death rather than surrender [her] ideals of life."[7] Goldman criticized women's suffrage not because women were incapable of political activism but because the right to vote was not enough for equality. Indeed, woman suffrage could not improve an already corrupt system.[8] Goldman believed suffrage did not help while Barnard argued that suffrage was, for her, unnecessary. Neither of them believed the cause worth fighting for.

Where Barnard differed from some of her Progressive and Socialist allies was in her lack of support for women's suffrage. As a result, critics have described her as anti-suffragist. However, there is no indication that Barnard indeed *opposed* a woman's right to vote. She, like most of her contemporaries, believed strongly that women had the ability to alleviate the moral problems of their communities. She often referred to her ability "as a woman" to be more sympathetic to the less fortunate around her. Furthermore, she fought for the protection of women in the workplace. Barnard argued that before women married, they should work outside the home to develop a sense of self-reliance.[9] This self-reliance, she believed, could build confidence for women that would eventually help them within their homes as wives and mothers. For those women who remain unmarried, like Barnard, self-reliance allowed women to take on mantles of leadership, particularly in the area of social justice.

By her own admission, Barnard did not trust women, particularly because they had not supported her as she thought they should. "I never received very much valuable assistance in my work from women," she wrote.[10] Barnard recognized the gender limitations placed on women, but rather than campaign for political equality, she chose to focus on things that helped women in other ways, such as property rights and workers' rights as well as the appointment of police matrons and establishment of a higher age of consent for girls. Barnard understood that women's suffrage would benefit women, but, like other activists such as Emma Goldman, Barnard did not believe that suffrage was the most important goal for women to achieve. "I know that a great many women of the state think that I ought to drop my work and take sides with them in this struggle for suffrage," Barnard wrote, "but I do not think I am capable of assuming anymore load than I am now carrying."[11] Barnard was not willing to sacrifice her goals of protecting women within the home and the workplace to guarantee them a spot in the polling place.

Barnard had a mind of her own, deciding for herself what issues were worthy of her personal support and which issues to leave to others, and she decided that suffrage was best left to others. She was more willing to help racial minorities. Many Oklahomans, influenced particularly by the southerners among them, promoted Jim Crow laws that subjected Black Americans to second-class citizenship. Evidence shows Barnard did believe in the racial superiority of whites, but she also believed that a person's environment helped explain their circumstances. Though she campaigned neither for voting rights for Black Americans nor for the integration of races, she believed that the American—especially the Oklahoman—preoccupation with race was pointless. Barnard argued that all people, regardless of their race, should have the opportunities to fulfill their potential.[12] Later in her career, this very principle concerning Native Americans would cost Barnard her job.

Barnard's rise to prominence as a Progressive reformer happened just as Oklahoma Territory was granted the opportunity to apply for statehood in 1906. Barnard worked to ensure that those elected to the constitutional convention would pay due attention to the plight of the poor throughout the soon-to-be state. She asked reformers across the country to submit opinions for publication in the *Daily Oklahoman* describing how terrible the territory's social problems were and presenting possible solutions.

The larger context of the era is of particular importance. Many reformers saw the Oklahoma Constitutional Convention as a rare opportunity to establish Progressive ideals from the very inception of a state. Such reform-minded activists included onetime presidential candidate William Jennings Bryan, who traveled to the territory and campaigned for a constitution that Progressives everywhere could endorse. "It will be your own fault if you do not frame the best constitution ever written," Bryan warned the convention delegates.

As a part of her Progressive reform work, Barnard was an activist for temperance and other charitable causes women associated themselves with during the Progressive Era. However, as with other issues, Barnard defined her own activism rather than allow others to define it. Although Barnard and the Woman's

Christian Temperance Union shared the common goal of eliminating the influence of alcohol on the masses, leaders of the WCTU believed the vote would help women hold society accountable. But Barnard did not join their ranks. Progressive women activists who also identified as suffragists criticized Barnard's approach to leadership. For example, Julia Woodworth, a member of the Twin Territories Suffrage Association and the Oklahoma Federation of Women's Clubs, claimed that Barnard mismanaged her charitable organization and charged her with "impotence, cruelty, and dishonesty."[13] Woodworth's claims did not have the support of the media. "It seems a Mrs. Julia Woodworth saw fit to bring charges against Miss Barnard," the editor of the *Daily Oklahoman* wrote, "based as it seems on the ground that [Barnard] is too young to be safe herself in such a position." The article continued, "We do not know what the specific charges were the married lady brought against Miss Barnard after she had attempted to hire two private detectives, who refused to hunt damaging evidence, but whatever they were the board who heard scorned it and passed an unanimous verdict of confidence."[14] Although she was exonerated of all charges, the accusations made one thing very clear: Barnard might have been a reformer, but not all reformers agreed with her tactics.

Barnard joined the Democratic Party, although, as a woman, she was not permitted to register to vote or cast a ballot. Republicans controlled territorial politics until statehood, thanks in part to the political loyalty of Black Americans and the dominance of Republicans at the federal level.[15] Democrats used the 1890s and early 1900s to gain their own political momentum and, as a result, gained a political foothold. Of the 112 delegates elected to the convention, 99 were Democrats.[16] Territorial Democrats had organized locally to nominate candidates to serve as convention delegates. On August 22, 1906, Democrats gathered at the Shawnee city hall, where they heard from several speakers addressing the territory's most important issues.

Barnard was a Progressive Democrat, "a new breed of Democrat," as Crawford and Musslewhite describe her.[17] She was committed to fighting for social reforms and advocating on behalf of workers and farmers. She also did not necessarily see Black Americans as equal to white Americans, nor did she make it a priority to protect them. "She did not stress white supremacy," Crawford and Musslewhite write. "She neither advocated black disfranchisement nor raised the specter of black rule in her political campaigns."[18] Barnard was invited to speak in Shawnee, and in her very first public address, she described her work as a reformer. The new state constitution, Barnard argued, must be written with the poor in mind. "Change his conditions," she declared, "give him a 'square deal' and you make him a better neighbor, more useful citizen and a factor for good society."[19]

This speech was the first of many for Barnard. It gained attention not only among Democrats but among all Oklahomans. The *Daily Oklahoman* described her as being as "sweet and dainty as a wildflower and as refreshing as an Oklahoma breeze."[20] Indeed, Barnard's physical appeal was usually the first thing people noticed about her—not only the press, but her biographers as well. But Barnard was more than an attractive woman. She was a leader in both social and political circles, with a sincere interest in helping the poor and marginalized. She best demonstrated her leadership abilities at the state constitutional convention in 1906.

As delegates assembled to discuss the state constitution, Barnard found herself campaigning among the public to increase pressure on state delegates for reforms. Peter "Big Pete" Hanraty, a mine inspector, union leader, and vice president of the convention, had a long working relationship with Kate Barnard. According to Barnard, Hanraty created an opportunity for her to speak for a half hour at the convention, an unprecedented opportunity for a woman. "This speech," Barnard wrote, "marked an Epoch in my life. It enabled me to be the first woman in the world to draft planks for a constitution and secure their passage."[21] While she was aware of the significance of the moment, Barnard also knew that as a single voice, her arguments would have a limited impact. To shore up her position, she worked to create political alliances based on reforms that would pressure convention delegates to take action. In other words, she was creating a political lobby. This required Barnard to reach out to like-minded people, including women's organizations.

During the convention, Barnard primarily focused on three planks: child labor laws, compulsory education laws, and the creation of a government office to help the needy. She created these planks in partnership with her allies in labor unions, but Barnard prepared for backlash from Oklahoma farmers and workers who were dependent on children's labor and wages.

To answer these farmers, Barnard solicited women's organizations, asking them to join her efforts to lobby delegates and push for such Progressive reforms. Just a year earlier, to stir up more women's support for these reforms, Barnard had created the first Anti–Child Labor League in Oklahoma in October 1906. Two months later, she had established two new chapters of the Woman's International Union Label League, which would allow working women to speak out against child labor. Thus, Barnard had reached out to middle-class and working-class women for years in different ways. Her efforts paid off as these women from diverse economic backgrounds united to support legislation on the issue of child labor.

Barnard's talent of bringing opposing agendas together propelled her to the forefront of the convention. Because of her efforts, the convention delegates appointed a Joint Legislative Board, whose primary purpose was to compile a list of what laws the farmers and workers hoped to include in the constitution. The list included demands for laws that banned child labor and made education compulsory. Barnard then traveled throughout the territory, making forty-four speeches addressing poverty and injustice. And though she was not an elected delegate, Barnard successfully convinced supporters that such laws worked together for the benefit of all children and that these laws were therefore necessary.

Despite wide support, members of both political parties opposed the bills once they were introduced in the Oklahoma House of Representatives. Republicans believed that Progressive labor laws—particularly the child labor laws—would prevent Oklahoma's industrial development. Without the cheap labor of children, Republicans argued, industry owners would hesitate to invest in and create jobs for Oklahoma workers. On the other hand, Democrats opposed child labor laws on the premise that they would prevent children from working on their own families' farms. Farmers were heavily dependent on child labor to keep farms economically sustainable. Although the bill to banish child labor was passed, Governor Charles Haskell, who believed it was too extreme, vetoed the bill. It was revised later to allow children as young as fourteen to work. This received a better response from political leaders and eventually became law.

The third plank Barnard campaigned for during the convention was the creation of a new government department designed to help Oklahoma's most underprivileged citizens regardless of age or race. In support of her campaign, the convention delegates created the Department of Charities and Corrections. Although women did not even have the right to vote, delegates created an office for a woman who had demonstrated her leadership ability. Barnard did not hesitate to campaign for this position, which required the support of voters. However, Barnard's lack of support for the suffragists' push for equal voting laws at the convention sent conflicting messages about her activism. In fact, convention chairman William H. Murray and future governor Charles Haskell used her as an example as to why women's suffrage was unnecessary. "Katie

Barnard's life is a lesson that every suffragist should study," Haskell claimed. "And let me appeal to every mother that is in this audience to go back home to your boys, and continue to rock the cradle, and through that well-known medium continue to rule the world."[22] Barnard, who was unmarried and childless, nonetheless became an example of a woman attending to her "appropriate" responsibilities. Rather than vote, Barnard brought her issues directly to men and asked them to bring about reforms. This, according to Haskell, was how women could be most useful in politics.

While she stepped aside on the issue of suffrage, other women's organizations took it on, including at the state level. The WCTU, for example, had played a significant role in promoting women's political rights, encouraging women to unite so they might influence the greater society. By the late nineteenth century, the WCTU hoped to produce local leaders among the women in Oklahoma Territory. In 1895, in the wake of their success in Colorado, the National American Woman Suffrage Association sent workers to Oklahoma to gather support for the local suffrage movement. These activists hoped that Oklahoma legislators would be willing to pass a suffrage measure, but it ultimately failed. Perhaps legislators were not convinced of the necessity or success of suffrage. The movement lost momentum for the foreseeable future.

It was not until the Oklahoma Constitutional Convention of 1906 that suffrage regained momentum in the new state of Oklahoma. Suffragists had hoped to convince the seemingly Progressive leaders who were drafting the constitution that women's suffrage would benefit Oklahoma, as it had other western states where it was practiced. But state leaders had two major reservations that prevented them from passing the measure. First, they feared that equal voting rights would also enfranchise Black women, leading to racial equality. Southerners who had migrated to Oklahoma to participate in various land runs and land lotteries were unwilling to take that risk. Second, anti-suffragists feared that once women had the vote, they would align themselves with the Socialist Party, an already significant influence among farmers and workers in the state.[23] This was especially threatening to Oklahoma Democrats, who had until then enjoyed complete control over the local political climate. These arguments proved impossible for Oklahoma's political leaders to ignore; equal suffrage would have to wait.

What could not wait, however, was the issue of who would emerge as the Democratic nominee for Oklahoma's governor. The Democrats were split into two camps: those who supported Charles Haskell, the majority leader of the

Democratic Party, and those who supported S. O. Daws, the first president of Indiahoma Farmers' Union and leader of thousands of farmers, miners, and other workers from across the state. Charles Haskell and William H. Murray considered Daws to be "a radical" who would take the party to the extremes while Haskell and Murray considered themselves to be moderate Democrats. Daws carried enough support to win the nomination and quite possibly win the gubernatorial race. Haskell needed help and reached out to the one person he believed could sway the race to his favor: Kate Barnard. As Haskell knew, "the Labor Group had unquestioning faith" in her.[24] But she hesitated to help because she liked and trusted Daws as a friend and political leader. Daws also had the trust and support of "a hundred thousand loyal, desperate, mortgaged and over-worked, underfed men."[25] Discouraging Daws meant possibly alienating the thousands of poor workingmen who had also put their trust in Barnard.

Haskell, knowing that he needed to sway Barnard to pull her support from Daws and give it to Haskell, promised to support labor issues, including Barnard's demands for restricting child labor and making education compulsory. Barnard was caught in a difficult position. "How could I bite the hand so faithfully and generously extended to me" by Daws and his supporters, Barnard wrote. "On the other hand," she added, "Haskell was the most Powerful and Dominant personality, bar none, ruling and swaying Public Destiny in that critical hour."[26] Haskell was an experienced politician who knew how to get what he wanted. He also had access to money, an incredibly important asset for a politician. Furthermore, a split Democratic vote would all but guarantee a Republican victory, which Barnard could not bear to face. "The Republican Party were rejoicing," she wrote. "They saw utter route [sic] and ruin for the Democrats and a chance to destroy the Constitution they, and their Conservative backers, so hated."[27] She had to reach out to Daws.

In her conversation with Daws, Barnard pointed out that Haskell would never withdraw from the race. Furthermore, she argued, if farmers, workers, and miners wanted any chance of legal protection, a Democrat had to win. She pleaded with Daws to push workers to support Haskell. "If Haskell will not sacrifice Public Office for such high achievement to secure these Humane Laws for the people of our State," Barnard said to Daws, "I know you are big enough to make the Sacrifice."[28] The next day Daws withdrew his name from the race, giving Haskell the support of a hundred thousand labor votes. Although she was uncertain about the decision at the time and would later express worry over how her choice affected Daws's long-term political career, she later wrote,

> **MISS KATE BARNARD**
> "FRIEND OF THE POOR"
>
> DEMOCRATIC CANDIDATE FOR
>
> ## State Commissioner of Charities
>
> CLOTHED AND SCHOOLED 500 POOR CHILDREN. HOMED 2,000 OF
> OKLAHOMA'S POOR LAST YEAR. MEMBER OF
> TRADES AND LABOR ASSEMBLY.

Kate Barnard's campaign card for state commissioner of charities, circa 1907. Courtesy of the Research Division, Oklahoma Historical Society.

"Time proved its wisdom. Haskell was elected, the Constitution carried" by a majority of seventy thousand, and "I learned the fight had only just begun."[29]

Once the Democrats settled on Haskell as their nominee, Barnard began her own campaign as a candidate for the Department of Charities and Corrections. Her efforts proved worth her time and energy. She won the office by a greater plurality than any other candidate in the election. Indeed, she won her office by a margin of five hundred votes more than the governor had won his race. Barnard's victory was a reflection of a long-term relationship she had created with the Oklahoma public. As Deborah Bouziden reminds us, Barnard had created a strong alliance with the *Daily Oklahoman* and its readers. When she worked for her private charities and wrote articles or advertisements asking for help, readers gave generously. She relied on this same support when she became commissioner for Charities and Corrections.

Her electoral victory demonstrated the fluidity of power in the early years of Oklahoma statehood. Although women did not have the right to vote, Kate Barnard won state office by the largest plurality in that year's election. Such circumstances could not be duplicated elsewhere, and Barnard would learn this lesson for herself after spending some time in New York. When in the city to study its living conditions, Barnard announced that she had become a suffragist: "I've been a suffragist for only six months . . . and it's your horrid conditions here that have made me one."[30] People in New York were living in such dire circumstances that the only solution possible was women's suffrage. However, this was not the case in Oklahoma. "In Oklahoma," Barnard continued, "men will give us rights, but here it seems you must have the vote to get anything."[31] Women's suffrage, as Barnard's political career demonstrated, was not necessary to accomplish the social reforms she prioritized.

From the very beginning of her career as commissioner, Barnard made her priorities clear to the public. "I am especially interested in that class of legislation that will best protect the tiniest and frailest bit of humanity that is entrusted to our care," she wrote.[32] But while she was primarily concerned with children, her first course of action was to deal with Oklahoma prisoners. As commissioner, Barnard's responsibilities included overseeing jails, poorhouses, orphanages, rescue homes, and institutions for the care of children as well as blind, deaf, and mentally ill people across the state and at every level of government. Although the state had jails scattered throughout, it lacked a prison. Instead, the state paid the government of Kansas to take Oklahoma's prisoners. For forty cents a day per prisoner, Oklahoma prisoners served out their sentences in the Kansas Penitentiary in Lansing. Without giving advance notice to the warden or guards, Barnard decided to pay a surprise visit to the prison. After she paid an admittance fee, she was escorted to what prisoners referred to as the "show place of the prison." Barnard was not fooled, though. After her tour, she went to the warden's office, identified herself, and demanded a tour that would take her into the parts of the prison that were closed off to visitors. When asked under what authority she could make such demands, Barnard replied, "I am commissioned by a million and a half Oklahoma citizens to investigate this penitentiary. Either show me through as a state officer of Oklahoma, or order me out."[33]

As she made her way through the prison, inmates begged her to visit areas where they had been tortured. In one such place, nicknamed "the dungeons," prisoners worked extensive hours in the mines near or below the prison in extremely dangerous conditions. When prisoners were punished, they were forced into "cribs," small spaces where doors closed and isolated them for hours at a time. Other prisoners were dropped into holes where water was poured on them. Barnard was shocked to hear about the prisoners' experiences. She demanded to talk to every Oklahoma prisoner, some of whom were as young as fifteen.

Upon her return to Oklahoma, Barnard knew it was her responsibility to bring this issue to the attention of her fellow political leaders. She knew that in addition to describing the atrocious conditions of the prison, she would need to explain to state leaders the economic costs to Oklahoma taxpayers. Barnard reported that while Oklahoma paid Kansas 40¢ a day per prisoner, Kansas spent only 10.9¢ a day per prisoner for food. Furthermore, Kansas was using prisoners as a source of free labor. In other words, Kansas was profiting from the forced labor of Oklahoma prisoners in addition to the state's payments. It would be to the state's economic as well as moral benefit, Barnard argued, to build its own state penitentiary.

Although she made a clear argument, Governor Charles Haskell dismissed Barnard's report as nothing more than a woman being overly concerned with issues that did not need to be prioritized. "Miss Barnard is a good woman," Haskell claimed, "and a good industrious official and has a heart full of sympathy for the unfortunate, and her kindness of heart would make things look cruel to her more than an ordinary citizen would consider proper and necessary."[34] His dismissal of her concerns as nothing more than an overemotional woman's overreaction when faced with what he thought was a trivial issue was an indication of how he perceived Barnard and her role as a woman leader. While she was an elected official who had earned more votes than anyone else, himself included, he did not believe her priorities were important.

Haskell might not have taken Barnard's report seriously, but the public disagreed. Oklahomans contacted their legislators and demanded action. In response, the Oklahoma House of Representatives launched an investigation of its own. In its concluding report, investigators established that Barnard was correct in her assessment and that she had, in fact, addressed only half the horrors that prisoners experienced. As a result, the state legislature appropriated $50,000 to construct a state penitentiary in McAlester, Oklahoma.

From the beginning of her career as commissioner, Barnard demonstrated that her interests were not only for children; they were for all people who were marginalized by larger society. Barnard had successfully convinced the public that Oklahoma prisoners—who had been found guilty of crimes under the Oklahoma judicial system—were worthy of charitable acts. Their guilt did not rob them of their humanity, as she established.

Barnard's charity also extended to the mentally infirm. Norman, Oklahoma, located twenty miles south of Oklahoma City, was home to the Oklahoma Sanitarium. State officials appointed Dr. A. H. Clark as the superintendent of the hospital, whose primary responsibility was to oversee the treatment and care of its mentally ill patients. As commissioner of Charities and Corrections,

Barnard expected that the hospital was well equipped and its patients received the best care possible. Upon investigating the hospital, however, she learned that was not the case.[35]

According to Barnard's observations, hospital staff at the Oklahoma Sanitarium fed patients only beans and cornbread because they did not have access to fruits or vegetables. Some patients were locked in their cells without access to sanitation and were therefore locked in their rooms with their own excrement. Other patients were kept in cuffs or chains while some were placed in cribs, similar to what the Oklahoma prisoners experienced in Lansing, Kansas. When Barnard confronted Dr. Clark about the horrific conditions the patients lived in, he responded that the lack of funding made it difficult to give the patients the care they needed.

Barnard approached the state legislature and requested additional funds for the mentally ill, a community that had long been ignored and forgotten. However, learning from her experience advocating for prisoners, Barnard knew that a report alone would not suffice to guarantee additional funding. Instead, she employed a strategy that had worked for her when she was a charity fundraiser; she called on experts in the field to comment on the situation in Norman and to submit ideas of how to improve the hospital's conditions. After she presented her report to the state legislature in 1909, including written opinions from national experts, the state legislature agreed to increase the annual funding for the sanitarium. Confident that the patients would finally receive better care, Barnard felt satisfied that she had helped to resolve another problem.

However, when she returned to inspect the hospital in 1910, Barnard was shocked to learn that the hospital's superintendent, Dr. Clark, had done nothing with the increased funding to help his patients. "You send me a six-page letter dealing in generalities and not one single figure regarding your itemized expense of the profits or dividends declared," Barnard wrote to the superintendent.[36] In her letter, she listed the egregious conditions under which patients lived and nurses worked. "In the face of this fact," she declared, "the lack of bathing facilities, the high death rate and the absolute absence of scientific equipments, I have a right to know and I demand as commissioner of charities an accounting."[37] Infuriated that conditions had remained the same, Barnard fired the doctor and hired Dr. D. W. Griffin to replace him. The change in personnel created a new problem, though, because Barnard did not have the authority to fire or hire a superintendent. She once again faced the state legislature—this time in a battle over the extent of her authority. In the end, she won, and in the media she was a hero. According to writers for the *Daily Oklahoman*, "Conditions have in every way have been bettered, and almost $75,000 has been expended for new buildings, repairs, and equipment."[38]

Barnard's choices as commissioner did not always create friends. In fact, she often created political enemies, none greater than William H. Murray, once chairman of the state's constitutional convention and future governor of Oklahoma. Murray was a Democrat who still held a Jeffersonian view of America, favoring agrarianism and limited government. He was also Jacksonian in his approach to politics, embracing the power of the common people and rejecting Progressive views of government power. Furthermore, Murray felt no sympathy for any group that Progressives described as "disadvantaged." In his opinion, the government did not have any responsibility for women, children, minorities, or anyone else marginalized by society.

Barnard was also a Democrat, but a new breed of Democrat—one significantly different from Alfalfa Bill Murray. She had pledged herself to the goals of Progressive reform: she embraced industrialism but advocated to protect workers, and she fought for social justice and fairness throughout all strata of American society. Her ideals were deeply rooted in her Christian faith, and though she had not always been a suffragist, Barnard was confident that women had the ability to better the world with or without the vote. Her work reflected her values. While there were limitations to her Progressive stances, she stood in clear opposition to politicians such as Murray.

Murray had a reputation of speaking contemptuously about women, despite the fact that he benefited greatly from them. "Women have always embarrassed me," Murray once wrote.[39] He owed his economic advantage to his wife, Mary Alice Harrell, a citizen of the Chickasaw Nation. That marriage had made him eligible for land allotments and secured his political connections with important figures, such as the Chickasaw chief, who happened to be his wife's uncle. Mary Alice was better educated and came from a higher economic standing than her husband. Still, Murray insisted in the broadest generalization that despite their best efforts, women hurt society more than they helped. It is no surprise, then, that Murray and Barnard often clashed over politics.

Their rivalry had begun during the days of the constitutional convention and carried into the first legislature when Murray, then a state representative and Speaker of the House, argued that the Office of Charities and Corrections required very little funding. To his dismay, the House Appropriations Committee disagreed and recommended significant funding. But Barnard was ready to fight Murray if that was what she had to do. "I built up a regular organization," she wrote. "Every speech was prepared and one followed the other with the precision of a school entertainment."[40] Murray, infuriated by the committee's recommendation, took to the floor to debate the funding, but to no avail. In fact, Murray's willingness to humiliate a woman publicly cost the state even more. The legislature ultimately voted to appropriate $1,000 more than the amount the committee had recommended.

Barnard and Murray also clashed on the issue of child labor, but it was Governor Charles Haskell who would defeat her legislative proposal. In early 1908, Barnard actively campaigned for a child labor bill. Murray, long opposed to child labor laws, campaigned against it. Barnard successfully "out-politicked" Murray, but Governor Haskell, also long opposed to regulating child labor, vetoed the bill. Barnard did not take the defeat well, blaming Murray and obsessing over why she had lost. Ultimately, she decided that Murray and his political allies had purposely targeted her and her Progressive reforms. She chose to focus her efforts on revenge aimed at Murray and his colleagues' political careers. To this end, Barnard took to the campaign trail.

Murray did not seek reelection, but he did actively endorse his friends. After realizing that Barnard was targeting him in her campaign speeches, Murray attacked her social justice proposals, describing them as "freak legislation."[41] Murray did not want to be humiliated by a woman on the campaign trail, and Barnard would not waiver. In a speech to the Oklahoma Federation of Labor in July 1908, she criticized Murray's anti-labor policies and misogynist behavior. The organization, in response, officially declared Murray "an enemy to the masses of Oklahoma." Not to be outdone, Murray described the union members as "a bunch of grafters."[42] The Federation of Labor was aligned with the Farmers' Union, whose members renounced any support the organization received from Murray. Instead, they chose to follow Barnard's lead. She was so confident in her support and clout that she challenged Murray to a public debate. Murray chose to leave town instead.

Two years later, friends of Kate Barnard recalled that Murray's behavior had become quite hostile toward her. In letters to the *Daily Oklahoman*, her friends described threats he had made against her shortly after the Oklahoma Federation of Labor had passed resolutions against Murray. Barnard shared with her friends that "Murray had threatened to 'rotten egg' her if she came to Tishomingo [where Murray lived], that she had worked with him and knew his temperament, and that she was afraid he would carry his threat into execution."[43]

Still, Barnard did not allow his intimidation to stop her from expressing her opinion of him. "Every one knows Bill Murray's record on union labor matters," she said, "and I would be false to the cause I have so long advocated, if I would consent to support" Murray's gubernatorial campaign.[44]

In confronting Murray, Barnard showed her fearlessness in the political arena. Murray was a formidable politician, well known throughout the state and eventually across the nation, but Barnard was not deterred. Murray was a "keen, able, crude uncouth Political Leader who had much in common with the 'Common people' and represented them able [sic] and faithfully . . . most of the time."[45] But Barnard was most motivated to fight when the lives of innocent people were at stake. Nothing demonstrated this better than her next, and last, great political battle: protecting Native American orphans.

When Oklahomans contacted Barnard's office about seeing fairies in the woods, she knew immediately that she had to investigate. She discovered that the "fairies" were actually three orphaned Indian children who were starving, wearing rags, and homeless. Upon further investigation, Barnard discovered that the children had been assigned a legal guardian, but the guardian had no interest in actually caring for them. Indeed, the guardian was living on the allotment that had originally belonged to the children but made no effort to care for the children's welfare. Barnard was shocked to discover that this type of neglect was typical thanks to the practice of graft. In 1908, state judges had appointed guardians to control the estates of orphans or children whose parents were judged incompetent to manage their property. These appointments created an opportunity for grafters who preyed on elderly or orphaned Native Americans, hoping to gain access to their land and the resources therein.

Horrified, Barnard investigated and, with the help of attorney J. H. Stolper, exposed several cases of corruption to the public. She contacted orphanages and other state institutions to research records of the number of Indian children who had been assigned guardians. In all, 143 Indian children had the ability to pay for their own care but were living in poverty. Stolper took legal action against their guardians for mishandling the children's estates.[46] Their investigation exposed how extensively the corruption had spread. "The state, acting through Miss Kate Barnard," one journalist wrote, "has started a crusade to clean up the abuses of guardianship of Indian minors and to prevent the robbing of the minors by unscrupulous guardians."[47] Barnard's work continued for more than a year, through her reelection in 1910.

After her reelection, Barnard contacted tribal leaders, hoping they would be interested in protecting the rights of Indian children, but none of them responded to her requests.[48] State legislators, however, did respond by trying to slow and stop Barnard's meddling. While she worked to eliminate political and economic corruption, some state legislators attacked her and tried to eliminate her position. To their disappointment, Barnard was still a popular public figure—too popular to remove from office.

After contacting her allies in the Oklahoma state legislature, Barnard contacted her friends in the press. Newspaper articles and editorials exposed and denounced the practice of graft and praised Barnard's efforts. "No person in the state is more thoroughly familiar with Indian affairs in Oklahoma than Kate Barnard," one writer declared, "and no woman is more competent to comment upon their conditions than she."[49] Writers demanded that these so-called guardians be held accountable. If they were not held accountable, taxpayers would have to pay the bill to help provide for poor children who had been abandoned by their guardians, but it was necessary work. "That the Indian situation in Oklahoma is one of the most serious problems which the state is facing is being recognized by men who take a deep interest in such affairs."[50] As a result of Barnard's work, nearly $70,000 was restored to the orphans by late September 1911.[51]

Although the media responded positively to Barnard's work, state legislators did not. Her investigations into Indian orphans and their deceitful guardians only became more assertive. As her department's responsibilities expanded, Barnard submitted a request to the legislature for a public defender. According to Musslewhite and Crawford, the request sparked a debate on the floor of the state legislature. Critics did not agree with the necessity of the expense, and they did not believe that Barnard should have the final authority over the public defender. This continued on the senate floor as well.[52]

Unfortunately for Barnard, bouts of illness kept her away from the state capitol. She tried to relay to her allies in the house and senate her wish to expand the budget and power of her office so she could protect minor orphans. But her legislative opponents used her absence to their political advantage, campaigning instead to decrease her power as commissioner and reduce the size of her department. Indeed, the Oklahoma Senate unanimously adopted a resolution prohibiting lobbying of any kind by state officials in the interest of any legislation "that has to do with the affairs of their offices."[53] Although the resolution clearly targeted Barnard, she argued that her physical ailments prevented her from "making a canvass of the members of the senate individually." Barnard requested twenty minutes to speak on behalf of legislation that would affect her office. Her request was denied.

The tension between Barnard and the state legislature was an indication of how much more difficult her second term as commissioner would be. She was not able to influence legislators like she had in her earlier years. Furthermore, "after 1912, legislators became even more conservative and even less inclined to agree with reformist suggestions."[54] Rather than confront them directly, Barnard once again used the media to her advantage. She claimed that legislators were continually attempting "to defeat her appropriations and destroy the efficiency of her department" because they "failed to control the work of her office."[55] The contention, she believed, was because her department had been "a stumbling block to those who have sought to deprive innocent orphans of their birthright." But she pledged to continue her fight regardless of opposition from the state legislature.

By the time the legislative session was complete, the Department of Charities and Corrections was still standing, but just barely. Legislators had reduced the office's budget so that it could pay the salaries of only Barnard and one stenographer. By 1914 she had little left to work with, and to make matters more complicated, she was battling several chronic health problems. Although Barnard was certain she could win, she decided not to run for reelection. Instead, she focused the remainder of her time in office on protecting Native children from graft. She was convinced she could create a political storm that would force "the politicians and grafters" to "be completely whipped into submission." But her ideas to help Native people would require at least $10,000 of outside funding, an amount the Oklahoma state legislature was not willing to spend.

The last fifteen years of Barnard's life were difficult and, at times, overwhelming. Her diary entries reveal a woman who was depressed and disappointed by how her political career, and even her life, had unfolded. Indeed, Barnard described herself as "ostracized, isolated, hated, damned, and forgotten." She tried "desperately to regain her health and re-build her shattered life work, not knowing what the end will be."[56] She continued fighting for the rights of Native people, only to be met with disappointment and rejection. The more she fought, the more politicians resisted her. She once wrote to a friend, "But God knows there is no justice for Indians in Oklahoma. . . . Truly, I don't know why I was born. This battle is too much for me. It would kill a strong man."[57] She died alone on February 23, 1930. Her grave marker bears this inscription: "Intrepid pioneer leader for social ethics in Oklahoma." Indeed, she was. Rather than allow society, politicians, or even other women to define her, Kate Barnard created her own path and served as the leader she wanted to be.

While Jim Bissett does not address Kate Barnard's relationship with the Farmers' Union, he effectively describes the political chaos in the early years of Oklahoma statehood. While Oklahoma's Democrats hoped to gain support among Socialist farmers, the Oklahoma Socialist Party struggled to find its own footing. Furthermore, as Bissett points out, "agrarian radicals came to the Socialist Party with democratic ideas of decentralized power firmly in place, ideas that were immediately at odds with the way Party leaders routinely exercised their authority."[58] Despite not having the right to vote, Barnard fit into the chaos quite easily.[59] Her ability to influence the state's constitutional convention, to campaign and win more votes than any other official, and to confront corruption point to her ability to work both within and outside of existing gender norms. After convincing S. O. Daws to withdraw his gubernatorial nomination in favor of Charles Haskell, Barnard wrote, "I felt uncertain about this political move but time proved its wisdom.... Then I learned the fight had only just begun."[60]

NOTES

1. Kate Barnard, typewritten diary, Correspondence Concerning Kate Barnard, box 1, Kate Barnard Collection, Oklahoma Historical Society Research Division (hereafter cited as Barnard diary), 241.

2. Suzanne Jones Crawford and Lynn R. Musslewhite, "Kate Barnard, Progressivism, and the West," in *"An Oklahoma I Had Never Seen Before": Alternative Views of Oklahoma History*, ed. Davis D. Joyce (Norman: University of Oklahoma Press, 1994), 73.

3. The Farmers' Union was organized in 1902 in Texas and moved north into Oklahoma and Indian Territories. Jim Bissett, *Agrarian Socialism in America: Marx, Jefferson, and Jesus in the Oklahoma Countryside, 1904–1920* (Norman: University of Oklahoma Press, 1999), 4.

4. Barnard diary, 310.

5. Bissett, *Agrarian Socialism in America*, 3.

6. Barnard diary, 22.

7. Barnard diary, 214.

8. Emma Goldman, "Woman Suffrage," *Anarchism and Other Essays* (Auckland, New Zealand: Floating, 2008), 238.

9. Barnard to Cora J. Martin, February 16, 1909, Charities and Corrections Collection, State Archives of Oklahoma, Oklahoma City.

10. Barnard to Mary Wilkes Glenn, March 3, 1909, Charities and Corrections Collection, State Archives of Oklahoma, Oklahoma City.

11. Barnard to Judge Ben Lindsey, July 18, 1913, Charities and Corrections Collection, State Archives of Oklahoma, Oklahoma City.

12. Suzanne Jones Crawford and Lynn R. Musslewhite, "Progressive Reform and Oklahoma Democrats: Kate Barnard versus Bill Murray," *Historian* 53, no. 3 (Spring 1991): 473.

13. Lynn R. Musslewhite and Suzanne Jones Crawford, *One Woman's Political Journey: Kate Barnard and Social Reform, 1875–1930* (Norman: University of Oklahoma Press, 2003), 33.

14. "Kate Barnard Making Her Way in the World," *Daily Oklahoman*, November 18, 1906, 6.

15. Murray R. Wickett, *Contested Territory: Whites, Native Americans and African Americans in Oklahoma, 1865–1907* (Baton Rouge: Louisiana State University Press, 2000), 175.

16. Wickett explores this further and argues that Democrats instilled a fear in white Oklahomans that Republicans were turning over political control to Black Americans. Wickett, 192.

17. Crawford and Musslewhite, "Progressive Reform and Oklahoma Democrats," 10.

18. Crawford and Musslewhite, 15.

19. Musslewhite and Crawford, *One Woman's Political Journey*, 31.

20. *Daily Oklahoman*, August 23, 1906.

21. Barnard diary, 26.

22. Bob Burke and Glenda Carlile, *Kate Barnard: Oklahoma's Good Angel*, Oklahoma Statesman Series 8 (Edmond: University of Central Oklahoma Press, 2001), 21.

23. Suzanne Schrems, *Who's Rocking the Cradle? Women Pioneers of Oklahoma Politics from Socialism to the KKK, 1900–1930* (Norman, OK: Horse Creek, 2004), 1.

24. Barnard diary, 217.

25. Barnard diary, 217.

26. Barnard diary, 217.

27. Barnard diary, 219.

28. Barnard diary, 223.

29. Barnard diary, 224.

30. "Kate Barnard Is Now a Suffragist," *Daily Oklahoman*, September 22, 1909, 1.

31. "Kate Barnard Is Now a Suffragist."

32. Deborah Bouziden, "Catherine 'Kate' Ann Barnard: Child Advocate and Voice for the Poor," in *More than Petticoats: Remarkable Oklahoma Women* (Guilford, CT: Globe Pequot, 2013), 1.

33. Glenda Carlile, "Kate Barnard: The Good Angel of Oklahoma," in *Buckskin, Calico and Lace: Oklahoma's Territorial Women* (Oklahoma City: Southern Hills, 1990), 84.

34. Carlile, "Kate Barnard," 85.

35. Carlile, "Kate Barnard," 85.

36. "Accounting of Board Demanded," *Daily Oklahoman*, January 14, 1910, 11.

37. "Accounting of Board Demanded."

38. "Effective Work on Miss Kate Barnard," *Daily Oklahoman*, September 29, 1911, 28.

39. Crawford and Musslewhite, "Progressive Reform and Oklahoma Democrats."
40. Crawford and Musslewhite, "Progressive Reform and Oklahoma Democrats."
41. Crawford and Musslewhite, "Progressive Reform and Oklahoma Democrats."
42. Crawford and Musslewhite, "Progressive Reform and Oklahoma Democrats."
43. "Woman in Terror of 'Bill' Murray," *Daily Oklahoman*, July 29, 1910, 18.
44. "Miss Barnard Is a Foe of Murray," *Daily Oklahoman*, August 1, 1910, 1.
45. Barnard diary, 27.
46. Musslewhite and Crawford, *One Woman's Political Journey*, 149.
47. "Indian Orphans Fraud Victims?," *Daily Oklahoman*, November 19, 1910, 9.
48. Musslewhite and Crawford, *One Woman's Political Journey*, 150.
49. "Indians Robbed of $3,000,000," *Daily Oklahoman*, February 12, 1911, 36.
50. "Indians Robbed of $3,000,000."
51. "Much Aid Given Indian Orphans," *Daily Oklahoman*, September 27, 1911, 3.
52. Musslewhite and Crawford, *One Woman's Political Journey*, 153.
53. "Kate Barnard Attempts to Break Senate Rule of No Lobbies by Officials," *Daily Oklahoman*, January 17, 1913, 10.
54. Musslewhite and Crawford, *One Woman's Political Journey*, 155.
55. "Politicians Seek to Wreck Office, Says Miss Kate," *Daily Oklahoman*, May 8, 1913, 1.
56. Barnard diary, 21.
57. Bouziden, "Catherine 'Kate' Ann Barnard," 9.
58. Bissett, *Agrarian Socialism in America*, 61.
59. Women could not vote in legislative matters, but, according to the original state constitution, women could vote in school elections.
60. Barnard diary, 224.

FARINA KING

5
"LOYAL COUNTRYWOMAN"
Rachel Caroline Eaton, Alumna of the
Cherokee National Female Seminary

In the summer of 1910, Rachel Caroline ("Callie") Eaton traveled with Nellie Ross throughout Cherokee country in the northeastern part of Oklahoma, visiting historic places in order to study and gather sources for the Sequoyah Historical Society, which she had helped to organize in her hometown of Claremore, Oklahoma, only two years earlier.[1] Callie was pursuing a graduate degree in history at the University of Chicago, and although her academic and professional track would take her throughout the United States, she constantly returned to her home in Cherokee country—her motherland and birth nation. She had established the Sequoyah Historical Society for historical research focusing on "the former Indian Territory."[2] The stories and histories of Cherokee land kept drawing her back home, even when the Cherokee Nation was disbanded by American policies such as the Dawes (or Allotment) Act. She and Nellie Ross, as local newspapers in Oklahoma recounted, were both "Cherokees and intellectual ladies, who wish to perpetuate the history, traditions and memories of the once great Nation of Cherokees, who were a numerous and great people long before Columbus set foot on the western continent."[3] Another newspaper recounted the same story but described the Cherokees as "the first great nation."[4] As a Cherokee "intellectual lady," Callie applied her skills in the field of history to sustain Cherokee nationalism and peoplehood in conjunction with her American citizenship. Her life and work are examples of Cherokees' attempts to balance multiple, even conflicting, allegiances to both the Cherokee and American nations.

Callie Eaton was one of 212 women who graduated from the Cherokee National Female Seminary between 1851 and 1909. They constituted an exceptional group who spearheaded education for women not only in Indian Territory but also throughout the American West and beyond.[5] As the first Cherokee woman to earn a doctoral degree, Callie connected with and stood alongside fellow trailblazers and strong women whom the female seminary matriculated, such as Isabel ("Belle") Cobb, who was nine years her senior. Belle returned to her alma mater to teach from 1882 to 1887, during which time Callie Eaton was a seminary student.[6] After teaching at the female seminary, Belle pursued medical studies and became one of the first female physicians in Indian Territory. In 1892, Dr. Belle Cobb hoped to serve as the first woman physician at the Cherokee National Female Seminary. She signed her letter of interest, addressed to Colonel Johnson ("C. J.") Harris, principal chief of the Cherokee Nation, as "your loyal countrywoman."[7]

Women like Belle and Callie not only represented themselves individually but also evoked the many other accomplished Cherokee female seminarians. This chapter focuses on Callie and her accomplishments as part of a network of Cherokee "loyal countrywomen." In a groundbreaking study of the seminarians, *Cultivating the Rosebuds: The Education of Women at the Cherokee Female Seminary, 1851–1909*, Choctaw scholar Devon A. Mihesuah finds that many seminary alumnae engaged in social reform, leadership, and politics even before the Nineteenth Amendment solidified women's suffrage in 1920.[8] Historian Brad Agnew stresses how seminarians "had influence far beyond their actual numbers, and that influence reverberated through many generations."[9] Seminary alumnae, including Callie, dedicated their lives and work to bolstering the Cherokee Nation when American policies designed to integrate and dissolve tribal nations jeopardized Cherokee sovereignty between the late nineteenth and early twentieth centuries.

Rachel Caroline ("Callie") Eaton in 1896–97, when she was working as the first assistant to the principal of the Cherokee Female National Seminary. Courtesy of Northeastern State University Archives.

Callie, both an educator and historian, has been recognized as one of the first female county superintendents of schools in Oklahoma.[10] In her work, she valued oral tradition and her Cherokee identity, which many other academics underappreciated and even ostracized her for. Despite various challenges, she formed a hybrid methodology that celebrated and focused on Cherokee national history. Callie Eaton's life and work epitomize the complexities of being a "loyal countrywoman." She claimed allegiance to the Cherokee Nation and upheld her citizenship based on her Indigenous heritage while also embracing and navigating European American influences and dictates in her career and life. She exemplified ways that women shaped the Cherokee Nation as her people struggled to justify their existence to the United States as a "civilized tribe" through the early twentieth century.

Intersectional barriers marred the seminary alumnae's experiences through generations of graduating classes. Belle, for example, was never appointed physician at the seminary and struggled to maintain a private practice in her Indian Territory hometown near present-day Wagoner, Oklahoma.[11] The Cherokee Nation overlooked her as a candidate and hired a non–Native American man, Dr. Richard Fite, who was married to Nancy ("Nannie") Katherine Daniel—ironically a fellow Cherokee seminary alumna—and was therefore granted preference and "similar citizenship" in the Cherokee Nation.[12] Belle's great-niece Carol Payne Merriman and scholar Janice J. Sisemore both recognize how the sexism of this oversight impacted Belle. Sisemore asserts that Belle "was, however, a woman of intelligence and talent who used those gifts as a doctor, an educator and leader of her church and community."[13] Callie, who came from a later class of seminary graduates, also faced blocks to her professional goals as a Cherokee woman.

Despite the setbacks they faced as women, Cherokee seminary alumnae such as Callie carried the mantle of being "loyal countrywomen" of the Cherokee Nation. While scholars have asserted that the Cherokee National Female Seminary enabled them to obtain a white settler education and imbued them with European American customs and mannerisms, the seminary also ingrained in its graduates at least one significant aspect of an intergenerational Cherokee tradition—Cherokee peoplehood as separate from US nationalism. Devon Mihesuah recognizes that Cherokee alumnae held "multiple loyalties: to their white and Cherokee family members, to the Cherokee Nation, to the state of Oklahoma, and to the United States of America."[14] But the different loyalties of alumnae such as Callie Eaton were valued in ways that were not necessarily equal.

In her later work, Mihesuah refers specifically to these prominent alumnae: "Women such as Belle Cobb, Rachel Caroline Eaton, and Nannie Katherine Daniels [sic] went on to graduate from universities . . . but they did not use their extensive education to help their tribe."[15] While the United States government sought to dissolve the Cherokee Nation, however, these Cherokee alumnae continued to value and support their tribal nation, elevating some of their loyalties over others. By continuing to acknowledge Cherokee nationalism, Cherokee alumnae questioned and complicated American nationalism. Considering their multiple but unequal loyalties, this chapter examines the ways that Callie, like other female seminary alumnae, supported the Cherokee Nation through her work. The seminary instilled in its students a sense of the Cherokees' right to exist as both a people and a nation, which seminarians such as Callie honored throughout their lives, even when US officials aimed to terminate indefinitely all "Indian" nations as sovereigns, including the Cherokees. Cherokee scholar Kirby Brown highlights, for example, how Callie's historical writings support "a people's self-determined struggle to be 'still, a nation.'"[16] Callie contributed to the Cherokee Nation as both a storyteller and a writer of Cherokee history from the perspective of a "loyal countrywoman."

Nearly three thousand women attended the Cherokee National Female Seminary throughout its tenure, each with her own stories of accomplishments, setbacks, and everyday life.[17] Nannie Daniel Fite, who graduated in 1880, described fellow seminary alumnae, including Callie Eaton, as being part of an enduring sisterhood.[18] As an alumna, Nannie noted how many of the "old Seminary girls" had returned to the seminary as teachers, just as Callie would later do. Considering the graduating class of 1887 as an example of the successes and growth of the seminary, Nannie referred to "Callie Eaton, Lizzie McNair and Adda Ross," each of whom received her diploma at the Cherokee National Male Seminary after the fire of 1887 destroyed the female seminary building in Park Hill, Indian Territory. Despite this heavy loss, the Cherokee Nation rebuilt and opened the new female seminary building in Tahlequah by 1889. Callie returned nearly ten years later to work as first assistant principal under the respected educator and principal Ann Florence Wilson.[19]

Many Cherokee alumnae acknowledged Wilson's influence during her time as "a worthy helmsman" of the female seminary between 1875 and 1901.[20] Wilson engaged in politics by attending local political rallies and following contemporary issues, which students recognized and emulated.[21] The Cherokee National Council resolved to appoint her as principal of the female seminary for

Cherokee Female Seminary staff: Miss Florence Wilson, principal; Mrs. Eugenia Thompson, fifth assistant; Miss Nell Taylor and Miss Cora McNair, music teachers; Miss Oklahoma Spradling, third assistant; Miss Caroline Eaton, first assistant; Miss Bluie Adair, second assistant; and Miss Leila Morgan, fourth assistant, 1896–97. Courtesy Northeastern State University Archives.

life, but when US federal officials blocked this decision in 1901, Wilson resigned, displaying a sense of loyalty to the Cherokee Nation, which faced increasing restrictions and interference.[22] After graduating from the female seminary under Wilson's tutelage, Callie started her career as an educator then later returned to work with Wilson at the seminary for two years between 1896 and 1897.[23] Fite and others respected these women as "ladies [who] were selected on account of their ability as teachers and their personal characters."[24] Callie was thus part of a network of educated women who intentionally sought to shape their communities and the Cherokee Nation.

The seminary represented the growth and strength of the Cherokee Nation through its training of Cherokee women who would lead in various capacities in society. In a summary of 1887, the Cherokee Nation commended its self-determined and sovereign educational system: "Our higher schools are sending forth the majority of those engaged in this patriotic work."[25] Callie demonstrated this Cherokee patriotism by teaching in Cherokee schools and studying and writing Cherokee national narratives.[26] Fite acknowledged Cherokee ancestors who prepared the way for the seminarians like herself: "What other mistakes our ancestors might have made they took great pride in their daughters and saw that they were properly trained for the duties, the realities, and responsibilities of life."[27] She also hoped—for the seminary and seminarians—that the Cherokee "identity be not lost in the coming years."[28] This identity of "loyal countrywomen" centered on dedication to family, community, and the Cherokee Nation. Cherokee women and seminarians such as Callie also changed the tradition of Cherokees by becoming the first Cherokee and Native American women to pursue and excel in certain professions. Callie's identity, as an alumna of the Cherokee National Female Seminary and academic historian, also enabled her to connect with her Cherokee heritage.

In 1892, Dr. Belle Cobb received a letter signed by Kate O'Donald, one of her associates at Drury College in Springfield, Missouri. In the letter, Kate referred to Belle as "my dear Friend," and she mentioned Callie Eaton as a common acquaintance: "Callie, and Pink McClelland are still with us. Callie has no intention of returning next year as she feels she must get to work."[29] Callie eventually graduated with a bachelor's degree from Drury College in 1895. The reference to Callie in the letter seems minor, but it reveals a key point: seminary alumnae stayed in contact and updated one another about their lives and professional developments. Belle's sister Mattie wrote, in a separate letter dated 1898, how she hoped that Belle would attend the annual commencement for the female seminary. Like her older sister Belle, Mattie had also attended the female seminary. Mattie said she missed principal Ann Florence Wilson, and she inquired whether Callie still taught at the seminary.[30]

Such correspondence shows how Cherokee alumnae offered support and connections not only as a network of friends and kin but also as professionals, academics, and public intellectuals. This term, "public intellectuals," underscores their roles as public servants and contributors to society who offered services such as education and medicine, as would become the case for Belle, whom Mattie endearingly referred to as "Miss Physician."[31] In a similar way, Kate had acknowledged Callie's urgency "to work." These letters illuminate the ties between Cherokee seminary alumnae, which included Callie and her affiliations.

Maggie Culver Fry knew of Callie from the stories that her mother told her about being a former student of the seminary while Callie was a teacher there in the 1890s: "Miss Callie was forthright in her approach, and she had a quiet sense of humor. In addition to her personal attributes, she had impeccable manners."[32] Rosalie Mills, who interviewed Callie for a Claremore news article featuring her as the Rogers County school superintendent, "appreciated her more, because of her sweet, unassuming, modest manner."[33] Callie impressed and educated others with her example of humility.[34] In 1910, Callie identified herself as a "teacher"; then, in 1930, she referred to herself as an "author" and "independent" who was "working on own account."[35]

In 1936, only a couple of years before she died, Callie was inducted into the Oklahoma Hall of Fame, where she was celebrated as a "pioneer" and the "daughter of a Cherokee Indian."[36] In 1938, in honor of Callie's life, Choctaw intellectual Muriel H. Wright sketched a tribute to Callie as a fellow Native American woman historian: "Reticent in disposition and positive in her decisions, she was one of the outstanding personalities reared under the regime of the old Cherokee Nation as an Indian republic."[37] To a wide reading public, in the *Chronicles of Oklahoma*, Wright identified and celebrated Callie as a Cherokee nationalist. While Callie had witnessed the efforts to detribalize and disintegrate Cherokee nationalism in the wake of assimilationist policies, allotment, and Oklahoma statehood, she had nonetheless preserved the sense and spirit of the Cherokees as a nation through her life's work as a historian, writer, and educator.

Originally from the region of Indian Territory near Claremore Mound, Callie spent her early years in Cherokee country, an experience that shaped her pursuits and scholarly contributions. One of Callie's historical studies, "The Legend of the Battle of Claremore Mound Oklahoma" (1930), focuses on the Battle of Strawberry Moon, or the Claremore Mound Massacre, of 1817 in which Cherokees attacked Osage families in the village of Pasuga, which lay at the bottom of the hill. Callie's historical narrative reveals how her interests in Native American history began with the landscapes of her home. As a child, she had become familiar with remains of that "tragic encounter" and the destroyed village of the mound, which she continued to trace through her historical research.[38] Her "childhood was spent under the shadow of the historic hill, glossy-grass slopes and rock-rimmed summit," after her parents, George Washington and Nancy Williams Eaton, settled their family there in 1874.[39] Callie's earliest exposure to history came through Native American intellectual processes, as she learned the stories of the land and what Michi Saagiig Nishnaabeg scholar Leanne Betasamosake Simpson calls "land as pedagogy."[40] Indigenous epistemology, Simpson says, "takes place in the context of family, community and relations."[41] Indigenous education thus "comes through the land" as families and communities teach with the traditions, stories, and oral histories of their homelands.[42]

Callie received foundational lessons by listening to stories of the lands such as Claremore Mound and how Osage and Cherokee lived and fought over them. As a Cherokee historian, she constantly returned to learn from her homelands, family, and community, specifically, as Callie writes, about "traditions and fireside tales passed by word of mouth from generation to generation."[43] Callie learned from these various sources, which are archives of lands and community voices, and passed on the histories of violent struggles that took place when Cherokees were forced to relocate to ancestral Osage lands because white settlers encroached on their traditional homelands in the southeast.[44]

Callie recalled her young "pioneer days" with fondness, even if the everyday rigor came with deprivations. Since her family could buy only limited supplies from town, which had to last for months at a time, simple household ingredients such as sugar could be scarce. When her mother served the sugar that she hid for guests, Callie's brother exclaimed at the sight of the delicacy: "Whoopy! Sugar in your coffee."[45] In order to attend the "old West Point school" near present-day Claremore, Callie began to live "in a log cabin with [her] grandmother," most likely Lucy Ward Williams, whom Callie said was a "fireside historian" and an inspiration for her studies in Cherokee history.[46]

Callie was among a cohort of Cherokee and Native American students from Indian Territory who continued their higher education at Drury College in Springfield, Missouri, where she received her bachelors' of science with distinction in 1895.[47] In college, professor Edward M. Sheppard helped persuade Callie to study Native American history.[48] Callie later completed a master's degree in 1911 and a doctorate of philosophy in history at the University of Chicago by 1919, after which she became a distinguished historian and professor.[49] She served two terms as superintendent of public instruction in Rogers County, Oklahoma, after her election to the position in 1920.

Callie established herself nationally as a reputable scholar in higher education—"a woman of broad scholarship, rich experience, and splendid personality" as the *Waxahachie Daily Light* described her.[50] In 1916, the newspaper featured Callie after she was elected dean of women and chair of the History Department at Trinity University in Waxahachie, Texas.[51] The article praised Callie's "successful experience as a college teacher," referring to her assistant principalship at the Cherokee National Female Seminary and professorships at the State College of Columbus in Mississippi and later at the Lake Erie College in Ohio. The article also touted Callie as a "Texas woman" from Houston, which is not credited to a source but might refer to her father and other Eaton family members who originally came from that region.⁵² But Callie sustained ties with her home community in Cherokee country. As local newspapers indicate, her home community in Oklahoma followed and celebrated her accomplishments. In 1911, the *Morning Tulsa Daily World* recognized Callie for earning her master's degree.⁵³ The following year, local papers noted that Callie had returned to Claremore after completing her master's program in Chicago during the summer. She was visiting Claremore before heading back to her professorship in Columbus, Mississippi.⁵⁴ Newspapers also reported on Callie's visits with friends and family such as her sister Martha ("Mattie") Pauline York of Sageeyah, Oklahoma.⁵⁵ Callie came home to Claremore not only for socialization but also to research and learn histories of the Cherokee Nation.⁵⁶

One of Callie's greatest influences was her Cherokee grandmother Lucy Ward Williams, who first immersed Callie in oral traditions and histories. Callie respected her grandmother as "one of the last of the fireside historians of her race," referring to oral tradition, that is, the practice of passing on history through stories about Cherokees that had been memorized. In the preface to her book *John Ross and the Cherokee Indians*, Callie further defines how her grandmother and other "fireside historians" would "repeat their story in season and out of season until it was rooted and grounded in [her] memory from earliest childhood."⁵⁷ Through repetition and memorization, oral histories shaped Callie and her role as a storyteller. Kirby Brown explains how this "situates her study within a long history of Cherokee women as keepers and producers of knowledge and as insightful social critics."⁵⁸ Following her matrilineal line through her grandmother Lucy, Callie descended from strong Cherokee matriarchs, which included Granny Hopper, who came from the influential family of Cherokee leader Old Hop. Her family had close ties to the *Ghighua*, "beloved woman," Nanye'hi (also known as Nancy Ward) through marriage. Cherokees learned about and remembered the revered Cherokee warrior Nanye'hi, who led her people and represented them in early relations with the newly established United States between the late eighteenth and early nineteenth centuries.⁵⁹ Cherokees used the title *Ghighua* to distinguish women who had "the right to speak and vote in the councils of the nation with the men, in times of war and of peace."⁶⁰ As her great-grandmothers had done before her, Callie's grandmother Lucy Ward Williams fulfilled a pivotal role in passing on the histories of the people for posterity. Callie continued this tradition but transferred the oral sources to written forms. Although she transformed the medium of historical narratives, she perpetuated Cherokee knowledge and heritage—foundations for Cherokee peoplehood and nationhood—just as her predecessors had.[61]

Callie married and later divorced James Alexander Burns, who had supposedly attended the Cherokee National Male Seminary and graduated about the same time as Callie.[62] However, in a 1904 interview with the US Department of Interior Commission to the Five Civilized Tribes to confirm her "enrollment as a citizen by blood of the Cherokee Nation," Rachel C. (Eaton) Burns claimed that her husband, "A. J. Burns," was not a Cherokee citizen.[63] Callie had married Burns during the winter of 1901, and she was living with him in Nowata, Oklahoma, at the time of the application.[64] After the Curtis Act of 1898, the federal government required Cherokees and other Native Americans of the "Five Civilized Tribes" to identify themselves and enroll as Callie did, extending the Dawes (or Allotment) Act to dissolve their tribal land claims and sovereign governments in Indian Territory by 1906.[65] Callie's interview reveals that she assumed her husband's last name, Burns, for at least three years, through the precarious and tumultuous times of allotment and termination of tribal federal recognition. Callie also complied with the commission and enrolled as a Cherokee woman.[66]

Callie was an active member in the Federated Club, the Eastern Star, and the Tulsa Indian Women's Club as well as her Presbyterian church. The La-kee-kon Club of Tulsa designated her an honorary member, and she also joined the Quest Club of Claremore.[67] Her participation in clubs not only served social purposes but also supported her research and writing. As president of the Sequoyah Historical Society, for example, she actively researched histories of Cherokee communities on the society's behalf.[68] The clubs and societies also provided audiences for her work. While she was still at the seminary, she participated in church activities and started a branch of the Young Women's Christian Association with Bluie Adair, who later became second assistant principal at the seminary under principal A. Florence Wilson from 1896 to 1897. The YWCA supported devotional services and prayer meetings at the seminary. Callie's religious fervor and activism impressed those around her who envisioned her as a missionary, which Callie did consider becoming.[69] Callie learned such religiosity from the example of her grandmother Lucy Ward Williams, who promoted Presbyterianism to Cherokees.[70] But Callie continued her historical research and writing into retirement and even in her final days, leaving her last book, *The History of the Cherokee Indians*, unpublished when she died.

Kirby Brown's analysis of Callie's work underscores what others have deemed her significant contribution: Callie challenged the hegemony of the United States by illuminating the nationhood and sovereignty of her beloved Cherokee Nation at a time when the tribal nation faced one of the US government's worst affronts in the guise of allotment. She "recovers a history of *multiple sovereignties* in the Americas that state-national narratives explicitly deny."[71] Scholar Deborah Bouziden describes Callie in a way that emphasizes the inner tensions of Cherokee "loyal countrywomen": "While she was always loyal to her country, she knew not to trust the men who ran it."[72] Bouziden refers to the United States as Callie's "country," but Callie's primary country was the Cherokee Nation—a sovereign nation within the United States.

As various scholars consider Callie's life and work, they trace the tensions, the contradictions, and the constant balancing act that Cherokee seminarians such as Callie faced. Brown assesses Callie's limitations and her appropriation of overarching Eurocentric historical frameworks such as "the discourses of civilization, progress, and modernity." Her language in narratives about Cherokees, for example, celebrates them as "the most powerful and the most civilized of all the North American Indians."[73] She also appropriated the dichotomy of barbarism versus civilization that European Americans used to frame the tensions between Native Americans and white settlers. Despite these alignments with Eurocentric history, Callie intervened in histories of US settler colonialism by featuring Cherokee historical perspectives and sources. Callie made her mark, according to Brown, by focusing on the Cherokee Nation's relations with the United States to "reframe that history not as a clash between savagery and civilization but as a political contest between national sovereigns."[74] Her work *John Ross and the Cherokee Indians* presents "a counterhistory of Cherokee nationhood."[75] In the foreword to her study of John Ross, Callie asserts her support of the Cherokees' "struggle to maintain their tribal identity and ancestral domains."[76] Callie intervened and revised history by acknowledging and following Native American historical figures and their causes. Her work focused on Cherokee heroes, such as Chief John Ross, who defended their land, people, and sovereignty, and it undermined the triumphalist narratives of American expansionism and power.

Her essays about local history and the Claremore Mound, for example, examine Native Americans and intertribal dynamics. When the General Federation of Women's Clubs and *Chronicles of Oklahoma* printed her essay "The Legends of the Battle of Claremore Mound Oklahoma" in 1930, scholars and community members both locally and nationally acknowledged Callie's work.[77] During the twentieth biennial convention of the General Federation of Women's Clubs, held in Denver during the summer of 1930, scholars could receive prizes "for the best presentation on the historical background, traditions and culture of local Indians." Callie was one of the award-winning historians, probably for her article about the Battle of Claremore Mound.[78] These publications and prizes show that Callie engaged with the public and wide audiences as a scholar and historian.

Callie also contributed to the shaping of historiography, methodologies, and approaches to the academic study of history as a Cherokee intellectual. Some of her contemporaries praised her use of Cherokee sources and respected her as a Cherokee scholar who "had the privilege of seeing and hearing all of the principal chiefs of the nation since the Civil War."[79] Unlike many previous historians of Cherokee history, Callie was one of the first scholars from the Cherokee Nation who recognized and accessed Cherokee historical sources and methodologies. Callie navigated and applied different forms of knowledge from Native American history. She hybridized approaches, intermingling forms of "fireside" stories in the oral tradition and the practice of reading place, as someone who had grown up in the region, with her academic training, which prioritized written sources and archival documents. Scholar Peter Nabokov concludes, while considering Callie's case, that "Native historians must somehow combine and contextualize raw materials from an alien archival tradition, honor the authority of a specific geography, and interweave their own oral tradition's multiple genres."[80] These hybridized approaches shaped the counterhistories that embodied resistance to the ongoing efforts to delegitimize Cherokee sovereignty and force detribalization and full integration into the United States.

Callie experienced the impacts of US initiatives to detribalize and assimilate Cherokees firsthand, specifically through programs of education and allotment. In terms of allotment and the dissolution of Indian Territory, her family had lost 88 percent of their dividends when their original homestead of more than 1,000 acres was reduced to 120 acres by allotment.[81] Allotment crippled many Native American families, which scholars such as Angie Debo, who wrote *And Still the Waters Run* (1940), expose in their works.[82] In 1904, Callie filed a Cherokee allotment contest against Ioney Ross for a specific lot. The chief clerk of the Cherokee Land Office summarized the series of trials that followed until Callie and Ross came together to file "a stipulation and agreement that the land in controversy be divided between them."[83] The dispute shows how Cherokees, including Callie, struggled within their own communities over claims to allotments due not only to the changing policies but also to the continual affronts to Cherokee sovereignty and treaty rights—their ties to land.

Like other female Oklahoma authors of the early twentieth century, Callie had her work rejected by publishers and other scholars. The University of Oklahoma Press, for example, did not accept the manuscript on Cherokee history that she submitted in 1935. The publisher instead accepted another submission on Cherokee political history by a male scholar, Morris Wardell, claiming it was more "definitive." A reviewer criticized Callie's writing, which he claimed "occasionally revealed a bias," and called her work "too-partisan, pro-Cherokee." John Rhea, who studied these reviews of Callie's work, argues that the "sexual, racial, and cultural biases were clearly recorded in black and white."[84] Rhea emphasizes how Callie's impact on historiography and scholarship prevailed, nonetheless, because of her work's influence on scholars who focused on Cherokee and Native American historical perspectives, namely Angie Debo.[85]

In 1938, before Callie died, she expressed a wish to publish her last major work, *The History of the Cherokees*. According to John Rhea, this manuscript "advocates both women's suffrage and treaty and citizenship rights for the Cherokee freed people."[86] Her nephew, Grady York, promised to get her final manuscript printed, but he and relatives struggled to find a publisher. As of 2021, her family continues to pursue publication of the manuscript, which she barely completed before she lost her battle with breast cancer.[87] The *Tahlequah Citizen* honored Callie as an "authority on Oklahoma Indians." The local news announced, "At the time of her death [Callie] was writing a history of the Cherokees," indicating that people anticipated her work.[88] In 2017, Callie's work inspired her great-great-great-niece Patricia Dawson to start her doctoral studies of Cherokee history. After reading Callie's dissertation, Dawson realized that "there are still so many stories out there left to tell."[89] As Dawson explores the archives of her Cherokee family and heritage, her relatives have encouraged her to "[follow] in Aunt Callie's footsteps."[90] In her writing and research, Callie's legacy as a historian of the Cherokee Nation and exemplar to Native American intellectuals lives on.

In February 1920, several months before Congress ratified the Nineteenth Amendment, Callie was appointed to the Committee of Resolutions at the Democratic County Convention in Claremore, Oklahoma. She joined the Scott Ferris Club, which Democrats of Rogers County formed soon after the convention, and was elected its secretary.[91] Through her involvement in local, state, and national US politics, Callie navigated her own American citizenship and multiple loyalties. As part of the convention's leadership, she helped to draft declarations of support for Democrats and for Progressive changes such as women's suffrage. She and the other four members of the committee wrote resolutions that upheld "equal suffrage of men and women throughout the Nation."[92] They also demanded that the state of Oklahoma "[ratify] the proposal of Congress to amend the National Constitution so as to give women equal right of suffrage with men."[93] Callie and fellow Claremore Democrats promoted Cherokee politician Robert Latham Owen Jr. as a presidential nominee.[94] Owen was a citizen of the Cherokee Nation, and his mother, Narcissa Chisholm Owen, taught at the Cherokee National Female Seminary in the 1880s.[95] Owen came from Indian Territory, and he, like Callie, straddled the intertwined but conflicting sovereignties of the Cherokee Nation and the United States. Callie's endorsement for Owen implies ongoing ties of Cherokee nationalism within American hegemonic politics.

Rachel Caroline Eaton, a pathbreaking Cherokee seminary alumna, forged her way as one of the first Native American women to stand for women's equal footing with men as professionals and experts in Indian Territory and, later, Oklahoma. Cherokees and Oklahomans continue to celebrate her legacy and those of other Cherokee female seminarians.[96] In March 2019, Principal Chief Bill John Baker emphasized the impact of Cherokee women through past generations, referring specifically to alumnae of the Cherokee National Female Seminary, such as "loyal countrywoman" Belle Cobb:

> From Isabel Cobb, the first female physician in Indian Territory, to Mary Golda Ross, a NASA aerospace engineer who helped America win the space race, Cherokee women have been at the forefront of defining our success. In 1851, we opened the first institute of higher education for women west of the Mississippi River. The Cherokee National Female Seminary's curriculum was academically challenging, reflecting our tribe's vision of strong, educated women. Cherokee Nation is a matrilineal tribe, and reverence for women is deeply rooted in our culture.[97]

Cherokee seminary alumnae like Callie, in their everyday actions and decisions to push boundaries and contribute as professionals and as family, strengthened the Cherokee Nation. Many of them might not have pushed for radical changes, such as the immediate equal right to vote or Cherokee rights in direct testimonies to Congress, but they resisted US attacks on Cherokee sovereignty in simple but powerful ways, such as growing and sustaining ties to the Cherokee Nation and recognizing Cherokee citizenship after allotment and Oklahoma statehood.

In a stanza from a poem that Callie wrote, which became the club collect for the Tulsa Indian Women's Club, she emphasizes the role of contemporary Cherokee women as bridges between the Cherokee past and future: "We pride of race would cherish veneration / For ancient Knowledge, wisdom, legends, lore; / Would throw the torch each future generation / To grasp and pass, As in the days of yore."[98] Callie and her fellow female seminary alumnae continued the traditions of Cherokee women as carriers of knowledge and advocates for the people—the Cherokee Nation—as loyal countrywomen. In 1934, seminary alumnae prepared for their annual gathering at the remaining campus of the seminary, which had become Northeastern State Teacher's College. They elected "Doctor Rachel Caroline Eaton of Tulsa, historian" to be one of the officers of their alumnae organization, which had plans for a homecoming celebration to "commemorate the eighty-fifth anniversary of the dedication" of the Cherokee National Female Seminary.[99] While Callie explored new paths, she also came full circle by returning home, where the first steps of her journey had begun with learning and sharing stories of her land and people.

NOTES

1. "Organize Historical Society," *Shawnee (OK) Daily Herald*, August 6, 1910, 5.
2. "Sequoyah Historical Society," *Claremore (OK) Messenger*, April 3, 1908, 1.
3. "Sequoyah Historical Society," *Muskogee County (OK) Republican* and *Fort Gibson (OK) Post*, July 21, 1910, 8.
4. "Organize Historical Society."
5. Devon Mihesuah, *Cultivating the Rosebuds: The Education of Women at the Cherokee Female Seminary, 1851–1909* (Urbana: University of Illinois Press, 1993), 95.
6. "Cobb, Isabel (1858–1947)," *The Encyclopedia of Oklahoma History and Culture*, Oklahoma Historical Society, accessed August 21, 2020, https://www.okhistory.org/publications/enc/entry.php?entry=CO009.
7. Isabel Cobb to Hon. C. J. Harris of Tahlequah, October 29, 1892, Oklahoma Historical Society, Oklahoma City, copy in Beverly Cobb Collection, box 2, folder 3, Isabel Cobb Correspondence, Northeastern State University Archives (hereafter cited as NSU Archives).
8. Mihesuah, *Cultivating the Rosebuds*, 102–3.
9. Brad Agnew, "'The School Is in a Prosperous Condition,' 1887–1901," in *Northeastern: Centennial History* (Tahlequah, OK: John Vaughan Library, 2009), 7.
10. Muriel H. Wright, "Rachel Caroline Eaton, 1869–1938," *Chronicles of Oklahoma* 16 (December 1938): 509–10; Christina Berry, "Rachel Caroline Eaton—Cherokee Woman, Historian, and Educator," All Things Cherokee, January 2, 2001, accessed

August 21, 2020, https://www.allthingscherokee.com/rachel-caroline-eaton/. See also Maggie Culver Fry, *Cherokee Female Seminary Years* (Claremore, OK: Rogers State College Press, 1988), 73, in Northeastern State University Special Collections, Tahlequah, Oklahoma (hereafter cited as NSU Special Collections); her citation reads, "an excerpt from the *Rogers County Historical Book*, told by the Eaton family." Although Callie became a county superintendent by 1920, other women had been elected as county superintendents before then in Oklahoma. Zilpha Arrilla McClain, for example, was elected superintendent of schools in Cimarron County on November 4, 1914. See Joseph Bradfield Thoburn, *A Standard History of Oklahoma, Vol. 4* (Cambridge, MA: Harvard University, American Historical Society, 1916), 1712.

11. Carol Payne Merriman, "Cobb Family History" (unpublished manuscript, 1995), 12, typescript, Beverley Cobb Collection, NSU Archives.

12. Merriman, "Cobb Family History," 23.

13. Janice J. Sisemore, "Our People: Isabel Cobb, M.D., 1893," *Cherokee Quarterly* (Summer 1998), Beverley Cobb Collection, NSU Archives.

14. Mihesuah, *Cultivating the Rosebuds*, 107.

15. Devon Abbott Mihesuah, "Culturalism and Racism at the Cherokee Female Seminary," in *Indigenous American Women: Decolonization, Empowerment, Activism* (Lincoln: University of Nebraska Press, 2003), 63. See also Deborah Bouziden, *More than Petticoats: Remarkable Oklahoma Women* (Guilford, CT: Morris, 2013), 37.

16. Kirby Brown, *Stoking the Fire: Nationhood in Cherokee Writing, 1907–1970* (Norman: University of Oklahoma Press, 2018), 112.

17. Mihesuah, *Cultivating the Rosebuds*, 95, 117.

18. For more about Nancy Katherine Daniel Fite, see Donald Ricky, *Native Peoples A to Z: A Reference Guide to Native Peoples of the Western Hemisphere Vol. 8* (Hamburg, MI: Native American, 2009), 865–66. See also Eula E. Fullerton, "Mrs. R. L. Fite, 1862–1946," *Chronicles of Oklahoma* 27 (Spring 1949): 122–24; D. C. Gideon, *Indian Territory* (New York: Lewis, 1901), 724–25, cited in Daniel F. Littlefield, Daniel F. Littlefield Jr., and James W. Parins, *A Bibliography of Native American Writers, 1772–1924: A Supplement* (Metuchen, NJ: Scarecrow, 1985).

19. Maggie Culver Fry, "An Introduction to Rachel Caroline Eaton," 73, cited in Brown, *Stoking the Fire*, 71.

20. Isabel Cobb, "Cherokee Schools," (manuscript written and loaned by author, n.d. [1933]), Indian-Pioneer Oral History Project Papers, 65: 7–8, 184–218, NSU Archives, also accessible through Western History Collections, University of Oklahoma Libraries, accessed August 21, 2020, https://digital.libraries.ou.edu/cdm/singleitem/collection/indianpp/id/7958/rec/1. See also Thomas Lee Ballenger, *A Brief History of the Male and Female Seminaries* (Tahlequah, OK: Northeastern State University, n.d.), 7, NSU Special Collections.

21. Devon Abbott, "Ann Florence Wilson: Matriarch of the Cherokee Female Seminary," *Chronicles of Oklahoma* 67 (Winter 1989–90): 427–32.

22. Agnew, "'The School Is in a Prosperous Condition,'" 6.

23. Bouziden, *More than Petticoats*, 40.

24. Nancy Katherine Daniel Fite, "Historical Statement," in *An Illustrated Souvenir Catalog of the Cherokee National Female Seminary, Tahlequah, Indian Territory, 1850 to 1906* (Chilocco, OK: Indian Print Shop), reprinted in *Journal of Cherokee Studies* 10, no. 1 (Spring 1985): 124, NSU Archives.

25. "Summary," *Cherokee Advocate* (Tahlequah, Indian Territory), October 26, 1887, 2.

26. Sean Rowley, "Cherokee County Has Long History of Educating Women," *Tahlequah (OK) Daily Press*, March 18, 2017.

27. Fite, "Historical Statement," 124–25.

28. Fite, "Historical Statement," 125.

29. Kate O'Donald to Isabel Cobb, May 22, 1892, Beverly Cobb Collection, box 2, folder 3, PC Cobb (Isabel Cobb) Correspondence, NSU Archives.

30. Mattie and Clement [Clarke] to Isabel Cobb, January 31, 1898, NSU Archives.

31. Mattie and Clement [Clarke] to Isabel Cobb, January 31, 1898.

32. Fry, "An Introduction to Rachel Caroline Eaton," 73.

33. Rosalie Mills, "Head of Rogers County Schools," *Claremore (OK) Progress*, September 14, 1922; see also Christa Rice, "Dr. Caroline 'Callie' Eaton—Cherokee Author and Educator," Explore Claremore History, March 8, 2019, accessed August 21, 2020, https://exploreclaremorehistory.wordpress.com/2019/03/08/dr-caroline-callie-eaton-cherokee-author-and-educator/.

34. Fry, "An Introduction to Rachel Caroline Eaton," 75.

35. See "Caroline R Eaton," 1910 United States Federal Census, Claremore Ward 2, Rogers, Oklahoma, roll T624 1273, p. 33B, enumeration district 0168, FHL microfilm 1375286, Ancestry; "Rachel Carolyn Eaton," 1930 United States Federal Census, Claremore, Rogers, Oklahoma, p. 2B, enumeration district 0007, FHL microfilm 2341658, Ancestry.

36. "In Hall of Fame," *Daily Oklahoman*, July 7, 1936, 2.

37. Wright, "Rachel Caroline Eaton," 510. For more background on Muriel H. Wright, see Patricia Loughlin, *Hidden Treasures of the American West: Muriel H. Wright, Angie Debo, and Alice Marriott* (Albuquerque: University of New Mexico Press, 2006).

38. John M. Rhea, *A Field of Their Own: Women and American Indian History, 1830–1941* (Norman: University of Oklahoma Press, 2016), 152. See also Kay Little presentation, cited in Roseanne McKee, "Women Who Made Their Mark on Oklahoma," *Pawhuska (OK) Journal-Capital*, August 4, 2019, accessed August 21, 2020, https://www.pawhuskajournalcapital.com/lifestyle/20190807/women-who-made-their-mark-on-oklahoma.

39. Rachel Caroline Eaton, "The Legend of the Battle of Claremore Mound," *Chronicles of Oklahoma* 8, no. 4 (December 1930): 369–77. See also Mills, "Head of Rogers County Schools"; Bouziden, *More than Petticoats*, 35.

40. Leanne Betasamosake Simpson, "Land as Pedagogy: Nishnaabeg Intelligence and Rebellious Transformation," *Decolonization* 3, no. 3 (2014): 7.

41. Simpson, "Land as Pedagogy," 7.

42. Simpson, "Land as Pedagogy," 9.

43. Eaton, "The Legend of the Battle of Claremore Mound," 369.

44. Wright, "Rachel Caroline Eaton," 510.
45. Eaton, cited in Mills, "Head of Rogers County Schools."
46. Eaton, cited in Mills, "Head of Rogers County Schools."
47. Bouziden, *More than Petticoats*, 40; Rhea, *A Field of Their Own*, 153.
48. Eaton, *John Ross and the Cherokee Indians* (Menasha, WI: George Banta, 1914), preface. See also Bouziden, *More than Petticoats*, 40.
49. Brown, *Stoking the Fire*, 71.
50. "Ms. Eaton Elected to Chair of History," *Waxahachie (TX) Daily Light*, July 7, 1916, 8.
51. Trinity University was relocated to San Antonio, Texas, by the late twentieth century.
52. Bouziden, *More than Petticoats*, 35; "Ms. Eaton Elected to Chair of History," 8.
53. "Oklahomans Get Degrees," *Morning Tulsa Daily World*, June 16, 1911, 2.
54. "Miss Caroline Eaton Left Saturday for Columbus, Miss.," *Rogers County (OK) Leader* and *Rogers County (OK) News*, September 27, 1912, 5.
55. "Mrs. Caroline Eaton of Chicago, Is Visiting Friends in the City and Her Sister, Mrs. J. M. York, of Sageeyah," *Claremore Progress* and *Rogers County Democrat*, January 9, 1914, 6.
56. For her first book publication Callie also relies on Cherokee sources, including oral histories that she learned by visiting and working with Cherokee community; see Eaton, *John Ross and the Cherokee Indians*, preface. She acknowledges former principal chief of the Cherokees Colonel J. C. Harris "for access to the Cherokee National Records at Tahlequah," for instance.
57. Eaton, *John Ross and the Cherokee Indians*, preface. See Brown, *Stoking the Fire*, 98.
58. Brown, *Stoking the Fire*, 98.
59. Martha Berry, e-mail correspondence with Farina King, September 21, 2020. As the daughter of Grady York, Callie Eaton's nephew, Martha Berry is Eaton's great-niece. See Elisha Sterling King, *The Wild Rose of Cherokee; or, Nancy Ward, 'The Pocahontas of the West.' A Story of the Early Exploration, Occupancy and Settlement of the State of Tennessee. A Romance, Founded on and Interwoven with History* (Nashville: University Press, 1895), 119, cited in *Terra Incognita: An Annotated Bibliography of the Great Smoky Mountains, 1544–1934*, ed. Anne Bridges, Russell Clement, and Ken Wise (Knoxville: University of Tennessee Press, 2014), 17. Elisha Sterling King claims to repeat the stories that an elderly Cherokee woman, one of Nanye'hi's granddaughters, told him. For more about Nanye'hi, see Michelene E. Pesantubbee, "Nancy Ward: American Patriot or Cherokee Nationalist?," *American Indian Quarterly* 38, no. 2 (2014): 177; Virginia Moore Carney, *Eastern Band Cherokee Women: Cultural Persistence in Their Letters and Speeches* (Knoxville: University of Tennessee Press, 2005).
60. Wright, "Rachel Caroline Eaton," 510.
61. Eaton, *John Ross and the Cherokee Indians*, preface; see also Brown, *Stoking the Fire*, 98. For more about the practices of oral tradition and storytelling as significant ways of preserving and disseminating Cherokee history, see Joyce Conseen Dugan, foreword, *Living Stories of the Cherokee*, ed. Barbara R. Duncan (Chapel Hill: University of North

Carolina Press, 1998), xi. For more about Cherokee peoplehood and sovereignty, see Ellen Cushman, "'We're Taking the Genius of Sequoyah into This Century': The Cherokee Syllabary, Peoplehood, and Perseverance," *Wičazo Ša Review* 26, no. 1 (2011): 67–83; Julie L. Reed, *Serving the Nation: Cherokee Sovereignty and Social Welfare, 1800–1907* (Norman: University of Oklahoma Press, 2016); Fay A. Yarbrough, *Race and the Cherokee Nation: Sovereignty in the Nineteenth Century* (Philadelphia: University of Pennsylvania Press, 2013); Andrew Denson, *Demanding the Cherokee Nation: Indian Autonomy and American Culture, 1830–1900* (Lincoln: University of Nebraska Press, 2004); William G. McLoughlin, *After the Trail of Tears: The Cherokees' Struggle for Sovereignty, 1839–1880* (Chapel Hill: University of North Carolina Press, 1993).

62. Rhea, *A Field of Their Own*, 153.

63. Rachel C. Burns, interview with Department of the Interior, Commission to the Five Civilized Tribes, Tahlequah, Indian Territory, May 9, 1904, Ancestry. Eaton is also listed in the Cherokee rolls of the Final Rolls of Citizens and Freedmen of the Five Civilized Tribes in Indian Territory, dated 1902, as having 1/64 blood quantum. See "Rachel C. Eaton, in the U.S., Native American Citizens and Freedmen of Five Civilized Tribes, 1895–1914," Ancestry.

64. Burns interview.

65. For more background about these acts and allotment in Indian Territory, see Tabatha Toney, "'Until We Fall to the Ground United': Cherokee Resilience and Interfactional Cooperation in the Early Twentieth Century" (PhD diss., Oklahoma State University, 2018); Kent Carter, *The Dawes Commission and the Allotment of the Five Civilized Tribes, 1893–1914* (Orem, UT: Ancestry, 1999); Angie Debo, *And Still the Waters Run: The Betrayal of the Five Civilized Tribes* (Princeton, NJ: Princeton University Press, 1940).

66. For more about the significance of these detailed commission interviews and lists of Cherokees and Native Americans, see Melinda Miller, "Dawes Cards and Indian Census Data," *Historical Methods: A Journal of Quantitative and Interdisciplinary History* 48, no. 4 (October 2015): 214–29.

67. Wright, "Rachel Caroline Eaton," 511.

68. "Over the State," *Evening News* (Ada, OK), July 30, 1910, 3.

69. Bouziden, *More than Petticoats*, 38; see also Wright, "Rachel Caroline Eaton," 510.

70. Wright, "Rachel Caroline Eaton," 510.

71. Brown, *Stoking the Fire*, 112.

72. Bouziden, *More than Petticoats*, 37.

73. Eaton, *John Ross and the Cherokee Indians*, 6.

74. Brown, *Stoking the Fire*, 69.

75. Brown, *Stoking the Fire*, 68.

76. Eaton, cited in Bouziden, *More than Petticoats*, 40.

77. Eaton, "The Legend of the Battle of Claremore Mound." See also Kay Little, cited in McKee, "Women Who Made Their Mark on Oklahoma."

78. "Prize Winners," in "Indians Must Be Allowed to Use Their Art Commercially, Women's Federation Is Told," *Albuquerque Journal*, June 7, 1930, 1.

79. Mrs. Sam to James Thoburn, n.d., cited in Bouziden, *More than Petticoats*, 41.

80. Nabokov, *A Forest of Time*, 215.
81. Bouziden, *More than Petticoats*, 37.
82. Loughlin, *Hidden Treasures of the American West*, 93–94.
83. Chief Clerk, Cherokee Land Office, Muskogee, Indian Territory, Department of the Interior, Commissioner to the Five Civilized Tribes, December 6, 1906.
84. Kirby Brown, cited in Rhea, *A Field of Their Own*, 91. See also Rhea, 160–61.
85. Rhea, *A Field of Their Own*, 161.
86. Rhea, *A Field of Their Own*, 158.
87. Kay Little, cited in McKee, "Women Who Made Their Mark on Oklahoma." See also Brown, *Stoking the Fire*, 73. Shelli Freeman was a graduate student in the history MA program at the University of Central Oklahoma in 2004 when she started to connect with Rachel Caroline Eaton's relatives to work on her thesis about Eaton, but she did not complete the thesis. One of Callie Eaton's relatives, Patricia Dawson, is pursuing a PhD in history at the University of North Carolina at Chapel Hill, and Dawson has openly expressed how Eaton inspires her work and studies of Cherokee history. The descendants of Eaton's nephew Grady York and Dawson are preparing the manuscript for publication.
88. *Tahlequah (OK) Citizen*, September 29, 1938, 1.
89. Patricia Dawson, cited in Will Rimer, "Meet a New Tar Heel: Patricia Dawson," Dynamic Minds, August 16, 2017, accessed December 1, 2019, https://www.unc.edu/discover/meet-a-new-tar-heel-patricia-dawson/.
90. Patricia Dawson, "Tales from the Archive: An Unexpected Archive," *Traces: The UNC Journal of History* 7 (2019): 126.
91. "Scott Ferris Club Formed," *Claremore Progress*, February 5, 1920, 1.
92. "Democratic Convention Held Here Saturday," *Claremore Progress*, February 5, 1920, 1.
93. "Democratic Convention Held Here Saturday."
94. "Democratic Convention Held Here Saturday."
95. See Narcissa Owen, *Memoirs of Narcissa Owen, 1831–1907* (Charlottesville: University of Virginia Press, 1907); Karen L. Kilcup, ed., *A Cherokee Woman's America: Memoirs of Narcissa Owen, 1831–1907* (Gainesville: University Press of Florida, 2005); Stephen J. Brandon, "'Mother of U.S. Senator an Indian Queen': Cultural Challenge and Appropriation in *The Memoirs of Narcissa Owen, 1831–1907*," *Studies in American Indian Literatures* 13, nos. 2–3 (Summer/Fall 2001): 5–22; Mark A. Bolin, "Four Pillars of Identification: Redefining Cherokee People by Traditional Standards" (MA thesis, Northeastern State University, 2019), 64.
96. See Kay Little, cited in McKee, "Women Who Made Their Mark on Oklahoma."
97. Principal Chief Bill John Baker, "Cherokee Nation Celebrates the Women Who Make Us Strong," speech, March 4, 2019, Cherokee Nation, Tahlequah, Oklahoma, accessed December 1, 2019, https://www.indianz.com/News/2019/03/04/bill-john-baker-cherokee-nation-celebrat-1.asp.
98. Rachel Caroline Eaton, untitled poem "published as the club collect in the Tulsa Indian Women's Club, yearbook, 1976–77," cited in Christina Berry, "Rachel Caroline

Eaton—Cherokee Woman, Historian, and Educator," All Things Cherokee, January 2, 2001, accessed November 8, 2020, https://www.allthingscherokee.com/rachel-caroline-eaton/.

99. Mildred Pfaff, "Seminary Students Plan Homecoming: Celebrating Will Commemorate Eighty-Fifth Anniversary of Dedication," *Cherokee County (OK) Democrat-Star*, April 13, 1934, 3.

PART TWO

THE GENDERED POLITICS OF CIVIL RIGHTS

Part Two examines the place of gendered politics in civil rights activism in Oklahoma from the 1920s through the 1960s. Just as the fluidity of power in the years immediately surrounding statehood afforded new opportunities for women, so, too, did new opportunities emerge for African Americans. In fact, nearly fifty all-Black towns were established in Oklahoma between 1865 and 1920. Many of them had disappeared by the 1920s, but others, like Langston and Boley, thrived economically and culturally. So strong and vibrant were the all-Black towns on the eve of statehood that African American leaders proposed the admission of Oklahoma to the union as an all-Black state. This dream proved short-lived, but the simultaneous power and suppression of African Americans persisted in the decades that followed. It is within this framework that Black women activists experienced—and ultimately challenged—segregation in Oklahoma.

This portion of the book contextualizes the place of racial politics in shaping Oklahoma women's activism. Despite the possibilities and momentary opportunities that the Progressive era generated, obstacles to racial and gender equality only increased in the following years. Melissa Stuckey's analysis of California M. Taylor reveals much about the transition of Oklahoma in the period before and after the worst race massacre in American history. After Taylor's arrival in Boley in 1904, she, along with other Black women, began fashioning their identities and defining what it meant to be a Black middle-class woman in a prosperous all-Black town. Yet, in the years following her arrival in Boley, Taylor witnessed the entrenchment of segregation and disenfranchisement. By the 1940s, she had become the town's most active member in the NAACP. She knew well the complexities of being a Black woman and challenging segregation in a state that was especially hostile to change.

During the Tulsa Race Massacre of 1921, Ada Lois Sipuel Fisher's light-skinned mother stood across the street, watching her home burn to the ground, until a white militia officer, who mistook her for a white woman, warned her to go "back to the white part of town before the niggers get ahold of you."[1] Ada Lois's parents relocated to Chickasha, where they raised their family, never forgetting the horrors of that night. In examining the significance of Ada Lois Sipuel Fisher to the civil rights movement in the United States, Cheryl Elizabeth Brown Wattley describes the smart, spunky, outspoken Ada Lois and her role as a plaintiff in the NAACP lawsuit in the mid-1940s to integrate the University of Oklahoma College of Law. While Sipuel Fisher succeeded in her effort, the journey to get there came at a cost. She endured death threats, hate mail, and an uncommon level of public scrutiny. Reviled by anti-integrationist whites and idolized by hopeful African Americans, Sipuel Fisher bore an immense burden in her quest to see the equal protection clause of the Fourteenth Amendment finally realized in higher education in her home state.

Often described as the mother of the Oklahoma civil rights movement, Clara Luper led the first lunch counter sit-in in the entire country in 1958 at Katz Drug Store in Oklahoma City. Rachel E. Watson examines Luper's gendered activism as a mother, teacher, and NAACP Youth Council sponsor, but she also offers a deeper examination of how Black feminism and decolonization tools shaped her pedagogical approaches within and outside Luper's history classroom. Luper played a decisive role in the desegregation of Oklahoma City as well as the cities of Lawton and Tulsa.

Luper's passion for civil rights and unwillingness to accept no for an answer proved contagious, and she found many a willing volunteer, including a badly disfigured white woman named Rosie Gilchrist. In her chapter, Sarah Eppler

Janda describes the evolution of Gilchrist's activism and the price she paid for it when she was committed to a mental institution for five years because she tried to sell her house to a Black man. When she was released in 1968, it was largely due to the fact that a Black man, civil rights attorney E. Melvin Porter, had risen to a prominent enough position in Oklahoma politics to demand her release. Each chapter reveals the interplay between race and gender in the Oklahoma civil rights movement. By the time Gilchrist was released, segregation in Oklahoma was no longer legal, but the place of women and notions of equality continued to generate much debate.

NOTE

1. Ada Lois Sipuel Fisher, *A Matter of Black and White: The Autobiography of Ada Lois Sipuel Fisher* (Norman: University of Oklahoma Press, 1996), 12.

MELISSA N. STUCKEY

6

FREEDOM ON HER OWN TERMS

California M. Taylor and Black Womanhood
in Boley, Oklahoma

In June 1904, California Minnie Brock, née Taylor, a thirty-six-year-old African American woman from Houston, Texas, alighted from a railcar on the Fort Smith and Western Railroad and into Boley, an all-Black town established barely a year earlier.[1] Located in what was then Creek Nation, Indian Territory, Boley had been established as a cooperative venture between African Americans seeking freedom from the privations of the Jim Crow South, landowning African Creeks, and entrepreneurial white investors. In his efforts to populate Boley with other talented freedom seekers, Boley's chief founder, Thomas M. Haynes, invited "all good men and women, of our race wherever they may be and under whatever conditions they may be constrained" to settle in Boley.[2] Along with her father, Hilliard Taylor; her husband, Charles Brock; and at least two of her four brothers, California answered this call with dramatic flair. The group carried with them a cotton gin owned by her father and husband and had plans to settle in Clearview, another Black town located along the railroad line.

When railroad officials learned about their highly desirable cargo, however, they bypassed the Clearview stop and sent the train directly to Boley, the Black town that the railroad line was unofficially backing. Upon the family's arrival at Boley, Haynes, a fellow Texas expat, offered Hilliard and Charles two free lots abutting the railroad depot to set up their business and, in this way, convinced the clan to settle in the burgeoning Black town.[3]

Amid the hubbub surrounding her father and husband and their cotton gin, California's arrival in Boley appears to have gone unrecorded. The men and their cotton gin represented the masculinist elements of the Black nationalist chords sounded by Boley's founding cohort, a group usually identified as all male. In the first issue of one of the town's first newspapers, the *Boley Progress*, which had the motto "All Men Up, Not Some Down," editor Oniel H. Bradley issued an appeal to Black men to leave the South, where they could "exercise no rights of manhood," and move to Boley, where they could be "business men, professional men, farmers, merchants and wage workers" and exercise their "rights and privileges" as American citizens "in the broadest term."[4] To be sure, Black women were included in the Black nationalist vision of Boley endorsed by Bradley and others. As articulated by many Boley men and women, the town's women would be role players, helpmates particularly charged with the responsibility of raising children who would be equipped to participate in the work required to raise up the race. In a 1906 *Boley Progress* issue that dedicated several columns of front-page space to Boley's women, "true mothers" were praised as "the hope of the race," capable through their childrearing practices of being a "race builder" or a "race destroyer."[5] In their roles as town promoters, elected officials, newspaper editors, and business owners, men played an outsize role in shaping Boley's public discourse and image. Paralleling the image of Boley that was shaped by early town leaders, Boley's men have received the bulk of the scholarly attention by historians seeking to unpack the meanings of Black towns to the early twentieth-century Black freedom struggle.[6] Significantly less attention has been devoted to the role of Boley's women as leaders in shaping the town's early trajectory and its long-term prospects.

Intertwined as it is with the history of Boley, the life story of California M. Taylor (also known as California M. Brock and eventually California Taylor-Turner) provides an opportunity to better understand the contributions of Black women to the town's early success and, especially, to its perpetuity. Telling such a story requires a tremendous amount of sifting through a wide variety of primary sources.[7] The contours of California's life as well as her thoughts and sense of purpose can be gleaned from sifting through, with the finest of sieves, newspaper clippings, censuses, vital records, city directories, university catalogs, correspondence, photo albums, interviews, and myriad ephemera. Such sifting is required to usher forth a female-focused narrative of Boley, one that hopefully serves to add more balance and nuance, and different insight into Boley's early twentieth-century rise and subsequent decline.

California M. Taylor's life in Boley spanned nearly forty-four years. Like many of Boley's first female settlers, she was an entrepreneur, a businesswoman, and a clubwoman. Early Boley women could be found running the post office, operating small businesses, teaching schoolchildren, tilling the land, building homes, and raising families.[8] Their labors contributed tremendously to Boley's early growth and development. California's life in Boley was deeply intertwined with the lives of other Boley women and was, in some ways, very similar to theirs. She came to Boley as part of an extended family unit, worked in town, engaged in town life with a sense of great purpose, and was devoted to her church community. In other ways, however, California stood out. In Boley, she reinvented herself by shedding old identities that no longer suited her and by taking on new challenges. She blazed trails into careers, such as notary public work and pharmacy, that were just opening up on a national level to white women but were still generally closed to Black women. She used her education to chronicle Boley's story, and in her later years she became an outspoken leader in Boley's branch of the National Association for the Advancement of Colored People (NAACP). She stood out in her personal life as well. She did not have children, divorced her first husband, reinvented herself as an unmarried woman, took on a married lover, and eventually, after an undoubtedly rocky courtship, married again. Significantly, California remained in and contributed to Boley's survival long after her father, her two husbands, and other leading men of Boley died or otherwise departed from the town.

California Minnie Taylor, the eldest of six children, was born to Houstonian freedpeople Hilliard Taylor and Emily Ferguson in 1868.[9] The Taylors were part of an emergent middle-class community of freedmen and -women in Houston's Fourth Ward. California's mother died in 1900, and little is known about her life, but her father was ambitious, politically active, and community oriented. Together, the couple, who married in 1867, raised six children. They perhaps revealed their hopes for their firstborn's future in freedom by naming her after the mythical Black warrior queen Calafia, whose island home of California became the namesake for the western territory that had entered the union as a free state in 1850.[10] They could not know then that she would spend the second half of her life defining freedom on her own terms in a different place—Indian Territory, which later became the state of Oklahoma.

In the meantime, Hilliard and Emily did their best to make the world a place of possibility and opportunity for California and her siblings. After receiving her primary education in Houston's segregated public school system, California completed two years of coursework at Fisk University in Nashville, Tennessee. In 1885, she returned to Houston and taught school for six years before moving on to work for herself as a dressmaker. In 1896, she married Charles Brock, a blacksmith and mechanic for the Houston and Central Texas Railway. As members of the same church and with fathers who were both active in Reconstruction-era Republican politics and foundational community work, such as the establishment of Houston's famed Emancipation Park, the two would have known each other since childhood. The newlyweds set up their household near California's parents and siblings but raised no children; California experienced only one pregnancy, which ended in either miscarriage, stillbirth, or early-childhood death.[11]

What must California, who had thus far lived the entirety of her life within the carefully guarded confines of southern, urban, middle-class African American society, have thought of Boley in those early years? The town was raw, with tree stumps and a community well breaking up the expanse of Pecan Street, its main road, which would not be paved for several decades. Only a few houses and commercial buildings had been erected. Many newcomers lived in and worked out of canvas tents until they had the time and materials necessary to build more permanent structures. Over time, these rough-hewn and rapidly built wooden homes and businesses were replaced by more commodious buildings constructed of higher-quality material, much of it imported and milled by Hilliard Taylor and Charles Brock, who had purchased a sawmill to accompany their cotton gin business.[12]

Thomas Haynes's aggressive recruitment campaign resulted in a steady stream of new settlers. One 1905 arrival, Hallie Smith Jones, described subsequent arrivals she witnessed thus: "In the years of 1905 and 1906 people came to Boley by train loads. In some instances eight and ten families would alight from the same train. Their luggage would fill the depot platform and would be piled six and seven feet high. . . . Many persons of the town would meet the trains to welcome the new comers."[13] California herself took part in these types of welcoming parties. One instance, described in the *Boley Progress*, featured a walking tour designed to introduce Boley to Mrs. M. L. Chandler and her daughter Eva. Mrs. Chandler had brought young Eva to Boley to join her husband, William L. Chandler, the newly hired manager of the Fort Smith and Western Railroad station in Boley. The tour featured visits to established businesses and residences, the lot upon which the Chandlers' home would be built, and also the lot that would soon be home to Prewitt Chapel, the permanent edifice of Boley's Methodist Episcopal church. In the meantime, California could assure Mrs. Chandler that there was weekly church service in Boley and that she was one of Prewitt's four Sunday school teachers.[14]

The community California proudly introduced Mrs. Chandler to was vitally important to her as well. California was very active in the Methodist Episcopal church. Although by the late nineteenth century most African American Methodists were members of African American–controlled denominations, the Brocks, Taylors, Chandlers, and others who worshipped at Prewitt's Chapel in Boley represented the small percentage African American Methodist congregations that remained affiliated with the segregated Methodist Episcopal Church. In addition to serving as one of Prewitt's Sunday school teachers, California was an active member of its Women's Home Missionary Society. Established in Cincinnati, Ohio, in 1880 by white Methodist Episcopal women for "the amelioration of the conditions of the freed-women of the South," the Women's Home Missionary Society quickly grew in scope and membership.[15] California and her church sisters were part of a cadre of African American women who forged their own identities within the organization. At Prewitt, they took responsibility for church services on the first Sunday of each month, which included arranging the musical and literary selections. They also held charitable events and capital fundraisers, such as concerts, suppers, and socials. One elaborate fundraiser, a five-day bazaar that took place in November 1909, featured ornate displays and booths selling everything from clothing and jewelry to novelty items as well as hearty meals, cake, and sangria. With the assistance of several others, California ran a postcard booth at the event.[16]

In addition to church-sponsored activities, California and other Boley women participated in many different kinds of community-building and -sustaining organizations. Some, like the Boley Women's Club, were single-sex organizations and part of the burgeoning national Black women's club movement. Others, like the Boley Literary Society, were open to men and women alike. Regardless of the membership, these organizations were future-focused and grounded in the Progressive and nationalistic principals that undergirded Boley's existence. In one early meeting of the literary society, members debated whether or not "the [N]egro should celebrate George Washington's birthday." The team that was assigned to the negative side of the debate won. On another occasion, Mrs. H. R. Rogers of the Boley Women's Club delivered a paper on the theme of work. In it, she offered the following impassioned plea: "Let us teach our girls to work in our homes and beautify them. God bless the girls and hasten the time when in Boley we may have a Phillis Whitten [Wheatley]. We should teach them to be modest in life. Let our young ladies be the life of Boley."[17]

California also made a niche for herself as a career woman in Boley. Abandoning her earlier vocations of teaching and dressmaking, she became part of the vanguard of Black women entering professional work, much of which required specialized training. The trails Black women blazed in fields like education, social work, and nursing have been well documented, but California pursued different and more entrepreneurial paths in professions in which Black women were exceedingly rare. She first took on civil service work as a notary public and soon after added news correspondent to her repertoire. Later she became a pharmacist and drugstore manager. In each of these roles, California provided vital services to her community and demonstrated the public modes of leadership with which Black women engaged in Boley life.[18]

Almost as soon as she settled in Boley, California became a federally commissioned notary public and therefore a government representative in Indian Territory. As a notary, California played a vital role in her community. Between 1898 and 1907, the federal government orchestrated a massive tribal enrollment and land distribution program in Indian Territory. The goal was to privatize land ownership in order to end tribal sovereignty and transform this adopted tribal homeland into a US state. Boley, which had been established in Creek Nation, Indian Territory, was founded on land owned by Creek Indians and African Creeks who had successfully completed this process. As a notary, California facilitated the applications of local Creeks: in addition to other essential duties, she drew up and witnessed affidavits used to bolster their citizenship claims and typed letters for them.[19]

In taking on the role of notary public, California both aided others in their citizenship claims and quietly but demonstratively staked her own. Notaries were sworn public officers, and for this reason, well into the twentieth century, state legislatures across the United States grappled with the question of whether or not women—who collectively did not have the right to vote until the passage of the Nineteenth Amendment in 1920—could legally serve as notaries public.

MRS. C. M. BROCK,

❈ Notary Public ❈

All legal papers drawn and executed.

OFFICE IN MR. TURNER'S DRUG STORE.

Boley,   Indian, Ter.

Mrs. C. M. Brock's notary public advertisement. Between 1905 and 1906, California M. Taylor Brock regularly advertised her notary public business in the *Boley Progress*. She also operated the telephone in David J. Turner's drugstore. *Boley Progress*, May 10, 1906, available through the Sterling Memorial Library, Yale University, and the Oklahoma Historical Society.

California received her notary appointment through the federal government, but, as she was a woman, her right to maintain the position after Oklahoma statehood in 1907 had to be affirmed in the new state's constitution. Her citizenship claims, as made through her notary work, were all the more significant for taking place in a space where African American men were making powerful and vocal citizenship claims by voting, running for and holding elected offices, and advocating for Black male political power in the future state.[20]

To conduct her notary work, California rented office space in Turner's Drug Store, Boley's first drugstore, and she advertised her business extensively in the *Boley Progress*. Established in December 1904 by David J. Turner, the drugstore was a community hub, especially in Boley's early years. Day-to-day operations were managed by David and his wife, Minnie. A consummate entrepreneur, David Turner also rented office space to a local physician, became a licensed pharmacist, maintained a safe in which Boley citizens stored important papers and money, operated a soda fountain, and installed the town's first telephone within his establishment. California quickly became a vital worker in the drugstore. In addition to her notary work, she operated the telephone for customers and also used it to phone in Boley news to an African American weekly newspaper published in Guthrie, the capital of neighboring Oklahoma Territory. Because of this work, she is credited as being Boley's first news correspondent, working as she did before the *Boley Progress* began its operation in 1905.[21] During this time California also took courses, presumably by mail, at Highland Park College's School of Pharmacy in Iowa. In 1907, when Turner turned his attention to running the town's first bank and also to a real estate company he shared with Thomas Haynes, he turned over operations of the drugstore not to his wife, Minnie, but to California. She was well suited to the role, and under her watch, the drugstore remained a community gathering place. Customers could find her dispensing medication, selling tickets to club fundraisers, and keeping folks abreast of local and distant affairs. She was frequently complimented for her pharmacy work, her stock of goods and sundries, and her window displays and in-store decor. In 1911, perhaps feeling a bit outmatched, Boley newcomer and new *Progress* editor Henry Clay Gray praised her work in the pharmacy but also observed that "if she ever [took] the notion to give her whole time to newspaper work, she'[d] have the people busy, one half reading and the other half thinking." He concluded, "The *Progress* man is a blue hen's chicken and a game one at that, but he hasn't beat Miss Taylor yet."[22]

The drugstore might also have been the stage upon which monumental dramas in California's personal life took place, at least in part. In 1906 cracks began to emerge in her marriage with Charles Brock. After a visit to Houston in April, California returned to Boley and sued Brock for misappropriating nearly $1,200 of her personal money. The estrangement hinted at in this lawsuit only grew in the ensuing years. The couple ultimately divorced in January 1908, and Brock remained in Boley for only a few more months.[23] He briefly entered the newspaper business, co-operating a new weekly called the *Boley Beacon*, and tried his hand at real estate. These new ventures were likely signs that his business partnership with Hilliard Taylor was also a casualty of the divorce. Soon his residence in Boley was at an end as well. Before the year was over, Charles Brock had permanently returned to Houston.[24]

California remained in Boley and reinvented herself as an unmarried woman. Her new status as a divorcée, however, brought forth certain anxieties about respectability. She maintained her independence by continuing her drugstore work and safeguarded her reputation by renting a room in a boardinghouse run by Mariah Foster, the wife of Baptist minister L. P. Foster. She also reclaimed her original surname and went by "Miss Taylor." Townspeople accepted this renaming and, in doing so, effectively erased any remnants of Charles Brock's brief presence in the town. Nevertheless, in 1910, census taker and fellow Boley citizen Fleming B. Jones recorded her marital status as "widow." Since Jones undoubtedly knew she was divorced and not widowed, he, like many others in town, seems to have participated in forming a veil of protection around California, ignoring the divorce by embracing the never-been-married implications of "Miss" and by representing her as widowed in government documents.[25] California's divorce from Charles Brock had some negative social implications, however. In October 1908, twenty-four married women in Boley established the Ladies Industrial Club. Members met twice a month to socialize, do needlework, and engage in community service activities. Their most lasting achievement was the establishment of Boley's public library, one of three public libraries established by Black Oklahomans during the era of segregation. They limited their membership to married women only and, pointedly, forbade divorced women, even those who had remarried, from ever joining.[26]

California's personal life underwent other upheavals over the next two decades. Her father suffered a paralyzing stroke in 1911 and died two years later.[27] And, at some point during this period, she entered into an extramarital affair with David J. Turner (perhaps the reason for the snub by the Ladies Industrial Club). David and his wife, Minnie, had been married sometime around 1895 and had five children together. David, Minnie, and California likely all worked together closely in Turner's Drug Store during its first few years of operation, but by 1910, Minnie no longer worked outside her home.[28] David, a handsome and talented entrepreneur who was seven years younger than California, was described by one visitor to Boley as "a fine specimen of manhood, standing slightly more than six feet tall, with broad, manly shoulders"; he was also "easy to talk to" and had "an interesting and engaging personality." Townspeople described him as both "a man of honesty, unselfishness, keen vision and quite the best business man in the state" and a man who would "curse you out and then turn right around and do more for you than anyone else."[29] An original investor in Boley's first bank, the Farmers and Merchants' Bank, David took on a series leadership positions within the organization and was eventually elected bank president in 1916. While maintaining his position of bank president, he also served as Boley's mayor from 1917 to 1920 and again from 1929 until his death in 1932.[30] We can only speculate as to when California and David became lovers, but what is certain is that in 1921, Minnie Turner sued her husband for divorce on charges of "cruelty, threats, and infidelity" and named California as a co-respondent in the suit.[31] In spite of the sensational nature of the case, its resolution is not entirely clear. The Turners and California all continued living in Boley for several more years. Minnie Turner presided over the Turner family home until her death in 1926. In the meantime, however, California moved to Missouri in 1924 to live with her sister and brother-in-law. Prior to her departure, she was feted by friends and fellow Prewitt Chapel congregants and honored for her contributions to Boley.[32] At the time, she might have believed this to be a permanent relocation, and she lived her life accordingly, enjoying, among other things, travel across the United States; she even ventured across the ocean to England and France in 1926.[33] Soon after her return, however, she and David Turner reconnected. The couple wed in Kansas City, Missouri, on July 28, 1927, and returned to Boley together.[34]

This period was an even more tumultuous one for the Boley community. Oklahoma statehood strained the freedom dreams that Boley's original settlers had brought with them. In 1908 California would have witnessed the Fort Smith and Western Railroad building a partition to create a "whites only" section in the town's iconic railroad depot. Nearly three years later, she saw her father and the other men of Boley disfranchised through the execution of a grandfather-clause election law, which forced Black men to take literacy tests in order to qualify to vote. The very next year California and her community were brought to their knees by the lynching of Laura Nelson and her twelve-year-old son, L. D., whose family lived on outskirts of Boley. In the years that followed, the town was rocked again by the development of two major migration movements resulting in the departure of hundreds, if not thousands, of African Americans from Boley and other parts of the county who moved to Canada and the Gold Coast of Africa. The outmigration trend continued during and after World War I as residents found new economic opportunities in urban areas of the United States to the north and west. By 1930, even Boley's chief founder, Thomas M. Haynes, had moved away.[35]

Now married to the bank president and once and future mayor, California Taylor-Turner (or, as she signed her name during this period, "Mrs. Calif. Taylor-Turner") reentered Boley society with a flourish. She did not return to her notary and pharmacy work. Instead, she immersed herself in club work through her participation and leadership in the Women's Home Missionary Society, the Ladies Coleridge-Taylor Choral Club, the Flower Garden Club, and the Organization of Eastern Stars. She was even welcomed as a guest at Ladies Industrial Club meetings.[36] It was her political voice, however, through the Boley branch of the NAACP, that shined through most during this period. Her voluminous correspondence with the organization also provides a clear window through which Boley's post-boom years can be seen and understood.

California became secretary of the Boley branch of the NAACP in 1929 and held the office, sometimes unwillingly, for the better part of the next eleven years. Her first bit of correspondence with the national office, dated October 16, 1929, was written on the eve of the stock market crash that ushered in the Great Depression. In it, she expressed "hope of new life and activity" within the Boley branch.[37] Unfortunately, California soon realized that her task would be a difficult one. Mirroring the town itself, Boley's NAACP branch had fallen on hard times. It had been established in July 1919 in an attempt to engage the civil rights organization in the voting-rights struggle in Boley. Unfortunately, over the years, the New York–based national office of the NAACP had shown only fitful interest in taking on the voting-rights fight in Okfuskee County in which Boley is located. Instead Boleyites slowly chipped away at their disenfranchisement through a combination of lawsuits and backroom dealmaking. These economic and political circumstances resulted in a population of Boley residents who, by the late 1920s, exhibited a general unwillingness to devote its scarce resources to the NAACP.

The majority of California's NAACP branch work took place during the worst economic years the people of Boley had faced thus far. For this reason, her primary challenge was simply keeping the branch functional and in good standing with the national organization. This entailed maintaining a minimum of fifty members and paying the branch's annual five-dollar apportionment used to defray costs for the annual national convention. In April 1931, two years into her tenure as secretary, she updated the national office on her current progress toward these goals and explained the economic reasons behind the shortfalls:

Possibly California M. Taylor Turner, undated. Although there are no confirmed extant photographs of California M. Taylor, this image, found in one of several photograph albums owned by California's Houston family, shows a woman who may be her. California's brother, James B. Taylor, visited Boley several times, and there is photographic evidence of these trips in the albums. This woman is fair-skinned (Taylor was described as "mulatto" in census records), wearing a long pearl necklace, and carrying an umbrella and what appears to be a newspaper, items indicative of the woman's economic means and education. Behind her is a flat landscape featuring a few one-story buildings, scrubby brush, and a dirt road, a landscape that aligns with that of Boley. Hilliard Taylor Collection. Courtesy of the African American Library at the Gregory School, Houston Public Library.

"So far we haven't been able to get our drive on foot. So little money and so many claims to be met. Boley's financial status has never been so weak." She closed the missive with an expression of hope that she would get her neighbors to join or renew their memberships, but by November, she found herself explaining that "if the balance of the apportionment does not reach you before Dec. 31st it will be no fault of mine. All efforts at entertainments have failed. There has never been a time when a dollar was so difficult to get.... All pledges are like piecrust."[38] In April 1932, a year after her first complaint of financial woe, she reiterated the town's financial plight: "It is with sincere regret that so little is raised by the Boley Branch, but a dollar is a dollar here. No weekly or monthly payroll and the few possessing a dollar or so, have been forced this Spring to help feed and clothe many. Boley has never been in such a plight as now." Although the community managed to rally to her call in 1934 in order to make a showing at the national convention, held in Oklahoma City, Boley's overall economic slump and subsequent branch moribundity continued indefinitely.[39]

Although her efforts to reanimate the branch proved impossible, California achieved a degree of success functioning as Boley's unofficial NAACP organizer. She used her positions in the Women's Home Missionary Society and the Ladies Coleridge-Taylor Choral Club to run NAACP membership drives; she organized a very successful "penny-caucus" (which earned her recognition in *The Crisis*); and she even conducted a letter-writing campaign asking Oklahoma congressman Percy L. Gassaway to support a federal anti-lynching bill. On her own, she went door-to-door to collect funds for NAACP legal campaigns, such as the 1932 defense of Louis and Elbert Blake, sharecroppers convicted of murdering their landlord in Camden, Arkansas, and the 1934 appeal of Jess Hollins's rape conviction in neighboring Okmulgee County.[40] When all else failed, she marshaled her personal resources. In 1931, she paid the five-dollar apportionment out of her own funds, noting that although this was her usual annual contribution to the organization, she wished for it to be credited to the Boley branch that year. She also sent in personal contributions toward causes as varied as the 1932 Mary White Ovington gift campaign and the 1933 the Scottsboro defense fund, purchased NAACP Christmas seals, and subscribed to *The Crisis* and other organization literature.[41]

Ultimately, California's labors proved both frustrating and exhausting. She found the people of Boley to be increasingly inward facing. At her request, the branch president issued calls for meetings, but they went unheeded, and he did little to produce better results. Others were worse. Upon hearing of her clubs' letters to Congressman Gassaway about the anti-lynching bill, members of the Ladies Industrial Club, which had frozen her out of their company so many years ago, wrote to him as well. Their request was not for his support for the anti-lynching bill but instead solicited a donation for the completion of the town's library, which California dismissed as a "little . . . shack about 16 × 20 that has been under construction 10 years."[42] She found the men and the young people of the town to be equally impossible to mobilize. To Walter White she wrote, "I regret to say our men will not 'act.' I've exhausted my patience trying to keep the Branch alive and have failed. . . . The Professional, and the young people just will not function, and to turn loose a dollar is out of the question, unless an immediate return is in sight. Promises from them is all you get. I regret the state of affairs but I have no remedy. We have *no Branch*."[43]

California resigned from her position as Boley NAACP secretary in 1936 and returned the chapter's charter to the national office. The branch was reestablished three years later, however, and California, who was not even present during the organizational meeting, was unwittingly elected back to the position of secretary. She accepted the drafting and trudged along for a few more years, dealing with the same level of officer and membership inactivity that had plagued the branch before. In a 1940 letter, she complained, "A peculiar situation exists in this all NEGRO Town. What is called the Intelligent and Better-class have the least interest."[44] Finally, in 1941, after eleven years of carrying the branch, California had had enough. She made a final effort to raise the annual convention apportionment because the convention was to take place in Houston, "her native home," and, "if alive," she intended to attend.[45] Even this closely held desire was stunted by the Boley branch's failure to thrive. A few days before the conference began, she sent what she had managed to collect of the apportionment along with a penultimate missive in which she stated, "I will tell you, I am heartily ashamed of Boley and I've done what I could. One can not pull the load." Shortly after sending this message to the national office, California was involved in a car accident. She spent the next several months convalescing in a private hospital in Guthrie. During her absence, the Boley branch withered away again. It would periodically be revived with the aid of the national office, but California had, in effect, retired from her labors on its behalf. Her final words on the subject were simply "It is very pitiful that Boley will not be interested in the Branch; I've done what I could."[46]

Even as California transitioned out of her role in the Boley NAACP, she remained active in Boley in ways that advanced rights for the people of the town. Between 1940 and 1948 she served three times as precinct clerk at polling places in town. During this period she also served as Boley's correspondent with the *Okemah Daily Leader.* Tucked amid her newsy items about activities and comings and goings in Boley were her most direct surviving observations about the state of race relations in the United States. In one column she critiqued the shortsightedness of white Americans who remained committed to the color line even if it threatened the nation's war efforts. Quoting an unnamed "White scholar," she noted that this dogged commitment to excluding or segregating African Americans led to "shortages of manpower, of nurses for our armed forces, of blood donations." In brief, she stated, "What America is really [short of] is common sense. Unless America reduces its surplus prejudice and increases its supply of common sense more blood will be spilled in the post[war] era and not on foreign soil."[47] In another column, which was published shortly after Presidents' Day in 1944, California soberly reflected on the legacies of presidents George Washington and Abraham Lincoln and the unfinished business of the struggle for Black freedom. "Both Washington and Lincoln," she wrote, "had their personal ideas about race relation[s]. Washington freed his individually owned Negroes before he died and urged others to do the same. Lincoln set in motion the machinery for freeing the Negroes of the nation but his program is still to be finished."[48]

In this reflection on US presidents, representing the United States as they did, and the unfinished business of Black freedom in America, California perhaps unwittingly mirrored a conversation that had begun in a debate held in Boley almost forty years before. It was a conversation that, in her own way, she had strived to shape throughout her life and career in Boley. In her various pursuits, she had pushed toward expanding opportunities for African American people to experience personal, economic, and political freedom in Boley. Over time, as the notion faded that Black towns like Boley would be the ultimate solution to the racial discrimination, inequities, and injustices that African Americans faced in the nation, she worked to reconcile Boley's path toward Black freedom through separation with the town's place in an expanding African American civil rights struggle. By 1948, however, when, at the age of eighty, California retired from public life, these challenges, at least within Boley, remained unresolved. Sometime between then and 1955, she moved back to Houston and spent her final years living in her brother's home. There she died of breast cancer on December 17 and was buried in Oak Park Cemetery in the city of her birth.[49]

NOTES

1. *Topeka Plaindealer*, March 6, 1908.
2. Melissa N. Stuckey, "All Men Up: Race, Rights and Power in the All-Black Town of Boley, Oklahoma: 1903–1939" (PhD diss., Yale University, 2009); Melissa N. Stuckey, "Boley, Indian Territory: Exercising Freedom in the All-Black Town," in "African American Migration and Mobility after the Civil War, 1865–1915," ed. Kendra Field, special issue, *Journal of African American History* 102, no. 4 (Fall 2017): 492–516; *Boley (OK) Progress*, May 17, 1906.
3. Testimony of Hilliard Taylor, "In the Matter of the Application Made by Josiah Looney, Guardian of Abigail Barnett, a Minor, for the Unrestricted Alienation of the NE-1/4 of Section 29, Township 12 North, Range 8 East, for Townsite Purposes in the Town of Boley, Creek Nation, Indian Territory," April 4, 1905, Dawes Commission Townsite Records, Boley, Creek Nation, February 5, 1905–June 13, 1905, box 115, folder 7, Oklahoma Historical Society (hereafter cited as OHS); "Trimble, Jay C.," *Indian Pioneer History* 112, no. 9565, OHS.
4. *Boley Progress*, March 23, 1905.
5. *Boley Progress*, March 17, 1906; Michele Mitchell, *Righteous Propagation: African Americans and the Politics of Racial Destiny after Reconstruction* (Chapel Hill: University of North Carolina Press, 2004); Kevin Gaines, *Uplifting the Race: Black Leadership, Politics and Culture in the Twentieth Century* (Chapel Hill: University of North Carolina Press, 1996).
6. William E. Bittle and Gilbert Geis, "Racial Self-Fulfillment and the Rise of an All-Negro Community in Oklahoma," *Phylon Quarterly* 18 (1957): 247–60; William E. Bittle and Gilbert Geis, "Alfred Charles Sam and an African Return: A Case Study in Negro Despair," *Phylon Quarterly* 23 (1962): 178–94; William E. Bittle and Gilbert L. Geis, *The Longest Way Home: Chief Alfred C. Sam's Back-to-Africa Movement* (Detroit, MI: Wayne State University Press, 1964); Norman Crockett, *The Black Towns* (Lawrence: Regents Press of Kansas, 1979), 187; Kenneth Marvin Hamilton, *Black Towns and Profit: Promotion and Development in the Trans-Appalachian West, 1877–1915* (Urbana: University of Illinois Press, 1991).
7. The relative paucity of sources about Black and Native American women in this region and era is discussed in "Where Were the Women?" in Sarah Deutsch, "Being Black in Boley, Oklahoma," in *Beyond Black & White: Race, Ethnicity, and Gender in the U.S. South and Southwest*, ed. Stephanie Cole and Alison M. Parker (College Station: Texas A&M University Press, 2004), 112–15.
8. Linda W. Reese, "Working in the Vineyard: African American Women in All-Black Communities," *Kansas Quarterly* 25, no. 2 (1994): 7–16; Linda W. Reese, "Lifting as We Climb," in *Women of Oklahoma, 1890–1920* (Norman: University of Oklahoma Press, 1997), 144–84.

9. 1870 US Bureau of the Census (Population Schedule), Fourth Ward, Houston, Harris County, Texas, Dwelling 253, Family 280, "Hilliard Taylor Household," JPEG image, accessed June 15, 2019, Ancestry; License to Marry or Solemnize Marriage of Hilliard Taylor and Emily Ferguson, December 7, 1967, Harris County, Texas, Marriage Records, Harris County Clerk's Office, Houston, Texas, accessed February 14, 2020, Ancestry.

10. Edward Hale Everett, "The Queen of California," *Atlantic Monthly* 13, no. 77 (March 1864): 265–79.

11. *Catalogue of the Officers and Students of Fisk University: Nashville, Tennessee, for the College Year 1883–4* (Nashville: Marshall & Bruce, 1884), 10, Birney Anti-Slavery Collection, Johns Hopkins University, accessed September 9, 2019, Internet Archive; *Catalogue of the Officers and Students of Fisk University: Nashville, Tennessee, for the College Year 1884–5* (Nashville: Marshall & Bruce, 1885), 18, Birney Anti-slavery Collection, Johns Hopkins University, accessed September 9, 2019, Internet Archive; *Annual Report of the Public Schools of the City of Houston, 1890–91* (Houston: Gray's, 1891), 13, accessed September 9, 2019, Houston Public Library Digital Archives; *Morrison & Fourmy General Directory of the City of Houston, 1895–96* (Galveston: Morrison & Fourmy, 1895), 325, accessed September 9, 2019, Houston Public Library Digital Archives; Marriage Record for California M. Taylor and Charles H. Brock, Harris County Clerk's Office, Houston, Texas; *Harris County, Texas, Marriage Records*, accessed June 3, 2019, Ancestry; 1900 US Bureau of the Census (Population Schedule), Third Ward, Houston, Harris County, Texas, Dwelling 267, Family 286, "Charles Brock Household," JPEG image, accessed June 15, 2019, Ancestry.

12. Hallie Smith Jones, "A History of Boley, 1904–1945," in *Stories of Early Oklahoma—A Collection of Interesting Facts, Biographical Sketches and Stories Relating to the History of Oklahoma*, assembled by Hazel Ruby McMahan, State Historian for Oklahoma Society Daughters of American Revolution, 1945, OHS; *Boley Progress*, June 8, 1905.

13. Jones, "A History of Boley."

14. *Boley Progress*, March 9, 16, 1905.

15. Emily Apt Geer, "Lucy W. Hayes and the Woman's Home Missionary Society," *Hayes Historical Journal* 4, no. 4, Rutherford B. Hayes Presidential Library and Museums, accessed December 25, 2019, https://www.rbhayes.org/research/hayes-historical-journal-woman-s-home-missionary-society/.

16. *Boley Progress*, March 30, 1905, March 11, November 25, 1909.

17. *Boley Progress*, May 17, 1906.

18. Stephanie J. Shaw, *What a Woman Ought to Be and to Do: Black Professional Women Workers during the Era of Jim Crow* (Chicago: University of Chicago Press, 1996), 3, 11.

19. Deborah M. Thaw, "The Feminization of the Office of Notary Public: From *Femme Covert* to *Notaire Covert*," *John Marshall Law Review* 31, no. 3 (1998): 706–7. California's name can be found on several notarized documents related to African Creek citizenship and land claims filed with the Dawes Commission.

20. Thaw, 714–16. For Oklahoma's notary public laws, see Luther B. Hill, *A History of the State of Oklahoma, Vol. 1* (Chicago: Lewis, 1910), 464.

21. "The Town of Boley: A Community of Colored People, Bent on Demonstrating Their Good Citizenship, Their Town and Their Business Houses," *Fort Smith (AR) Times*, May 31, 1905, reprinted in *Boley Progress*, June 8, 1905; *Boley Progress*, March 9, 1905; Velma Dolphin Ashley, "A History of Boley, Oklahoma" (MA thesis, Kansas State Teachers College, 1940), 20, 45.

22. *Boley Progress*, August 24, 1905, December 22, 1910, May 5, 1911; Ashley, "A History of Boley, Oklahoma," 20; *Topeka Plaindealer*, May 7, 1915, March 31, April 7, 1916. A "blue hen's chicken," in this context, can be interpreted as a tough fighter.

23. *Chandler (OK) News*, July 26, 1906; *Plattsburg (MO) Leader*, January 24, 1908.

24. *Boley (OK) Beacon*, February 20, March 19, 1908.

25. Darlene Clark Hine, "Rape and Inner Lives of Black Women in the Middle West: Preliminary Thoughts on the Culture of Dissemblance," *Signs* 14, no. 4 (Summer 1989); 1910 US Bureau of the Census (Population Schedule), "Boley Township, Boley City, Okfuskee County, Oklahoma, Dwelling 191, Family 191, L. P. Foster Household," JPEG image, accessed June 15, 2019, Ancestry.

26. Ashley, "A History of Boley, Oklahoma," 69; Louise S. Robbins, *The Dismissal of Miss Ruth Brown: Civil Rights, Censorship, and the American Library* (Norman: University of Oklahoma Press, 2001), 39.

27. *Boley Progress*, October 26, 1911; "Hilliard Taylor," Memorial, Find a Grave, https://www.findagrave.com/memorial/60115048/hilliard-taylor.

28. 1900 US Bureau of the Census (Population Schedule), "Township 10, Seminole Nation, Indian Territory, Dwelling 119, Family 130, David J. Turner Household," JPEG image, accessed April 22, 2007, Ancestry; 1910 US Bureau of the Census (Population Schedule), "Boley Township, Boley City, Okfuskee County, Oklahoma, Dwelling 240, Family 240, D. J. Turner Household," JPEG image, accessed April 22, 2007, Ancestry; 1920 US Bureau of the Census (Population Schedule), "Paden Township, Boley City, Okfuskee County, Oklahoma, Dwelling 178, Family 185, D. J. Turner Household," JPEG image, accessed April 22, 2007, Ancestry.

29. *Pittsburgh (PA) Courier*, September 13, 1930.

30. *Topeka Plaindealer*, April 7, 1916; *Okemah (OK) Ledger*, November 1, 1917; "A Great Treat for Boley!," May 16, 1919, box 18, folder 9, record group 8-D-1-1, Governor's Office Records, Oklahoma State Archives, Oklahoma Department of Libraries, Oklahoma City; Ashley, "A History of Boley, Oklahoma," 44; *Chicago Defender*, December 3, 1932.

31. *Tulsa Daily World*, September 6, 1921.

32. "Minnie Turner," Memorial, Find a Grave, accessed March 5, 2020, https://findagrave.com/memorial/39115785/minnie-turner; *Black Dispatch* (Oklahoma City, OK), November 27, 1924.

33. "Taylor, California," List of United States Citizens, S. S. *Majestic*, Sailing from Southampton, August 19, 1926, Arriving at Port of New York, August 25, 1926, accessed November 28, 2019, Ancestry; *Pittsburgh Courier*, September 4, 1926.

34. Application for License to Marry, California M. Taylor and David J. Turner, Missouri State Archives, Jefferson City, Missouri; Missouri Marriage Records (Microfilm), accessed June 3, 2019, Ancestry; *Topeka Plaindealer*, August 5, 1927.

35. Stuckey, "All Men Up"; R. Bruce Shepard, *Deemed Unsuitable: Blacks from Oklahoma Move to the Canadian Prairies in Search of Equality in the Early 20th Century, Only to Find Racism in Their New Home* (Toronto: Umbrella, 1997); Kendra Taira Field, *Growing Up with the Country: Family, Race, and Nation after the Civil War* (New Haven, CT: Yale University Press, 2018); Bittle and Geis, *The Longest Way Home*.

36. 1930 US Bureau of the Census (Population Schedule), "Paden Township, Boley City, Okfuskee County, Oklahoma, Dwelling 49, Family 50, D. J. Turner Household," JPEG image, accessed July 15, 2019, Ancestry; 1940 US Bureau of the Census (Population Schedule), "Paden Township, Boley City, Okfuskee County, Oklahoma Dwelling 86, California Turner Household," JPEG image, accessed July 15, 2019, Ancestry; California Taylor-Turner to Roy Wilkins, April 16, 1935, NAACP Branch Files, Boley, Oklahoma, box I:G172, folder 6, National Association for the Advancement of Colored People records, Manuscript Division, Library of Congress, Washington, DC (hereafter cited as NAACP manuscript records); California M. Turner et al. to Hon. P. L. Gassaway, May 19, 1936, NAACP Boley Branch I:G172, 6, NAACP manuscript records; California M. Turner and Mrs. Mayme Jones to Hon. P. L. Gassaway, May 19, 1936, NAACP Boley Branch I:G172, 6, NAACP manuscript records; *Okemah Daily Leader*, March 6, June 26, 1942.

37. Calif. Taylor-Turner to the NAACP, October 16, 1929, NAACP Boley Branch I:G172, 3, NAACP manuscript records; California Taylor-Turner to Walter White, May 20, 1936, NAACP Boley Branch I:G172, 6, NAACP manuscript records.

38. California Taylor-Turner to the NAACP, April 22, 1931, NAACP Boley Branch I:G172, 4, NAACP manuscript records; California Taylor-Turner to the NAACP, November 17, 1931, NAACP Boley Branch I:G172, 4, NAACP manuscript records.

39. California Taylor-Turner to the NAACP, April 1, 1932, NAACP Boley Branch I:G172, 5, NAACP manuscript records; Roy Wilkins to California Taylor-Turner, April 9, 1932, NAACP Boley Branch I:G172, 5, NAACP manuscript records; California Taylor-Turner to the NAACP, June 12, 1934, NAACP Boley Branch I:G172, 5, NAACP manuscript records.

40. California Taylor-Turner to the NAACP, May 19, 1934, NAACP Boley Branch I:G172, 5, NAACP manuscript records; California Taylor-Turner to the NAACP, February 20, 1934, NAACP Boley Branch I:G172, 5, NAACP manuscript records; "Penny Fund," *Crisis*, 41, no. 12 (December 1934): 377; California M. Turner et al. to Hon. P. L. Gassaway, May 19, 1936, NAACP Boley Branch I:G172, 6, NAACP manuscript records; California M. Turner and Mrs. Mayme Jones to Hon. P. L. Gassaway, May 19, 1936, NAACP Boley Branch I:G172, 6, NAACP manuscript records; California Taylor-Turner to Juanita E. Jackson, June 5, 1936, NAACP Boley Branch I:G172, 6, NAACP manuscript records; California Taylor-Turner to the NAACP, April 1, 1932, NAACP Boley Branch I:G172, 5, NAACP manuscript records; Blake v. State, 52 S.W.2d 644 (Ark. 1932); California Taylor-Turner to the NAACP, October 15, 1934, NAACP Boley Branch I:G172, 5, NAACP manuscript records; Hollins v. State, 1934 OK CR 140 38 P.2d 36.

41. California Taylor-Turner to Mary White Ovington, August 8, 1931, NAACP Boley Branch I:G172, 4, NAACP manuscript records; California Taylor-Turner to the NAACP, April 24, 1932, NAACP Boley Branch I:G172, 5, NAACP manuscript records; California

Taylor-Turner to Roy Wilkins, May 29, 1933, NAACP Boley Branch I:G172, 5, NAACP manuscript records; California Taylor-Turner to Walter White, May 20, 1936, NAACP Boley Branch I:G172, 6, NAACP manuscript records; California T. Turner to NAACP, December 18, 1940, NAACP Papers, Sterling Memorial Library, Yale University, New Haven, CT (hereafter cited as NAACP Papers), part 26 (microfilm), reel 17, frame 00549; California T. Turner to William Pickens, June 5, 1940, NAACP Papers, part 26 (microfilm), reel 17, frame 00547.

42. California Taylor-Turner to Juanita E. Jackson, June 5, 1936, NAACP Boley Branch I:G172, 6, NAACP manuscript records.

43. California Taylor-Turner to Walter White, May 20, 1936, NAACP Boley Branch I:G172, 6, NAACP manuscript records.

44. California T. Turner to NAACP, December 18, 1940, NAACP Papers, part 26 (microfilm), reel 17, frame 00549.

45. California T. Turner to Walter White, January 6, 1941, NAACP Papers, part 26 (microfilm), reel 17, frame 00551.

46. California T. Turner to NAACP, June 17, 1941, NAACP Papers (microfilm), part 26, reel 17, frame 00555; California T. Turner to E. Frederic Morrow, October 22, 1941, NAACP Papers, (microfilm), part 26 reel 17, frames 00558–59.

47. *Okemah Daily Leader*, August 2, 1944.

48. *Okemah Daily Leader*, February 25, 1944.

49. *Okemah Daily Leader*, April 1, 1948; Death Certificate of California Taylor, Texas Department of State Health Services, Austin, Texas, accessed June 3, 2019, Ancestry.

CHERYL ELIZABETH BROWN WATTLEY

7
MAKING HISTORY AS AN NAACP PLAINTIFF

Ada Lois Sipuel Fisher

Even though she was only six years old in 1930, Ada Lois Sipuel Fisher always remembered the lynching of Henry Argo. She had known Henry. He had lived in her town, Chickasha, Oklahoma. He was the son of the ice delivery man. He had been falsely accused of raping a white woman. But a mob of two thousand angry white people went to the jail, burning it down. They then shot and stabbed Argo to death.

    African American parents gathered their children, shielding them in homes protected by rifles and pistols. Other families came to the Sipuels' house. The doors were locked. Ada Lois and other children lay on pallets on the floor so that they would be below window height. Her father and other men stood by windows, standing guard, fearful of another destructive riot like that one that devastated the Greenwood District of Tulsa in 1921. The riot that had destroyed the Sipuel home and church and forced their departure from Tulsa.

Born in 1924, Ada Lois grew up in Chickasha, Oklahoma, in the 1930s and early 1940s. A child of segregation, she lived a life constrained by racially based restrictions, prohibitions, and violence. Yet a sense of self-worth, a drive for fairness, a passion for equality, burned within her. She volunteered to be a plaintiff in landmark litigation against the State of Oklahoma. A lawsuit that helped to end segregation.

A lawsuit that would also make her a target. She had to ignore the hate-filled stares. The letters addressed to "Nigger, Chickasha, Oklahoma" that were delivered to her. The threatening phone calls that caused "shivers to run up her spine."[1]

But Ada Lois actively embraced her role, driving miles across the state of Oklahoma for meetings at local chapters of the National Association for the Advancement of Colored People (NAACP). She made national appearances, traveling to New York to share her story. She became the face and voice of the fight for equality. But she hadn't been asked to be the plaintiff.

In 1945, Roscoe Dunjee, owner of the state's leading African American newspaper, the *Black Dispatch*, and head of the Oklahoma NAACP, invited Thurgood Marshall to speak at the state convention. He wanted Marshall to personally appeal to the NAACP members to recruit a plaintiff for a desegregation lawsuit. Marshall told attendees that the suit would be the easiest case to win that could ever be filed in Oklahoma.[2] It was time to attack educational segregation in Oklahoma.

Dr. W. A. J. Bullock, regional director of the Chickasha-area NAACP, heard Marshall's statements. He thought he knew the perfect person to be the NAACP's plaintiff: Lemuel Sipuel. A graduate of Langston University, the state university for African Americans. A soldier who had served in World War II. A man who wanted to be a lawyer.

But Lemuel wanted to get on with his life. The war had interrupted his studies, and he was ready to go to law school. He didn't want to spend years fighting Oklahoma, putting his life on hold. He declined Dr. Bullock's request.

Ada Lois, his younger sister, overheard the conversation.[3] She knew what Dr. Bullock was asking Lemuel to do. She was willing to say yes. She was willing to be the NAACP's plaintiff—after all, she had been a member of the NAACP for years. She was also a strong student: an honors graduate of the all-Black Lincoln High School in Chickasha and a graduate of Langston University. She wanted to be a lawyer. This would be her chance to attend law school in Oklahoma. She stepped forward and asked Dr. Bullock whether she could be the plaintiff. When he said yes, she was so excited that she danced in circles and clapped her hands.[4]

Ada Lois Sipuel Fisher around the time of her first application to the University of Oklahoma College of Law, 1946. Courtesy of the Fisher family.

Ada Lois's childhood had prepared her to step forward. She had been raised in segregated Chickasha, which had clearly defined white and Black sections of town. She knew the signs that read "colored only." She had climbed the stairs to the balcony of the movie theater, the Black section. She knew that she couldn't swim in the municipal swimming pool. Or see the animals at the city zoo. Or go to Shannon Springs, the city park.

But she had grown up sustained by the vibrancy of the Black Chickasha community. There were six churches, including the Church of God in Christ congregation pastored by her father, Travis B. Sipuel. Black professional organizations such as the Negro Chamber of Commerce, the Prince Hall Masons, the Odd Fellows Lodge, the Flower Lovers Federated Club, and the NAACP focused on the community needs of African Americans. There were grocery stores, barber shops, cleaners, drugstores, restaurants and cafés, and funeral parlors. There was a movie theater, a skating rink, and baseball fields. Doctors, dentists, and lawyers had offices. The schools offered many activities: band, choir, student government.

Her mother, Martha Bell Sipuel, was a strong, determined, involved woman. She had refused to work as a maid when the homeowner told her that she had to use the back door. Instead, she opened a grocery store in the house next to the Sipuel residence. She was active in the NAACP. When the local sheriff ran for election, she put a sign in her car urging people not to vote for him because he had been involved in Henry Argo's lynching.

Bishop Travis B. Sipuel, Ada Lois's father, was the son of former slaves. He had run away from Mississippi at the age of ten to settle in Arkansas. After he and Martha married, they moved to Tulsa, where he established a Church of God congregation. When their home, church, and neighborhood were destroyed during the assault on the Greenwood District of Tulsa, they moved to Chickasha. Bishop Sipuel became even more active in the Church of God denomination, eventually becoming the church's statewide leader.

But their status did not blind the Sipuels to the prejudice and racial segregation that were intrinsic to Oklahoma's existence. They had known of the early hopes of recently emancipated slaves who had flocked to Oklahoma after the Civil War to establish more than fifty all-Black townships. They were aware of the public notices proclaiming that African Americans could not reside in certain cities. They were conscious of signs publicly stating that Black people were not welcome after the sun set, the notorious "sundown towns." They had lived with Oklahoma's separate systems of schools, segregated transportation, and restricted seating in the back of the bus.

Ada Lois's parents made certain that she knew the importance of activism. She had participated in demonstrations and protests at Langston University and served as a panelist in public discussions about race relations. She had been associate editor of the school paper, and she had pledged the Alpha Kappa Alpha sorority, the first Greek organization for Black women.

Most of all, she dreamed of becoming a lawyer in her home state. She was willing to confront any risks and assume any burdens because she knew that "separate but equal" was a fiction that served only to deny African Americans an equal education. This would be her chance. She would be the NAACP's plaintiff.

The end of World War II had brought new opportunities to the NAACP to continue its fight against educational segregation. It had already successfully represented Donald Murray and Lloyd Gaines in lawsuits attacking segregation in graduate educational programs.[5] But in 1945 Thurgood Marshall was "more than worried about our inability to get cases started."[6]

Being a plaintiff in an NAACP lawsuit that challenged decades of racial segregation was not easy. Efforts to intimidate a plaintiff could come from many directions. White employers could fire them from their jobs. Lenders could demand payment on outstanding loans or refuse any more credit. White landlords could evict them or put pressure on Black landlords to do the same. Segregation supporters could confront them with shouts, taunts, and hate-filled jeers. White mobs could use violence; African Americans were still being lynched.

These consequences were well known in the Black community. Lloyd Gaines had mysteriously disappeared after the Supreme Court ruled in his favor. Ada Lois, who had a mother active in the NAACP and subscribed to its organ *The Crisis*, was exposed to these realities. And yet she stepped forward and asked if she could be the plaintiff.

Dunjee had to approve Ada Lois's selection. Within days Dr. Bullock was driving Ada Lois to Oklahoma City to meet with Dunjee. As they drove, Ada Lois knew that this would be one of the most important meetings of her life.

She had to show Dunjee that she was smart enough to handle law school courses. She had to persuade him that she could stand the pressure of being the only African American student in an all-white school. She wanted him to see that she could be his partner in traveling across the state, talking with the NAACP branches, and raising the money to fund the litigation. She needed him to see that she had the courage to ignore the hate mail and angry taunts and jeers from people who supported segregation. She had to make him realize that she had the ability, determination, and steadfastness to stay the course.

Ada Lois's high school and college transcripts were reviewed. She was academically qualified. She would receive financial support from her husband and father. Her husband, Warren Fisher, was a soldier in the United States Army, her father a bishop. Because they could provide for her, Ada Lois would not be vulnerable to retaliatory threats of unemployment.

It didn't hurt that Ada Lois was female. She was attractive and demure and had a pleasing personality. She would not present a threat. At the end of the meeting, Dunjee was convinced: he had found the right person to lead the challenge against Oklahoma's segregated education.

On a cold January morning in 1946, Ada Lois made history; she was the first African American to apply for admission to the University of Oklahoma College of Law. Dunjee and Dr. Bullock walked alongside her. As she walked from the parking lot to the steps of the administration building, she recognized the gravity and importance of her actions. With each step she understood the risks that she faced and the dangers that surrounded her. She understood that there were few women lawyers. Here she was, Black and female. But it was her race that targeted her under the law. She couldn't help being a little anxious and apprehensive.[7]

They entered the Registrar's Office, where a line of students stood, waiting to enroll. Ada Lois took her place in line, then handed over her transcript when she finally reached the front. With her announcement that she was there to apply to the law school, she, Dunjee, and Dr. Bullock were escorted to the President's Office.

Dr. George Lynn Cross had been anticipating this day. After Marshall's appearance at the state convention, the university's Board of Regents had issued a direct order to Dr. Cross to deny any such applications. Oklahoma's segregation statutes made it a criminal offense for white and Black students to be taught in the same classes, so admitting any Black student would expose administrators and teachers to daily fines.

After introductions were made, Dr. Cross began to read aloud the statutes that required him to deny Ada Lois's application. Dunjee cut him off abruptly, telling him that they knew the law and that all they wanted was a letter stating that Ada Lois was being denied because of her race. Dr. Cross, with full understanding of the significance of his words, affirmed that Ada

Lois was academically qualified for admission; the only reason she would not be accepted was her race.

Dr. Cross knew that his letter would be the basis for a federal lawsuit. He discussed with Ada Lois and Dunjee the specific words that should be used to strengthen any legal claim. He wrote:

> Dear Miss Sipuel:
>
> This will acknowledge receipt of your application for admission to Law School of the University of Oklahoma. However, I must deny you admission to the University for the following reasons:
> 1. Title 70, Sections 452–464, inclusive, of the Oklahoma Statutes, 1941, prohibits colored students from attending the schools of Oklahoma and makes it a misdemeanor for school officials to admit colored students to white schools, to instruct classes composed of mixed races, or to attend classes composed of mixed races.
> 2. The Board of Regents has specifically instructed the president of the University of Oklahoma to refuse admission to Negroes, giving as a basis of their decision the statutes of Oklahoma.
>
> Cordially yours,
>
> G. L. Cross, President

Cross supported her application even if he had to reject it.[8] And, as Dunjee had predicted, Dr. Cross saw Ada Lois as "chic, charming, and well poised."[9] To NAACP officials, Dr. Cross's comments were important because they reflected a positive assessment of Ada Lois. Dr. Cross did not view her as a threat.

With Dr. Cross's letter in hand, Dunjee eagerly drove back to Oklahoma City. He excitedly typed a letter to Marshall to tell him of the day's events. He wrote, "Here's your case and I think it's what one would call a natural."[10] Dunjee described the meeting to Marshall, giving special attention to the discussion with Dr. Cross:

> Confidentially, I received a lot of cooperation from the president of the college. He told me in the presence of Dr. Bullock and Miss Sipuel that he was sympathetic and wanted to cooperate with us in having just what we want to get into the federal court for relief. . . . The president and the Dean of Admissions certify that Miss Sipuel's scholastic credits are nearly perfect and President Cross wrote the letter in such a way that there could not be any claim that she was not qualified."[11]

Cross's support, though, had to be carefully shielded. If it were known that he was sympathetic to Ada Lois's cause, he would most likely be terminated.

Ada Lois's application immediately received attention. Before the group left campus, students from the YMCA and YWCA supplied them with box lunches so that they could all eat together. No restaurant in Norman would serve African Americans. Pictures were taken of the students greeting Ada Lois.

The state's largest newspaper, the *Oklahoman*, ran a front-page story about Ada Lois's futile attempt to enter OU. The article contained significant details about Ada Lois, including her academic record, extracurricular activities, and interests in reading and hunting. She was described as a "tall, slim and pretty girl."[12]

Students on OU's campus joined in discussions about the admission of African Americans to the university. School-wide debates were held. Editorials appeared in the student newspaper. One editorial stated that separate school systems were "impractical, undesirable, and unnecessary."[13] Another posed the question of whether a Black student could ever be comfortable at OU when Norman was a sundown town, requiring Blacks to be out of the town before the sun set.

Finally, by early April 1946, it was time to file the lawsuit. A Black attorney from Tulsa, Amos Hall, had been hired as local counsel. Hall, Dunjee, and Ada Lois drove to Norman to file the petition that would begin her quest to attend the law school. Her petition stated that she desired to study law at OU, was academically qualified to be admitted, and would pay all costs and expenses related to her enrollment. Her denial because of her race violated the equal protection clause of the Fourteenth Amendment. She asked the judge to enter an order requiring Oklahoma officials to admit her to the law school.[14]

The judge entered an order requiring the state to file an answer within thirty days. Oklahoma claimed to need more time. The state wanted to explore whether it could expend the resources to create a separate law school for African Americans. After receiving the additional time, the state filed its answer. It did not contest that Ada Lois was academically qualified for admission. It did not deny that the sole reason she was not admitted to the law school was her race. But the state did deny that Ada Lois's constitutional rights had been violated.

In July 1946, almost six months after Ada Lois applied to OU, a hearing was held before Judge Ben Williams in the Cleveland County Courthouse in Norman. The air-conditioned courtroom was packed with spectators, both Black and white. Whispering and quiet murmuring could be heard. All eyes were on Ada Lois when she finally walked into the courtroom.

Marshall had not been able to travel to Oklahoma, so Dunjee and Hall escorted her into the courtroom. They made their way through the crowd to the tables for lawyers and clients. Representing the state were Mac Williamson, Oklahoma's attorney general; his first assistant, Fred Hansen; and Maurice Merrill, acting dean of the law school.

Hall spoke first. It was undisputed that Ada Lois was qualified. It was admitted that Oklahoma had not made any plans or taken any steps to create a segregated law school. Based upon the Supreme Court ruling in the *Gaines* case, Oklahoma was required to provide Ada Lois a legal education within the state. She had a constitutional right to study law in Oklahoma because white students were being afforded a legal education within the state. The injustice being imposed upon Ada Lois, Hall said, could only be corrected if judges had the courage to make the right ruling.[15]

Judge Williams was offended by Hall's argument, particularly the insinuation that he lacked courage. He took the unusual step of dictating a reply into the official record: "This Court feels that he has the courage to do his duty in this or any other judicial proceedings."[16] He then recessed court. At 7:45 P.M., Judge Williams returned to the courtroom to announce his decision. He would not order state officials to violate Oklahoma law and admit Ada Lois to the law school. The state had met its obligations when it gave the Board of Regents the authority to set up a separate law school.

Ada Lois was disappointed by the decision. The NAACP attorneys were surprised. The Supreme Court in the *Gaines* case had made it clear that a state had to provide a legal education to its African American citizens, not simply go through the motions. Oklahoma wasn't providing Ada Lois that opportunity to study law. Judge Williams's decision ran against the ruling of the United States Supreme Court because he did not require Oklahoma to provide Ada Lois with a legal education. His ruling had to be appealed. But it would be months before oral arguments would be scheduled before the Oklahoma Supreme Court.

While Ada Lois was waiting for that hearing, her father died suddenly. He had not been ill. There had been no warning signs. Two of her strongest supporters had died in the same year, her father and Dr. Bullock.

And Ada Lois needed support. She was being called "nigger." She was receiving threatening letters that described what would happen to her if she continued to fight to enter OU. There were death threats.

But these things did not weaken her resolve. She and Dunjee made appearances across the state. At every event, she was applauded for her bravery and sacrifice and encouraged to keep fighting. Money was raised. Audiences contributed to show their faith in her.

She became a central figure in the annual statewide NAACP conference, the very conference where a year earlier Marshall had issued the call to find a plaintiff. This year the conference was held in Chickasha at her old high school. She gave a keynote address titled "Why I Desire to Enter Law Classes at Oklahoma University." She promised the crowd that she would pursue the litigation to the highest court if need be.[17]

A surprise presentation came from a young white man, Ben Blackstock, a student at OU.[18] His speech was "Why the White Students at Norman Welcome Ada Lois Sipuel." He told the audience that students at OU supported her admission. The school newspaper had written an editorial encouraging the enrollment of Black students.

Ada Lois and Ben Blackstock stood together on the stage of that segregated high school. They were surrounded by about forty white people who had traveled from Norman as well as the members of the state NAACP who were on the stage. This interracial endorsement was evidence of the growing support for her admission to law school. It was a testament to the confidence that people had in her and Dunjee's belief that she would not be viewed as a threat. It signaled the coming change in white attitudes about her enrollment. Five student organizations would ultimately support her admission.

Later that year, Ada Lois was nationally recognized by the *Chicago Defender*, a Black newspaper. It named her one of the twenty-five outstanding contributors to democracy. In one year, she had gone from relative obscurity to national recognition and celebrity status.

The oral arguments before the Oklahoma Supreme Court were heard in March 1947. Seven of the nine justices were graduates of the University of Oklahoma law school. All seven of those justices served on the Board of Directors of the OU Alumni Association.[19]

The courtroom was again packed with Black and white observers. This time Marshall had flown to Oklahoma to give the oral argument. Marshall told the justices that because Oklahoma did not have a separate law school at the time Ada Lois applied, OU was obligated to admit her. Students who had applied at the law school at the same time had already completed a year of legal study.[20] This was a violation of her constitutional rights.

The justices pressed Marshall with questions: When should the state have created a separate law school? When it established OU? Did its segregation laws violate the Constitution? Marshall handled each question with an eloquence and logic that made Ada Lois dare to dream that the court might actually rule in her favor.

But it was only a dream. About a month after the arguments, the denial of her petition was upheld. Segregation had not been outlawed. Oklahoma was willing to provide Ada Lois with a legal education in segregated facilities equal to those of white students. It was not required to do more.

Ada Lois's disappointment was lessened by an understanding that this ruling was needed in order to take the case before the United States Supreme Court. Perhaps, before those justices, her constitutional rights would be recognized and enforced. Perhaps they would issue a ruling that would allow her to start her life as a law student.

The Supreme Court granted the petition for certiorari, scheduling the case for early January 1948. Oklahoma's lawyers again urged officials to create a separate law school. The university's Board of Regents expressed a desire to provide programs of higher education for African Americans once there was funding. Until then, there was not any money to create a separate law school.

Almost two years to the day after she had walked across OU's campus to hand her application to Dr. Cross, Ada Lois's case was heard before the United States Supreme Court. She had written Marshall a letter, asking if she could attend the arguments, a request that was quickly granted. The two walked up the steps together, the words over the door, "Equal Justice under the Law," having special meaning on that day. As she watched the justices file in, she realized that the "august body was assembled that morning because of [her]—to recognize and affirm [her] rights of citizenship."[21]

Marshall spoke first. His argument was straightforward and concise. The contrast between the treatment of white and Black applicants was obvious. A white student merely applied. A Black student had to request the creation of a school and then wait for its establishment. He argued that "equality under a segregated system is a legal fiction and judicial myth."[22]

When the attorneys for Oklahoma rose to speak, they were peppered with questions from the justices: Did students of other races apply for the creation of a new school? The state had known for two years that she wanted to go to law school; what had it done to create a school for her? Why should she be required to do more than a white student? If the court were to issue an order that she be admitted to law school this semester, would the state do that?[23]

National newspapers noticed the tone of the justices' questions to the Oklahoma lawyers. Articles called it a "severe hazing."[24] *Time* described the questions as "phrased to badger the attorneys for the state of Oklahoma."[25] The *Oklahoman* declared that the "justices ripped attorneys for the state of Oklahoma with a running fire of hostile questions . . . [that] had seldom been duplicated."[26]

As she left, Ada Lois had reason to be optimistic. She didn't have long to wait. Four days later, the Supreme Court issued a one-page per curiam decision:

> The petitioner is entitled to secure legal education afforded by a state institution. To this time, it has been denied her although during the same period many white applicants have been afforded legal education by the State. The State must provide it for her in conformity with the equal protection clause of the Fourteenth Amendment and provide it as soon as it does for applicants of any other group.[27]

The court ordered that its mandate be issued immediately, without the customary delay for formal printing.

The ruling, and the speed with which it was issued, received nationwide attention. The Supreme Court was sending a crushing and stinging rebuke to bigotry and expressing a loss of patience with the "evasions and prejudices of Southern states."[28] *Newsweek* said the court decision "cracked down firmly . . . on discrimination against Negroes."[29] Anticipating her actual enrollment, another paper wrote, "Miss Sipuel is a young woman of brains, charm, and guts who rates a bow from Negro America and its prayers for her success, for in her success she will open doors for hundreds."[30]

The NAACP declared the ruling to bring "educational equality one step closer."[31] On the university campus, the student newspaper headline boldly declared, "SIPUEL WINS CASE!" It predicted that "barring any last-minute devices on the part of the state to circumvent her entrance Ada Lois Sipuel will enroll in OU's law school this next semester."[32]

Ada Lois was ecstatic. The two-year fight had ended. The roller coaster of hopes and dashed dreams had come to an end. Oklahoma had to provide her with a legal education. The United States Supreme Court had said so. She told reporters, "I'm going to be a lawyer, I'm going to learn. . . . The few on the campus at the university who call me names—why, I won't even hear them. . . . I don't think I'll be alone for long. Somebody had to be first. It will be hard but maybe soon there'll be other Negroes with me."[33] In another interview, she said, "I plan to enroll as soon as I can get there. Naturally I am very, very happy about the Supreme Court's decision. I have won a fight that started two years ago."[34]

And she wasn't the only one who interpreted the opinion to require her immediate admission to OU. That was the consensus of the lawyers, the reporters, and the students at OU. She could finally have her life back and begin her studies. It was over.

But those who believed that Ada Lois would be entering her first law school class in just a few days underestimated the stubborn determination of Oklahoma state officials to maintain a strict system of educational segregation. The United States Supreme Court's order was sent back to the Oklahoma Supreme Court for implementation.

The Oklahoma justices seized upon the language requiring that it "provide her with a legal education . . . as soon as it does" white students. They were presented with three options: (1) order that Ada Lois be admitted to OU's law school, (2) suspend all legal studies at OU, or (3) create a segregated law school for Ada Lois. To them, the solution was clear: create a segregated law school. Ignore the fact that in May and then again in December 1947 state officials had determined that they could not fund a segregated law school. Disregard the statement by the state's attorney at the Supreme Court argument that it would take time to create a separate law school. Disavow their attorney's statement that if the Supreme Court ordered Oklahoma to provide Ada Lois with a legal education, she would be admitted to OU. The justices decided to issue an order to the Board of Regents to create a separate but equal law school for Ada Lois.

On Saturday, January 17, 1948, the Oklahoma Supreme Court ordered that

> plaintiff, and all others similarly situated, [be given] an opportunity to commence the study of law at a state institution as soon as citizens of other groups are afforded such an opportunity, in conformity with the equal protection clause of the Fourteenth Amendment of the Federal Constitution and with the provisions of the Constitution and statutes of this state requiring segregation of the races in the schools of this state.[35]

"In conformity with . . . segregation" were the key words of the Oklahoma Supreme Court's order. It was ordering the creation of a segregated law school. The very law school that state officials had twice determined could not be funded. And, unless it was going to suspend legal studies at OU, the segregated school had to be created before OU's classes began in a little more than a week.

That Monday morning, undaunted by the Oklahoma Supreme Court's ruling, Ada Lois, accompanied by Marshall and Hall, again drove to Norman. Dunjee, who had been so involved in every step of her fight, was too ill to travel with them. Ada Lois again walked across the campus on a cold January morning. She again stood in line, waiting to file her second application for admission to the university law school. She again presented her transcripts in support of that application. She was again firm in her declaration that she was there to apply for admission.

This time her application was accepted. The university issued a statement that her application would be considered once a directive had been received from state educational authorities as to how to proceed.

On that same day, state education officials met to chart a course of action. Classes were scheduled to begin the following Monday. They had to act quickly. A resolution was passed declaring "that there is hereby established as one of the functions of Langston University, a school of law to be known as the Langston School of Law, which law school shall be located at Oklahoma City, Oklahoma."[36] The course of study "shall be substantially equal to the course of study and standards now in existence at the University of Oklahoma School of Law." The registration period would be identical to the registration period for enrollment at OU. And with that resolution, Langston Law School was created, a separate law school for African Americans.

In addition to passing that resolution, education officials created a special committee to establish the Langston Law School. Meeting immediately, the committee was assured that the dean of the OU law school would provide advice and guidance, that the State Board of Public Affairs would arrange for storage rooms in the capitol building to be cleaned out to be used for faculty offices and a classroom, and that the capitol library could be used by students of the law school. The committee then adjourned. It had met for one hour.[37]

Within days, $15,000 in funding was identified, a dean and two part-time faculty were hired, and certification was obtained from the Oklahoma Board of Bar Examiners. The facilities were declared to be even better than those at OU. A regent affirmed that the state was "making a bona fide effort to provide opportunities for a legal education" and that the school was "entirely adequate to meet all demands."[38] In fact, one regent declared that the opportunities at the new school were superior in many respects to OU's law school.

On Monday, January 26, 1948, Langston Law School officially opened for enrollment. Ada Lois was sent telegrams informing her that Oklahoma was prepared to offer her a legal education. A segregated law school, absurdly declared "substantially equal," had been created just for her.

Ada Lois recognized the ploy for what it was. A blatant end run around the United States Supreme Court ruling. The new law school was a law school in name only. It was all form, no substance.

Rejecting that insult and refusing to attend Langston Law School, Ada Lois traveled again to Norman to visit with university officials. She was informed that her application had to be denied because a "substantially equal" law school existed in the state to provide her with a legal education. She would not be entering OU.

News of the state's creation of Langston Law School rapidly spread across the nation. There was blistering criticism from national media. Most important, Oklahoma students were galvanized to protest. At OU more than a thousand students publicly staged a symbolic burning of the Constitution and sent the ashes to President Truman. That demonstration was reported in the *New York Times*, the *Washington Post*, the *Pittsburgh Courier*, the *Atlanta Daily World*, the *Daily Mirror*, *Time*, and *Newsweek*.[39] At Langston University, war veterans wrote a letter of protest and sent it to the president. For the first time, African Americans obtained a demonstration permit and picketed the state capitol.[40] Students at the all-white Phillips University organized a chapter of the NAACP and became a central organizer of a statewide student conference on racial integration.

Ada Lois was once again in the limelight. A local sorority presented her with flowers and praised her:

> The NAACP cannot do its fine work for the advancement of our people without individuals who are willing to make the sacrifice for a cause. We need more Ada Lois Sipuel Fishers. We are supporting the NAACP in our local chapter and as a national group, but we do know that we are indebted to you, and in our humble way we shower you with flowers as an expression of our appreciation for your fight for equal education in our state.[41]

She attended community meetings and fundraisers. She gave speeches in Lawton, El Reno, and sites of other NAACP branches. She received words of encouragement from Black newspapers as she was applauded for not applying to the "makeshift" law school. She received a commendation from the southwest conference of NAACP branches. She was a featured guest at a Langston University fundraiser. But, despite the United States Supreme Court order, she was not able to enter the University of Oklahoma law school. Her life was again on hold.

While Ada Lois was still trying to gain admission to the law school, on the last day of the January registration period, six other African Americans sought admission to various graduate programs at OU. They were relying upon the express language of the United States Supreme Court ruling in Ada Lois's case. Oklahoma had to provide them the same opportunity for study at the same time that those educational opportunities were made available to white students. They wanted to pursue graduate degrees in education, sociology, and chemistry. Oklahoma couldn't possibly create separate and substantially equal educational programs in every academic field of study. These applicants would force Oklahoma to grant them admission to OU.

Ada Lois's legal case continued to proceed. In May 1948, a trial was held to address the issue of whether Langston Law School was substantially equal to OU's law school. To Marshall and the NAACP, that was a ludicrous proposition. How could a makeshift law school, created in seven days and without any students, be substantially equal to a law school that had existed for forty years and had an alumni base and a student body?

The NAACP gathered legal education experts from across the country to travel to Norman to testify. Deans of nationally recognized law schools—Harvard, the University of California–Berkeley School of Law, the University of Wisconsin, the University of Pennsylvania, Columbia University, and the University of Chicago—appeared as witnesses. Each of them testified that Langston Law School was not substantially equal to OU.

OU law professor Henry Foster Jr. powerfully denounced Langston Law School. Foster testified, "In my opinion, only the prejudice of an academic minded person could conceivably find the slightest substance to say that the two schools are at all comparable, let alone substantially equal or equivalent." The segregated school was an attempt "to manufacture on paper and copy and ape a superficial indicia of a college without having anything in substance to back it up. It is a fake, it is a fraud, and it is a deception, and to my mind [it] is an attempt to avoid the clear-cut mandate and orders of the Supreme Court of the United States. It is indecent."[42]

The NAACP also had a surprise witness: Paige Keeton, the dean of OU's law school. Under questioning from Marshall, Keeton testified that he "did not believe that the opportunities of the student at [Langston] would be equal or substantially equal" to those provided at the University of Oklahoma."[43]

Despite this evidence and testimony, Cleveland County judge Justin Hinshaw found that Ada Lois had been given an opportunity to study first-year law courses that were substantially equal to the offerings at OU. Once again, Ada Lois's hopes of entering OU were crushed. Once again, her life was on hold as the NAACP prepared to appeal to the Oklahoma Supreme Court and, ultimately, to the United States Supreme Court.

While she waited, a federal court in Oklahoma ordered the admission of George McLaurin to the graduate program in education based upon the Supreme Court's ruling in Ada Lois's case. In October 1948, because of Ada Lois's courage and tenacity, McLaurin became the first African American to attend the University of Oklahoma. Other Black students enrolled in graduate courses the following semesters.

It took more than a year and a half for Ada Lois to finally be admitted to OU. The legislature reluctantly decided that it was time to stop funding the unused Langston Law School and closed it. Oklahoma had to admit Ada Lois to OU. She had been able to stay the course because, as she said, "My driving force was that I believed in democracy and citizenship according to my concept that citizens require equality of treatment. There is no such thing as separate but equal."[44]

In June 1949, Ada Lois finally walked up the stairs to OU's Monnett Hall, which housed the law school. She commuted from Chickasha because Norman was still a sundown town. She was two weeks behind in her studies because classes had begun before Langston Law School had officially closed. She sat in her designated seat in the roped off "colored" section in the back of the classroom. She was restricted from access to the law library and the student union. She studied under the professor who had argued against her admission before the Oklahoma and United States Supreme Courts but who would eventually become an important mentor.

Most significantly, for the very first time in her life, she was in classes with white students. Not all the students welcomed her presence. She would sometimes hear "nigger" muttered as she walked by. There was a group of students who reached out to help her catch up on the material that she had missed, providing her with notes, and allowing her to read their books. But mainly she was alone, sitting off by herself, not even befriended by the two other female students.

Like all law students, she was taking a rigorous course of study. Unlike any of her classmates, the nation was watching her academic performance. Could she pass her courses? Would she actually graduate? Admission did not end the pressure. Enrollment did not remove the spotlight.

Ada Lois Sipuel Fisher on her first day at OU College of Law, 1949. Courtesy of the Fisher family.

Ada Lois did graduate from the OU College of Law. She passed the bar and became a practicing attorney. Now she was the attorney handling desegregation cases, challenging restrictions on public parks in Oklahoma City and denials of admission of African American students to colleges. But developing a lucrative client base proved difficult.

Ada Lois eventually left the practice of law and spent most of her professional career as an administrator and professor at Langston University, where she had completed her undergraduate studies. In 1992, in a historic appointment, Ada Lois was named to the Board of Regents for the University of Oklahoma.

An appointment to the very board that had fought her admission showed the progress that had been achieved because of her courage, determination, and steadfastness. As she said, "I thrive on adversity. . . . If you tell me I can't do that, I'm going to do it. Was it worth it? Most certainly yes. Would I do it again? Yes."[45] Because Ada Lois had said yes, legally sanctioned racial educational segregation had been ruled unconstitutional. Millions of children and young people were now able to learn from each other in integrated schools and colleges. Never again would a person be lawfully told that they could not attend a school because of their race.

NOTES

1. "Ada Lois Sipuel," *Black Dispatch*, August 11, 1951, 4.

2. "State NAACP Conference Plans Bold Attack upon Education Inequalities in Sooner State," *Black Dispatch*, November 8, 1946, 1.

3. Throughout this chapter, I use "Ada Lois" rather than "Sipuel Fisher" because I want to present her as the young woman that she was, not the icon that she became. She took a courageous stand and found within herself the strength, determination, and resolve to fuel her commitment.

4. Ada Lois Sipuel Fisher, *A Matter of Black and White: The Autobiography of Ada Lois Sipuel Fisher* (Norman: University of Oklahoma Press, 1996), 78–79.

5. Pearson et al. v. Murray, 169 Md. 478, 182 A. 590 (1936); State of Missouri ex rel. Gaines v. Canada, 305 US 337 (1938).

6. Memorandum to Walter White, October 24, 1945, NAACP Papers, part 3, reel 1:682, Library of Congress.

7. Sipuel Fisher, *A Matter of Black and White*, 81.

8. George Lynn Cross, *Blacks in White Colleges: Oklahoma's Landmark Cases* (Norman: University of Oklahoma Press, 1993), 36–38.

9. Cross, *Blacks in White Colleges*, 36.

10. Roscoe Dunjee to Thurgood Marshall, January 15, 1946, NAACP Papers, part 3, reel 13: 342–43.

11. Dunjee to Marshall, January 15, 1946.
12. "Negro Barred from Enrolling at University," *Oklahoman*, January 15, 1946, 1, 5.
13. "STUDENT OPINION: A Clear Cut Issue," *Oklahoma Daily*, January 15, 1946, 2.
14. Petition, Ada Lois Sipuel, Petitioner, vs. Board of Regents of the University of Oklahoma, filed April 6, 1946, https://digitalprairie.ok.gov/digital/collection/sipuel/id/377/+6.
15. "Ada Lois Sipuel Denied Right to Enter Law School at the University of Oklahoma," *Black Dispatch*, July 13, 1946, 2.
16. "Original Case Made Part 2 *Ada Lois Sipuel v. OU Board of Regents*," 43, https://digitalprairie.ok.gov/digital/collection/sipuel/id/353/rec/19.
17. "Presenting the Oklahoma NAACP in Chickasha," *Black Dispatch*, November 23, 1946, 1.
18. "Separate Schools: Oklahoma University Youth Makes Impassioned Address to State NAACP Conference," *Black Dispatch*, November 16, 1946, 1.
19. "Oklahomans at Home and Abroad," *Sooner Magazine* 5, no. 9 (June 1933): 267.
20. "Oklahoma Law School under NAACP Fire," March 7, 1947, NAACP Papers, part 3, reel 14:035.
21. Sipuel Fisher, *A Matter of Black and White*, 119–20.
22. "Asks High Court End School Segregation," *New York Times*, January 8, 1948, 23.
23. Enrollment for the spring semester would begin in just two weeks, on January 26, 1948.
24. "Supreme Court Questions Oklahoma Counsel on Banning Negro Girl from Law College," *Washington Post*, January 9, 1948, 12.
25. "Ada's Day in Court," *Time*, January 19, 1948, 62.
26. "High Court Caustic on OU Negro Ban, Early Rule Hinted," *Oklahoman*, January 9, 1948, 1.
27. Sipuel v. Board of Regents of the University of Oklahoma et al., 332 US 631 (1948).
28. "Walter White: People, Politics and Places: A Crushing Rebuke," *Chicago Defender*, January 31, 1948, 15.
29. "The Court and Color," *Newsweek*, January 19, 1948, 86.
30. Roy Wilkins, "The Watchtower," *Los Angeles Sentinel*, January 22, 1948, 5.
31. "Sipuel Victory Brings Educational Equality Step Nearer, Says NAACP," NAACP Papers, part 3, reel 14:74.
32. Quinton Peters and Ed O'Brien, "SIPUEL WINS CASE!" *Oklahoma Daily*, January 13, 1948, 1.
33. "Court Ruling 'Wonderful,' Says Negro," *Chicago Daily Tribune*, January 15, 1948, 20.
34. "'Behind Scenes' Talks Continue in Negro Case," *Norman Transcript*, January 15, 1948, 1.
35. Sipuel v. Board of Regents of University of Oklahoma, 190 P.2d 437, 199 OK 586, (1948).
36. Oklahoma State Regents for Higher Education, Resolution no. 142, January 19, 1948.

37. Minutes of First Meeting, Regents' Committee on Langston University School of Law, January 19, 1948.

38. "Regents Name Oklahoma City Trio to Operate New Law School for Negroes," *Oklahoman*, January 25, 1948, 1.

39. "Oklahoma Students Protest Negro Ban," *New York Times*, January 30, 1948, 25; "Burn Fourteenth Amendment," *Washington Post*, January 30, 1948, 14; "Open New Attack on U. of Okla. Bias: White Students Cremate Copy of 14th Amendment," *Pittsburgh Courier*, February 7, 1948, 1; "An Example for Elders," *Atlanta Daily World*, February 1, 1948, 4; "Whites Burn Law in Protest as Negress Ban," *Daily Mirror* (London), January 30, 1948.

40. Allan A. Saxe, "Protest and Reform: The Desegregation of Oklahoma City" (PhD diss., University of Oklahoma, 1969), 88.

41. "Ada Lois Sipuel Fisher Accepts Token from Sigma Gamma Rho Sorority," *Black Dispatch*, February 14, 1948, 3.

42. *Ada Lois Sipuel*, no. 14807, Transcript of Oral Proceedings, May 24, 1948, Oklahoma Archives, 123.

43. *Ada Lois Sipuel*, no. 14807, 141.

44. "Courage," *Oklahoman*, February 26, 1995, 2.

45. "Courage."

RACHEL E. WATSON

8

BEYOND THE WALLS

From Sit-Ins to Integration in the
Activism of Clara Luper

On August 19, 1958, members of the NAACP Youth Council walked into Katz Drug Store and requested to be served at the counter. Katz Drug Store had no problem serving white people at its lunch counter, but refused the group of thirteen children, the youngest of whom was six, because they were Black. After a few days of the group sitting in the drugstore until closing time, Katz decided to desegregate the chain of stores throughout the region, marking a victory for the Youth Council.[1] Clara Luper is best known for the work she did to grow the NAACP Youth Council and support her students through the fight for integration, first with a letter-writing campaign politely asking that store owners serve Black people of their own volition and then, when letters failed, with sit-ins. However, Luper's anti-racist beliefs and activism took her beyond downtown Oklahoma City, and few people know that she was responsible for integrating parts of Tulsa and Lawton and was instrumental in the negotiations between Oklahoma City and sanitation workers during the 1964 sanitation strike.

Clara Luper's actions and activism were largely responsible for the desegregation of public spaces in Oklahoma City. Her work as a teacher and a Youth Council adviser stemmed from a pedagogy of resisting anti-Blackness on interpersonal and institutional levels.[2] The same beliefs that drove her classroom also moved through her activism, where she supported her students' desire to realize freedom in Oklahoma. Previous studies of her work emphasize the way she challenged anti-Black racism on an individual level but leave out the ways she challenged inherently problematic institutions. These studies also sideline her work in the classroom and her beliefs in favor of naming her more public-facing actions.

Luper's name frequently comes up in discussions of Oklahoma history, particularly in discussions centered on the Oklahoma civil rights movement or Black women in Oklahoma.[3] Much of the scholarship on Clara Luper barely scratches the surface of the extent of her involvement in desegregation. While some recent scholarship is shifting toward acknowledging or emphasizing the role of Black women in the civil rights movement, the majority of the work on Luper and the sit-ins in Oklahoma City is repetitive. The work presented here is a shift from traditional histories of Luper's activism to a history that centers her as a Black feminist leader, using decolonial and feminist tools to analyze her pedagogy and methods. This chapter also aims to remind readers of Clara's work beyond Oklahoma City; she led marches in Lawton and Tulsa and worked for causes beyond desegregation in public accommodation.

Clara Luper was born in 1923 in Okfuskee County, Creek Nation, in east-central Oklahoma, formerly Indian Territory. Her parents, Ezell and Isabell Shepard, worked primarily blue-collar jobs to support their family. Luper's father repeatedly expressed to her the belief that one day Black people would not have to be subservient to white people. He died in 1957, and, when making the decision to initiate the sit-ins, Luper thought of how he told his children that someday they would be able to go to restaurants, parks, and zoos.[4] Even though he had fought for his country, her father had never been able to sit down and eat a meal in a restaurant. Segregation in Oklahoma meant that any sit-down restaurants were white-only, and Black people had to take their food to go in a brown paper bag.

Her early schooling at Hoffman, a one-room schoolhouse for African American students, was far from ideal, using discarded textbooks from the white elementary school. Living in segregated Oklahoma meant racial separation in all aspects of private life, and Luper's parents taught her how to survive under white supremacy. After graduating from her segregated high school, Luper attended Langston University, majoring in mathematics and minoring in history, earning her degree in 1944. In 1950, she became the first Black student in the University of Oklahoma's graduate history program, earning her MA degree in 1951. She taught in Oklahoma City public schools until her retirement in 1989.[5] For twenty years she continued to deliver public lectures on racial justice. She died in 2011, survived by her children, Calvin Luper, Marilyn Hildreth, and Chelle Wilson.[6]

To understand how Luper and her students tore down the walls of segregation, we must first learn more about core beliefs that she sought to pass on through her classroom and in her role as NAACP Youth Council adviser. Luper believed that education was an essential step in encouraging the kind of activism that she and her students used to accomplish substantial change in their community. One cannot be an activist without proper education about the issues, and Luper believed that an education in history outside the textbooks often assigned to classrooms was particularly necessary. As she stated in an oral history interview in 2005, "The textbooks must be changed. For example, the Oklahoma history books, before 1980, hardly had anything about women, and women were the backbone of the state. The more you know about women, the more you know about blacks, the more you know about Indians, the better off you are. History books have been written by white men."[7] The employment of an inclusive anti-racist history in her classroom made it easier for Luper to mobilize her students for the change she sought to make in Oklahoma regarding segregation. She taught a history that was inclusive of women and people of color even though the textbooks she relied on did not include those narratives. She knew, however, that many educators did not understand that, which explains the need for a change in the textbooks.[8] Her classroom was just as important to her activism as the sit-ins, because without her pedagogy of anti-racism, she would not have been able to mobilize young students against white supremacy.

Being in the classroom in order to have direct relationships with students was very important to Luper as teaching was what she loved to do. In the summer of 1970, her position as a teacher at Northwest Classen High School was threatened by the Oklahoma City Public Schools Board of Education when it offered her a position as a research assistant rather than a teacher for the upcoming school year.[9] Luper refused the research position, despite the pay increase that accompanied it, because, as she stated, "As a teacher, I feel that my greatest contribution comes as a result of my direct contact with the human product. . . . My first and only love has always been the student."[10] In the classroom, Luper centered her students and their needs rather than the curriculum, making her attentive to the students and the problems impacting her community. Doing so is what enabled her action in Oklahoma to be so effective in accomplishing desegregation and equal access to public spaces. The majority of white educators she worked with were not aware of the needs of the Black students.[11]

Luper's position enabled her to teach about broader racism in the United States, beyond the anti-Blackness that she and most of her students personally experienced during the sit-ins. Whiteness operates to the disadvantage of all people of color, not just Black people, and evidence that Luper taught about the discrimination other people faced because of white supremacy is best seen in a speech written by one of her students.[12] Barbara Posey, the president of the NAACP Youth Council in 1960, discussed the racism experienced by American Indians in a speech at the Fifty-First Annual NAACP Convention: "We will go back to Africa *when* the English go back to England, the Irish back to Ireland, the French back to France and when the white man gives America back to the Indian and goes home. Until then, we, the youth of America, will carry out our plans for a democratic America."[13] The protesters were often told to go back to Africa, and this response calls attention to the colonization of the Americas and the land stolen from Indigenous peoples. Barbara Posey, as Luper's student, was knowledgeable about the oppression others faced and recognized that Blackness and Redness are in conversation because of the way white supremacy positions them.

An integral part of Clara Luper's pedagogy was viewing whiteness and Blackness as traits of individuals independent of skin color. One of her central tactics in dismantling segregation was asking white people who benefited from systemic anti-Blackness to join the struggle against white supremacy. Luper described a fellow protester, Earl Temple, as a man who was Black by choice, because "blacks come in all colors."[14] Luper's argument was not that his skin had physically gained more melanin but that he had access to white spaces and instead chose to disavow that access in favor of protesting with those who were refused service. Individual actions also had far-reaching impact in the Black freedom struggle, and desegregation in Oklahoma City would not have been accomplished if not for the belief that individuals can make substantial, enduring changes. One prime example of this is the first Black person to eat at the Anna Maude Cafeteria, one of the restaurants that took the longest to change its segregation policies: a Black baby who was smuggled into the restaurant by a white woman. This action elicited strong reactions from the white community.[15] White

Barbara Posey Jones (*left*), Clara Luper (*middle*), and Alma Posey Washington (*right*), 1983. Photograph by Roger Klock. Courtesy of the Research Division, Oklahoma Historical Society.

individuals breaking away from white civil society to protest white supremacy were a major component of the change-making mechanisms for the removal of explicit anti-Black codes from various restaurants in Oklahoma City.

For Luper as well as her students, the Black freedom movement was about an end to white supremacy. Luper imparted anti-racism to her students through her teaching that white supremacy ought to be resisted. Gwendolyn Fuller, the president of the NAACP Youth Council in 1958 and one of Luper's students, stated, "I do not believe the managers of John A. Brown's [department store lunch counter] and other restaurant owners will continue to hold on to a long lost dream of white supremacy. Rather I believe and pray that they will join with the organization and people who are working to make democracy and Christianity work in Oklahoma City."[16] Fuller's words echoed much of Luper's rhetoric; in many places in her book *Behold the Walls*, Luper discusses the people who opposed the sit-ins as being victims of a system of white supremacy.[17] Clara Luper stood firmly against white supremacy and resisted it wherever possible, and her students, like Gwendolyn Fuller, adopted that message and imitated Luper's resistance. This can also be seen in the NAACP Youth Council platform during Fuller's presidency; she and Barbara Posey articulated the Youth Council's goal as freedom through the elimination of segregation in public accommodations.[18]

Sit-in participants frequently had to remind their opposition that the protests were for the end of white supremacy, a call frequently articulated as a call for freedom. Luper relates some of the harassment protesters faced: "'Don't you wish you were white so you could eat at John A. Brown's?' the white Central High School students said. 'No,' Lynzetta Jones said, 'I don't want to be white, I just want to be free.'"[19] Several parts of the interaction here need to be analyzed. First is the white students' assumption that the desire for equal access to public spaces is the same as the desire to have white skin. The demand that civil society not discriminate against persons based on skin color is not the same as wanting to be a part of the oppressive and privileged groups in civil society. The white students' implication is that Oklahoma City's racial tensions are because of the existence of Black people and people of color, not because of the discrimination against them. The second part of this is the demand that Black humanity become a part of white civil society. Lynzetta Jones does not want to lose part of herself, her Blackness, in order to achieve total freedom but rather is calling for an end to anti-Black racism. Jones's response clarifies that Blackness and Black people are not the problem. The problem is the systemic anti-Blackness that whiteness perpetuates.

As a more effective method of achieving freedom, Clara Luper called in, rather than called out, individuals who enforced anti-Black store policy.[20] John A. Brown's was one of the most contentious loci of protest from August 1958 to late 1959, and its owner, Della Brown, was one of the people most resistant to integration.[21] She finally agreed to integrate as a result of a one-on-one conversation with Clara Luper in which Brown began to embrace Black humanity.[22]

White people in positions of power who decided to resist white supremacy were essential to integration efforts.

These core views—that knowing histories of oppression can help undo it, that people's skin color does not prevent them from fighting white supremacy, and that her relationships with students were a valuable part of her work—shaped the way Clara Luper supported students in Oklahoma City and how she moved against segregation in Tulsa and Lawton.

Before the thirteen children walked into Katz Drug Store on August 19, 1958, Luper had taken them on a trip that showed them how the world could be different. She was then a history teacher at Roscoe Dunjee High School, a majority-Black school, and used her position to teach about injustices in the world and how to correct them. In 1957, Luper wrote and directed a play called *Brother President*, which she would later turn into a film. *Brother President* showcased the nonviolence doctrine of Dr. Martin Luther King Jr.[23] The play's performance drew high turnout from all over the state, filling Dunjee High School's auditorium. After this success, the students presented the play again at East Sixth Street Christian Church, where the national youth director of the NAACP, Herbert Wright, saw it and asked them to present *Brother President* at a "Salute to Young Freedom Fighters" rally in New York City.[24] Luper planned their trip to New York City to maximize its educational value; on the way there, they took a route through mostly northern states that did not have segregation laws, meaning that many of the cast members were able to eat in restaurants and at lunch counters for the first time.[25] On the return trip, they went to Washington, DC, and visited the Tomb of the Unknown Soldier, where one student pondered, "What do you think would happen in this country if the Unknown Soldier's casket was opened and they would find out he was black?"[26] This significant moment shows that the students were beginning to imagine different possible futures for themselves and for Oklahoma. After returning from that trip, the Youth Council met and decided that they would work for freedom in downtown Oklahoma City.[27] The play and the trip's planning both contributed to the students' ability to identify a problem and decide to fix it.

Luper wrote that her position as a teacher was essential to her recruitment abilities.[28] She had ample access to young people, which enabled her to recruit Youth Council members, and she empowered them to make decisions about how to proceed. Throughout the sit-ins, both the NAACP and Luper believed that the youthfulness of the protesters allowed the group to circumvent violence;

white opposition might have been more violent or stronger if the participants had been adults.[29] In fact, when the demonstrations first started, Luper reported that the white servers and manager of Katz Drug Store accosted her for being involved because she was older and should "know better."[30] Having a group of young people engage in sit-ins and lead the majority of the protests kept the situation nonviolent, not only because of their nonviolence training but also because the opposition was reluctant to acknowledge that the children had agency and were knowingly challenging segregation.

When the Youth Council decided to protest, sit-ins were not their first course of action. They waited eighteen months after they first explicitly stated that their goal was freedom in the form of eliminating segregation in public accommodations.[31] Their first tactic for reaching this goal had been calling and writing letters to individual restaurants, requesting that individual business owners choose to desegregate.[32] They felt this tactic had the potential to work because Oklahoma City's segregation was not a municipal law, but a policy enforced by the owners, supposedly because they would lose white business if they opened their restaurants to people of color.[33] They began with this because Luper's doctrine of nonviolence was rooted in recognizing white humanity, that is, acknowledging that people with white skin are humans and can be called to combat white supremacy.[34] Luper refused systemic racism and encouraged others to refuse to participate in anti-Blackness by changing their policies. Doing so in this way offered owners an opportunity to change their segregation policies before facing other, more direct means of challenge.

The movement's goal was not to shame people into changing anti-Black policies but rather to fight against the explicitly harmful segregation codes. Barbara Posey, serving as secretary of the NAACP Youth Council in 1958, told the manager of Katz Drug Store, the first store to be targeted for sit-ins, "We don't intend to cause you or your store any embarrassment. We only want to be served."[35] Posey used the first person, "we," to articulate the demand for equal service, emphasizing the protest and the desire for change. She illustrated the unflinching anti-racist demand by highlighting the demand and pointing out that the intention was not to negatively impact store owners. Posey redirected the conversation from the focus on white business owners to the lager concern of systemic anti-Blackness in downtown Oklahoma City.

Through many years of activism against the walls of segregation, Luper and the Youth Council successfully desegregated public places in Oklahoma City. The city council passed an ordinance against segregation in public accommodations in Oklahoma City months before Lyndon B. Johnson signed the 1964 Civil Rights Act into law.[37] However, there were other issues that Luper needed to address.

On the surface, the issues of attaining fair pay for sanitation workers and integrating businesses in major urban areas might seem unrelated, but for Luper, they both fell squarely in the realm of tearing down the walls of racial inequality. At least 80 percent of sanitation workers were Black, but none of their supervisors were. Black men were barred from higher-paying positions such as driving, and they worked longer hours in lower-paying jobs. Many earned less than $500 a month, and chief among their concerns was a pay raise. They also had requests for a five-day, forty-hour work week.

Luper became involved in negotiations on behalf of the sanitation workers in a roundabout way. In 1964, she and Cecil L. Williams were appointed to a new minority employment committee to advise the city manager on how to increase minority employment. The committee met monthly to make recommendations; however, they did not have the ability to carry out any of the recommendations, so dedication among committee members waned, and they slowly stopped meeting. In 1969, new city manager Robert Oldland brought the committee back together and gave its members the power to examine and correct inequities in city staffing. They quickly discovered the treatment of Black workers in the sanitation department and recommended a pay increase as well as the promotion of Black workers into vacant supervisory positions.

Because of Luper's role on the committee, sanitation workers came to her office to meet and express their feelings about their roles in the sanitation department. She took these concerns to the committee, but the city council was reluctant to take action and address the grievances.[38] Over the course of a week, around two hundred sanitation workers came to Luper's office, asking her to speak on their behalf and deliver their demands to city hall. She agreed on the condition that the men begin a personal journey of improving their perceptions of their value as sanitation workers. She asked them to repeat after her:

"I MIGHT CARRY GARBAGE,
BUT, I AM, I AM
I AM SOMEBODY.
I MIGHT BE UNDERPAID

BUT I AM, I AM SOMEBODY."
HOLD UP YOUR HEADS.
THERE IS AS MUCH DIGNITY IN CARRYING GARBAGE
AS IN BEING CITY MANAGER.[39]

This, along with her agreement to be the spokesperson for the workers, illustrates her unwavering commitment to equality and the intrinsic value of each person, irrespective of skin color or occupation. Supporting the self-esteem of the disgruntled employees was an essential part of empowering them to agitate for themselves against the injustices they faced.

At the next meeting of the Minority Employment Committee, things were tense as Luper brought up the issues of the sanitation department. Oldland initially made some concessions, but he eventually decided that Luper was not an authorized spokesperson for the sanitation department. His early concessions included a trial period of three five-day work weeks and a three-person collection crew, but he offered no pay increase. The committee was split by race on the question of whether or not there was racial inequality in the sanitation issue, and if they could not agree on that, it would be impossible to take steps to fix those inequalities. All the Black committee members affirmed the racial inequity, while the white members voted to deny its existence. Joe Wharton, the assistant city manager, requested that Luper disclose the names of people complaining as well as the dates and times of incidents to investigate, but Luper viewed the request as an attempt to find and retaliate against any agitators.

With the committee locked in tension over whether or not there was actually a problem to discuss, it became clear that more aggressive negotiations would be necessary to make any changes to the workers' pay. The workers informed city hall of their intention to strike if demands were not met. Luper and the NAACP Youth Council organized in support of the striking workers, planning ways to feed workers and their families and agreeing to stand or lie down in front of garbage trucks to prevent strikebreakers from running their routes. The personal conflict between Luper and Oldland also escalated; in the committee meeting where Luper raised the issues, she gave incorrect numbers regarding the current pay of the sanitation workers, and Oldland used that slipup to accuse her of being "uninformed" and unable to serve as the spokesperson for the strikers.[40] Their personal dislike for each other permeated meetings and negotiations, with Luper contending that Oldland's Equity Committee was a worthless endeavor and Oldland continuing to publicly and privately refuse to recognize Luper as the spokesperson for the movement. Between August 2 and August 19, tensions increased, and Oldland promised to fire any sanitation workers who walked off the job. In the interim, A. D. Taylor, a Black man, was hired to a supervisory position, which was under the director of sanitation but overseeing four collection teams. This did little to quell the conflict.

These tensions culminated in the Black Friday strike, the protest that took place on August 19, 1969. A key difference between the Black Friday strike and the sit-ins in years prior was that this time the NAACP supported the workers' action against the walls of segregation from the beginning. During the sit-ins, the Youth Council had been taking unauthorized, unsupported action up until they proved that the sit-ins were an effective means to achieve desegregation. For Black Friday, the NAACP supported Luper and sent national officeholders to assist in organizing and demonstrating on behalf of the sanitation workers. So, while Oldland did not view Luper as a representative of the strikers, the NAACP did and helped her work with the sanitation workers to achieve their goals.

In the lead-up to Black Friday, Luper and the sanitation workers took extensive measures to prevent strikebreakers from running their garbage routes. The Youth Council, sanitation workers, and supporting community members, including Senator E. Melvin Porter and a number of local clergy, as well as representatives from the NAACP national office gathered daily at five A.M. in front of the sanitation center to stand in front of garbage trucks and prevent them from going out. Many people, including Luper, were arrested for these demonstrations, supposedly for trespassing, although there were no trespassing ordinances in effect.[41] The mayor attempted to prevent these demonstrations by passing an emergency ordinance making it illegal for groups of three or more to gather in certain locations, including city hall and the sanitation center. Police were aggressive in their arrests. Even after a garbage truck bumped Clara Robertson and pulled her fifty feet, injuring her, the police beat and arrested her, leaving her wounded in a cell. One sixty-year-old man held a plastic American flag as he lay down in front of a truck, and the police tore the flag from his hand as they cuffed him.

Luper and other strike organizers had aimed as best they could for the protest and march to be nonviolent. She drew on many of the current Youth Council members to teach what they had learned in nonviolence training to the children who came out just for the Black Friday protests. This included how to practice nonviolence in the face of massive police presence and resistance. The strike was accompanied by boycotts and marching; the Black community across Oklahoma

City gathered to march and support the workers in whatever ways they could, converging on city hall to demonstrate support for those on strike. During the strike, forty-three men decided to continue hauling garbage, and Oldland commissioned ninety-six volunteers from other city departments to maintain garbage collection routes.[42] Despite the strikebreakers, the many arrests and the ongoing boycott eventually led city hall to agree to move up the scheduled pay raise, and strike leaders negotiated for the sanitation workers who would otherwise be fired to be moved to other city departments.

Tulsa posed a greater challenge to Luper. It was more difficult for her to bring down the walls of racism there, given its distance from Oklahoma City, the center of her activities. Tulsa also had a different history of racial tensions; in 1921, white citizens of Tulsa had systematically burned down what was then called Black Wall Street, killing between thirty-six and three hundred Black people. Oklahoma City did not have the same history of violence, and whereas Luper had a rapport with the Oklahoma City police and city officials, which might have reduced the risk of violence faced by protesters in Oklahoma City, she had few connections in Tulsa.[43] Despite all this, Luper did not hesitate to agree when Shirley Williams Scoggins, a former student of Luper and the youth director of Tulsa's Congress of Racial Equality (CORE) chapter, called to ask for help organizing against discrimination in Tulsa.

Because the aim for Tulsa was similar to what they had worked for in Oklahoma City, so were the tactics. The NAACP Youth Council organized a bus trip to Tulsa, where Williams and others had been working to gather local supporters. Despite more than four hundred people locally joining in the march and rally, the Tulsa NAACP Youth Council distanced itself from the consequences of the demonstration, blaming the NAACP Youth Council's Oklahoma City chapter and CORE for organizing the event without their involvement. The demonstration was Tulsa's first civil rights parade, and the police presence was heavy. This might have been because a segregationist group, the White Citizens' Council, had applied and been rejected for a parade permit at the same times and locations, leading some to think they might make an appearance.[44] The *Oklahoman* did not note their presence, but Luper indicated that there was an angry crowd of White Citizens' Council members gathered as the freedom marchers moved toward their destination, Borden's Cafeteria.[45] Regardless, the freedom marchers' nonviolent intentions and the police presence, including at least seventeen officers on motorcycles, helped ensure that there was not a conflict between the White Citizens' Council and the freedom march participants.

While the demonstration did not turn violent, Luper and many of those who traveled with her from Oklahoma City were among the thirty-three people arrested for trespassing. After speaking at the rally, a small group attempted to enter Borden's Cafeteria in the Northland Shopping Center, where the staff refused to let them in. Luper and a few others found the rear entrance unlocked and entered through the kitchen, where they stayed, singing hymns and reciting the psalms, after being blocked from the dining room. The group that was gathered outside recited the Pledge of Allegiance and attempted to enter when the employees tried to let their white customers leave.[46]

After months of demonstrations, just before the 1964 Civil Rights Act made discrimination illegal nationally, Tulsa passed an accommodation law banning discrimination.

After the Civil Rights Act made segregation in the NAACP Youth Council's previous battlegrounds illegal, the group turned its attention to Lawton. That city offered a context where the discrimination Black people faced felt even more unjust. As home to Fort Sill, a military base, most of the patrons to Lawton businesses were servicemen and their families. One business in particular, Doe Doe Amusement Park, where white troops would often spend a weekend of fun when they had time off, refused to allow Black customers. This persisted even after the passage of the Civil Rights Act; a district court had decided, based on a lawsuit over the issue, that the park was exempt from the public accommodations provisions.[47] The owners were still free to exclude customers based on the color of their skin.

It made sense then that the group chose Lawton for its next fight. Attorney and key organizer Archibald Hill had moved to Lawton and revived its inactive NAACP chapter, beginning his organizing efforts with voter registration drives. He said, "Man, Lawton, Oklahoma is Jim Crow's headquarters and we've got to do something."[48] Similar to businessowners in Oklahoma City and Tulsa, the owners of Doe Doe, Ben Hutchins and his son, Ben Hutchins Jr., had the power to decide independently whether or not to integrate. The reborn NAACP in Lawton had organized a number of protests and even met with Major General Harry Critz, who oversaw Fort Sill at the time, to ask if he would declare the park off-limits to servicemen.[49] However, months of marches, gatherings, protests, and petitions had not produced the desired results.

The most publicized effort to integrate the amusement park came early in the summer in the form of a march from Oklahoma City to Lawton. E. Melvin Porter, Clara Luper, and the leaders of the NAACP Youth Council collectively decided to march one hundred miles to support the continued desegregation efforts. They dedicated the march to Willie J. Cole, a fellow organizer and graduate of Douglas High School who had been killed fighting in Vietnam during the first week of June. It really hit home with the students that Black soldiers could fight and die for the United States but could not swim at Doe Doe.[50] Beginning June 16, 1966, the youths and their supporters, including Porter, gathered at the state capitol, sharing in speeches and songs before setting off on their long march. Luper reported that the children were largely eager and determined to keep to their goals and complete the march but that Porter had a very difficult time making the trek and was the primary reason for slow progress. At one point in the trip, the weather report predicted that there would be rain, and Porter asked the group to turn around and give up on account of the weather. They took a vote, and ninety-nine out of one hundred voted to press forward in spite of the expected poor conditions. They were determined to complete the demonstration.

As the group walked, they encountered very different reactions from some of the towns on their route. They passed through Tuttle under the watchful eye of four highway patrolmen, the Tuttle City Police Department, and many white onlookers, most of whom were silent. The notable exception was a group of white boys shouting, "Hey niggers, what are you doing in my town? This is my town and I don't need any niggers in my town."[51] This is in stark contrast to the reactions of those in Chickasha, where supporters, most of whom were Black, gathered at City Park, singing:

> Freedom, Freedom, Everybody wants Freedom
> Chickasha wants Freedom.
> Lawton wants Freedom.
> Everybody wants Freedom.[52]

Supporters from Oklahoma City, Lawton, and Chickasha pooled their resources to provide the group with a hearty meal during their visit to City Park, and the show of love for the demonstrators' efforts gave the group a new sense of hope and a sense of the importance of their work.

The Youth Council's arrival in Lawton became a celebration; people from all over Oklahoma traveled to welcome the group and join them as they converged outside Doe Doe Amusement Park. While the spirits were high and the NAACP firmly believed in the importance of the demonstration, ultimately Ben Hutchins and his son were unmoved by the march. It was not until 1968, two years after the hundred-mile march, that Ben Hutchins Jr. announced the integration of the park, largely in response to Fort Sill's decision earlier that year to make the park off-limits to all personnel because it served only white patrons.[53] It remains unclear why General Charles P. Brown, who succeeded General Critz as Fort Sill commander, decided to place Doe Doe off-limits when Critz had claimed that such an act was out of his jurisdiction. When reflecting on integration forty-two years after the fact, Ben Hutchins Jr. stated that his father had been a stubborn man and only wanted to wait for the Supreme Court decision on whether or not the Civil Rights Act applied to the amusement park.[54]

Clara Luper's life and work were dedicated to tearing down the walls of injustice that she and her students regularly encountered while living in Oklahoma. Her activism and organizing were driven by her anti-racist beliefs, which she also fostered in her students. With the help of many other activists, leaders, and, of course, the students in her chapter of the NAACP Youth Council, she tore down the walls of segregation in Lawton, Tulsa, and Oklahoma City and spent her life fighting for freedom.

NOTES

1. Joel Edward Baehler, "Organizing the 'Living Dead': Civil Rights in Oklahoma City and Tulsa, Oklahoma, 1954–1964" (MA thesis, Oklahoma State University, 2012), 57.

2. In this chapter, whiteness and Blackness are understood as ontological foundations of civil society, particularly in the United States. Anti-Blackness specifically operates on different levels, between individuals and organizations that favor whiteness over Blackness. Whiteness and anti-Blackness also have gendered implications, meaning gender is a necessary tool for deconstructing these ontologies. This is drawn from theorists such as Frank Wilderson III, Tiffany King, Alexander Weheliye, and Sylvia Wynter, who in turn draw on the works of Frantz Fanon, whom Luper might have read. See Frantz Fanon, *The Wretched of the Earth* (reprint; New York: Grove, 2005); Frank Wilderson III, *Red, White, and Black: Cinema and the Structures of U.S. Antagonisms* (Durham, NC: Duke University Press, 2010); Tiffany King, "In the Clearing: Black Female Bodies, Space, and Settler Colonial Landscapes" (PhD diss., University of Maryland, 2013); Alexander Weheliye, *Habeas Viscus: Racializing Assemblages, Biopolitics, and Black Feminist Theories of the Human* (Durham, NC: Duke University Press, 2014); Sylvia Wynter, "Unsettling the Coloniality of Being/Power/Truth/Freedom: Towards the Human, After Man, Its Overrepresentation—An Argument," *CR: The New Centennial Review* 3, no. 3 (2003): 257–337.

3. The term "civil rights movement" refers to the period of the Black freedom struggle, roughly 1954–1968, but it is important to acknowledge that the struggle for Black rights began well before 1954 and continues to this day.

4. Clara Luper, *Behold the Walls* (Oklahoma City: Jim Wire, 1979), 5.

5. Linda Williams Reese, "Clara Luper and the Oklahoma City Civil Rights Movement: 1958–1964," in *African American Women Confront the West: 1600–2000*, ed. Quintard Taylor and Shirley Ann Moore (Norman: University of Oklahoma Press, 2003), 328–32.

6. Dennis Hevesi, "Clara Luper, a Leader of Civil Rights Sit-Ins, Dies at 88," *New York Times*, June 11, 2011.

7. Clara Luper, interviewed by Rose Aguilar, August 1, 2005, Clara Luper Collection, Research Division, Oklahoma Historical Society.

8. Clara Luper, interview by Karen M. Scott Clark, March 31, 1994, partial transcript, in Scott Clark, "The Contributions of African American Women in Education in Oklahoma" (PhD Diss., Oklahoma State University, 1996), 108.

9. "Clara Fired? Boss Says No," *Oklahoman*, August 14, 1970.

10. Clara Luper to Robert Cheney, August 18, 1970, Clara Luper Collection, Research Division, Oklahoma Historical Society.

11. Luper, interviewed by Scott Clark, 108.

12. Critical race theorist Frank Wilderson III identifies Blackness, whiteness, and Redness as the three structures that are the foundation for United States civil society. It is necessary to discuss the three in conversation because of the historical foundation of the United States. Tiffany King gives a better explanation of how all three work together, explaining that the Settler/Master clears Native flesh and enslaves Black flesh. See Wilderson, *Red, White, and Black*; King, "In the Clearing."

13. Barbara Posey, untitled speech, 51st Annual NAACP Convention, Minneapolis, Minnesota, June 24, 1960, quoted in Davis W. Houck and David E. Dixon, eds., *Women in the Civil Rights Movement, 1954–1965* (Jackson: University Press of Mississippi, 2009), 122, emphasis in original.

14. Luper, *Behold the Walls*, 77.

15. Luper, *Behold the Walls*, 66–67.

16. "NAACP Youth Council Questions and Answers," *Black Dispatch*, October 10, 1958.

17. Luper, *Behold the Walls*, 146.

18. Luper, *Behold the Walls*, 2–3.

19. Luper, *Behold the Walls*, 25.

20. "Calling out" refers to the practice of pointing out problematic behavior in another person, usually publicly, to get them to stop that behavior. Conversely, "calling in" is usually done privately to educate a person about their errors and get them to change their behavior after self-reflection.

21. "NAACP Sets New Moves," *Oklahoman*, September 21, 1959.

22. Luper, *Behold the Walls*, 51–53.

23. Luper, *Behold the Walls*, 1–2.

24. Luper, *Behold the Walls*, 7.

25. Luper, *Behold the Walls*, 1–2.

26. Luper, *Behold the Walls*, 2.

27. Luper, *Behold the Walls*, 3.

28. Luper, *Behold the Walls*, 1.
29. "Cities' Negros Ponder Future of 'Sitdowns,'" *Oklahoman*, August 31, 1958.
30. Luper, *Behold the Walls*, 9.
31. Luper, *Behold the Walls*, 2–3.
32. Carl R. Graves, "The Right to Be Served: Oklahoma City's Lunch Counter Sit-ins, 1958–1964," *Chronicles of Oklahoma* 59, no. 2 (Summer 1981): 153–54.
33. Barbara Posey and Gwendolyn Fuller, "Protest Drug Counter Discrimination," *Crisis* 65, no. 10 (December 1958): 612.
34. Luper, *Behold the Walls*, 7.
35. Posey and Fuller, "Protest Drug Counter Discrimination," 613.
36. Graves, "The Right to Be Served," 154.
37. "OC Ordinance Wins Approval," *Daily Ardmoreite* (Ardmore, OK), June 3, 1964.
38. Luper, *Behold the Walls*, 211.
39. Luper, *Behold the Walls*, 213.
40. Luper, *Behold the Walls*, 218.
41. Luper, *Behold the Walls*, 231–32.
42. "Committee Urges Friday Cutoff to Regain Jobs," *Oklahoman*, August 20, 1969.
43. "Pair Were Best of Adversaries," *Tulsa World*, November 28, 1989.
44. "Tulsa Arrests 33 in Demonstration," *Tulsa World*, March 31, 1964.
45. Luper, *Behold the Walls*, 186.
46. Luper, *Behold the Walls*, 186.
47. "Doe Doe Owners Integrate Pool," *Lawton (OK) Constitution*, May 3, 1968.
48. Luper, *Behold the Walls*, 189.
49. "General Won't Put Park Off-Limits," *Oklahoman*, August 28, 1966.
50. Luper, *Behold the Walls*, 197.
51. Luper, *Behold the Walls*, 203.
52. Luper, *Behold the Walls*, 204.
53. "Lawton Park Voluntarily Integrated," *Oklahoman*, May 4, 1968.
54. "42 Years Ago Today, a March towards Equal Opportunities," *Oklahoman*, July 4, 2008.

SARAH EPPLER JANDA

9

"TO SPEAK SO FORTHRIGHTLY AS TO OFFEND"

The Civil Rights Activism and Confinement of Rosalyn "Rosie" Coleman Gilchrist

"Patient has been mentally ill since January 1958" but has "become much worse," asserted the 1963 notation in the "Allegation" box on the first page of Rosalyn Coleman Gilchrist's file at Central State (Griffin Memorial) Hospital. The complaint against Gilchrist maintained that she was "giving away all their furniture and belongings to help the cause of the colored race" and that she was planning to "sign over their home to them" as well. To be sure, the "Allegation" box contained multiple inaccuracies, including the claim that she "leaves her teenage boys alone and makes no provisions for them" and that she "says her family does not matter as much as the cause."[1] Most striking, however, is the simple fact that a divorced mother of three would find herself confined to a mental institution for five years because of her civil rights activism. While there is a long history of women being confined to mental institutions for failing to adhere to the gender or religious norms of a given period, there are multiple factors that make Gilchrist's confinement—and release—particularly remarkable.[2] In order to understand that, however, it is first necessary to examine how she came to support civil rights and how this, in turn, became a socially constructed—and persecuted—label of insanity.

Rosalyn "Rosie" Coleman was born on December 11, 1910, in Vernon, Texas, where she grew up and later married John Gilchrist. They had a son, Gordon, and twin boys, Jim and Joe (the latter of whom later changed his name to Coleman). In 1954, the family settled in Warr Acres, a small suburb of Oklahoma City, and after two years, John Gilchrist began working in Nashville, which kept him away from the family much of the time. In his memoir, *Spoke: A Mother. A Son. Civil Rights. Vietnam.* (2013), Coleman describes the more relaxed atmosphere that existed during his father's long absences, concluding, "On his visits, we'd bear our father's unceasing wrath for two miserable days, and then we'd promptly forget he was ever there when he boarded the plane on Monday to return to Nashville." Coleman described his father's stilted interactions with the rest of the family: "I have no recollection of my father laughing. He never hugged or kissed. I can't recall a single instance of his showing affection to my mother or any of his kids."[3]

While Coleman recounts happy memories in their home during his father's absences, the strain on the family during those visits home reached an entirely new level on June 6, 1959. Coleman recalled being awakened in the middle of the night by the sound of his parents arguing. When he woke the next morning, he and the rest of the family began getting ready for church until he heard a loud sound coming from the bathroom. At first, he thought the bathroom was on fire, but then he realized that it was his mother. She was rushed to the hospital with third-degree burns over 90 percent of her body and was not expected to survive.[4] Coleman and other family members thought it might have been a suicide attempt, but they quietly ignored it at the time. Dr. Hubert M. Anderson, an intern at Baptist Hospital in Oklahoma City, used experimental new treatments for severe burn victims in an effort save Gilchrist and reduce her pain. She spent more than five months in the hospital and returned for two dozen additional surgeries over the next few years until she finally decided she did not want to undergo any more operations despite still being badly disfigured.[5]

By the time Gilchrist decided to forgo any further surgeries, she had already begun participating in the civil rights movement. She learned about the civil rights activism going on in Oklahoma City through her friendship with the African American nurses who cared for her at Baptist Hospital. These nurses spent almost three years taking care of her during her numerous hospital stays.

Coleman does not recall any white nurses attending to his mother during that period. The African American nurses were friendly to him, and they seemed to take a genuine interest in his mother and her family.[6]

While Gilchrist became friendly with many of her nurses, one in particular, Mrs. Fulbright, played an especially important role in her care. Coleman recounts Fulbright consoling his mother during her first stay at Baptist when she was in so much pain that she wanted to die. Fulbright prayed for Gilchrist and reminded her that her sons needed her to live.[7] This friendship took on even greater significance to Gilchrist once she attempted to settle back into life outside the hospital. Coleman poignantly describes his mother's painstaking preparation to return to the family's church for the first time after the fire only to discover that she was not welcome. Reverend Garrell Dunn called Coleman's father after the service to ask that Rosie not return to the church because having her there "was too disruptive." He said that her appearance "scared the children and some of the adults."[8] Mrs. Fulbright's congregation, however, expressed no such concerns when the nurse invited Rosie to attend Calvary Baptist Church. After all, the congregation had been praying for Gilchrist's recovery for years at Fulbright's request.[9]

As her relationships with African American activists deepened, Gilchrist's marriage continued to unravel. Coleman described his father as being controlling and disapproving of his mother.[10] After many unhappy years of marriage, Rosie filed for divorce. The May 27, 1963, divorce decree noted the court finding, which stated that "the material allegations contained in the plaintiff's petition are true" and that Rosalyn Gilchrist was therefore granted an "absolute divorce" on grounds of incompatibility. She was awarded the family home at 5416 Northwest Forty-Fourth Street in Warr Acres near Oklahoma City as well as the household furniture and full custody of her teenage sons. The court directed John Gilchrist to pay her the sum of $200 monthly in child support.[11] Following her divorce, she began rebuilding her life with her sons. However, for friendship and acceptance, Gilchrist had to look beyond her all-white suburban neighborhood. She quickly found herself spending time with a growing number of African American friends while simultaneously discovering that her white friends had all but disappeared.[12] Gilchrist became committed to the civil rights movement. She participated in demonstrations, attended meetings, and eventually held meetings in her own home, which drew hostility from city officials and neighbors. A white woman inviting African Americans into her home seemed not only inappropriate but downright threatening. Coleman recalls one incident in the spring of 1963 that "greatly alarmed the neighbors." A bus carrying a group of African American teenagers from the NAACP Youth Council arrived at their house. Coleman explained that the neighbors thought it was "bad enough" that she "had been receiving black visitors one at a time, but now they were coming by the busload."[13]

Much of Gilchrist's activism remained a mystery to her sons. She did not include them in it, and they asked her no questions about it. The most thorough—if frequently inaccurate—record of her activism in 1962 and 1963 is in her medical records from the mental hospital. Ironically, the record of her activism appears as evidence of her "schizophrenic reaction, paranoid type" diagnosis.[14] Details of her activism served only to justify her confinement, not to provide serious consideration for the sacrifices she made to challenge segregation in Oklahoma City. For Gilchrist, 1963 started as a year of possibility. She found a community that accepted and supported her, and she used her experience as a burn victim to relate to others who suffered persecution and loathing. But 1963 also marked the start of her long confinement to a mental institution for acting on the very compassion that aided in her recovery. Evaluations of Gilchrist noted her "sympathy for the under-privileged," suggesting that this perhaps stemmed from "her feelings of being unloved or grief stricken in her early years."[15] That hospital personnel used this characterization as context for her diagnosis as a "schizophrenic, paranoid type" reveals much about racial and social attitudes of the time period. The notion that Gilchrist's sympathy toward African Americans constituted a sort of psychosis seems extraordinary even given the racial climate in Oklahoma at the time.

The year 1963 not only marked the start of Gilchrist's confinement, it proved pivotal in framing the direction of the civil rights movement, both in Oklahoma and nationally. Demonstrations against segregation in Oklahoma had already been underway since 1958 when Clara Luper, along with her children Calvin and Marilyn and others in the NAACP Youth Council, launched the first lunch counter sit-in in the United States at Katz Drug Store in Oklahoma City.[16] Luper and the NAACP Youth Council continued their efforts to challenge segregation in Oklahoma City and around the state. And Luper found willing allies in Rosie Gilchrist and others, such as Jodey Bateman, who supported the cause of equality.

In the summer of 1963, Jodey Bateman had just finished his freshmen year at the University of Oklahoma, where he had helped found the first chapter of Students for a Democratic Society (SDS) in the state.[17] He had become increasingly active in the civil rights movement and met Clara Luper during her effort to organize a demonstration at the Wedgewood Amusement Park in Oklahoma City. Bateman recalled the demonstration, explaining that "a bunch of us were taken to jail" and that African American civil rights attorney "E. Melvin Porter got us out." Bateman also met Rosie Gilchrist at Clara Luper's home, where they gathered to discuss the Wedgewood Amusement Park demonstration.[18]

While fifty people, including Bateman, were arrested for demonstrating against the segregation policy at the Wedgewood Amusement Park on June 22, Gilchrist was not one of them.[19] Her medical file notes that she "demonstrated with the marchers twice at Wedgewood Park," but there is no indication in her file that she was ever arrested for her participation.[20] Coleman supports this as well, saying, "My mother was never arrested." White women, explained Coleman, were often viewed as "misguided" and simply sent home for participating in demonstrations like the one at Wedgewood.[21] Jodey Bateman was also white, but he was young, male, and involved in numerous demonstrations and soon became the subject of intensive surveillance. A disfigured, middle-aged white woman's activism might have been dismissed as misguided, but Bateman's activism, and that of others like him, was viewed as subversive and even treasonous.[22] The racial and gendered conceptualization of activism and the implicit threat matrix that infused reactions to that activism reveal the extent to which paternalistic attitudes toward women dominated public discourse and actions by law enforcement.

On the one hand, the failure to arrest Gilchrist for her activism speaks to a larger societal paternalism that sought to undermine women's agency by trivializing it. On the other hand, her activism was later used to justify confining her to a mental ward precisely because her actions no longer seemed trivial but rather threatening to the status quo. Following the Wedgewood Amusement Park demonstrations, both Bateman and Gilchrist made plans to join Luper and a large group of young people to travel to Washington, DC, in August 1963 to participate in the March on Washington where Reverend Dr. Martin Luther King Jr. delivered his "I Have a Dream" speech. Bateman said that what he remembered most about listening to King speak is that "there was loud cheering and a whole sea of handkerchiefs held aloft and waving in the air."[23] It is impossible to know what Gilchrist felt as she listened to the speech from her nearby position. She never spoke about it with her family. She could not have realized it at the time, but this trip marked the end of her work with Luper and the NAACP Youth Council.

As important as it must have been to Gilchrist to accompany Clara Luper and the NAACP Youth Council to the March on Washington, her decision not to discuss it with her sons resulted in bitter disappointment and confusion. While Gilchrist was away, her son Gordon and his pregnant wife stayed in her house to keep an eye on Coleman and Jim. Coleman recalls not understanding his mother's decision to go. He felt "hopeless, deserted, and angry," and he "didn't understand where she was going or why."[24] The lack of communication between Gilchrist and her sons provided an opening for community leaders who opposed her growing involvement in the civil rights movement and, perhaps most of all, her willingness to invite African Americans into her home in *their* white neighborhood.

Despite her sons' confusion and frustration about the trip, Gilchrist nevertheless returned home believing that she had settled on a good solution to her family's growing financial difficulties, beyond whatever other satisfaction she had gained from the experience. The trip held multiple unforeseen consequences for Rosie Gilchrist, who was the only white female serving as an adult chaperone on the trip to Washington, DC. At some point during the trip, she met James West, a young African American doctor in Oklahoma City who was also acting as a chaperone. When Gilchrist learned that West wanted to buy a house closer to where he worked, she agreed to sell him hers.[25] According to Coleman, his father had stopped sending the court-mandated child support to his mother. Gilchrist took in ironing, and both Coleman and Jim got summer jobs to help pay bills.[26] Given how difficult it was to make ends meet, it is unsurprising that Gilchrist jumped at the opportunity to sell her house so that she and her two youngest sons, who were now fifteen, could move into a small apartment. Mrs. Fulbright had helped her find a job, which necessitated them moving anyway, so this perhaps seemed quite fortuitous.[27] Coleman recalled how difficult their financial situation had become: "The phone was shut off. Then the lights. And there was little food."[28]

From a purely financial standpoint, selling the house and moving made perfect sense. It is hard to imagine such a decision being deemed anything but responsible and utterly *sane*. However, Gilchrist's decision to sell her house was never understood as strictly—or even largely—a financial decision. And perhaps it was not. Warr Acres was a small, tightly controlled all-white suburb. According to Coleman, neighbors had already voiced dissatisfaction over African Americans visiting their home, but the possibility of an African American family living there set off alarm bells. As Coleman explained, "The wagons

Rosie Gilchrist (*front seat, wearing dark glasses*) on the NAACP Youth Council bus to the March on Washington in August 1963. Photograph by Johnny Melton. Courtesy of the Research Division, Oklahoma Historical Society.

started circling in Warr Acres."²⁹ Whether or not Gilchrist viewed her plan as an act explicitly challenging segregation is unclear. Even if she appreciated the social, political, and economic implications of selling her house to a Black family, she could not have foreseen the reaction from public officials and community leaders. Many neighborhoods already required that clauses be included in the sale of homes to prohibit homeowners from selling to African Americans, but this appears not to have been the case in Warr Acres. Custom alone had sufficed until Gilchrist decided to sell.

Shortly after returning home from the March on Washington trip, Gilchrist began preparing her house to be sold. While Gilchrist busied herself with cleaning the house and getting rid of unneeded items, town leaders turned their attention to her fifteen-year-old sons. Coleman recounts how he and Jim were called out of classes for private meetings about their mother. He explains, "First there was our dad. Then Nelson Beckett, the Warr Acres police chief. Then Eldon Lawson, the town mayor and its leading real estate developer. Finally, Garrell Dunn, our minister." Coleman's father described Gilchrist as being "not well" and needing help. He urged Coleman to go to Chief Beckett, and Chief Beckett in turn told Coleman and Jim, "We need to do something about your mother."[30] Reverend Dunn even picked Coleman and Jim up from school one day to take them out for lunch. He told them that "he and a lot of other people were watching out for" them, adding, "When you can't take it anymore, just go see Chief Beckett. We'll take care of it." Coleman said that he did not understand what this meant, but as things grew tense at home with his mother obsessively cleaning the house in preparation for the inspection and the pending move weighing on him, he decided that the time had come for action. And so, much to his deep and lasting regret, he went to see Chief Beckett.[31]

The town leaders moved quickly. Chief Beckett arrested Rosie Gilchrist and held her in the city jail overnight in advance of her hearing. Coleman and Jim spent the night at their minister's home, and the next day Reverend Dunn drove them to the Oklahoma County Courthouse for their mother's hearing. Coleman described the hearing as taking place "not in a courtroom, but in the private chambers of Judge Harold Theus." In addition to the judge, Jim, Coleman, their brother Gordon, Reverend Dunn, Mayor Lawson, and Chief Beckett were present. Coleman recalls that his mother "sat alone against a far wall, ignored, silent, dazed, and disbelieving" while community leaders made their case to the judge, saying, "Rosalyn Gilchrist is crazy. She's consorting with colored people. She attends a Negro church. She's had colored people over to her house. She's been arrested at Negro protests. She has gatherings of Negro children in her home. She rode a bus filled with coloreds night and day all the way to Washington and back. She's trying to sell her house in Warr Acres to a nigger doctor."[32]

Following the hearing, Judge Theus ordered Rosie Gilchrist to be confined, and she was transported to Central State (Griffin Memorial) Hospital in Norman, Oklahoma, where she spent the next five years of her life. Coleman describes how this came as "a complete surprise" to his mother, writing, "It'd never have occurred to my mother that her vengeful ex-husband and his soulless Warr Acres pals would be vile enough to have her declared insane in order to prevent her from selling her home to a black couple." He sums up the prevailing sentiment that underpinned Gilchrist's confinement, explaining that "this scarred, crippled woman was expendable, while the racially pure sanctity of their community was not."[33] Less than five months after she had been characterized by the court as truthful and granted a divorce, custody of her children, and her home, Gilchrist lost everything. Custody of her sons reverted to her husband, and she lost her house. Despite having lived in the house since 1954 and being its sole owner, the address listed in her admission file was that of her oldest son. Less than a year after her confinement, Gilchrist's home was auctioned off for the sum of $950 by Gordon, who was repeatedly referred to in the sale as the appointed "guardian of the estate of Rosalyn Gilchrist, an incompetent person."[34] There is no evidence that she received any of the proceeds from the sale.

One can only imagine the shock Gilchrist felt as she went through processing at the mental hospital, less than two months after hearing Martin Luther King Jr. speak about freedom during the March on Washington. Freedom, or rather the absence thereof, had taken on a whole new meaning for Rosie Gilchrist. Records indicate that she underwent both physical and psychiatric exams upon her arrival. Her psychiatric diagnosis was "schizophrenic reaction, paranoid type." Yet the extent of her treatment and medication remains unclear. The treatment notations are confusing at best. On the date of her release in 1968, her file indicates that she was being given phenothiazine, a tranquilizing drug commonly used to treat mental illness. However, in another portion of her file from 1967, "chemotherapy and milieu" are listed under "Treatment Summary." A few lines down, under the heading of "Recommendations," it lists medication as "none."[35]

According to later conversations between Coleman and his mother, it appears that for the first six months of her confinement, Gilchrist was kept in a wing of the hospital reserved for the criminally insane, "a wing that resembled a jail, with iron bars on the doors and windows."[36] Gilchrist also told her son on multiple occasions that she "never received any kind of therapy while in the hospital, and that she went for months, sometimes years, without seeing a doctor." As Coleman notes, the medical records he obtained for his mother in 2009, which the facility assured him were her "complete" records, offer no challenge to Gilchrist's characterization of her experience.[37] As for the notations about Gilchrist's medication, it is possible that she simply did not remember being given medication. However, it seems unlikely that hospital staff routinely administered any medication to her given that she did not take medication with her during any of her numerous furloughs away from the hospital.[38]

Several pages of Gilchrist's short medical file recount her social history and the allegations against her that resulted in her court-directed confinement. And several factors bear consideration here. First, the framing of her case reveals the interconnectivity of racial and economic motives behind Gilchrist's confinement. Second, her confinement reveals the precarious nature of freedom for women who fail to adhere to norms. Third, her case raises serious questions about mental health practices for a patient who might well have benefited from counseling given her family's assumption that the 1959 fire was a failed suicide effort. Fourth, her case reveals the intersectionality of racial, gender, and disability discrimination in the development of Gilchrist's predilection for activism.

The interconnectivity of racial and economic motives in Gilchrist's confinement are profound. No doubt town leaders opposed Gilchrist selling her home to an African American doctor because they wanted to maintain their all-white community, but so, too, did they have reason for economic concerns. Historically, when African American families moved into previously all-white neighborhoods, real estate values also dropped.[39] Eldon Lawson, the mayor of Warr Acres, also developed real estate and certainly had an interest in protecting his investments. The broader racial fear—beyond economics—reveals a much deeper element of racism at work, and this is apparent in the varying ways in which the planned sale of Gilchrist's home is characterized in her medical file. The initial complaint against Gilchrist describes her as "preparing to sign over her home to them."[40] In an assessment of her "present illness" that was written a week after her confinement at the hospital, Gilchrist is described as having made plans to "turn over" her house "to the NAACP organization in order that they might move to her part of town." Her plan to "sign her house over to the NAACP," the report explains, ended when "her son had her picked up and she was brought before a sanity hearing and sent to this hospital by court commitment."[41]

Three days after the characterization of Gilchrist as planning to sign over her home to the NAACP, yet another (slightly more accurate) account emerged. Social worker Clara Tatge described Rosie as trying to "give away her house to a negro doctor," identifying James West by name. Tatge offers a narrative of events that, while inaccurate in many regards (including the fact that Gilchrist planned to sell, not give away, her home), nevertheless provides a compelling glimpse into the clearly stated justification for Gilchrist's confinement, which had less to do with her consorting with African Americans and more to do with the pending sale of her house. According to Tatge, Gilchrist's "sons were quite indignant because she was asking so many negro people into the house and embarrassing them and she would punish the sons by refusing to give them any meals." This, Coleman, explains is simply untrue. Tatge goes on to explain that the older son talked to the court (this also is contradicted by Coleman's own role in the arrest of his mother) and that the court "suggested admission here as one way of keeping her from getting rid of all their resources."[42] In multiple places, Gilchrist's interactions with her sons are mischaracterized. However, one thing that is revealed in the last sentence is that the court, not the sons, identified the confinement of Gilchrist as a viable solution for stopping the sale of her house. The power of the state to not only support but enforce white supremacy is both shocking and profound.

While much of the attention in Gilchrist's medical file centers on her civil rights activism and her plan to sell her house to James West, another central complaint against her that emerged was her interest in and empathy for lepers. Her concern for lepers is noted in several areas. Coleman explains that his mother believed her scars and disfigurement resembled those of lepers, and she wanted to do something to help them. Given her own experiences of ostracism within her church and community, she understood all too well what it was like to have people either stare at her or ignore her altogether. In fact, she appears to have encouraged the doctor who treated her burns to help lepers.[43] This, too, is found in her medical file as further evidence that she was delusional. As one entry in her chart explains, "She is delusional in that she is trying to influence people, her doctors, to give up their jobs and go where she thinks they can do the most good."[44] In the same way that Gilchrist's civil rights activism was cited as evidence of her insanity, so, too, was her support for lepers. And so her emerging efforts at disability activism served only to further justify her confinement in the unsympathetic minds of those medical professionals who evaluated her.

Similar manifestations of her compassion and kindness appear elsewhere in Gilchrist's medical file as evidence of mental illness. Social worker Lela Jones describes her as "very demanding," and the evidence that follows includes her leaving the hospital on a pass and securing a "donation of $50.00 to put in a washing machine for the ward."[45] In yet another notation, under the heading "Reason for Hospitalization," is the false assertion that Gilchrist gave away much of the family's income when her husband worked away from home. Clara Tatge described Gilchrist as "spending money extravagantly for the less fortunate" and claimed that Gilchrist gave away much of the money to "a few really handicapped young people she knew, including her son's best friend."[46] While

Tatge greatly exaggerated Gilchrist's use of the family's money to help those less fortunate, it is nevertheless telling that she used Gilchrist's generosity as evidence of mental illness.

One day gave way to the next for Gilchrist as she struggled to adjust to her life of confinement in a mental hospital, even as she received occasional furloughs. Her file notes that "her sons were interested in her and did take her home on visits."[47] They visited the hospital when they could, and Gordon and his wife, Beverly, checked Rosie out of the hospital for weekend visits every few months before they moved out of state.[48] In year three of her confinement, her twin sons graduated from high school, and Coleman headed to Cornell University on a scholarship while Jim enrolled at Oklahoma State University. The lives of her sons moved forward even as her status in the mental hospital remained perplexing. In February 1967 and again in April, John Tawes, the reimbursement officer at Central State Hospital sent letters to Gordon (at the wrong address), requesting financial support from the family for Rosie's continued care. There is no evidence that Gordon responded to or even received the letters. And it is unclear from the letters how much information Tawes possessed about Gilchrist. He requested her social security number and asked whether she had any insurance. He wanted to arrange a payment plan with the family so they could help pay for her care.[49] Despite the lack of response from the family, Gilchrist's confinement continued.

Meanwhile, attempts to secure her own release proved futile. Gilchrist wrote letters to the governor and to various legislators asking for their help but instead found herself temporarily sent to a smaller facility in Vinita, Oklahoma (farther away from her family), and denied visitation rights. According to Coleman, hospital administrators told his mother that she would not be allowed to return to Norman unless she stopped writing letters and seeking her release.[50] And so she stopped. Perhaps the most telling problem Gilchrist faced in challenging her confinement appears in the following assessment of her mental state. Ward psychiatrist Louise Farr concluded that Gilchrist's "insight lacks reality" because "she does not believe that she is mentally ill."[51] Such circular reasoning made it impossible for Gilchrist to defend herself. Disability designations, including institutionalization, have historically been weaponized to challenge the power and autonomy of those considered inferior. As historian Kim Neilson explains, "At varying times, African Americans, immigrants, gays, lesbians, poor people, and women have been defined categorically as defective citizens incapable of full civic participation."[52] Gilchrist's refusal to view herself as insane became a weapon in the hands of those who sought to maintain her confinement.

Just as 1963 proved a germinal year—both for King's "I Have a Dream" speech and for Gilchrist's confinement—so, too, did 1968. Despite the plethora of personal accounts and scholarship on the impact of King's 1968 assassination, it remains difficult to fully appreciate the wide-ranging ripple effect that it had on so many lives, including those of Coleman and his mother. A week after King's assassination, Coleman wrote a letter to the Oklahoma City Draft Board and violated federal law by returning his draft card to them. Inspired by King's eloquent critique of the Vietnam War, his mother's civil rights activism (which he now understood much better), and his own growing belief in the fundamental injustice of the war, Coleman embarked on a painful and highly publicized journey of draft resistance.[53] He left Cornell and returned to Oklahoma to face charges for his refusal to retain his draft card. This, in turn, led to a chance encounter with an old acquaintance of his mother's from her days as a civil rights activist. And this proved to be the key to her release.

After delivering a speech about draft resistance, Coleman found himself exchanging introductions with E. Melvin Porter, who asked whether he was any relation to Rosie Gilchrist. Porter wanted to know what had become of her because it had been several years since he had last seen her, and "she just seemed to drop off the face of the earth."[54] Finally, Coleman had encountered someone who could help his mother. Porter had a law degree from Vanderbilt University. In 1961, he had been elected the president of the Oklahoma City chapter of the NAACP. He became a well-known and highly respected civil rights attorney. And by 1968, Porter was serving his second term as an Oklahoma state senator, having become to the first African American elected to the state senate in 1964.[55]

When Coleman shared his mother's story, Porter offered to help get Rosie released, and things progressed quickly from there. Coleman told Porter everything he knew, including the name of the judge and the city leaders involved in his mother's hearing. Porter researched the case but found no record of Gilchrist's arrest, hearing, or commitment, so he contacted Central State Hospital and made an appointment to visit with the head administrator.

Coleman also contacted Paul Rahe, a journalist with the *Oklahoma Journal*, and asked him to accompany them to the appointment at Central State.[56] Coleman knew Rahe from high school debate as well as from Cornell, where they had both been students. In 1968, Rahe had returned to Oklahoma for the summer and found a job as a reporter.[57] He covered a range of stories, including

Coleman's draft resistance, which is why Coleman reached out to him about the effort to secure Rosie's release. Coleman described the trip that he, Porter, and Rahe made to Norman on September 3, explaining that Senator Porter "quietly and directly" demanded his mother's "immediate release." Porter told the hospital administrator that "if she wasn't released, he'd file suit that afternoon in Oklahoma County, and Paul Rahe would print the story of her illegal incarceration in the *Oklahoma Journal*." Rosie was quickly released.[58] On the final page of her medical file—dated that same day—Dr. Ernest G. Shadid wrote simply, "Psychiatric evaluation of this patient does not reveal any evidence of an overt psychosis. This patient will be discharged with restoration of mental competency." Of course, as Coleman noted, there was no final evaluation of his mother. She was released within thirty minutes of their arrival at the hospital.[59]

"The psychiatrists knew full well that Rosie was in no way deranged," recalls Paul Rahe. By the time of her release, she had "become a kind of unpaid assistant, helping to take care of other patients." Rahe viewed her confinement as a political act intended to stop her from selling her house and—by extension—integrating her all-white neighborhood. He describes Rosie as "a woman of considerable intelligence" who was "perfectly sane." The way that people reacted to her disfigured appearance "made her sensitive to the treatment of blacks," which is why she got involved in the civil rights movement in the first place, explains Rahe.[60]

After five long years, Rosie Gilchrist was free to go home, but she no longer owned a house. Everything she owned fit "in a single tattered suitcase."[61] Her release came as suddenly and almost as effortlessly as her confinement had. Much had changed in Oklahoma and across the country during those five years. The civil rights movement had resulted in many victories, including adoption of the Twenty-Fourth Amendment, which banned the poll tax; the 1964 Civil Rights Act; the 1965 Voting Rights Act; and the 1968 Civil Rights Act (more commonly known as the Fair Housing Act), which banned discrimination in the rent or sale of homes. And Oklahoma had elected its first African American state senator. That an African American man wielded enough power to secure the release of a white woman from a mental institution illustrates well that much had changed.

Perhaps it would be gratifying to end the story here, but history is rarely so simple or triumphant. The confinement and release of Rosie Gilchrist leave lingering questions and uncomfortable insights. During the five years that Gilchrist spent in a mental hospital for trying to sell her house to an African American doctor, she appeared to have vanished from the minds and memories of the

African Americans whom she had demonstrated with, worshiped with, and invited into her home. Clara Luper's book *Behold the Walls* (1979) contains the names of hundreds of individuals who participated in civil rights demonstrations and sacrificed for the movement. Gilchrist's is not there.[62] Multiple members of the NAACP Youth Council have no memory of her. Jodey Bateman vaguely remembers a meeting at Luper's house around the time when Gilchrist was confined. Luper had addressed Rosie's absence, saying she was worried that Rosie's family was trying to have her committed to a mental institution. That was the last Bateman heard about her.[63] How could a woman, whose whiteness alone—not to mention her obvious scars and physical discomfort—made her stand out at civil rights demonstrations, be forgotten so quickly and completely? E. Melvin Porter had no idea what had happened to Gilchrist. There is no indication that Luper or Fulbright or any of Rosie's other African American friends came to visit her at the mental hospital.

Years later, when Coleman reached out to Clara Luper and her children, they began to recall Rosie, but not what had happened to her.[64] The suggestion here is not that the Lupers or any of the other African Americans who knew Rosie Gilchrist purposely turned their backs on her. Rather, the urgency of the civil rights movement proved so great and so pervasive that African American civil rights activists in Oklahoma did not have the luxury of sustained worry or curiosity about Gilchrist's disappearance. They were so focused on challenging discrimination and so fearful about the possibility of violence (which never erupted in Oklahoma in that era to the same extent that it did in other parts of the country) that they simply forgot about a woman who happened to pay a much higher price than most for attempting to integrate an Oklahoma neighborhood.

Another disquieting aspect of Gilchrist's experience that cannot be ignored is that she died less than three years after her release, possibly from suicide, as Coleman suspects. She was living in New York at the time, where she worked at the *Catholic Worker* (made possible through friends of Coleman's). Coleman was serving a prison sentence for his draft-resistance efforts when he learned that his mother had died from falling off a roof on July 15, 1971. Perhaps it was an accident, but Coleman and Rosie's coworkers were aware of the depression and physical pain that she lived with each day. In her obituary, Jan Adams and Kathy Schmidt described Rosie as "a lively, complicated individual" whose "fearless openness" sometimes "led her to speak so forthrightly as to offend."[65] It is worth remembering that her forthright speech and action are the very things that led to her confinement. Rosie's obituary also notes her continued effort to use her

Rosie Gilchrist (*pictured from behind*) as she participated, seemingly unnoticed, at a demonstration against segregation at the Anna Maude Cafeteria, circa 1962–63. Photograph by Johnny Melton. Courtesy of the Research Division, Oklahoma Historical Society.

own scars as part of a campaign to help other burn victims and lepers. Adams and Schmidt referenced her civil rights work as well and asserted, "Long before civil rights became a popular cause, when most Oklahomans still spoke of black people as 'niggers,' Rosie worked toward justice for those who were for her just other people." Prior to her death, Rosie told her friends that "she was glad she had been hurt so much because it had taught her that we simply must care for and forgive one another."[66] Rosie Gilchrist leaves a complicated legacy. Her experiences reveal the ease with which women could be so easily silenced well into the 1960s and how compassion and support for equality could be twisted and refashioned as mental illness, even as actual mental health needs went unaddressed. Many people saw Rosie Gilchrist without really seeing her at all; their eyes looked no farther than her scars, including on her eyelids, which she could never fully close after the fire. Perhaps others saw her as a well-meaning white woman who just stopped coming to civil rights meetings one day. Whatever the case, the uncomfortable invisibility of Rosie Gilchrist complicates the narrative of the interplay between race, gender, and sacrifice in the Oklahoma civil rights movement.

NOTES

1. Roslyn Coleman Gilchrist Medical File, Central State (Griffin Memorial) Hospital, 1963–1968, 1, Coleman Family Private Papers (hereafter cited as Gilchrist medical file). This file was obtained from the hospital by her son Coleman, who has graciously allowed the use of it for this project.

2. See Elaine Showalter, *The Female Malady: Women, Madness, and English Culture, 1830–1980* (New York: Pantheon, 1985); Phyllis Chesler, *Women and Madness* (Chicago: Lawrence Hill, 2018).

3. Joe Gilchrist changed his legal name to Coleman and is referred to as such throughout this chapter; Coleman, *Spoke: A Mother. A Son. Civil Rights. Vietnam.* (Mineral Point, WI: Little Creek, 2013), 27, 25.

4. Coleman, *Spoke*, 28–30.

5. Coleman, *Spoke*, 39–41, 44.

6. Coleman, interview with the author, September 16, 2019. For a discussion of racial politics and discrimination in nursing, see Charissa J. Threat, *Nursing Civil Rights: Gender and Race in the Army Nurse Corps* (Chicago: University of Illinois Press, 2015). While Threat's focus is on army nurses rather than civilians, many of the themes hold true in civilian hospitals. For example, African American nurses routinely found themselves relegated to the least desirable jobs, which makes it unsurprising that Gilchrist's nursing care was provided solely by African American women.

7. Coleman, *Spoke*, 42.

8. Coleman, *Spoke*, 43.

9. Coleman, *Spoke*, 45.

10. Coleman interview.

11. Rosalyn C. Gilchrist v. John T. Gilchrist, No. D 116192, District Court in and for Oklahoma County, May 27, 1963.

12. Coleman, *Spoke*, 26; Coleman interview. Coleman notes that Edna Pevehouse was the one exception to this. She was a member of their church who was shunned by most of the community because she and her family lived in a shack and collected junk in their front yard. Gilchrist's friendship with Pevehouse continued even after her confinement.

13. Coleman, *Spoke*, 48.

14. Gilchrist medical file, 3.

15. Gilchrist medical file, 9.

16. Clara Luper, *Behold the Walls* (Oklahoma City: Jim Wire, 1979). See also chapter 8.

17. For a discussion of Jodey Bateman's activism, see Sarah Eppler Janda, *Prairie Power: Student Activism, Counterculture, and Backlash in Oklahoma, 1962–1972* (Norman: University of Oklahoma Press, 2018).

18. Jodey Bateman, e-mail to the author, January 12, 2019.

19. "50 Arrested at City Park," *Daily Oklahoman*, June 23, 1963, 1.
20. Gilchrist medical file, 13.
21. Coleman interview.
22. Janda, *Prairie Power*, 76–90.
23. Bateman e-mail.
24. Coleman, *Spoke*, 55.
25. Gilchrist medical file, 9.
26. Coleman, "Annotations on the 'Complete' Medical Record of Rosalyn Gilchrist from Central State Hospital," April 13, 2009, 4, courtesy of Coleman. This document was put together by Coleman after he gained access to his mother's medical records. In it he offers a page-by-page assessment of the content of his mother's records.
27. Coleman, *Spoke*, 57.
28. Coleman, *Spoke*, 56.
29. Coleman, *Spoke*, 57
30. Coleman, *Spoke*, 57.
31. Coleman, *Spoke*, 58.
32. Coleman, *Spoke*. It should be noted that while the accusations against Gilchrist include the statement that she had been arrested for engaging in civil rights demonstrations, there is not actually any record of her having been arrested.
33. Coleman, *Spoke*, 168–69.
34. Guardian's Deed, Book 3008, p. 695, no. 136269, August 7, 1964, Oklahoma County Clerk.
35. Gilchrist medical file, 3–4. Here it should be noted that the term "chemotherapy," as it was used in the 1960s, refers to the use of chemical agents to treat a medical or mental disorder, so it is perhaps the case that this is another way of referring to phenothiazine. However, the notation on the same page of "no medication" is harder to explain.
36. Coleman, "Annotations," 8.
37. Coleman, cover page.
38. Coleman, "Annotations," 3.
39. See, for example, Michele Norris, *The Grace of Silence: A Family Memoir* (New York: Vintage, 2011). Norris recounts the impact on housing prices when her parents became the first African American family to move into a Minneapolis neighborhood.
40. Gilchrist medical file, 1.
41. Gilchrist medical file, 13.
42. Gilchrist medical file, 9; Coleman, "Annotations," 9.
43. Coleman interview.
44. Gilchrist medical file, 14.
45. Gilchrist medical file, 11.
46. Gilchrist medical file, 8
47. Gilchrist medical file, 11.
48. Coleman, *Spoke*, 168.
49. John P. Tawes to Gordon E. Gilchrist, February 9, 1967, April 12, 1967, in Gilchrist medical file, 6, 7.

50. Coleman, e-mail to the author, October 23, 2019.
51. Gilchrist medical file, 14.
52. Kim E. Neilson, *A Disability History of the United States* (Boston: Beacon, 2012), xii.
53. Coleman, *Spoke*, 107–9.
54. Coleman, *Spoke*, 141.
55. Larry O'Dell, "Porter, Edward Melvin," *The Encyclopedia of Oklahoma History and Culture*, Oklahoma Historical Society, https://www.okhistory.org/publications/enc/entry.php?entry=PO017.
56. Coleman, *Spoke*, 142–43.
57. Paul Rahe, interview with the author, October 27, 2019.
58. Coleman, *Spoke*, 143.
59. Gilchrist medical file, 22; Coleman, "Annotations," 22.
60. Rahe interview.
61. Coleman, *Spoke*, 143.
62. Luper, *Behold the Walls*.
63. Bateman e-mail.
64. Coleman interview.
65. "Rosie Gilchrist, RIP," *Catholic Worker* 37, no. 6 (July 1971): 2, https://thecatholicnewsarchive.org/?a=d&d=CW19710701-01.2.7&srpos=1&e=-------en-20--1--txt-txIN-rosie+gilchrist------.
66. "Rosie Gilchrist, RIP."

PART THREE
CONTESTED NOTIONS OF EQUALITY

Part 3 explores how both regional and national political forces shaped, and were shaped by, women in the areas of Indigenous rights and sovereignty, the Equal Rights Amendment, feminism, LGBTQ+ rights, and conservative politics, from the 1970s until the 2010s. The civil rights movement brought the issue of equality to the center of public discourse on race and in so doing raised questions about gender equality and eventually LGBTQ+ rights. But it also complicated understandings of Indigenous rights and sovereignty with characterizations of Native Americans as another minority challenging discrimination.

LaDonna Harris got married, graduated from high school, and then moved to Norman in the summer of 1949, just as Ada Lois Sipuel Fisher was finally admitted to law school at the University of Oklahoma. Harris identified with Sipuel Fisher and other African Americans fighting against segregation and saw similarities between them because of her experiences with discrimination as a Comanche woman. Yet, as Amanda Cobb-Greetham demonstrates, Harris's activism and commitment to a restoration of tribal sovereignty lay firmly within her Comanche values and culture. Cobb-Greetham examines how Harris's culturally based values system and identity as a Comanche matriarch shaped her commitment to training future tribal leaders—first with Oklahomans for Indian Opportunity and later with Americans for Indian Opportunity. Harris supported equality for African Americans as well as women, but in both instances her understanding of equality stemmed from her Comanche worldview.

When Congress ratified the Equal Rights Amendment (ERA) in 1972, Wanda Jo Peltier Stapleton, a farmer from rural Oklahoma turned college English professor, became a leading figure in the fight for ratification in Oklahoma. As Chelsea Ball reminds us in her timely chapter on the ERA in Oklahoma, Wanda Jo Peltier is an unexpected and self-proclaimed "radical American feminist," and she broadened the notion of what it meant to be a feminist in Oklahoma. Peltier identified as a feminist and, at the same time, was married to a Baptist preacher in rural Oklahoma, was a college professor, and supported reproductive rights and LGBTQ+ rights. For Peltier, as Burroughs explains, the ERA just made sense for women in Oklahoma. Yet Oklahoma became one of the battleground states for the STOP ERA campaign, which ultimately prevailed in the effort to halt further ratification of the amendment. Despite the eventual defeat of the ERA, Peltier's grassroots organizing emphasized how the amendment would support women without a separate income and protect property rights and social security benefits. As president of the Oklahoma Women's Political Caucus in the early 1980s, Peltier helped transform the organization into one of the fastest-growing chapters in the country.

The growing conservatism in Oklahoma in the 1970s and 1980s ultimately helped secure the defeat of the ERA and, by extension, further marginalized the LBGTQ+ community. Lindsey Churchill examines the life of Barbara "Wahru" Cleveland, founder of the Oklahoma City–based lesbian feminist activist group, Herland Sister Resources. Churchill details how Cleveland responded to her own marginalization as a Black lesbian by creating a "womyn only space" in conservative Oklahoma. Founded in 1983 by Cleveland as a feminist bookstore, Herland Sister Resources in Oklahoma City is a womanist organization—all women are welcome—with a strong lesbian focus, though not restricted to lesbians. Herland started as a bookstore and grew to become a lending library, meeting space, and organization for women. Churchill explains that Herland provides a physical space beyond the bar scene for the lesbian community in Oklahoma City to engage in political activism, including organizing to end sexual violence and promoting tolerance and safety for women and the entire LGBTQ+ community.

The growing conservatism that stifled Peltier's work and seemed to necessitate Cleveland's actually enhanced and legitimized the activism of Mary Fallin. Patricia Loughlin examines Fallin's background and political strategy as a Republican woman politician who intentionally used the politics of motherhood in her campaigns. Her career in elected public service spanned three decades, beginning in 1990 as a member of the state house of representatives, then lieutenant governor, US congresswoman, and then governor in the 2010s. Loughlin notes that early in her career, Fallin encountered attacks within her own party for being a young pregnant woman. But she quickly turned this to her advantage by using the rhetoric of motherhood as a strength while navigating the political landscape in Oklahoma and in the United States more broadly. Fallin's significance is part of a larger movement of conservative women activists in the late twentieth century who saw the ways that government directly impacted their lives and saw a need to get involved and prompt change, joining the ranks of the Republican Party and holding elected positions in the state and nationally.

Collectively, the chapters in this section reveal the tensions at play—both nationally and in Oklahoma—over the meaning of equality and the place of women in society. Both Harris and Fallin successfully used maternalism to create their own activist spaces; Harris through rematriation and Fallin by simultaneously traditionalizing and politicizing motherhood. Peltier and Cleveland engaged in political activism as a means to foster greater rights and protections for women, but both did so within a hotly contested framework of public discourse on equality, citizenship, and gender.

AMANDA COBB-GREETHAM

LADONNA HARRIS
Comanche Leader, Activist, Matriarch

LaDonna Harris first gained national attention as the wife of Fred Harris, who served as state and then US senator from Oklahoma during the late 1960s and early 1970s. As a team, LaDonna and Fred Harris strongly supported Indian issues in Congress and made national headlines during the civil rights era, but LaDonna's activism did not end with the end of that era or their marriage. Her work as an institution builder, such as her creation of the first intertribal nonprofit advocacy organization in Oklahoma, Oklahomans for Indian Opportunity (OIO), in 1965, shaped federal policy in ways that supported stronger tribal self-determination and built a legacy that continues to this day through her national advocacy organization, Americans for Indian Opportunity (AIO), founded in 1970. Known for her tremendous personal warmth, powerful charisma, and gracious style, LaDonna Harris—as a Comanche woman and matriarch—has had a tremendous and well-recognized impact throughout Indian country. In recognition of this, she was recently inducted as a member of the first class of the National Native American Hall of Fame.

That she is considered a leader is undisputed, but an analysis of *why* her leadership is effective demands that we complicate our understanding of what "leadership" and "activism" are and how they function in specific contexts. As I have discussed in my previous research regarding Harris's rhetorical style, the woman does not fit neatly within the Western conceptualizations of either leader or activist.[1] Such conceptualizations of "leadership" tend to privilege one person in a hierarchical position of power within a given system and honor that person for their accomplishments as an *individual*, based on highly valued and Western notions of masculinity, rugged individualism, and singular genius. Although conceptualizations of "activism" highlight those who explicitly work outside or against a system rather than within it, activists are no less grounded in the same individualistic value system and hierarchical structure of power. Frequently, when a woman is given attention as a leader—either within a system or in active opposition to it—it is because she is a *woman*, frequently the *first* woman in a position that has been customarily held by men, or is otherwise perceived to have met criteria for success within this individual-normative value system.[2]

Harris is different. She has never received a college degree. She has never held an elected or appointed office in tribal, federal, or state government. She has never led a protest or a political movement. Instead, she began by using her position as the wife of a US senator and the proximal power it vested in her as a platform from which to restructure and give shape to American Indian policy from "inside" the system; she cultivated key relationships during this period from which she built broader networks to influence policy makers' decisions. To the ears of many of my current undergraduate students, this work may not sound "radical" or even particularly "Progressive." And, indeed, an afternoon in the archives reading OIO grant proposals from the 1960s or even early AIO policy papers from the 1970s can be disconcerting to scholars who came of age at a time when theoretical discussions of sovereignty, settler-colonial power structures, and decolonization were commonplace. Reviewing OIO or early AIO documents is striking in the lack of language that fits neatly in current academic conversations. In fact, much of the language outlining the goals of OIO, as noted by historian Sarah Eppler Janda, could be described as "quite conservative in doctrine and practice," rooted as it is in the concepts of integration and even assimilation.[3] Yet the leadership program for Native youths established in OIO and the leadership program for young Native professionals established in AIO represent what many consider to be Harris's greatest contribution and legacy to Indian country. What, then, did Harris accomplish through these programs? What is the nature of her legacy? How are these leadership programs illustrative of her activism and leadership? How can we best understand the modality of her leadership?

Context is critical.

When Harris arrived in Washington, DC, the federal government generally treated tribes as archaic social and programmatic units whose problems were "handled" by the paternalistic Bureau of Indian Affairs (BIA), an agency which, as often as not, perceived the continued existence of tribes *as* the problem. Treating tribes as sovereign governments was not imagined as an option. In fact, the term "tribal sovereignty" might have existed as legal doctrine, but it was denied and avoided as policy and not used in any practical sense within the federal-tribal relationship, let alone any state-tribal relationship. This was, after all, the "termination" era of federal policy toward tribes; government officials were much more focused on termination, i.e., cutting off any kind federal-tribal relationship altogether, than they were in engaging tribal sovereigns as polities deserving of respect and possessing legal rights. Janda reminds us of this important context, contending that "Harris is a product of both termination and self-determination policies, and the growth of her activism can best be understood with the context of the shift in federal Indian policy from the former to the latter."[4] While I agree that Harris is, in part, a product of termination policies in that she grew up as a Comanche woman in Oklahoma during a period of strict assimilation policies, I disagree with the proposition that Harris is a *product* of self-determination policies. She is, instead, a *producer* or agent of change. Further, I argue that LaDonna Harris and her particular mode of leadership and activism—embedded in and springing from her understanding of herself as a Comanche matriarch within a uniquely Comanche value system—were critical elements in opening the way for the growth of the self-determination era.

Scholars born after 1970 do not personally remember a time when "tribal sovereignty" was a new and radical term, when long-standing ideological belief in the essential inferiority of Native Americans and Native cultures and in the inevitable disappearance of Native people led policy makers to enact laws explicitly designed to expedite that disappearance. This is not to suggest in any way that the ideological work to combat the forces of erasure is done. Without a doubt, many—too many—in our society continue to hold those damaging ideological beliefs. And it is true that many—too many—face and fight the oppression that is hardwired into our institutions. But it is also true that our tribal governments are no longer puppets of the BIA, that our children are no longer captives of assimilationist boarding schools, and that the bones of our ancestors are no longer part of museum displays. "Most of the federal Indian policy," as Harris poignantly wrote about the period in which she came of age, was explicitly and expressly designed "to make us go away."[5]

That federal policy ever dictated such oppression and cruelty is unconscionable, and yet *it did*. Harris felt the trauma wrought by these policies in her physical person, describing at various points in her life how "the pain comes back, like posttraumatic stress syndrome. Makes me feel like I have to throw up, like food turns sour."[6] She describes her pain as a catalyst for her work: "These are the things I worked all my life to rid other people of so they wouldn't hurt."[7] That federal Indian policy shifted so dramatically, so radically, through the 1970s and beyond represents the profound changes engendered by LaDonna Harris and her colleagues who developed insight into their situation without the benefit of graduate classes in postcolonial or settler-colonial theory. Harris saw quite clearly that the "New World" was not new, that the frontier was not empty, and that the closing of the frontier—which, ironically for Harris, was marked by the opening of Indian Territory and the establishment of Oklahoma as the forty-sixth state—did not end the devastation wrought by physical conquest; as she has noted, "We Indians are past the colonialism *physically*, but we are not necessarily out of it *politically*."[8] As Native studies scholars Dale Turner and Audra Simpson explain, for Indigenous people, colonialism "continues to define the relationship between our people and the European newcomers.... Indigenous peoples live the practical, and philosophical, effects of colonialism in the *present*."[9] In the context of American settler colonialism, settlers first imposed power through the dispossession of land, then declared the acquired territory a new "homeland," and worked diligently to erase or eliminate Native people through every kind of policy, including treaty making, forced removal, warfare, land allotment, and ultimately sweeping assimilation policies expressly constructed to *erase* or eliminate Native languages, religions, histories, and cultural value systems. By *replacing* them with their own languages, religions, and histories, most certainly with their own cultural value systems, settlers became "native" to their new homeland and Indigenous people were firmly relegated to a mythologized past.

These aggressive assimilation policies were firmly in place during Harris's formative years. As she explains, "In the 1950s we Indians were supposedly fading away so rapidly that there wouldn't be Indians around much longer and this process was designed to help it along."[10] Her articulation of government officials' firm conviction that Native Americans would eventually disappear into a mythic premodern past underscores her understanding that Native Americans *were not supposed to have a future*. Thus, colonization results not only in the dispossession of Indigenous land and the erasure of Indigenous histories but also in the foreclosure of Indigenous futures. For Harris, the pain of that realization is palpable, physical. She acknowledges, however, that healing from trauma is an ongoing process and that it is far from easy, stating simply, "To live in this world, I have to take a deep breath."[11] As Harris has suffered from asthma all her life, this statement is especially meaningful. In other words, the pain in the world is capable, literally and figuratively, of taking her breath—her life—away. Sometimes, taking a deep breath—remembering the past but choosing the future—is a conscious choice of more significance than the physical act itself.

Harris's effectiveness as a leader and activist is based on her unwillingness to give up either her history or her future. A Comanche woman from Oklahoma, rooted firmly in Comanche values, Harris has always known exactly who she is and has understood exactly where she was—in a position to *make history* by envisioning a *different future* for Native Americans and, in particular, for Native youths.

In this chapter, I first describe Harris's expression of her Comanche value system, interpreting the exercise of those values in her role as a Comanche matriarch as a powerful counter to settler-colonial erasure. Using this matriarchal lens, I consider LaDonna Harris's legacy and the modality of her leadership by examining elements of two leadership programs with which Harris is associated, both of which underscore her persistent focus on cultural heritage, values, and identity. Although Harris, a founder of OIO, transitioned to her national platform, AIO, after only a few years, an analysis of the origins of OIO's youth leadership program highlights Harris's early attempts to embed Native values squarely in her advocacy efforts. An analysis of AIO's leadership program for young professionals, which she created almost thirty years later, emphasizes Harris's growth and ability to fully articulate core cultural values in her work and to explicitly share those values with Indian country's emerging leaders, mentoring and guiding them to exercise those values in all aspects of their work. Applying a matriarchal lens to Harris's vision and goals for each leadership program clarifies the evolution of her modality as a leader and underscores the nature of her legacy, the restoration of core cultural values—what I call

LaDonna Harris with Comanche matriarch Wick-kie Tabbytite—her grandmother, role model, and mentor—and her niece, Donna Hooper Stark, 1965. Courtesy of the Research Division, Oklahoma Historical Society.

the *rematriation* of those values—in order to forge and reenergize Indigenous kinship systems, thus ensuring Indigenous futures.

As a Comanche woman from Oklahoma who was married to a US senator, Harris occupied a unique position. As an Indian person, she was considered, by law, to be a ward of the federal government; as a woman from Oklahoma, she was perceived to be a poor country girl; but as the wife of Fred Harris, she was considered, by virtue of marriage to a sitting US senator and onetime presidential candidate, to be part of the power structure, the very same power structure that was trying to erase Native people. Significantly, she embraced all aspects of her identity, remarking once that "My being an Indian . . . born to a poor family and the wife of a candidate for President are as much a part of me as being a woman."[12] While she was all these multifaceted pieces, she relied upon her understanding of her Comanche worldview to synthesize and unify seemingly disparate elements of her identity, writing, "I filter everything through Comanche values."[13]

Born on a Comanche allotment in southern Oklahoma, formerly Indian Territory, in 1931, just twenty-four years after Oklahoma statehood, Harris was raised primarily by her grandparents, Wick-kie and John Tabbytite, whom she cites as the source of her Comanche values. Born in 1883 and 1872, respectively, her grandparents lived through the period in American history characterized by the Dawes Allotment Act and the Indian Wars fought across plains in the aftermath of the US Civil War. Both allotment and wafare resulted in the fracturing of tribal governments, the containment of decimated Native families on reservations, and the separation of their children through the federal boarding school system. For Harris, the "conquest" of the West—and all that the idea encompasses—was not part of a mythologized national past. Instead, through her grandparents, it was part and parcel of her present upbringing, the dinnertime conversations with which she was raised.

As I point out to my students, while one hundred years may seem too long ago to care about, it is also the possible length of one person's life. Indeed, when history is interpreted through "lifetimes," the concept of "a long time ago" collapses very quickly. Harris, who understood her own identity in relationship to the identities of her grandparents, very clearly understood the structure of colonization and keenly felt its impacts. Additionally, she was fully immersed in Comanche culture and understood herself, first and foremost, as a Comanche person. According to Harris, the biographical "facts" of her life cannot be understood without some understanding of her Comanche values and worldview.

In considering this, it is important to emphasize that Harris does not subscribe to an essentialist notion of what it means to be Comanche, nor does she believe that all Comanche people know and manifest these values in precisely the same way. She has chosen to describe these values as she was taught them and as she experiences and exercises them. For LaDonna Harris, being a Comanche woman is not merely something you are; it is something you *live*.

Harris's upbringing, and particularly her close relationship to her grandparents, brought the values of kinship and responsibilities to the forefront for her. She writes that we understand our own identities "through our families and clans and the particular responsibility that comes with each relationship."[14] She continues to explain that for Comanches, "a child is brought up by the entire extended family, as well as the larger community.... We learn our way to contribute through our relationships to family members.[15] For Harris, acknowledging those relationships by "being a good relative" and "knowing your responsibilities" is of prime importance as the functioning of the entire community is based on those relationships and the special responsibilities that come with them.

She understood Comanche women to play a special role, saying, "I grew up surrounded by strong women.... I remember her [my great-grandmother] sitting with her cane, the empress of all her domain. Every man, woman and child in our family respected that." She believed her grandmother would one day assume the same role, noting, "Both of them were matriarchs, great-grandmother and then grandmother. They assumed the responsibility of keeping the family together." Harris identified them as her role models and acknowledged that her own role in the family was to become like them and behaved accordingly: "I would go with her [my grandmother]. I would do some of the things that were recognized as the matriarch's role.... Going along with her would honor me—rub off—and the fact that I was with her and doing those things meant that she recognized something in me."[16]

Harris's stories about her grandmother demonstrate the ways in which the bonds of kinship pass through lifetimes. Interpreted through the lens of lifetimes, "history" is not long ago but directly imbedded in families and passed from person to person. She illustrates this point: "To this day, people come to me and cry. They remember my grandmother, and it ties me to them. They think of me as the legacy of my grandmother, and they hold me and cry."[17]

Another value, one Harris identifies as having special meaning to her, equality, is manifested through relationships. According to Harris, "Relationships among men, women, and children were based on harmony, and women and children were equal partners to men in Comanche culture."[18] Her belief in and exercise of equality as a value are evidenced in the early years of her marriage. She married Fred Harris, a high school sweetheart, in 1949 and moved to Norman, where he attended the University of Oklahoma. After he received his law degree in 1954, the couple moved to Lawton, Oklahoma, and started their family, which includes three children—Kathryn, Byron, and Laura. Fred Harris practiced law and served on the Oklahoma state senate for eight years, at which point, in 1964, he won a special election to serve out the remainder of the unexpired term of US senator Robert Kerr, who had died in office. He then won a full term in 1966. LaDonna and Fred Harris were well known for their teamwork; she was integrally involved in Fred's political life, not merely as a campaigner but as a true partner, giving advice, helping Fred read people and situations (they spoke to each other in Comanche on the Senate floor for privacy), taking her own stance on issues, and becoming an increasingly public advocate for Indian issues. It was in this capacity that she established Oklahomans for Indian Opportunity in 1965 as one of the first intertribal advocacy organizations in the history of the state, and it was highly regarded for its youth leadership program.

Through her experiences as a senator's wife and Indian advocate, LaDonna Harris began to come to a fuller understanding of how she could best make a contribution to the community—another Comanche value. Harris firmly believes that "every person in the society, even a child, has something to contribute, some special role to play."[19] She writes, "The role any person plays is based on that person's own inner strength or 'medicine.' Everyone's medicine is different, and the tribe recognizes that it needs different kinds of leaders with different strengths for different types of societal responsibilities."[20]

As a value, contribution highlights the importance of an individual's identity and special role within a collective tribal identity and the relationship of each individual to others. Harris views relationships in an ever-widening spiral. Seeing all things as being part of a web of relationships, she feels a responsibility to her family and clan, to the Comanche Nation, to other tribal nations, and to society in general. Recognizing her own special talent, or medicine, in her seemingly innate ability to bring people together, Harris established Americans for Indian Opportunity in 1970 to fulfill her need to contribute, this time on a national platform.

During this period, Fred Harris maintained an ambitious Senate agenda, becoming increasingly outspoken on poverty and civil rights issues. After eight years in office, however, he chose not to seek reelection to the Senate and instead mounted a run for the 1976 Democratic presidential nomination, campaigning as a "new populist." After he lost the primary race to Jimmy Carter, the Harrises moved to New Mexico, where he began a much-respected career as a political scientist at the University of New Mexico.[21] They divorced soon after, and Harris returned to Washington, DC, where she blossomed as an activist in her own right and without a relationship to a sitting US senator. In this period, she actively participated in the National Urban Coalition and Common Cause and ultimately, if unsuccessfully, ran for vice president in 1980 on the Citizens Party ticket with Barry Commoner.[22] After this brief foray into formal electoral politics, she refocused her work on Native American issues and advocacy, the area in which she believed she could make the greatest contribution.

Returning to the more organic model of relationship building she preferred, Harris continued to develop and expand the work of AIO, which in many ways became her life's work. Through AIO she produced many programs and initiatives as well as a notable body of literature on Indian issues. She felt, and continues to feel, driven by a need to share—a value she sometimes calls "redistribution." Sharing, or redistribution, is based on the belief that "Comanches are not supposed to own anything we are not willing to give away.... As a matter of fact, the greater the wealth a person has, means the greater the responsibility that person has to the rest of the community."[23] For Harris, sharing wealth does not refer merely to material resources but also to the sharing of perspectives and ideas, personal medicine, and the cultural value system that sustained and guided her. She created Americans for Indian Opportunity, as well as the earlier Oklahomans for Indian Opportunity, in order to share her energies and her Comanche value system. As such, the organizations are both manifestations of her generative power as a matriarch within her Comanche value system and a powerful exercise of those values in the broader community.

Harris resisted the erasure of all things Indigenous that was demanded by federal policies by resolutely refusing "to go away" and by intentionally embracing her own identity. Further, she asked other Native Americans to embrace their identities, too, and thus to embrace a notion of intertribal kinship, along with all the responsibilities kinship relationships entail. Harris expanded her circle of kinship by creating two organizations to make what was very nearly erased *visible*. The creation of OIO and AIO forced government officials to see the continued existence of Native people and, more significantly, to acknowledge the persistence of Native nations as culturally distinctive entities. And by concentrating OIO's and AIO's programmatic initiatives on Native youths, Harris set up a system through which she could make the greatest contribution possible as a matriarch by sharing her single greatest gift—her own set of core cultural values—with upcoming generations of Native people. If colonization had, to any degree, divested Native people of cultural value systems, then Harris's singular mission was to restore those values—to *rematriate* them, a term I use intentionally to contrast with "repatriation," though both are key to decolonization and healing.

LaDonna Harris created OIO's youth programs and AIO's leadership program in ways that honored matriarchal knowledge. Through rematriation—that is, through the restoration and transmission of core cultural values—Harris restored to young Native leaders their own sense of belonging to their communities and cultures. Before discussing these organizations as products of Harris's particular modality of Native advocacy, let me explore what my reference to rematriation signifies. "Repatriation" is a more commonly encountered term. It is common parlance, particularly in Indian country due to its use in the Native American Graves Protection and Repatriation Act (NAGPRA, 1990), which provides for the "repatriation and disposition" of Native American human remains, funerary objects, sacred objects, and objects of "cultural patrimony" held by museums, universities, and other institutions. In other words, the law provided a way for tribal governments to recover bones and funerary objects—taken from the graves of Native ancestors—which were bought and sold, collected and displayed, or warehoused and studied as part of the larger settler-colonial project and rationalized by a persistent belief in the inevitable disappearance of Native people. The enactment of NAGPRA was the result of decades of dedicated Native activism and advocacy. The law itself, particularly its use of the term "repatriation," highlights notions of ownership and property that spring from Western, colonial, and legalistic understandings of rights and objects.

By using the term "rematriation," I am specifically drawing attention to Harris's understanding that colonial policies were designed to dispossess Native people of land as well as a person's access to cultural knowledge or participation in continued tribal kinship relationships. The colonial project conceptualized cultural knowledge as the property of a person—as a tangible *belonging* that could be bought, sold, collected, or destroyed. Harris's work implicitly rejects that notion. Her conceptualization of cultural knowledge also highlights *belonging* but situates it instead, and more actively, as part of her system of kinship, making cultural knowledge not about *ownership* but about *relationships*.

Relationships, in this sense, are not about an *object's belonging* to a person but of a *person's belonging* to a people, culture, and community. Her efforts to restore core cultural values should, therefore, be described using a term I interpret as consistent with and growing from that value system—"rematriation."

Harris's rematriation project, manifest in her vision for Oklahomans for Indian Opportunity, grew out of a set of community-organizing experiences that began with a weeklong seminar on civil rights and race relations at the University of Oklahoma's Southwest Center for Human Relations Studies in the early 1960s. Attending in place of her husband, a state senator at the time, Harris become viscerally upset during the discussions when she discovered that, in the minds of her supposedly "learned" colleagues, Native Americans did not need to be included in their conversation. Native Americans, they believed, were already taken care of by the BIA. Knowing the extreme poverty and the daily discrimination experienced by Native Americans in Oklahoma in spite of the supposed care taken by the BIA, Harris's frustration grew. Unable to articulate her feelings, Harris burst in to tears: "They couldn't see that they were part of the problem.... I so wanted them to understand."[24] Although embarrassed by her reaction, she effectively changed the course of the conversation, which turned first to the organization of programs as part of the center and then evolved and grew over time into an active group of community advocates. "Out of that nucleus we started Oklahomans for Indian Opportunity," Harris remembered, noting that the organization began—in true Harris style—"in her living room."[25]

Harris and her new cohort recognized President Lyndon B. Johnson's War on Poverty and vision of a Great Society as an opportunity to spotlight Native issues as they related to poverty and racial discrimination. The Office of Economic Opportunity (OEO) became the means through which Johnson's grand vision was operationalized. Much of the funding provided by the OEO was funneled into Community Action Programs (CAPs), which were intended to situate the locus of power over funding and decision making within the communities themselves. For many reservation tribes, which were included in the scope of the OEO's work, CAPs provided a virtually unprecedented opportunity to bypass the paternalistic authority of the BIA, engage in community organizing and decision making, voice their own needs, and determine possible paths forward. For many tribal nations, in fact, participation in CAPs reenergized tribal leadership, who appreciated that engaging the federal government through OEO could, and eventually would, lead to a shift in the federal-tribal relationship away from termination and toward policies of self-determination.[26]

Tribes in Oklahoma were not, however, eligible for OEO funds. The logic behind their exclusion was based on Oklahoma's status as a nonreservation state—if Oklahoma, once Indian Territory, did not have Indian reservations, then it must logically follow that the state no longer had Indian people, that the settler-colonial project of Native elimination and erasure was complete. Officials of the federally run OEO believed Oklahoma Indians no longer existed; many Oklahomans, like Harris's aforementioned fellow board members, believed that the while Indians still existed, the BIA "took care of them." If Harris's initial response to this vicious circle was to burst into tears, demonstrating her inability to articulate her insights in a way her audience would understand, her second response, the creation of OIO, was much more complicated, concentrated, and deliberate.

A close look at the one of OIO's earliest documents, a 1966 proposal for an operational grant from the OEO for the development of a social-educational skills training program for Oklahoma Native youths, contains the seemingly contradictory goals of helping Native youths integrate and even assimilate into the broader society and of encouraging Native youths to embrace their cultural heritage. I argue that Harris, who had once so badly "wanted to make them understand," utilized the language of her audience intentionally. Even the name of the organization, Oklahomans for Indian Opportunity, mimics the name of the office that had been created to administer Great Society policies, the Office of Economic Opportunity. By naming her organization Oklahomans for Indian Opportunity, Harris and her cohort made nonreservation Indians in Oklahoma *visible* to OEO officials. Accordingly, OIO outlined two primary goals of its organization, which included "improving conditions for Oklahoma Indians" and "helping to draw them more fully into Oklahoma's economy and culture," goals that mirror those articulated by the OEO as part of the Great Society.[27] Additionally, the specific terms and language that OIO used to express its goals often mirror the language used by the OEO, which, as rightly noted by Janda, sometimes "smacked of assimilation."[28] For example, in a paragraph describing reasons for the isolation of Native people in Oklahoma, the authors wrote, "The problems faced by Indians are perhaps peculiar to them because of their heritage." That could be interpreted as identifying heritage itself as the problem, especially in light of the next few sentences, which read, "Though their culture is anachronistic to the twentieth and approaching twenty-first centuries, they have not been able to divest themselves of it. . . . Within it they find the security which their lack of skills prevents in the greater social order."[29] Such language can easily be interpreted to reflect an ideological belief in inevitable disappearance, disappointment in failed assimilation policies, and even blame for their own isolation due to a perceived lack of skills.

However, the next few sentences demonstrate a larger, more nuanced purpose by placing the blame for this toxic dynamic elsewhere—namely by arguing that "the non-Indian traditionally has not been sensitive to the plight and needs of the Indian" and thus pointing out an overall lack of awareness of historical realities. The document goes one step further by observing that "hardened, hostile attitudes have been consistently demonstrated through discriminatory practices which have greatly reduced the opportunity for Indians to gain access to mainstream activities."[30] Harris and her colleagues could have easily ended their narrative at that point, having shifted the blame from themselves to the racism of their individual neighbors; instead, they further complicated the matter by evoking the realities of years of colonial policies, writing, "An accumulation of bad experiences, including disappointments with governmental and private agencies, has produced among many a kind of withdrawal and self-imposed isolation."[31] The authors' proposed solution significantly calls for Native leadership, pointing out, "Too many undertakings . . . have sought to impose solutions and provide synthetic leadership from the outside," a noteworthy shift toward what would soon become the language of self-determination.[32]

By mimicking the OEO's language, Harris and her cohort ensured that Oklahoma Indians would be heard—interposing, in effect, a Native advocate in federal bureaucrat's clothing. And by then extending and complicating the language and argument, they introduced an important distinction between "assimilation" and "integration." Introducing this distinction in the grant proposal was critical as it allowed Harris and her colleagues to educate their audience in a nonadversarial manner, taking an important step away from the language of assimilation, which demands cultural erasure, and toward integration, which, Harris argued, does not.

Harris herself has refused to assimilate or deny her own identity as a Comanche woman. And, as an active participant in the larger society, she likely saw no reason why other Native people should not or could not do the same. The problem, as identified by Harris, was "the whole colonial madness." Recalling an early OIO project examining the high dropout rate among Native children, Harris remembered, "The children said they felt humiliated almost every day by teachers calling the 'squaws' and using all those other old horrible terms."

Addressing the ways in which the children internalized this discrimination, she remarked, "These kids felt something was wrong with them . . . They learned that the Indian culture had no value, and that because they were part of that culture, they had no value."[33]

The answer to this problem, for Harris, was to "take away their pain" *by restoring their engagement with and pride in cultural heritage.* Thus, Harris and her colleagues further complicated the language of the proposal by outlining the following two goals: "To help young Oklahoma Indians develop adequate self-concepts and pride in their cultural heritage" and "To help young Indians develop a positive self-concept of themselves as Indians and worthy individuals."[34] That Harris and her cohort included such starkly anti-terminationist goals in a federal grant proposal during the termination era is remarkable in and of itself and underscores the boldness of their advocacy. That the grant was awarded is testament to the agency of Harris and others like her who used such opportunities to educate government officials and move federal policies forward, one step at a time—from assimilation to integration, from integration to self-determination, and from self-determination to sovereignty.

For Harris, the goals as stated also represent a very important step away from bursting into tears as a child might because she "couldn't articulate" how she felt. Instead, Harris moved forward on her path toward becoming a mature matriarch who fulfills her obligation to care for children and all kin—in the manner expected of her by her great-grandmother and grandmother. Because her own self-worth came from her cultural identity, she desired to give that identity away—Comanche style—to Native children who so clearly struggled to be seen and heard in spite of the weight of "the colonial madness." Harris's inclusion of these goals, while not expressly framed in terms of cultural values, represents a significant, if less than fully formed, expression of her cultural values and her rematriative efforts.

If OIO was born of frustrated tears and the co-opting of federal terminationist rhetoric, AIO's leadership program, which Harris created in 1993, almost thirty years later, reveals a fully articulated, eloquently wrought, and matured conceptualization of Harris's core cultural values—the powerful expression of a Comanche matriarch who has embraced her given role and the responsibilities inherent to it.

The AIO leadership program, titled the American Indian Ambassadors Program: Medicine Pathways for the Future, is organized entirely around four specific core cultural values, often referred to as "the Four Rs": relationships, responsibility, reciprocity, and redistribution.[35] Harris and other AIO members, representing a diversity of tribal affiliations and cultural backgrounds, determined that these four values have manifested repeatedly in Indigenous cultures across time and place despite myriad cultural differences and distinctions and committed to their use in the Ambassadors Program. Each value is described as an "obligation," and each is related to and builds on the others in turn. The first, relationships, defined as the "kinship obligation," recognizes that at our roles in society are based on our relationships to others. Responsibility, the second, is considered the "community obligation," the understanding that your role determines your responsibility to other people. The third value, reciprocity, acknowledges the "cyclical obligation" each person has to others while the final value, redistribution, is the term Harris uses for the "sharing obligation," her lifelong belief that knowledge is a gift to be shared with others. Knowing Harris's early life and formative development with her grandparents, these values can be clearly understood as deriving from her understanding of herself and the Comanche worldview she internalized as a child.

For Harris, the Ambassadors Program is not only rooted in those four values and intentionally organized around them; the program and its values are also designed to be shared as a gift. She writes that Americans for Indian Opportunity considers "the Ambassadors Program to be a precious gift that continues to grow and give with each class. . . . Ambassadors are expected to honor this gift."[36] This statement both models the idea of sharing as a value and stipulates the appropriate relationship response and expectation in the same way a grandmother or family matriarch would.

Each of the ambassadors in a leadership class (sixteen per class) is expected to attend four, sometimes five, "gatherings" over a prescribed period of time, usually a year or two, each of which is designed to make ambassadors cognizant of their relationships to others—relationships they might not be aware they are in. For example, the activities at the first gathering push each ambassador to examine their individual relationship with their family, clan, and tribe and their role and responsibilities in those systems. By holding the first gathering in her own home in New Mexico, Harris is able to address family and kinship head-on. Introducing herself as "Mama LaDonna" and stressing that the ambassadors are part of the "AIO family," Harris spends every waking hour with the group, asking each member to answer a single question: "Where did you get your medicine?" As previously noted, Harris believes that each individual's inner strength, or "medicine," determines that person's role in their tribe. By asking ambassadors where their medicine comes from, she is asking them to identify and verbalize their inner strength and to reflect on how that strength was developed.

The second gathering, held in Washington, DC, concentrates the special relationship between Native nations and the federal government. Harris—keenly aware that during her formative years, federal policies defined her as a ward of the government—demands that ambassadors understand that, as Native studies scholar Jace Weaver aptly notes, "Aside from his or her relation to family, clan, or tribal nation, an Indian's most significant relationship is with the federal government."[37] By holding the gathering in Washington, DC, introducing ambassadors to individuals in each branch of government, and sharing her own stories, Harris not only underscores the instability of the federal-tribal relationship but highlights, as well, that Native people have the power to shape and reshape that relationship, just as she did.

The focus of the third gathering is on the relationships between and among Indigenous people globally. For this purpose, Harris accompanies each ambassador class to an international location, where they engage with a given Indigenous community and, in addition to developing personal relationships with community members, reflect on that community's culture and kinship system and relationship to their nation-state. Locations have included Venezuela, Guatemala, Bolivia, New Zealand, and others. Because Harris strongly believes that "Native Americans can influence the global discussion," she asks ambassadors to consider the ways in which sharing Indigenous core cultural values could be of benefit to others, writing, "As many minorities throughout the world struggle for autonomy and as tribal and ethnic strife becomes the focus of unrest on nearly every continent, Tribal America has a unique opportunity to make positive contributions."[38]

This statement illustrates just how much Harris has grown and evolved since bursting into tears so many years ago. Contending that Native people have "a unique opportunity to make positive contributions" goes far past the two goals outlined in the 1966 OIO proposal: "To help young Oklahoma Indians develop adequate self-concepts and pride in their cultural heritage" and "To help young Indians develop a positive self-concept of themselves as Indians and worthy individuals."[39] By advocating for Indigenous global engagement, Harris makes clear that her efforts to decolonize through the rematriation or restoration of core cultural values to Native Americans only *partially* fulfills her sense of responsibility and obligation. Harris's early distinction between assimilation and integration revealed her desire for Native people to fully participate in the world, in any way and in any place, *without giving up* their cultural identities or Indigeneity; she calls on Native people to internalize and manifest core cultural values "in all arena of contemporary life."[40] Her statement on global engagement demonstrates a notable shift in her rematriative efforts. Her initial goal was to rematriate core cultural values and share them with Native youths; her vision, as implemented through AIO, is for the ambassadors—who are trained and encouraged to express those core cultural values—to contribute to the restoration of Indigenous cultural values globally in an effort to care for others. She notes that tribes are the "miners' canaries of the global system," stressing that Native people have continued in spite of colonialism because of a reliance on Indigenous values and knowledge systems. Harris, situating all people as her circle of kinship, expresses a sense of greater responsibility and a broader sharing obligation, asserting, "If we create a system which nurtures us, then probably we will have created a system capable of nurturing everyone."[41]

At the final gathering, which is usually held on a tribal reservation in order to emphasize a return home to tribal land, Harris asks ambassadors to synthesize their experiences and to show that they understand their identity, role, and contribution by developing a community initiative that "weaves their traditional tribal values into a contemporary reality."[42] The community initiative represents a key element in Harris's rematriative efforts by providing evidence of her intended outcome—to "help you get to another level of consciousness . . . to move to another place [in life]."[43] Further, by asking ambassadors to develop an initiative for their community based on the needs of that community, she provides the opportunity for them to immediately express their core cultural values and to exercise the obligations associated with them.

Each aspect of the leadership program clarifies to the participants just why they are called "ambassadors." Throughout the program, each has been asked to act as a representative of their tribal nation by embodying the core cultural values of that nation and by establishing relationships—and expanding their circles of kinship—at each gathering. The name, then, serves to constantly remind participants of the specific role they play and the responsibilities they have to their sovereign nations, even after leaving the program.

Almost thirty years have passed since AIO welcomed its first class of ambassadors into the AIO family. A look at the work of ambassador alumni illustrates the far-reaching scope of Harris's vision and the extent to which ambassador alumni have "honored the gift." Alumni have gone on to serve as elected and appointed tribal government officials, federal government officials, and lawyers; practicing artists, musicians, filmmakers, radio hosts, and television producers; directors of museums, cultural centers, and language revitalization efforts; professors and academic administrators; CEOs and nonprofit directors; and board members for virtually every organization in Indian country. And, most significantly, the large majority of ambassador alumni continue to work directly on behalf of Native nations—shaping the government-to-government relationship between tribes and the federal government through their active participation in it, regardless of where they are geographically situated. Harris's rematriative process significantly restores core cultural values to a person so that wherever they may live, they are at home in the sureness of their own identity—rooted in tribal values and fulfilling kinship obligations.

Harris acknowledges that the Ambassador Program may be her most important legacy, her greatest strike against the colonial policies of erasure and elimination. By devoting herself to undoing and healing the pain of internalized oppression that she herself felt, she has safeguarded cultural heritage and ensured cultural continuance. Harris remarked on just how surprised the architects of assimilation and termination must have been to find out, fifty years later, that Native people never disappeared: "Little did they know . . . we are growing bigger and better."[44]

LaDonna Harris, as previously noted, has never held elected or appointed office or led a protest or movement. She is often referred to as a leader or activist, and an analysis of the vision and goals of the OIO and AIO leadership programs clearly evidences her leadership abilities and persistent advocacy. Yet neither term clarifies the nature of her legacy or the modality of her leadership. That she is a leader is undisputed, but she is something more: she is a *matriarch*, and it is this identity that best explains her legacy and modality. Her status as a matriarch extends well beyond the Comanche Nation. She is cherished throughout Indian country and treated much the same way her own family treated her great-grandmother. By using a matriarchal lens to analyze Harris's vision and goals for each leadership program, the evolution of Harris's distinctive modality as a leader becomes clear as does the remarkable nature of her legacy—the rematriation of core cultural values and the re-creation and forging of kinship relationships and obligations, thus foreclosing colonial erasure and generating—not terminating—a distinctly Indigenous future.

NOTES

1. Amanda J. Cobb, "Powerful Medicine: The Rhetoric of Comanche Activist LaDonna Harris," *Studies in American Indian Literature* 18, no. 4 (Winter 2006): 63–87.
2. Cobb, "Powerful Medicine," 65.
3. Sarah Eppler Janda, *Beloved Women: The Political Lives of LaDonna Harris and Wilma Mankiller* (DeKalb: Northern Illinois University Press, 2007), 39.
4. Janda, *Beloved Women*, 39.
5. Janda, *Beloved Women*, 92.
6. LaDonna Harris, *LaDonna Harris: A Comanche Life*, ed. Henrietta Stockel (Lincoln: University of Nebraska Press, 2000), 66.
7. Harris, *LaDonna Harris*, 66.
8. Harris, *LaDonna Harris*, 116, emphasis added.
9. Dale Turner and Audra Simpson, "Indigenous Leadership in a Flat World" (paper, National Centre on First Nations Governance, May 2008), 8, emphasis in the original.
10. Harris, *LaDonna Harris*, 92.
11. Harris, *LaDonna Harris*, 99.
12. Janda, *Beloved Women*, 56.
13. Harris, *LaDonna Harris*, iii; Cobb, "Powerful Medicine," 63–87.
14. Harris, *LaDonna Harris*, 12; Cobb, "Powerful Medicine," 63–87.
15. LaDonna Harris, "Looking within Ourselves: Civil Societies and Core Cultural Values" (paper, Conference on Civil Society and Durable Development, Fez, Morocco, February 14–16, 2002), 2.
16. Harris, *LaDonna Harris*, 3.
17. Harris, *LaDonna Harris*, 3.
18. Harris, *LaDonna Harris*, 2.
19. Harris, "Looking within Ourselves," 1; Cobb, "Powerful Medicine," 63–87.
20. Harris, "Looking within Ourselves," 1–2.
21. Richard Lowitt, *Fred Harris: His Journey from Liberalism to Populism* (New York: Rowman and Littlefield, 2002), 257–65.
22. Harris, *LaDonna Harris*, 110–16; Cobb, "Powerful Medicine," 63–87.
23. Harris, "Looking within Ourselves," 2.
24. Harris, *LaDonna Harris*, 56–57.
25. Harris, *LaDonna Harris*, 59.
26. Annelise Orleck and Lisa Gayle Hazirjian, eds., *The War on Poverty: A New Grassroots History, 1964–1980* (Athens: University of Georgia Press, 2011); Daniel M. Cobb, *Native Activism in Cold War America: The Struggle for Sovereignty* (Lawrence: University Press of Kansas, 2008).

27. Oklahomans for Indian Opportunity, "A Proposal Designed to Develop and Implement a Social-Educational Skills Training Program for Indians of Oklahoma," 1966, box 283, folder 4, 1, Fred Harris Collection, Congressional and Political Collections, Carl Albert Center, University of Oklahoma, Norman.

28. Janda, *Beloved Women*, 39.

29. Oklahomans for Indian Opportunity, "A Proposal," 10–11.

30. Oklahomans for Indian Opportunity, "A Proposal," 7.

31. Oklahomans for Indian Opportunity, "A Proposal," 4.

32. Oklahomans for Indian Opportunity, "A Proposal," 5–6.

33. Oklahomans for Indian Opportunity, "A Proposal," 59–60.

34. Oklahomans for Indian Opportunity, "A Proposal," 14, 25.

35. Americans for Indian Opportunity, "Working for Change through Traditional Tribal Values," in *Projects and Initiatives* (Bernalillo, NM: Americans for Indian Opportunity, 2000/2001), 3.

36. Americans for Indian Opportunity, "Working for Change," 4.

37. Jace Weaver, *Other Words: American Indian Literature, Law, and Culture* (Norman: University of Oklahoma Press, 2001), ix.

38. Americans for Indian Opportunity, "Working for Change," 4.

39. Oklahomans for Indian Opportunity, "A Proposal," 14, 25.

40. Americans for Indian Opportunity, "Working for Change," 2.

41. LaDonna Harris and Jacqueline Wasilewski, *This Is What We Want to Share: Core Cultural Values* (Albuquerque, NM: Americans for Indian Opportunity, 1992), 5.

42. Harris and Wasilewski, *This Is What We Want to Share*, 2.

43. Harris, *LaDonna Harris*, 125.

44. Harris, *LaDonna Harris*, 92.

CHELSEA BALL

11

"UNTIL WE ORGANIZED"

Wanda Jo Peltier Stapleton and the Equal Rights Amendment Debate in Oklahoma, 1972–1982

At first glance, Wanda Jo Peltier Stapleton is probably not what one would expect a "radical American feminist" to look like. If you tell her this, even at eighty-five, she laughs and says, "You have to growl when you say it so it sounds more intimidating."[1] Peltier Stapleton has been called quite a few things over her long career of political activism. After being labeled a communist by a state representative for asking him to meet with her about the Equal Rights Amendment (ERA), she began to call herself a Radical American Feminist, or RAF. Yet, on closer examination, Peltier Stapleton's political career has been highly reactive, responding to the variety of everyday challenges and gender discrimination that women in Oklahoma and across the country faced in the 1960s and 1970s. A widow and displaced homemaker with two children by age twenty-six, she faced major obstacles in her personal life that were largely out of her control. It was in her professional life that Wanda Jo found her path to create change by advocating for women's rights and eventually the ERA. From her sex discrimination lawsuit victory against Oklahoma Baptist University to her focus on helping homemakers and farmwives, Peltier Stapleton challenged the "women's libber" radical stereotype that was thrust upon feminists by conservative New Right leaders by the 1980s. As a mother, Baptist Church member, and housewife supporter, she was far from anti-family. Yet she was liberal in her own right, supporting unorthodox and often humorous grassroots tactics to campaign for the ERA. In doing so, she aided in the creation of a sort of Oklahoma feminism, one that married southern family values and religion with the independent spirit of western women. Peltier Stapleton led the grassroots ERA movement on behalf of the Oklahoma Women's Political Caucus and many other local feminist organizations, challenging the conservative or watered-down image of the movement perceived by many state representatives. And, like hundreds of women on both sides of the ERA issue, she was inspired by this ratification campaign to serve in public office.[2]

Born Wanda Jo Gramlich during the height of the Dust Bowl and living on her own by age fourteen, Peltier Stapleton was no stranger to hard times, yet she remained highly motivated and independent. After she was born in 1933 on a small farm outside Checotah, Oklahoma, her father would spend $0.35 of his $1 a day wage to purchase Eagle Brand milk for his only child.[3] Two years later, after Wanda Jo's sister and only sibling, Vanda, was born, the family migrated to California to find work in the cotton fields. For the next eight years, the family bounced around nearly every state in the southwest, often returning to Oklahoma for short stints to stay with family. Her father was an alcoholic who developed a gambling problem, and this, combined with the instability caused by constantly moving, drove Peltier Stapleton's mother to suffer a "nervous breakdown." With a highly absent father and a hospitalized mother, Peltier Stapleton and little sister Vanda went to live with their aunt and uncle in Checotah. Once they realized the family already had five other children in their care, Peltier Stapleton and her sister found their own apartment in town. With the help of their teachers and by working various waitressing jobs, they managed to pay the rent.[4] The sisters always made it a point to attend school wherever they were living, which was often a challenge. Yet Peltier Stapleton was an incredibly bright student, graduating from Checotah High School in 1949 at the age of sixteen.

After graduation, she married her high school sweetheart, William Wilson, and had two children. She enjoyed working with her husband on their family farm and supporting him on Sundays when he preached at a local church.

Peltier Stapleton was not a particularly political person in her early years, but in the late 1950s she became interested in the League of Women Voters after a fellow church member invited her to a meeting. It was at this meeting that she learned for the first time of her legal vulnerability as a farmwife in Oklahoma. Under state law, Peltier Stapleton was considered a dependent of her husband, with a legal status similar to that of their children. Because of a specific "Head of Household" law, a wife did not have automatic legal access to property the couple acquired during their marriage and, if challenged by her children, could be subject to probate court and inheritance taxes on her own property.[5] Farmwives and housewives like Peltier Stapleton were particularly at risk, as their work was tied to this property but often not viewed as a legitimate career. Nor did this type of work pay into social security, leaving housewives even more vulnerable in old age. Upon learning this, Peltier Stapleton immediately returned home and had her husband draw up a will naming her as the sole beneficiary of his estate. As unfortunate circumstances would have it, Wilson soon died from an undiagnosed heart condition at age twenty-six. Widowed, with two children to support and no real work experience or training, Peltier Stapleton decided to return to school, a place where she had always found success.[6]

Despite heartbreak, financial difficulties, and the task of raising two daughters on her own, Peltier Stapleton was an excellent student. She graduated from Oklahoma Baptist University in 1963 at the top of her class, earning not only her degree in English but the Shakespeare Award, the Latin Award, the Robinette Award for future teachers, and a fellowship for a master's program at the University of Kansas. After graduating with her master's degree in English, Peltier Stapleton returned to her home state so that she could begin working on her doctorate at the University of Oklahoma. She finished her coursework at OU and married her close friend Gerald Peltier, then returned to Oklahoma Baptist University in 1968, this time as a faculty member in the English Department. It was there that Peltier Stapleton noticed a pattern. Year after year, while male colleagues who had no doctoral work and less teaching experience received tenure and promotion, Peltier Stapleton remained untenured and without a pay raise. After five years of waiting, she decided to file a complaint with the new Equal Employment Opportunity Commission. Although the commission took four years to return a ruling, Peltier Stapleton won her case. The decision read, "The Commission finds reasonable cause to believe that the Respondent University (Oklahoma Baptist University) has violated Title VII by discriminating against women because of their sex with reference to promotion and tenure practices, wages, and retirement/insurance plans. There is also reasonable cause to believe the respondent violated Title VII by failing to hire women in certain departments."[7]

The ruling not only recognized Peltier Stapleton's experiences and verified her charges but clearly established for every woman at OBU the right to equal pay and equal hiring and promotion practices.[8] Not wanting to wait around for the backlash, Peltier Stapleton moved on from OBU and prepared for her doctoral exams. While she did receive a small cash payout from her lawsuit, she found her reputation in the academic world highly tarnished. Her adviser and committee members at the University of Oklahoma became impossible to work with, refusing to meet with her about her comprehensive exams or give her feedback despite the university administration's positive reviews of her exam answers.[9] Without her committee's approval, Peltier Stapleton would not be able to finish her doctorate.[10]

Fed up with academia, Peltier Stapleton left the university and started her own technical writing business, Peltier Pen Productions. As a former English professor, Peltier Stapleton used her writing skills to aid those who, as she recognized through firsthand experience, were highly vulnerable in her community—women. She was particularly concerned with helping displaced housewives: women who, through death or divorce, unexpectedly found themselves in their thirties, forties, and fifties without a husband bringing in an income and no job experience or training of their own. She developed a training course to aid these women in basic job and life skills, from help with writing a résumé and filling out job applications to seminars on how to negotiate for a raise. Initially holding classes at vocational centers, Peltier Stapleton developed a curriculum that was eventually adopted and distributed nationwide through the Women's Educational Equity Act in 1980 because of its success in the Oklahoma City metro area. She also used her writing skills to obtain more than $6 million in grants over her lifetime for women's resource centers and education curricula for numerous underprivileged Oklahoma communities, including five American Indian tribes and one all-Black town. Her experience empowering working mothers and housewives as well as her exposure to the needs of minority women through her writing center and tutoring work made Peltier Stapleton increasingly aware of the unending legal work it would take to amend sexist laws at the state and local levels. It is no surprise that she jumped at the chance to lobby on behalf of the Equal Rights Amendment after its passage by Congress in 1972.

The Equal Rights Amendment, or ERA, a constitutional amendment written and proposed by suffragist Alice Paul in 1923, would outlaw discrimination based on sex. The amendment did not obtain congressional approval until fifty years after its first introduction to legislators. By the early 1970s, when the United States was well into the so-called rights revolution, both the Democratic and Republican Parties endorsed the amendment because of its straightforward wording; it seemed like a moderate way for politicians to support the women's movement.

Within hours of its congressional passage, the ERA made its way to the individual states for ratification. In a highly unusual move, the Oklahoma Senate was one of the first state legislative bodies to immediately approve of the amendment, giving the ERA a voice vote of "yea" that very same day. In the first month, fourteen states ratified it. By the end of the year, that number had risen to thirty. Only eight more states needed to ratify the amendment to add gender discrimination protections to the Constitution; the situation looked hopeful.[11]

After easy passage through the senate in Oklahoma, there was little reason to believe that the ERA would have any trouble in the state house. National and local politicians labeled the state's endorsement an easy win for the ERA for a few important reasons. The highest-ranking state officials, Governor David Hall and Speaker of the House Dan Draper, publicly endorsed the amendment and encouraged legislators to do the same.[12] With a newly formed Governor's Commission on the Status of Women and a legacy of female leadership in the local civil rights movement, many Oklahomans assumed that civil rights for women was naturally the next step for legal justice in the state. After all, Oklahoma, like many western states, had given women the right to vote before the Nineteenth Amendment went into effect; it was written in the state's history and culture. Yet, despite all these signs, the Oklahoma house of representatives became the first legislative body in the nation to vote down the ERA, stating that the amendment needed more research.[13] This defeat sparked the beginning of the battle over the Equal Rights Amendment in Oklahoma.

After the amendment failed in the house of representatives, Peltier Stapleton went straight to the Oklahoma state capitol to share her story and offer support. In an oral history interview conducted by Oklahoma State University, Peltier Stapleton described that experience: "We thought if we looked good, if we smelled good, if we made sense, it was a done deal. Well, about all we got at first were pats on the head. That is, until we organized."[14] Peltier Stapleton's fight for women's rights in her home state was only just beginning. Along with

Wanda Jo Peltier (Stapleton) speaking to a crowd of ERA supporters in front of the Oklahoma State Capitol, June 6, 1982. Activists hoped to encourage Governor George Nigh to call a special legislative session to give the amendment one last chance to pass in Oklahoma. Courtesy of the Women of the Oklahoma Legislature Oral History Project, Oklahoma State University.

many other pro-ERA activists, she turned to local organizations and grassroots campaigning as the mechanisms with the best chance of lobbying for the amendment's ratification.

By 1975, Oklahoma's pro-ERA activists had organized statewide. Coming from different women's organizations, churches, and occupations, women and men alike united into various lobbying and support groups, the largest of which were OK-ERA and the Oklahoma Women's Political Caucus (OKWPC). OK-ERA, formed in 1976 by Edna Mae Phelps and Dorothy Stanislaus, was an umbrella organization that united local women's groups (e.g., the Oklahoma League of Women Voters, Common Cause, the American Civil Liberties Union) that supported the passage of the ERA. Because of the large groups involved, OK-ERA remained the most powerful lobbying organization for ratification until 1980. OKWPC, cofounded by state representative Cleta Deatherage in 1971, included other important leaders, such as activist Shirley Hilbert-Price and University of Oklahoma journalism professor and writer Junetta Davis. The OKWPC was also involved in several non-ERA projects aimed at assisting Oklahoma women but would become larger and much more focused on the amendment later in the decade.

Aside from Democratic Party support and the formation of early pro-ERA women's organizations in the state, politicians and citizens alike were confident that the ERA would gain approval in Oklahoma because there was a lack of organized opposition to it in the early 1970s. The ERA was largely a nonpartisan issue until Ronald Reagan rescinded Republican support for it when he became president in 1981. Before this, the ERA had the support of President Jimmy Carter, members of both political parties (although more Democrats than Republicans), and almost every governor, including Oklahoma's David Boren (1975–79) and George Nigh (1979–87). It had, after all, only been in late 1973, with the passage of *Roe v. Wade*, that the ERA had become associated with the ideas of the early women's liberation movement and began to face real opposition. After the United States Supreme Court ruled abortion legal, conservatives and religious fundamentalists began to unify against the ERA as a common enemy.[15]

Sociologist and women's historian Ruth Murray Brown argues, "The anti-ERA organization which became the nucleus of the pro-family movement was born the weekend after the ERA's defeat in Oklahoma" in 1972.[16] Unlike the ERA supporters, those in opposition did not have already-established organizations that they could convert to work against the ERA. By 1975, though, the pro-family supporters in Oklahoma were fully united in their fight against the amendment. United by a frustration with their sex being misrepresented in the media and at the state capitol, conservative women entered the public sphere, battling the ERA as a form of protest against feminism. Feminists, they argued, did not represent the wants and needs of American women. Rather, conservative women and mothers—who highlighted their differences from men as what made them unique—represented a majority of America's women. In the 1970s and early 1980s the ERA offered conservative activists a highly public and symbolic feminist issue to defeat, which laid the foundation for the eventual development of the pro-family movement into the New Right.

The difference between those in favor of the ERA and those against was a very old issue that had plagued the women's movement since the 1920s after the passage of the Nineteenth Amendment. The debate over whether women are fundamentally the same as or different from men split the women of the 1970s. Most feminists believed that women were capable of the same activities as men and that it was society that created and designated the sex roles that continued to constrain women. Those against the ERA thought that men and women were biologically different and, as a result, women were more suited for motherly roles and housework.[17] In order to defend their way of life as homemakers, pro-family supporters in Oklahoma organized OK STOP ERA. As the most powerful anti-ERA group in the state, it attracted support from other groups, including Women Who Want to Be Women, the Farm Bureau, and, most important, Phyllis Schlafly's Eagle Forum. OK STOP ERA owed much of its success to Phyllis Schlafly's conservative organization and its publication the *Phyllis Schlafly Report*. Schlafly was a "conservative author, newspaper columnist, attorney . . . and self-professed housewife" with a husband and six children. During the ERA debate Schlafly went on multiple speaking tours, several of which landed her in Oklahoma, urging women to stay in the home, where God wanted them.[18] With ERA opposition growing throughout the nation, Schlafly ruled her anti-ERA organizations almost like a dictator. She was the only official leader and face of the movement, making the pro-family program highly united, efficient, and successful.[19]

With the New Right increasing in numbers, it became obvious to Peltier Stapleton that the logic-based arguments supporting the ERA were no longer effective. Most opponents of the amendment disagreed with constitutional equality of the sexes because they believed either that it was an unnecessary reach of federal power or that it went against the Bible. Fundamentalist Christians viewed the ERA as a direct attack against their religion and the morality of the nation, based on their literal interpretations of the Bible. These fundamentalists (largely the Church of Christ, Baptist, Mormon, and Methodist denominations) accounted for 43.3 percent of Oklahoma's population and 74 percent of the ERA protesters within the state.[20]

A majority of the female pro-family defenders had viewed politics as no place for ladies in the past (even the famed "Goldwater girls" of ten years earlier had not had much say in political strategies and the running of campaigns themselves), but the ERA debate brought them into a political realm that extended beyond just voting. They were now involved in lobbying, campaigning, and fundraising for political issues and the candidates who supported them. Overall, the ERA represented the conservatives' fear of an anti-family, anti-God nation made reality. Equal rights for women meant that women would no longer hold an elevated status and that they would be less respected by men. As *Tulsa Tribune* writer Jeffrey Hart wrote in 1980, "The New Right is a political 'phenomenon' focused more on cultural than political issues. They are defenders of a way of life that has merged with the new mass evangelical Christian to produce a new and powerful political force on the American scene."[21] The pro-family supporters waged war against abortion, pornography, prostitution, homosexuality, sex education in schools, and busing; somehow the ERA began to represent the wellspring of all of these evils. Convincing legislators that American women did not want feminism became more important than avoiding the highly public and often male realm of politicking.

Frustrated with anti-ERA activists controlling the perception of the amendment, many ERA supporters began to push back. One of the tactics used early on by Oklahoma pro-family women to sway legislators while also highlighting their femininity was to bake breads, cookies, and other treats and distribute them at the state capitol. Not wanting to come off as unladylike by lobbying legislators directly, they would set up big tables with anti-ERA signs along with their goodies, and the strategy was successful. To counter this, pro-ERA women also began delivering baked goods and pies during the last few years of the campaign. According to Mattie Morgan, former vice-chair of the Governor's Commission on the Status of Women and official ERA spokesperson for United Methodist Church, the women mimicked STOP ERA's big tables of food, except their signs read, "Baked by Liberated Women." During the 1981 and 1982 legislative terms, many ERA supporters also pinned white flowers to the lapels of legislators who supported the amendment (white and green were the colors of ERA supporters, similar to the suffragists, while those opposed always wore red).[22] As the lively baked goods competition between the factions became more noticeable, Peltier Stapleton challenged the pro-family women of the "Housewives League" to a bake-off. Although none of the members would engage Peltier Stapleton in her competition, several other women (and one man) volunteered to face her. She won and was awarded an Equal Rights Amendment apron.[23] In another pointed jab at the opposition, who had accused pro-ERA women of being unladylike, the OKWPC held a fashion show fundraiser in the governor's mansion in 1978. Modeling high-end clothing from Ruth Meyers, a prominent dress shop in downtown Oklahoma City, the participants attracted an impressive crowd of men and women. Above the catwalk hung a banner that read "Current Trends in Fashion and the Law."[24] Not only were these grassroots campaign techniques good for public support, they also gave ERA supporters a chance to reclaim their femininity in front of their opponents.

Wanda Jo Peltier Stapleton identified with pro-family women and understood what drove them. She had been a church member for most of her life and had come to understand that those against the ERA were simply ignorant of the needs and realities of women, especially single mothers. Peltier Stapleton dealt with ERA opposition by emphasizing how the amendment would help homemakers and farmwives, not put their way of life in jeopardy. She stressed how the ERA would protect women who didn't have a separate income but contributed to the home, because it would create social security benefits and make them equal property owners with their husbands. She viewed the amendment as logical: the ERA made sense for Oklahoma women. To battle this logic, anti-ERA proponents largely used the fear of unisex bathrooms, women being drafted, and men's lack of accountability to their families to gain attention and followers. However, the more the OKWPC, OK-ERA, and Peltier Stapleton repeated what the ERA would and would not do, the more they looked defensive to the public. In a newspaper interview, Penny Williams, the president of OK-ERA, was asked what the biggest barrier was to the amendment's passage Oklahoma. She replied, "It is the misunderstanding of what the ERA is, and what it will do. It has been made an aberration instead of a coherent, harmonious part of the constitution."[25] By the end of the 1970s many Americans were fed up with social change and protests. The conservative women who came out against the ERA capitalized on this.

When ratification had not been achieved by 1976, it became clear to many ERA supporters that this was not going to be the easy fight that politicians had predicted. Lobbying, organization, and educational pamphlets had not garnered the necessary support in the Oklahoma legislature. OK-ERA and the OKWPC quickly decided that campaigning for pro-ERA candidates and even their own organizations' members in the 1976 and 1978 state legislature elections was the best option for ratification as the deadline approached.[26] Like the New Right organizers who opposed the amendment, the women in support of the ERA began to cut their political teeth in public office and lobbying. Even for more progressive-minded women, the ERA debate would be the first time many of them conducted meetings, spoke publicly, met with their representatives, and campaigned for themselves or others.

Like her fellow Oklahoma feminists, Peltier Stapleton supported the grassroots campaigns for pro-ERA legislators as well as other woman-based projects like rape crisis centers, domestic violence shelters, and education resources for single mothers. She already held a reputation as a dedicated lobbyist, so she was no stranger to the state capitol. Peltier Stapleton had now lost two husbands, each time having to fight for her right to their properties and pensions, which only emboldened her commitment to the amendment's ratification. Along with lobbying and campaigning, Peltier Stapleton worked on many state-based programs to help better the lives of Oklahoma women. One of her first projects was establishing rape crisis centers for women who were victims of sexual abuse. After being nominated to the Governor's Commission on the Status of Women, Peltier Stapleton also helped women in Oklahoma penitentiaries gain access to work and recreational facilities equal to those afforded to their male counterparts.[27]

Wanda Jo Peltier Stapleton's grassroots organizing gave many Oklahoma ERA supporters renewed hope for ratification. In 1980, she became chairwoman of the OKWPC, a position to which she dedicated herself. The ERA deadline had just been extended until 1982, meaning both sides of the debate were preparing for the final push in the battle over ratification. During her four years of leadership in the OKWPC, Peltier Stapleton expanded the organization at a phenomenal rate. In 1982 alone it raised more than $16,000 to aid the ERA fight, logged in five thousand campaign hours, and built the OKWPC into the third-largest state organization of its kind measured on a per capita basis.[28] As president of what was now the most powerful pro-ERA group in the state, Peltier Stapleton utilized this newfound power to pressure Oklahoma leaders into taking a stand for the ERA.

In July 1981, Peltier Stapleton attended the tenth annual National Women's Political Caucus Convention in Albuquerque, New Mexico. The goal of the conference was to come up with a strategy that would grab the attention of states that had yet to ratify the ERA. The delegates had less than one year before the amendment would expire. Coincidentally, the annual National Governors' Conference would soon be meeting in an unratified state: Oklahoma. The delegates of the NWPC decided to contact all the governors from the thirty-five ratified states and urge them to boycott the National Governors' Conference in support of the ERA and to pressure Oklahoma legislators to change their votes.[29] When the national leaders called the motion to a vote, Peltier Stapleton did not give her support. She knew the measure would come off as bullying, radical, and highly influenced by pro-ERA forces from outside the state (which would not be well received by Oklahomans). Despite her protests, the delegates voted in favor of the measure, and Peltier Stapleton decided to support her organization and write the letters.[30]

Peltier Stapleton's letters were met with mixed responses from the governors. Most explained that the ERA was near and dear to their hearts, but punishing Oklahoma businesses was not the answer. Others saw the boycott as absurd; after all, the governor did not get a say in how its state legislators voted. However, an article in *US News and World Report* stated that a few governors were feeling "reluctant to commit themselves to attending" because their wives did not appreciate that the meeting was to be held "in a state that refused to ratify the ERA."[31] In the end, none of the lobbied governors boycotted the meeting, and Peltier Stapleton had to deal with a very angry governor, George Nigh of Oklahoma.

In the final years of the ERA debate, supporters and opponents intensified their publicity and influence. Propaganda inundated citizens of unratified states in the form of pamphlets, radio and television advertisements, rallies, and newspaper articles. While pro-ERA groups stuck to the logical approaches of education and facts, the pro-family representatives in Oklahoma, led by national leader Phyllis Schlafly, presented the ERA as an immoral threat to homemakers and their families that would lead to all women being forced into the workplace and a rise in abortion, promiscuity, and child abandonment. Schlafly also connected the ERA to gay rights and campaigned heavily against homosexuals being allowed to teach in secondary schools. While those in favor of the ERA in Oklahoma also experienced aid from national ERA groups and supporters, ironically, national influence seemed to hurt the local movement more than it helped. Peltier Stapleton and other local feminists also dealt with setbacks from national ERA leaders and movements. Like the failed letter-writing campaign, the disconnect between what the ERA meant to Oklahomans and what it meant nationally became more apparent after the National Organization for Women (NOW) began its ERA Countdown Campaign.

NOW, established in 1966, was the first civil rights group created to lobby and pressure the government on behalf of women.[32] The organization grew exponentially in the late 1960s and early 1970s with chapters across the nation, but it seemed to be losing touch with working-class and minority women as the women's liberation movement took off. Focused on working women and federal legislation and protections, NOW's message did not always resonate strongly with Oklahoma's large homemaker and farmwife populations. As for the Equal Rights Amendment, NOW had always supported its passage and made it the top priority after 1972. As the issue got down to the wire and approval was still needed from three states in 1981, NOW decided to spend the remaining year working on what it called the ERA Countdown Campaign. The organization sent representatives, resources, and funds to the four unratified states they thought most likely to ratify the ERA: Oklahoma, Florida, Illinois, and North Carolina.[33] National president of NOW Eleanor Smeal thought the organization's assistance in the states that were on the fence would finally give the ERA the backing and support it needed. NOW opened ERA Countdown Campaign offices in Oklahoma City, Tulsa, and Norman, each with its own out-of-state leader and personnel. Even the national NOW-nominated leader for the state of Oklahoma, Ruth Adams, was brought in from Indiana. Consequently, the local groups, the OKWPC and OK-ERA, were not happy about the infiltration. Peltier Stapleton was informed that NOW would be taking over lobbying legislators from the major metropolitan areas of Oklahoma while her local group could work on the rural representatives, who were less significant for the campaign's success. As the 1982 deadline approached, both local and national ERA organizations focused their efforts on those states that supposedly had the most potential. Unfortunately for Peltier Stapleton, the arrival of NOW and other out-of-state activists damaged the support and trust she had been building for the previous eight years.[34]

In October 1981, NOW began a media blitz throughout the state, buying radio and television advertisements promoting the ERA.[35] It also paid celebrities to come into Oklahoma and endorse the amendment. Actor Alan Alda held a speaking tour across seven Oklahoma cities, and singer and actress Mary Kay Place held an ERA rally at the University of Tulsa. As Peltier Stapleton had warned her National Women's Political Caucus delegates the year before during the governor boycott discussion, Oklahomans did not respond well to outside promoters. Many locals saw NOW as trying to throw money at the amendment and did not like celebrities and other national leaders being brought in to influence their opinions. One woman, angry at the spotlight NOW had put on Oklahoma, wrote to the *Tulsa Tribune*, arguing that the state could make up its own mind and saying she worried that her fellow citizens were not "thinking for themselves."[36]

Overall, NOW spent an estimated $200,000 on the ERA Countdown Campaign in Oklahoma and had little to show for it. The national groups also continued to exclude Peltier Stapleton from meetings and strategizing. She was conveniently left off guest lists for conferences, and when she would show up and try to work with national leaders, she was ignored. Due to her continued marginalization, Peltier Stapleton's OKWPC lost much of its influence within the state, and the movement lost many supporters whom she had worked so hard to bring on board. A few weeks before the June 30, 1982, deadline, a combined thirty-five thousand ERA supporters marched across the state capitols of the big four: Oklahoma, Illinois, Florida, and North Carolina. The Florida march was led by Governor Bob Graham and his wife while the Illinois protesters chained themselves to the senate doors. In Oklahoma, Wanda Jo Peltier Stapleton marched with more than ten thousand ERA supporters and gave one last impassioned speech for the amendment.[37] During the ten-year battle, the ERA had been submitted to the Oklahoma legislature sixteen times, with the closest tally only three votes short of approval. But the day of legal equality for women did not ultimately come to Oklahoma or the United States.

When Congress ratified the ERA in 1972, Wanda Jo Peltier Stapleton had become a leading figure in the fight for ratification in Oklahoma. Using her own personal experience with sexist laws and grassroots politicking, she lobbied for the ERA on behalf of farmwives and homemakers who would benefit greatly from provisions of legal protection that the amendment would afford. As the organization's president in 1980, Peltier Stapleton helped transform the Oklahoma Women's Political Caucus into one of the fastest-growing chapters in the country and was a fierce advocate of some of its most controversial political tactics, including a nationwide boycott on travel to all unratified states.

Gloria Steinem and Wanda Jo Peltier Stapleton at the tree-planting ceremony in honor of Chief Wilma Mankiller, Oklahoma City University, October 6, 2011. Courtesy of Jo Davis.

Peltier Stapleton, through her activism and commitment to local women's issues, redefined what it meant to be an Oklahoma feminist. It meant that you could be married to a rural Baptist preacher and still support reproductive rights and the rights of sexual minorities. It meant supporting the needs of housewives and farmwives as a part of the larger women's liberation movement and recognizing the particular needs and rights of women in your area. This ideology challenged the New Right definition of feminism both within the state and across the country.

Although her battle for the Equal Rights Amendment in Oklahoma ended in 1982, Peltier Stapleton still had some fight left in her. In 1986 she decided to run for a seat in the Oklahoma House of Representatives for District Ninety-Three in south Oklahoma City. For more than a month straight, Peltier Stapleton walked door-to-door, shaking hands with her constituents and passing out voter registration cards along with her famous "Wanda Jo's Hot Hominy" recipe, a grassroots tactic she had long used. After winning the election, she remained a state legislator for ten years, working for women's rights and education until

1996. Peltier Stapleton continued to win elections due to her tireless reporting and availability to her constituents, to whom she sent monthly newsletters, as well as her focus on consumer rights and state fiscal responsibility. She claims that much of her political inspiration came from the vision of Betty Friedan, founder of the National Women's Political Caucus, the organization Peltier Stapleton had dedicated so much of her time to. In 2007, when asked what political advice she would give contemporary women, she stated, "Life is short, and we just go around once—and you know our first grade reader said, 'Run Dick Run.' I'd say, 'Run Jane Run.' You'll always regret it if you don't."[38] Like thousands of other women who came into the political realm through either their support or protest of the women's movement in the 1970s, Peltier Stapleton used her background as an activist as a launching point from which to participate in electoral politics, where she continued to advocate for women's rights and education. Peltier Stapleton, even in her eighties and long retired, can still be found speaking to the Oklahoma City Council and campaigning for human rights. In other words, she is still running.

In 2015 the Oklahoma Universal Human Rights Alliance, an affiliate of the Greater Oklahoma City Chapter of the United Nations Association of the United States of America, awarded Peltier Stapleton the Human Rights Hero medal for "being a constant champion of women's rights and the rights of ordinary people everywhere." Her dedication and work on the ERA in Oklahoma and nationwide through the Oklahoma Women's Political Caucus as well as her tireless service as a state representative were cited in her award description.[39]

NOTES

1. Wanda Jo Peltier Stapleton, interviewed by the author, February 29, 2016, Oklahoma City, Oklahoma; "Monks' Quiz Request Upsets Rights Group," *Oklahoma City Times*, March 5, 1981.

2. Only one other scholarly work has been written about the ERA in Oklahoma, a University of Oklahoma dissertation filed in 2010, which was later published. The author, Jana Vogt, emphasizes the conservative opposition to the ERA movement and its relationship to the conservative movement nationwide. Jana Vogt, "Oklahoma and the ERA: Rousing a Red State, 1972–1982" (PhD diss., University of Oklahoma, 2010); Jana Vogt Catignani, "Conservative Oklahoma Women United: The Crusade to Defeat the ERA," in *Main Street Oklahoma: Stories of Twentieth-Century America*, ed. Linda W. Reese and Patricia Loughlin (Norman: University of Oklahoma Press, 2013), 221–38.

3. Wonder Woman Awards 1984 Nomination Form, Miscellaneous Folder, Wanda Jo Peltier Stapleton Collection, Oklahoma Historical Society Research Center, Oklahoma City (hereafter cited as OHS).

4. Wonder Woman Awards 1984 Nomination Form.

5. Head of Household, Oklahoma State §32-2 (1910), repealed by law, 1988, HB 1193, c. 17, §1, emerg. eff. March 16, 1988. This law was an obvious target for ERA supporters in Oklahoma and was eventually repealed in 1988.

6. Wanda Jo Peltier Stapleton, interviewed by Tanya Finchum, Oklahoma State University, May 16, 2007, Women of the Oklahoma Legislature Oral History Project.

7. Wonder Woman Awards 1984 Nomination Form; "OBU Accused of Sex Bias, Case Cited as ERA Argument," *Oklahoma Journal*, March 23, 1977; "Complaint Charges OBU with Sex Discrimination," *Daily Oklahoman*, March 14, 1973.

8. "Women Advocate the ERA Bill from Both Viewpoints," *Daily Oklahoman*, October 23, 1981; Martha Sanguinette, "Personal Battle Prompts Fight for Women's Rights," *Tulsa Tribune*, n.d.; "OBU Accused of Sex Bias," *Oklahoma Journal*, April 1973, in Miscellaneous Folder, Wanda Jo Peltier Stapleton Collection, OHS.

9. Wonder Woman Awards 1984 Nomination Form.

10. Linda Williams Reese, historian and graduate of the PhD program at the University of Oklahoma in 1991, includes in a book chapter her insights about life in the same program in the 1980s, around the time Peltier was also a student. See Linda Williams Reese, "The Recognition of Women in Oklahoma History," in *Reshaping Women's History: Voices of Nontraditional Women Historians*, ed. Julie A. Gallagher and Barbara Winslow (Urbana: University of Illinois Press, 2018), 71–84.

11. Nick Thimmesch, "Supporters to Blame for ERA's Woes," *Daily Oklahoman*, June 6, 1978.

12. Junetta Davis, "Similarities Seen in Past and Present Women's Amendment Action," *Norman Transcript*, January 16, 1973.

13. "Opponents Celebrate ERA Demise," *Tulsa Tribune*, July 11, 1982.

14. Peltier Stapleton, interviewed by Finchum.

15. Ashlyn K. Kuersten, *Women and the Law* (Santa Barbara, CA: ABC-CLIO, 2003), 40.

16. Ruth Murray Brown, *For a "Christian America": A History of the Religious Right* (New York: Prometheus, 2002), 30. See also Marjorie J. Spruill, *Divided We Stand: The Battle over Women's Rights and Family Values That Polarized American Politics* (New York: Bloomsbury, 2017), 81–83.

17. For more on the same-versus-different debate, see Nancy F. Cott, *The Grounding of Modern Feminism* (New Haven, CT: Yale University Press, 1987), 49–50.

18. David Wilson, "ERA Debaters Play to Tulsa University Audience," *Tulsa Tribune*, October 26, 1979.

19. For more information on Phyllis Schlafly and the rise of the conservative New Right, see Donald T. Critchlow, *Phyllis Schlafly and Grassroots Conservatism* (Princeton, NJ: Princeton University Press, 2005), 37–68.

20. Brown, *For a Christian America*, 69–71.

21. Jeffrey Hart, "Two Big Stories Benefit Reagan," *Tulsa Tribune*, July 31, 1980.

22. Becky Patton, interviewed by Martha Skeeters, March 9, 2010, Red Dirt Women Oral History Project, University of Oklahoma; Mattie Morgan, interviewed by Martha

Skeeters, November 16, 2009, Red Dirt Women Oral History Project, University of Oklahoma.

23. Peltier Stapleton, interviewed by the author.

24. Penny Williams, interviewed by Dr. Martha Skeeters, April 8, 2010, Red Dirt Women Oral History Project, University of Oklahoma.

25. Caroline Johnson, "Oklahomans for, against ERA in 11th Hour Effort," *Tulsa Tribune*, undated clipping, ERA Collection, box 60, OHS.

26. Will Sentell, "Bills Die Early Deaths," *Tulsa Tribune*, February 17, 1978.

27. Junetta Davis, "Breaking the Bonds," *Oklahoma Monthly*, ERA Collection, box 37, folder 26, OHS.

28. Peltier Stapleton, interviewed by Finchum.

29. "Peltier Reveals Strategy," *Daily Oklahoman*, July 14, 1981.

30. "ERA Groups Split on Governors' Meeting," *Tulsa Tribune*, April 13, 1982.

31. "Several Governors Are Reluctant to Commit," *US News and World Report*, March 3, 1982.

32. "Founding the National Organization for Women, 1966," in Susan Ware, *Modern American Women* (New York: McGraw-Hill, 2002), 237–40.

33. Clay F. Richards, "ERA Could Survive If . . . ?," *Tulsa Tribune*, January 27, 1979. For more on NOW's strategies in detail, see Joseph R. Ewing's article in *NOW Report*, January 1, 1977.

34. Peltier Stapleton, interviewed by the author; "Ladies against Women," interview by Martha Skeeters, June 27, 2009, Red Dirt Women Oral History Project, University of Oklahoma.

35. "OK Targeted for Extensive Media Blitz for ERA," *Oklahoma Times*, October 10, 1981.

36. "Letters to the Editor," *Tulsa Tribune*, January 15, 1982.

37. "Marchers Back ERA in 4 states," *Tulsa Tribune*, April 7, 1982.

38. Peltier Stapleton, interviewed by Finchum.

39. Tom Guild, "Wanda Jo Peltier Stapleton: A Constant Champion of Human Rights," United Nations Association of Oklahoma City, December 7, 2015, http://una-okc.blogspot.com/2015/12/wanda-jo-peltier-stapleton.html.

LINDSEY CHURCHILL

12

BARBARA "WAHRU" CLEVELAND AND HERLAND SISTER RESOURCES

The Oklahoma City–based organization Herland Sister Resources currently describes itself online as a womanist organization with a strong lesbian focus.[1] However, the group also stresses on its current Facebook page that Herland is not restricted to just lesbians and that all women are welcome.[2] Herland was officially founded as a bookstore in 1983 by Barbara "Wahru" Cleveland, who worked with other friends and activists to create what would later become a lending library and meeting space.[3] Since the early 1980s, Herland has provided a space for book exchanges, political activism, community, and women's music and a physical site where Oklahoma lesbians could be themselves outside the bar scene.[4] Herland offered solace from the unsupportive and oftentimes dangerous cultural and political environment within Oklahoma in the 1980s. Indeed, to be a lesbian in Oklahoma in the 1980s meant that you had to be afraid to "lose your family, your job and often times your life."[5]

In a booklet created in 2003 to celebrate twenty years of activism, the founders of Herland wrote of the organization's beginnings: "Herland Sister Resources was born from an idea and an ideal. The womyn of Herland dreamed of a world where womyn's values, ethics, and perspectives would lead to more justice and less suffering. A world that was safe for all, including womyn and children. A world that recognized and valued difference."[6]

Barbara Cleveland knew a great deal about feeling marginalized for being different. She was born on April 2, 1945, in Oklahoma City. As an African American woman born during segregation, she remembers feeling the impact of discrimination on her family. Her parents divorced when she was young, and even though her mother had some college experience, according to Cleveland, she never found a decent job. Cleveland spent a lot of time with her grandmother and learned how to "fetch the eggs and catch a chicken for dinner."[7] Due to the fact that her mother would leave for prolonged periods of time, Cleveland started school in Geary, Oklahoma, later than the other children her age. She remembers wanting desperately to leave Geary, which in 1960 only had a population of 1,416.[8]

Cleveland noticed early that she was not like the other girls in her class. She recalls, "Heck, I was the best tire roller, tree climber, and runner in the neighborhood. I could even make a better paper plane than the boys."[9] She was thrilled when her mother took her away from Geary and they moved to Oklahoma City, where Cleveland finished elementary school. As a teen Cleveland participated in civil rights activism in Oklahoma. Indeed, in the late 1950s, the support of young African Americans proved integral to the activism of Clara Luper, a schoolteacher and leader of the NAACP's Youth Council who challenged segregation in Oklahoma City's restaurants.[10]

In 1962, at the age of seventeen, Cleveland decided to enroll at Central State College (which would later become the University of Central Oklahoma) instead of attending Oklahoma's only historically Black college, Langston University. Cleveland says she did this in part to continue her activism and fight for integration in Oklahoma. She recalls that instructors at Central State worked actively to flunk out the four African American students involved in the science program. During her college years Cleveland also remembers experiencing police harassment on several different occasions and having a police officer pull a gun on her at the University of Oklahoma Health Sciences Center, where she worked as a lab supervisor.[11] She also has some positive memories of some of her classmates at Central State who supported her while she struggled with having enough money to pay for college and eat:

> [I was] part of a group who decided to go Central State College instead of Langston. I had some real struggles there, trying to make ends meet by working and getting loans. My influence came with the women athletes (many of whom started out being bad to me because I was the only Black). They gave up one meal a day to keep me fed when I could not get my room and board paid on time. Your meal ticket was pulled if you were late. There was not reimbursement when you got it paid. I became very sick and lost lots of weight from not eating. They took turns in the morning going to the cafeteria to pick [up] sack lunches. I lived on sandwiches, chips and an apple many days. Then they, the women athletes, came and got me and took me to the person who was in charge of food services for the college. They had gone to him and explained my situation. I started eating after that. One of the other athletes worked for a doctor on the weekends. She took me to him and I got free service. They picked me up on weekends so I could practice field hockey. They took me home when I was stranded on campus. They are still my friends.[12]

Despite these hardships, Cleveland eventually graduated college with a BS in chemistry, biology, and medical technology. Her life would take a different path, however, as she became more focused on music and activism. In the summer of 1982, when Cleveland was thirty-seven, a group of women connected with the feminist and lesbian publications *Brazen Hussy Rag* and *Sister Advocate* as well as the groups La Salle des Femmes and Let's Talk Women came together to create a women's bookstore. Although the group had difficulty convincing the building owner to let them open a storefront, Cleveland, who had been collaborating with the group, convinced the building owner, Murray, as they called her, to allow for a women's bookstore.[13] Cleveland remembers being inspired by a bookstore she had seen in Nashville and wanting her store to include women of all sexualities. She hoped to connect activists from the local National Organization for Women (NOW) and the Women's Political Caucus with the women of Herland. Cleveland recalls, "[Some of the women] wanted mostly a lesbian bookstore. My feeling was that . . . and it still is my feeling, that we need to be more inclusive and not exclusive in our movements because one of my phrases is that every movement out there that has merit, needs our help, and we need their help."[14]

This portrait of Barbara "Wahru" Cleveland hangs in the Women's Research Center and BGLTQ+ Student Center at the University of Central Oklahoma, where one can see some of the books donated by Herland Sister Resources. Portrait by Suzanne Gallagher. Courtesy of the Women's Research Center and BGLTQ+ Student Center, University of Central Oklahoma.

Cleveland recalls that Murray was in her eighties, and her husband had recently died. She lived in the back of the storefront, which, at the time, housed many antiques.[15] Murray liked Cleveland but gave her only one month to get the store ready. This involved doing the physical work of construction on the storefront as well as procuring books for the new bookstore. In order for others to learn about the new store, Cleveland wrote a one-page newsletter that promoted the women's music and books that would be available in Herland Bookstore. The Oklahoma chapter of the National Organization for Women included the newsletter with theirs in order to let their members know about Herland.[16] The self-published Herland twentieth-anniversary book describes Cleveland's early work for the store:

> During the first few years, Barbara took Herland books to many different womyn's places and events including NOW, Women's Political Caucus meetings, African American women's organizations, and even bars. She tried to reach womyn interested in a diverse range of issues and get them to see the strength that could come from working together. After some time, she realized that Herland had the potential to be a very strong nonprofit organization that could provide resources to many different types of women.[17]

By 1984, the Herland Sister Resources book collection included journals and books about women's and lesbian issues such as *Sinister Wisdom*, *Broomstick*, *Women and Therapy*, *Women and Politics*, *Off Our Backs*, *Women: A Journal of Liberation*, *Signs: A Journal of Women and Culture in Society*, *Calyx*, *Maenad*, *Heresies*, and *Women and Health* to name a few. They also subscribed to free publications including *Conscience: Catholics for a Free Choice*, the *Women's Legal Defense Fund Newsletter*, the *Independent Advocate*, *Oklahoma Families*, the *Committee for Gender Research*, *Congresswoman's Caucus Update*, and *Everywoman: Career and Vocational Guide*.[18] The store also included books that were banned or considered pornographic at the time, such as *The Joy of Lesbian Sex* and *Torch Song Trilogy*.[19] At this time, Herland also created a library club that allowed participants to pay five dollars for access to more than 150 titles for a full year.[20]

By having such an expansive feminist library, Herland allowed women who might not have had exposure to academic journals or publications to access feminist, lesbian, and pro-women writings from around the world. It also helped to show that many organizations throughout the country and even in Oklahoma continued to challenge the anti-woman and anti-LGBTQ+ stance of many who served in positions of political power in the early 1980s. Though the political climate of Oklahoma remained largely repressive for the LGBTQ+ community as well as women in general, the bookstore and Herland Sister Resources offered not only an alternative inclusive narrative of gender and sexuality but a space to politically organize and create a new vision for solidarity.

While Cleveland helped to create Herland Bookstore, she also worked on another passion—producing music. She worked with female country musicians and remembers reactions she received at the time: "What they're seeing is a black woman [in the early 1980s] producing country and western music, so we had to deal with that."[22] In addition to Cleveland's involvement with music, Herland always played a significant role in supporting and promoting local women artists. As a Herland newsletter from 1984 explained, "Herland sponsors and provides support services for the production of music concerts, poetry readings, coffeehouses, film/video showings, speakers, and slide shows."[23] Herland supported new women artists and hosted more established female artists as well.

For example, the front page of a December 1984 *Herland Voice Newsletter* advertised a two-dollar concert for musicians Hawkins and Delear and their "thought provoking feminist music." The Sisters, as group members called themselves, marketed events such as these that they sponsored as an "evening of entertainment for the Oklahoma women's community."[24] In 1983 Cleveland worked with Herland Bookstore to bring Odetta, who has been referred to as the "voice of the civil rights movement," as well as Austin-based singer-songwriter Nancy Scott to the Women's Resource Center in Norman, Oklahoma. In November 1985 Cleveland worked with Herland to bring in jazz artists Gayle Nature, Mary Reynolds, and Elyse Angelo.[25] In 1984 the *Oklahoman* referred to Mary Reynolds as "a musician with enough irons in enough fires to make a fire marshal blanch, keel over and die in a fit of apoplexy."[26]

In 1986 Cleveland and Herland presented "gospel-reggae to jazz-soul-country" musicians Casselberry-DuPreé at the Civic Center's Freede Little Theatre in Oklahoma City.[27] These concerts represented more than just music to the members of Herland. They offered a chance for women to experience female-centered music and support women artists.[28] When asked about the overall mood concerning women's music in the 1970s and '80s, the president of all-woman recording label Olivia Records Judy Dlugacz asserted, "We were reaching out to an audience that wanted to be found, but not necessarily identified." Indeed, as lesbians' sexuality was still very much illegal, Olivia Records and other women-centered music offered a means for community. It is important to note that as these concerts took place, Herland Sister Resources also hosted very progressive and inclusive activities for early-1980s Oklahoma, such as workshops on heterosexism and screenings of films about lesbian motherhood.[29]

Music also informed and inspired the activism of Herland. Peggy Johnson, a musician and Herland Sister, recalled when a group traveled to Wichita, Kansas, to counter anti-choice protesters at Dr. George Tiller's clinic, which performed late-term abortions.[30] She was surrounded by screaming protesters outside the clinic and responded with Holly Near's "Mountain Song." Despite feeling fear of being attacked or worse, she responded with song. Johnson's singing was not unusual since she always sang loudly and has utilized singing as a form of protest, but this time her Herland friends circled around her and sang "Mountain Song" along with her into the faces of the anti-choice protesters. Stories like these consistently emerge about the connection of music and activism in Herland. They demonstrate the importance of perseverance and activism in a time when many of those who fought for social change felt the pressure of overwhelming odds against them.

Cleveland and others who started Herland in the early 1980s also dealt with a political climate in Oklahoma that included the fight for the Equal Rights Amendment (ERA) as well as the rise of the so-called Moral Majority and their million-dollar campaign against what they deemed the "gay peril."[31] Several members of Herland advocated passionately for the passage of the ERA, an amendment to legally support women's equality. In 1981 only three more states needed to ratify the ERA for it to become an amendment to the United States Constitution. In January 1982 the Oklahoma Senate rejected ERA ratification by a close vote of 27–21. To the chagrin of many who had fought for the ERA, the Oklahoma House of Representatives refused to vote on the issue.[32]

In Oklahoma and throughout the United States, the National Organization for Women hosted countdown rallies to encourage states to ratify before the deadline of June 30, 1982. In order to garner support for the ERA, activist and author Gloria Steinem and NOW president at the time and cofounder of the Feminist Majority Foundation Eleanor Smeal visited Oklahoma in hopes of rallying support for the ERA's ratification. On June 6, 1982, more than eleven thousand people went to the state capitol in Oklahoma City to rally for the ERA. Activists asked Governor George Nigh to convene a special session to have the legislature vote on the amendment.[33] This failed to inspire the Oklahoma legislature to ratify the ERA by the deadline, and ultimately the ERA never succeeded as a constitutional amendment. During this time, the Oklahoma City metro area overall showed signs of resistance as more than 1,500 protesters showed up at the capitol to speak out against Ronald Reagan's 1982 visit, during which he spoke to the legislature about his "new federalism."[34]

Locally, the political climate in Oklahoma also influenced support for programs that encouraged research and advocacy involving women. According to the *Herland Newsletter*, during the 1983–84 school year, the University of Oklahoma's overall budget cuts totaled 9 percent. The College of Arts and Sciences (which housed the Women's Studies Program) usually cut around 16 percent or less on average. However, this time the Women's Studies Program received a 36 percent reduction in wages for its faculty and a 50 percent cut in funding for operations. The university also completely cut funding for a teaching assistant and an instructor to teach the Introduction to Women's Studies course. The *Herland Newsletter* reported that several Women's Studies faculty planned to look for other employment due to the budget crisis and the university's treatment of the program. Despite this devastating setback, the May 1984 newsletter included the many Women's Studies courses being taught in the fall of 1984, such as Human Sexuality, Women and Madness in Literature, Contemporary Parenting, Multicultural Counseling, Roman Women of the Republic, the Possible Human, and Mothers and Daughters in Literature to name a few.[35]

Around this time, the University of Oklahoma also engaged in a legal battle that went to the Oklahoma Supreme Court over the rights of OU students to have an LGBTQ+ student group on campus. OU Regents banned the Gay Activists Alliance even though it had gone through all proper procedures to become a student organization.[36] In 1982 the Oklahoma Supreme Court ruled that the OU Regents could not stop the creation of the Gay Activists Alliance. This ruling so infuriated Oklahoma state representative Bill Graves that he introduced legislation to stop funding for any state universities that allowed student organizations that "advocate sexual relations between unmarried people or conduct which would violate the law." This law targeted the LGBTQ+ community on campuses throughout Oklahoma. After the Florida legislature attempted to introduce a similar law that was shot down by the Florida Supreme Court as unconstitutional, Graves's bill stalled.[37]

Cases and laws such as these proved extremely important to Herland as the meeting space and community the group offered challenged the extremely repressive climate of Oklahoma. This climate, as Cleveland reiterated continually, is one reason why Herland was so important to create and sustain. Court case rulings and laws introduced by the Oklahoma legislature indicated that members of the LGBTQ+ community should not express their identities and should in some cases be eradicated. This repression did not stop the Herland community from growing and expanding. By March 1984 the *Herland Newsletter* reached more than 250 subscribers. The newsletter requested that anyone interested in being on the mailing list come to Herland Bookstore and sign up.[38] The newsletters always came in paper bags in order to ensure subscribers' privacy.[39] This was understandable considering the climate toward lesbians in Oklahoma in the early 1980s.

In their interviews, some Herland Sisters expressed the worry they had felt over being fired from their jobs for their sexuality. Some of the Herland Sisters worked as public school teachers, and they had to be extremely careful to hide their personal lives and sexualities. Cleveland understood this danger as well and expressed genuine surprise that the organization did not receive protesters. This fear was in part due to an Oklahoma statue that allowed schools to fire teachers who participated in "public homosexual activity or conduct." In 1985 the US Court of Appeals for the Tenth Circuit reversed part of these former rulings, claiming that they infringed on free speech. The court did, however, support prohibiting "public homosexual activity."[40] This represented just another way that Oklahoma law paved the way for legal discrimination against LGBTQ+ individuals.

While Oklahoma remained a repressive place for lesbians and feminists, Herland Sisters found a space in which to fight the oppressive nature of many laws and court rulings at the time. They demonstrated, time and again, agency and resilience against what often seemed like overwhelming odds.[41] Some examples of events that Herland helped to host or support include a women and madness conference and a gay film festival at the University of Oklahoma as well as a conference with Langston University titled "Sisters: Voices of a Different Color." Collaborations such as these were important because Herland was never particularly racially diverse regarding membership. The Sisters reported being diverse in terms of class but not race.[42] Although founded by an African American woman, Herland's membership remained overwhelmingly white.

Herland Sisters also took an active role in Take Back the Night rallies to end sexual violence. Herland members remained committed to combating domestic violence and sexual assault through their activism even though one member reported that lesbians had been "purged" from the domestic violence movement in the 1980s. These events hosted hundreds of participants. Herland also facilitated lesbian support groups in Oklahoma City and held therapy sessions at the Herland house.

A newsletter from 1984 announced the arrival of a new counseling service at Herland. The counselor set up a private practice at the bookstore and offered her services to women in need. She charged on a sliding scale and took a feminist approach in her work: "I do a combination of cognitive behavior and feminist counseling. Cognitive behavior helps people restructure how they think about things and how they make decisions. I define feminist counseling as our right to control our lives."[43] At this time, offering any sort of counseling, particularly outside of a Christian context, was very rare. Beyond this, advertising and offering feminist counseling represented a very revolutionary act for Herland.

Herland did not only demonstrate feminist and LGBTQ+ solidarity through activism. The group itself implemented a model that included women's-only spaces. Part of this model included the women-only retreats that the group hosted. Herland Sisters would go to various parks, usually in Oklahoma, and camp for a few nights. Cleveland remembers these retreats fondly, as do the other Sisters we interviewed. The Sisters never invited grown men into these spaces as Herland Sisters truly hoped to create a space that larger society would not allow.[44] This exclusion of adult men sometimes made people uncomfortable or seemed counterintuitive to a movement that was demanding that society accept difference. In her blog entry about feminism and its exclusion of lesbians from the movement, Susanna Sturgis explains the importance of women-only spaces, especially in the 1980s:

> Nevertheless, talk of women-only space makes moderates, liberals, and progressives— and all too many feminists—nervous. It implies exclusion, and exclusion is seen as illiberal. But men excluding women from positions of power is not the same as women excluding men from groups aimed at empowering ourselves. This sort of exclusion is crucial to identifying oppression and organizing against it. Workers trying to organize a union don't want bosses and owners in on the process. Black people organizing against Jim Crow did not solicit support from white segregationists.[45]

Indeed, one consistent thread comes from the oral histories that were documented from the former and current members of the Herland Sister Resources: the nostalgia for the retreats. The retreats still occur, but in the 1980s and '90s they offered an extremely important and rare space for women, particularly lesbian and bisexual women. Sisters reminiscence about really being able to be themselves at the retreats and getting to focus on women and also on themselves and their own personal growth. Some members commented on the deep pain Herland members had experienced because of men. The retreats offered an opportunity to escape this anguish and truly relax away from any worries about dealing with men. The consistent responses about the retreats were that they offered a space for just being yourself.[46]

Part of moving away from more masculinized spaces and modes of being also included an attempt to use a consensus model to come to an agreement as opposed to more common practices such as voting or having one clear leader making decisions. In fact, the group so eschewed these patriarchal, hierarchical modes of being that they created a rotating board. The group did not have president or vice president. Instead, they had Sister 1, Sister 2, Sister 3. These positions would rotate in order to avoid hierarchy within the group. Cleveland was not particularly a fan of the consensus model and has recalled:

> They wanted to look at a different way of calling everything so they came up with system one, system two, system three and the duty of system one, two and three. That's okay [because] I was leaving. I didn't find some things offensive. I think that they were trying to do [the] consensus model so I had to leave, you know, after a while because they couldn't come to a consensus. I think that there are some things that consensus works with, and a lot of things that consensus doesn't work with. . . . I thought well here is a new thing for you. You should probably come up with something that will work. They probably did I don't know but even today I had another group in Columbus, Ohio [who wanted to do the consensus model]. I said, in my experience consensus doesn't work.[47]

Others in the group did not particularly like the consensus model either, but they understood why it was important because of the different model that Herland hoped to create.[48] Though some of the Sisters' titles have changed, to this day, the board still has a rotating structure and remains committed to egalitarian ideals regarding its board and membership.

In September 1987 Herland purchased the house that it still utilizes for its organization. In 1988, the same year as the first gay pride parade in Oklahoma City, Barbara left Oklahoma to pursue her graduate degree in Ohio.[49] She returned periodically to continue to work with Herland. In 1997 she went to Herland's fall retreat at Lake Murray. By that time, she went by the moniker Wahru instead of Barbara. At the retreat, Cleveland led a drumming workshop. During this time the group continued to work on important projects such as the

Herland Legal Defense Fund (for which they were recognized by the ACLU), hosting groups such as the Oklahoma City Two Spirits Group for lesbian Native Americans and workshops for adoption for nontraditional families.[50]

One of Herland's most important projects in the 1990s was the support of a lesbian mother who was involved in the 1995 Oklahoma Supreme Court case *Fox v. Fox*. In 1982 the Oklahoma Supreme Court had ruled that a lesbian in Tulsa could not have her custody rights reestablished due to the notion that her sexual orientation created an unhealthy environment regarding the "moral" and "mental" welfare of her child. This created precedent that parental rights could be stripped from a person based on sexual orientation and activity. Herland played an integral role in the defense fund for Donna Jeanne Fox, a woman who had lost custody of her child because she was a lesbian and a had a girlfriend.[51] In *Fox v. Fox*, Donna Jeanne Fox's husband claimed that her "homosexuality was contrary to the children's moral and religious values and harmful to their psychological and emotional stability."[52] Ultimately, the earlier decision was overturned by the Oklahoma Supreme Court in 1995, setting the precedent that women could not have their parental rights taken away because they identified as lesbians. Herland raised more than $13,000 dollars for the legal defense of Donna Jeanne Fox.[53] Indeed, from its inception, Herland provided a space for mothers, particularly lesbian mothers who struggled to maintain custody of their children due to homophobic attitudes of the time. Newsletters provided information about support groups for mothers without custody, specifically a chapter at the Women's Resource Center in Norman, Oklahoma.[54]

After Cleveland moved to Ohio in 1988, she remained involved in women's organizations and activist groups and helped grow the National Women's Music Fest. She was also involved in civil rights and community activism. In 2016 a team of researchers sat down with Cleveland for several hours to talk about her experiences with Herland as part of an oral history project to document the stories of the many incredible women who acted as true pioneers and rebels in Oklahoma in the early 1980s. Against all odds, Herland had created not only a space for women and lesbians but a community that provided entertainment, discourse, and fellowship and a place for reading, debate, and discussion. Years later, in a follow-up interview, when Cleveland was asked what her greatest joy in creating Herland was, she responded, "The joy comes from finding out that I could actually do it. . . . I miss the activism in Oklahoma. I was in NOW, and the Women's Political Caucus. I miss how a handful of women would decide to do something and then go do it. True, this is not a real regret, but it's how I feel. I get lonely for Oklahoma."[55]

Indeed, from its creation as a bookstore and then its move to a house, Herland has consistently created a space for women to be activists and feminists. Through retreats, music, and fellowship, the group has provided a supportive space for lesbians to be open about their sexuality and connect with others. Through Cleveland's leadership and collaboration, her dream of creating a place that represented acceptance for radical women and lesbians in Oklahoma became a reality. In a climate that was not always accepting, Herland provided a revolutionary alternative to the conservative and many times stifling climate of Oklahoma.

NOTES

1. In 2016 I worked with the Oklahoma City–based organization Herland Sister Resources to secure the largest donation of books and materials in the history of the University of Central Oklahoma. The donation contained rare fiction and nonfiction books regarding women, gender, and sexuality, including a large collection of lesbian fiction. Receiving this donation and in turn creating the Herland Gender and Sexuality Studies Library helped to secure a physical space for the Women's Research Center and the BGLTQ+ Student Center (collectively known as "the Center") at UCO. The Center, which opened a physical location on campus in 2017, is unique in Oklahoma as it is a space that not only offers support to LGBTQ+ and female-identifying students but also has a library containing thousands of rare books and materials, many with only a few copies in existence. The donation of these materials occurred in large part because the members of Herland, many in their sixties, seventies, and eighties at the time, wanted to make sure the books they loved would be enjoyed, preserved, and appreciated by a younger generation. Their hopes have come to fruition as, on average, at least fifty unique titles are checked out every month during the school year from the Herland Gender and Sexuality Studies Library. Another important donation to the Women's Research Center and the BGLTQ+ Student Center is a portrait of Barbara "Wahru" Cleveland, who founded Herland Bookstore in the early 1980s. The portrait sits above a drum obtained from an auction at the National Women's Music Festival, which Cleveland donated to the Center in order to show how happy she was about the existence of the Center and its preservation of the history of Herland Sister Resources.

2. "About Us," Herland Sister Resources Facebook page, accessed December 15, 2019, https://www.facebook.com/pg/Herland-Sister-Resources-138897648960/about/?ref=page_internal.

3. Other individuals who helped with the storefront/bookstore include Theila Elliot, Marilyn Best, Donita Whitehead, Dona Williamson, Marilyn Sebek, Kevan Kiser, Deni McConnell, Nancy White, Paula H., Banika A., Beverly, Kathie, and Chris. For more, see Herland Sister Resources, *Herland: 1983–2003, Celebrating 20 Years* (Oklahoma City: Herland Sister Resources, 2003).

4. *Herland: Creating a Radical Lesbian Feminist Community*, directed by Jake Crystal and Mickayla Fisher (Edmond: University of Central Oklahoma Women's Research Center and BGLTQ+ Student Center, 2019). Part of the grant I received to document the stories and lives of the women of Herland Sister Resources included support for an oral history project. This project started in 2016 and was completed in 2019. Student researchers for the Center, Jake Crystal and Mickayla Fisher, worked alongside Herland member Ginger McGovern to complete a film from the interviews. *Herland: Creating a Radical Lesbian Feminist Community* was an official selection at the Palm Springs LGBTQ+ Film Festival in September 2019.

5. Crystal and Fisher, *Herland*.

6. Herland Sister Resources, *Herland*, 1.

7. Barbara "Wahru" Cleveland, e-mail to the author, May 13, 2019.

8. Merle Rinehart, "Geary," *The Encyclopedia of Oklahoma History and Culture*, Oklahoma Historical Society, accessed December 15, 2019, https://www.okhistory.org/publications/enc/entry.php?entry=GE001.

9. Cleveland e-mail.

10. "Oklahoma African Americans Sit-In for Integration, 1985–1964," Global Nonviolent Action Database, accessed December 15, 2019, https://nvdatabase.swarthmore.edu/content/oklahoma-city-african-americans-sit-integration-1958-64.

11. Barbara "Wahru" Cleveland, interview with the author, October 16, 2016, Oklahoma City, OK.

12. Cleveland e-mail.

13. Herland Sister Resources, *Herland*, 2.

14. Cleveland interview.

15. Cleveland interview.

16. Herland Sister Resources, *Herland*, 3.

17. Herland Sister Resources, *Herland*.

18. *Herland Voice Newsletter* 1, no. 4 (April 1984), Herland Voice Newsletter Archive, University of Central Oklahoma Library Digital Collections, https://library.uco.edu/archives/digital_collections/herland/pdf/HerlandVoice-1984-04_ocr.pdf.

19. Herland Sister Resources, *Herland*, 9.

20. *Herland Voice Newsletter* 1, no. 5 (May 1985), Herland Voice Newsletter Archive, University of Central Oklahoma Library Digital Collections, https://library.uco.edu/archives/digital_collections/herland/pdf/HerlandVoice-1985-05-v01-no05_ocr.pdf.

21. Crystal and Fisher, *Herland*.

22. Cleveland interview.

23. *Herland Voice Newsletter* 1, no. 3 (March 1984), Herland Voice Newsletter Archive, University of Central Oklahoma Library Digital Collections, https://library.uco.edu/archives/digital_collections/herland/pdf/HerlandVoice-1984-03_ocr.pdf.

24. *Herland Voice Newsletter* 1, no. 12 (December 1984), Herland Voice Newsletter Archive, University of Central Oklahoma Library Digital Collections, https://library.uco.edu/archives/digital_collections/herland/pdf/HerlandVoice-1984-12_ocr.pdf.

25. *Herland Voice Newsletter* 1, no. 7 (July 1984), Herland Voice Newsletter Archive, University of Central Oklahoma Library Digital Collections, https://library.uco.edu/archives/digital_collections/herland/pdf/HerlandVoice-1984-07_ocr.pdf.

26. Todd Webb, "Mary Reynolds Finds Time to Make Music," *Oklahoman*, August 2, 1984.

27. Herland Sister Resources, *Herland*, 10.

28. Crystal and Fisher, *Herland*.

29. Herland Sister Resources, *Herland*, 5.

30. In 2009 Dr. George Tiller was assassinated by an anti-choice extremist while at church.

31. Herland Sister Resources, *Herland*, 2.

32. Sarah K. Tyson, "Equal Rights Amendment," *The Encyclopedia of Oklahoma History and Culture*, Oklahoma Historical Society, accessed December 15, 2019, https://www.okhistory.org/publications/enc/entry.php?entry=EQ001.

33. Winston Williams, "Thousands March for Equal Rights," *New York Times*, June 7, 1982, https://www.nytimes.com/1982/06/07/us/thousands-march-for-equal-rights.html.

34. Herland Sister Resources, *Herland*, 4–5; Nicole Nascenzi, "Reagan Visited Oklahoma at Least 19 Times during His Life," *Tulsa World*, June 7, 2004.

35. *Herland Voice Newsletter* 1, no. 5 (May 1984), Herland Voice Newsletter Archive, University of Central Oklahoma Library Digital Collections, https://library.uco.edu/archives/digital_collections/herland/pdf/HerlandVoice-1984-05_ocr.pdf.

36. Gay Activists Alliance v. the Board of Regents of the University of Oklahoma, 638 P. 2d 1116, 162 (1981), https://law.justia.com/cases/oklahoma/supreme-court/1981/5110.html.

37. James Johnson, "State's Anti-gay Blueprint Loses in Florida," *Oklahoman*, February 5, 1982.

38. *Herland Voice Newsletter* 1, no. 3 (March 1984), Herland Voice Newsletter Archive, University of Central Oklahoma Library Digital Collections, https://library.uco.edu/archives/digital_collections/herland/pdf/HerlandVoice-1984-03_ocr.pdf.

39. Crystal and Fisher, *Herland*.

40. Board of Education of Oklahoma v. National Gay Task Force, 470, US 903 (1985), https://www.oyez.org/cases/1984/83-2030.

41. Crystal and Fisher, *Herland*.

42. Crystal and Fisher, *Herland*.

43. *Herland Voice Newsletter* 1, no. 8 (August 1984), Herland Voice Newsletter Archive, University of Central Oklahoma Library Digital Collections, https://library.uco.edu/archives/digital_collections/herland/pdf/HerlandVoice-1984-08_ocr.pdf.

44. Crystal and Fisher, *Herland*.

45. Susanna J. Sturgis, "Women = Books: In Defense of Woman-Only Space," Wellesley Centers for Women, accessed December 15, 2019, http://www.wcwonline.org/Women-=-Books-Blog/woman-only.

46. Crystal and Fisher, *Herland*.

47. Cleveland interview.
48. Crystal and Fisher, *Herland*.
49. Herland Sister Resources, *Herland*, 12.
50. Herland Sister Resources, *Herland*, 42–44.
51. Katja M. Eichenger-Swainston, "Fox v. Fox: Redefining the Best Interest of the Child Standard for Lesbian Mothers and Their Families," *Tulsa Law Review* 32, no. 1 (Fall 1996): 57–74. https://digitalcommons.law.utulsa.edu/cgi/viewcontent.cgi?referer=https://www.google.com/&httpsredir=1&article=2066&context=tlr.
52. Eichinger-Swainston, "Fox v. Fox," 60.
53. Herland Sister Resources, *Herland*, 40.
54. *Herland Voice Newsletter* 1, no. 4 (April 1984), Herland Voice Newsletter Archive, University of Central Oklahoma Library Digital Collections, https://library.uco.edu/archives/digital_collections/herland/.
55. Barbara "Wahru" Cleveland, interview with the author, May 13, 2019.

PATRICIA LOUGHLIN

13

"MY CHILDREN ARE MORE IMPORTANT TO ME THAN ANY OFFICE I MIGHT HOLD"

Mary Fallin's Use of Motherhood as a Conservative Political Strategy

Mary Fallin has never lost an election in almost three decades of public service, from Oklahoma state legislator, to lieutenant governor, to US congresswoman, to governor of Oklahoma. Her career in public service began in 1990 when she was elected to the Oklahoma House of Representatives and served two terms. In 1995 voters elected Fallin as Oklahoma's lieutenant governor, where she was the first woman and first Republican in that position, and she served for twelve years. Then she served in Congress, representing Oklahoma's Fifth District, from 2007 to 2011. In fact, Mary Fallin was the first woman since Alice Robertson in 1921 to represent Oklahoma in Congress, as Amy Scott's groundbreaking work on Alice Robertson and conservative maternalism reminds us in chapter 3. Later Mary Fallin served two terms as governor, beginning with her election in 2010. Throughout Fallin's political career, her role as a mother to her two children has remained front and center. As she said in 1999 while serving as lieutenant governor, "When I think about 'balancing' duties of my office with the responsibility I have to my children, there is no contest. My children are more important to me than any office I might hold. I think if you can set your priorities, and keep them, the 'balancing act' becomes much easier."[1]

As Mary Fallin has shared her experiences campaigning for political office from the 1990s through the 2010s, she has noted that campaigning was not easy. She was attacked within the Republican Party for being a young pregnant woman. "I actually had my son between the primary election and the general," she noted in an oral history interview in 2008 while she was serving in Congress and reflecting on her first campaign for the state house. "So on [primary] election night in August I was actually eight months pregnant. And my party had someone that ran against me on the Republican side because I was just this young woman who was pregnant running for office and she would never be effective and wouldn't be able to do the job. Actually it was pretty rough, because they pretty much campaigned against me as a young mother."[2] Mary Fallin's background and political strategy as a Republican woman politician in Oklahoma demonstrate how she intentionally and successfully used the politics of motherhood in her campaign.

The use of motherhood in political rhetoric is far from new, with origins in the early days of the American Republic. Embodied in Republican motherhood, women as mothers had a special role in American society and in the home, educating the next generation of citizens.[3] Mary Fallin's story is part of a larger movement of conservative women who became politically active in the late 1970s and 1980s who recognized the ways that government directly impacted their lives and saw a need to get involved and effect change, joining the ranks of the Republican Party and holding elected positions in Oklahoma and nationally. "Already in 1975, a new movement of social conservatism within the Republican Party was ascending," Catherine E. Rymph reminds us in *Republican Women: Feminism and Conservatism from Suffrage through the Rise of the New Right*, "one that would marginalize Republican feminists and succeed in moving the party away from its traditional support for women's rights. In 1980 delegates affiliated with the New Right dominated the Republican presidential convention, nominated Ronald Reagan for president, and approved new platform planks explicitly at odds with many of the goals of Republican feminists, including ERA and abortion rights."[4]

Mary Fallin was raised a Democrat in Tecumseh, Oklahoma, and became a Republican after college. Mary Copeland was born in 1954 at Whiteman Air Force Base in Warrensburg, Missouri, while her father was serving in the

United States Air Force. Soon after, the family moved to Muskogee and then Tulsa before returning to the small town of Tecumseh, where her parents and extended family had settled for several generations. "Growing up in rural Oklahoma and Tecumseh . . . was kind of considered on the edge of Little Dixie," she recalled in an oral history interview in 2008, "which is a very Democrat area. My mother and father were both Democrats and I can remember when I went to vote, my mother told me I should register as a Democrat because that's what they were and that's what rural Oklahoma [was], and in fact the majority of Oklahoma was Democrat during those days."[5]

Her father had attended Oklahoma Baptist University in Shawnee, and her mother attended Oklahoma College for Women in Chickasha. Both would go on to work for the state. "Most of my childhood life, my parents were both state employees," Mary Fallin said. "We used to joke how my mother worked at the welfare department and help people get welfare, while my dad worked at the unemployment service and helped put them on unemployment. We've got them covered with the social agencies that way."[6]

Both her father and her mother served as mayor of Tecumseh. When her father died in office, her mother took over mayoral duties. "My mother and father were not wealthy people," Mary Fallin recalled. "They were just small-town, good people. But they taught me the value of hard work and public service and giving back to your community and that one person truly can make a difference if they're willing to take a risk, take a chance, and work really hard."[7] The most influential person in her life was her mother. "I find reward in this job, making a difference. I saw my mother doing that as a social worker, helping people on welfare, helping people on food stamps, helping people in adoption, helping in cases of child abuse."[8] Both of Fallin's parents, but especially her mother, influenced her own understanding of her role as a politician in that she saw both kinds of work—social work and politics—as extensions of motherhood, family, and community services.

Mary Fallin attended Oklahoma Baptist University for two years, commuting from home, and then graduated from Oklahoma State University with a degree in family relations and child development in 1977. After graduation she moved to Oklahoma City for her first job with the state merit system, which is the state personnel agency. For three years she interviewed applicants for state jobs. The job offered opportunities for Fallin to interact with a variety of state agencies, including the Health, Corrections, and Welfare Departments. Then she worked for the Securities Commission as the office manager, gaining valuable experience in personnel and purchasing. Altogether she worked in state government offices for about five years.[9]

When she moved to Oklahoma City after college in the late 1970s, Mary Fallin registered as a Republican. What prompted the change? A friend had invited her to a Young Republicans meeting in Oklahoma City. There, she read the platform for the Republican Party and the platform for the Democratic Party and determined that she was a conservative Republican. "I liked fiscal discipline in spending," she said, "and I was conservative on social issues and believed in limited government. So I actually switched by the time I was about 21 or so to be a Republican."[10] In fact, she attended the inauguration of President Ronald Reagan.[11]

During the early 1980s Oklahoma experienced an oil and gas boom and bust. For about one year Mary Fallin worked for a private oil company, but then the state economy collapsed because of sinking oil prices by the mid-1980s, and the company closed. Next she received an offer from the Department of Tourism to be its state travel coordinator. She went to trade shows to represent the State of Oklahoma.[12] Then Fallin left the Department of Tourism when she received an offer to work for a hotel company. By 1989 she was district manager in Oklahoma for Lexington Hotel Suites. Within her first year as district manager, she received a national award in recognition of her work increasing revenue and maintaining costs.[13]

In the mid-1980s she married Joe Price Fallin II, or Joe Jr., a dentist. According to the standards of the time, Joe was an "old bachelor" at thirty-seven, and she was an "old bachelorette" at twenty-nine, almost thirty.[14] She continued to work. They had two children, daughter Christina Marie Fallin in March 1987 and son Joseph Price Fallin III in September 1990.

In the fall of 1989 Mary Fallin had been closely observing the debate surrounding House Bill 1017, also known as the Education Reform Act of 1990, which was a tax increase for education, and she was acutely aware of how government policies impacted her family's lives. Mike Hunter's seat representing District Eighty-Five in the Oklahoma House of Representatives opened up when Hunter decided he was not going to run for reelection.[15] His wife, Cheryl Plaxico Hunter, had been one of Mary Fallin's Kappa Alpha Theta sorority sisters at Oklahoma State University. Fallin told Mike Hunter that she would like to run for his seat, and he said to go right ahead. She wanted to focus on improving education, health care, the business environment, and criminal justice reform.[16] In December 1989 Mary Fallin announced that she was running. She had eleven months to campaign. She was still managing the hotels and doing a lot of volunteer work, and her daughter was almost three years old.[17]

Her first campaign team in 1990 for the Oklahoma House of Representatives consisted of volunteers—mainly women but some men—working out of her dining room. The volunteers took over the dining room table and filled it with voter lists and other information.[18] She started campaigning nights and weekends from January to August. By February she started feeling sick with nausea. It turned out she was six months pregnant:

> In fact I remember my doctor telling me at the time when he told me I was pregnant. Tears [were] running down my cheek. Well, aren't you excited about having a baby? Yes, but not now. It wasn't in my plans. He said, I can't think of anyone else I'd rather have for my elected official than a civic leader, a business woman, and a mother. I'll vote for you. I'll even give you a little money to help you get going. I think you should go ahead and run. If you have the stamina and courage to, then I'll support you running.[19]

She kept working full-time, managing hotels until June of that year and campaigning in her off hours. As the primary election approached, Fallin continued to campaign at eight months pregnant. "It was interesting to see the reactions of voters as I rang their doorbells and presented them with my campaign brochure and my ever-expanding self as a candidate for the legislature," Fallin recalled. "I was asked to step into many homes to rest my swollen feet and have much-needed refreshments."[20]

It is intriguing to observe the rhetoric Mary Fallin uses when talking about gendered stereotypes in politics, how she faced them, and how she moved through them. As she described it in Marianne Schnall's *What Will It Take to Make a Woman President? Conversations about Women, Leadership, and Power* in 2013:

> When I first started running for public office, back in 1990, there were some stereotypes of whether a woman could get the job done, whether a woman could be effective. And frankly when I ran for office back in my thirties, I was a young mother, I was a professional businesswoman, and I became frustrated with things that weren't happening at the Capitol, such as improving education and health care. And being a businesswoman, I thought we needed a better business environment for our state. I decided to run for office, and I was young; I was in my mid-thirties. I had a three-

year-old child at the time and worked my job full time, and then I would go out nights and weekends and campaign.[21]

Mary Fallin encountered critics within her own party who said that she would need to drop out of the race or have an abortion because young women with small children would be ineffective in office. They also said that she would not be able to get the job done. As she stated,

> I kept focus on what I wanted to accomplish in the end, which was to go to the Capitol and make changes on these different policy issues. So I kept running my campaign, and on election night I was eight months pregnant, and then I actually had my son between the primary and the general election in September—the election was in November. And I didn't have an abortion; I, of course, continued on with my pregnancy and that was twenty-three years ago.[22]

If Fallin had followed the advice of such critics within the Republican Party and had an abortion, public knowledge of such a thing could easily have destroyed her political career even a decade or two later. However, Fallin's use of maternalist politics was inadvertently strengthened by the implicit hypermaternalism of the pro-life platform within the Republican Party and supplanted conservative fears about working mothers with young children.[23]

In August 1990 Mary Fallin won the Republican primary and defeated attorney Mark Pruitt. Both were anti-abortion candidates, but at the time Fallin opposed abortion including cases of rape or incest.[24] She defeated Barbara Rupert, a pro-choice Democrat, in the general election in November. Mary Fallin remembered a lot about that campaign:

> It was hard for me to knock doors but I did knock doors, and my husband, and my mother, and everyone else. In fact, someone had a phone bank in the last month or so of the primaries. I came home around 10 o'clock that night and my mother said, I've had some strange phone calls. People have been calling our home asking if you are pregnant. I am pregnant and I hope you are telling them so. Why are they asking that? Well they are telling me that someone is conducting a phone survey asking if you'd rather have a pregnant woman or an attorney for your legislator. She was upset about it. They are all telling the phone survey that they'd rather have a pregnant woman rather than an attorney.[25]

This has everything to do with expectations of gender, motherhood, politics, and pregnancy. But Mary Fallin was defiant and unstoppable. "It actually went to my advantage," she recalled.[26] In 1992, Mary Fallin ran unopposed for a second term in the state house.

It is instructive here to examine the way Mary Fallin discusses her negotiation with motherhood and politics—how she made it all happen—and she did it in the 1990s: "I won the primary. My son, Price, arrived; and forty-five days later, I won the general election as the proud mother of a one-and-a-half-month-old baby boy and a three-year-old daughter. I was a state legislator!"[27] In an interview with the *Oklahoman* in 2010 while she was running for governor, Mary Fallin discussed balancing family and politics and noted that sometimes people wonder if she is tough enough for politics. "I say, you have a baby between the primary and general elections, then tell me how tough I am."[28] This notion of toughness is reminiscent of Sarah Palin's "mama grizzly" rhetoric, combining Republican women's leadership and empowerment with motherhood and protective impulses.[29] Throughout her political career Mary Fallin has frequently referred to giving birth between the primary and general election as an example of her own toughness and commitment to politics. And yet she deftly navigated the gendered politics of women politicians and motherhood beginning in the 1990s as she witnessed and participated in the state's shift from Democrat to Republican.

From Oklahoma statehood in 1907 through World War II and into the 1950s, Democrats dominated the political scene in Oklahoma. All Oklahoma governors had been Democrats, and the state had very few Republican legislators. But a shift in the one-party state from Democrat to Republican began to occur in the 1960s when Oklahoma elected its first Republican governor, Henry Bellmon, in 1962. By the 1990s the state had grown increasingly Republican, but women's representation in both parties remained minimal.[30] For example, during the early 1990s, Fallin was one of 3 Republican women in the Oklahoma House of Representatives out of 31 Republican members and one of 8 women altogether in a total of 101 house members. Then in 1993 and 1994 there were 7 women in the Oklahoma House—4 were Democrats and 3 were Republicans.[31]

It was not a difficult adjustment for Mary Fallin to serve as a state representative. She quickly acquired a reputation for getting things done: "I just believed in building consensus, selling people on why it was important to the state of Oklahoma and then working across both sides of the aisle because you had to, to get anything done. I know I was the only one with a brand new baby and a three year old working at the capitol."³² During her first term in the Oklahoma House, she got several bills passed, including stalker legislation, health care reform, and small business health insurance reform.³³

When asked about her most memorable moment during those years in the house, she said it was when the stalker legislation passed. "That was my law," she said.³⁴ Oklahoma was the second state after California to pass legislation that said if a person was being threatened or stalked, they could have some protection from that threat.³⁵

The second issue she worked on was health care reform as part of the larger national debate at the time with President Bill Clinton's administration. Fallin was active in the American Legislative Exchange Council, a bipartisan group, and she took the lead in Oklahoma, holding town hall meetings throughout the state and educating citizens about their options, which she described as "socialized medicine or free enterprise health care like we have now."³⁶ Fallin's work on health care and her statewide visibility participating in the town halls probably helped her gain name recognition with Oklahoma voters when the time came to run for lieutenant governor after serving two terms in the Oklahoma House of Representatives.

Mary Fallin's career in public service began in 1990. She served as a state representative for two terms before her election as lieutenant governor in 1995.

Running for lieutenant governor against other Republicans in the primary, Mary Fallin had to coordinate a statewide campaign for the first time. She relied on a whole host of volunteers. She could not afford to hire a political consultant for the campaign. She focused on specific counties that she knew would be important to win the primary. In that election, Mary Fallin won the runoff with Terry Neese, an Edmond businesswoman. Then she went into the general election against another woman, Nance Diamond, a Democrat from Shawnee, and Fallin won with 50 percent of the vote.³⁷ Mary Fallin become the first woman and the first Republican to serve as lieutenant governor in Oklahoma.³⁸ She served with Governor Frank Keating, a Republican, and later Governor Brad Henry, a Democrat. Although three of the four candidates for lieutenant governor were women, she hoped her victory would encourage more women to get involved in politics.³⁹ "I thought I was going to win," Mary Fallin said in an oral history interview in 2008 when recalling the campaign for lieutenant governor. "I wasn't in it just to be doing it for the heck of it. I'd given up my seat in the legislature. I couldn't go back. I'd given up that opportunity that I loved to run for lieutenant governor and to take that risk to do that. So I was in it to win and to be able to serve in that capacity."[40]

In her early years as lieutenant governor, Fallin worked on labor issues, including worker's compensation and right to work. For example, she established the Fallin Commission on Workers' Compensation Reform with the goal of bringing together representatives from business, industry, and government to discuss how to lower workers' compensation costs in Oklahoma and ensure that those injured on the job would receive workers' compensation benefits promptly.[41] With right to work Fallin exercised her constitutional privilege as lieutenant governor to preside over the state senate to help resolve the impasse between Republicans and Democrats:

> I took over the Senate to try and get them to vote on Right to Work and held up the Senate for three days. And all the senators walked out on me and didn't want to vote on that particular issue. And all heck broke loose on the Senate floor. But finally the Senate came back to vote on allowing the people of Oklahoma the right to vote on a ballot on whether they wanted to be a Right to Work state.[42]

She would exercise this right sparingly, and she maintained that she did it in the name of fairness, to allow Oklahoma's citizens to vote on right to work.[43]

Although Mary Fallin's political life was flourishing, her private life was unraveling. After fourteen years of marriage, she filed for divorce in 1998, citing irreconcilable incompatibility. During divorce proceedings, both parties accused each other of wrongdoing ranging from drug use to physical abuse to infidelity.[44] She had achieved political success as lieutenant governor, the highest woman in elected office in Oklahoma. But privately, her marriage was in turmoil. "My husband and I were battling many personal issues," she stated in her essay titled "The Lessons of Humility" in *Voices from the Heartland*. "Our relationship had become destructive, and finally we divorced. I lost most of my material possessions, including home and furniture. I received no financial help or child support after fourteen years of marriage."[45] Following the divorce, Mary Fallin and her former husband shared custody of the children, who split the week between their parents' homes and alternated weekends.[46] "I replaced my home," she stated. "I bought new furniture. I started a new life, as a mother and as a public official. I learned that faith does not mean simply expecting terrific things; it also requires accepting things that are far less than terrific."[47] And publicly, she won a third term as lieutenant governor in 2002.

Fallin was intentional and strategic in her political trajectory and timing, noting that she would not run for governor against an incumbent. She considered running for governor in 2002, but Congressman Steve Largent decided to run, and Republican legislators asked her to wait.[48] When Congressman Ernest Istook decided he would leave Congress to run for governor, Mary Fallin decided to run for his seat. She knew she would enjoy the work, and her teenage children supported her decision.[49] It was a competitive race, with six candidates in the Republican primary. Fallin ended up in a runoff and then beat Mick Cornett, who had just won the election for Oklahoma City mayor three months prior. She raised $1.5 million for her congressional campaign, and in the general election she handily defeated Democrat David Hunter with more than 60 percent of the vote.[50]

"I became the first woman in Oklahoma since 1920 to go to Congress," said Mary Fallin, in reference to Alice Mary Robertson, the first woman from Oklahoma to be elected to Congress some eighty-six years earlier.[51] A Republican from Muskogee, Oklahoma, Robertson had served one term in Congress. "And actually just this past week," Mary Fallin noted in an oral history interview in 2008, "our last week of session, I actually passed a resolution to honor her because she was the second woman elected to Congress and she was the first woman ever to sit in the Speaker's chair in the US House of Representatives. And she was a woman from Oklahoma, so I passed a resolution the last day of this session to honor her."[52]

Fallin's early congressional committee assignments included the Transportation and Infrastructure Committee and the Small Business Committee. In addition, she joined the Congressional Caucus on Women's Issues and the Congressional Anti-Terrorism Caucus.[53] In the beginning of her term she was also part of a congressional delegation to Iraq. She also served as one of the speakers at the Republican National Convention in support of Republican presidential nominee Senator John McCain. Following her reelection to Congress in 2008, Fallin married Wade Christensen, an Oklahoma City attorney, and welcomed his four children from two previous marriages into her family.

In the historic campaign for governor of Oklahoma in 2010, two women were running in a "groundbreaking election year for women in Oklahoma politics": Congresswoman Mary Fallin as the Republican candidate and Lieutenant Governor Jari Askins as the Democratic candidate. Both candidates had defeated men in the primary, and both candidates held similar centrist views on almost all major issues. During the first televised debate, Jari Askins called herself a workhorse, not a show horse, in an effort to draw a distinction between the two candidates. When Mary Fallin was asked what defined her as a candidate and what distinguished her from her opponent, she said, "I think my experience is one of the things that sets me apart as a candidate for governor. First of all, being a mother, having children, raising a family."[54] In this case, Mary Fallin privileged her own role as a mother and noted the absence of motherhood for Askins. This gubernatorial debate featuring two women—and this exchange about motherhood specifically—prompted a national discussion about the "Mommy Question." As Christine Pappas and Kyle Foster have argued,

> The Mommy Question dovetails into the voters' perceptions of these two female candidates because it was suggested that a woman could not really understand her constituents unless she had raised children herself. Mary Fallin, in invoking the motherhood role, seems to embrace the "Traditional" role for women, and thus "gender issue ownership." Jari Askins could not similarly embrace the role, but she states that her marital status or lack of children did not affect her "understanding of the issues of families in Oklahoma."[55]

In this case, Mary Fallin used motherhood as a political asset. When asked to defend her comments regarding her opponent, Fallin responded that motherhood helped her relate to other Oklahomans: "I was just explaining that these things give me a good perspective on the challenges Oklahomans face, and hopefully voters can relate to that."[56] As Brittany L. Stalsburg and Mona S. Kleinberg have explained, "Fallin's motherhood experience allows her to portray herself and be perceived by voters as relatable—she is a common woman who has experienced what most Oklahomans have also experienced—raising a family and thus becoming familiar with issues that affect families."[57] Mary Fallin won the election with more than 60 percent of the vote.

In the United States, the number of women serving as governor has historically been small, even in recent years. In 2011, when Mary Fallin became governor, only seven states were governed by women. Two years later, in 2013, only six states, or 12 percent, had women governors.[58] The highest number of women serving as governor simultaneously has been in 2004, 2007, and 2019, with nine each of those years.[59] In addition, when Mary Fallin became governor in 2011, she was only the fourth Republican in Oklahoma to hold the position since statehood in 1907. Moreover, only four Oklahoma governors, including Fallin, have served two consecutive terms. During Mary Fallin's second term,

Mary Fallin served two terms as governor of Oklahoma from 2011 to 2019. This photo from November 3, 2010, shows Governor-elect Mary Fallin during the Republican watch party in Oklahoma City with her son, Price, and daughter, Christina (*left*), and her husband, Wade Christensen (*right*). She never lost an election during her public life from the 1990s through the 2010s, and her role as a mother to her two children remained central to her politics. Courtesy of the *Oklahoman*.

her name even appeared briefly as a potential vice presidential candidate on the 2016 Republican ticket.[60]

While she was governor of Oklahoma, Mary Fallin's priorities included job growth and retention, education reform, and government modernization. Many of the plans outlined in her first State of the State address, including civil justice reform and workers' compensation system reform, passed during the legislative session.[61] She also served a second term as governor, capturing more than 55 percent of the vote. Her goals included improving public education and public health and reforming criminal justice to reduce the state's high incarceration rate. Nationally, she served on the National Governors Association Executive Committee.[62]

Mary Fallin has described herself as a risk taker, specifying three large risks during her political career. First, she took a risk by running for office while pregnant in the early 1990s. Second, she took a risk by leaving the legislature to run for lieutenant governor. Third, she took a risk by leaving the elected position of lieutenant governor to run for Congress when Oklahoma had not had a woman elected to Congress since 1920. "Financially, running for Congress was a huge risk, again," she pointed out in the 2008 oral history interview, "because I've been a single mom for ten years totally supporting myself, no help from anybody. I'd be risking losing my job one more time. My strong faith has given me the confidence to take these risks, trusting God to work all things for the good no matter what the outcome."[63] Again, within Mary Fallin's rhetoric, we see glimpses of themes that have remained constant in her life and in her politics—motherhood, campaigning during pregnancy and later as a single mom balancing work and family as an example of her political toughness, her faith in God, and her commitment to public service through elected political positions.

Mary Fallin's use of maternalist politics and traditionalism fits well within the status quo of conservative Republican politics in the late twentieth and early twenty-first centuries. It is true that her rhetoric fits within the framework of mainstream conservatism, but it is equally true that she *made* it fit. The fact that fellow Republicans suggested having an abortion would make her a better candidate than being a pregnant one speaks volumes about the lingering power of the "Mommy Question" and Fallin's astute ability to shift the narrative. While Mary Fallin may be characterized as a traditional Republican in many respects, it remains noteworthy that her activist maternalism transformed her vision of motherhood into a profoundly successful political tool.

NOTES

I would like to thank Sarah Janda, Jan Hardt, and John Wood for their helpful comments on the chapter. In addition, I acknowledge the work of research assistants Amanda Barnette and Alexis Landeros. Furthermore, I appreciate the productive conversations with other contributors at the two workshops held at the Gilcrease Museum's Helmerich Center for American Research and the Oklahoma Historical Society's Oklahoma History Center as the project developed.

1. "Mary Fallin: 'Making a Difference,'" *Oklahoman*, October 10, 1999, 10.
2. Mary Fallin, interviewed by Tanya Finchum, October 7, 2008, 7, Women of the Oklahoma Legislature Oral History Project, Special Collections and University Archives, Edmon Low Library, Oklahoma State University.
3. Linda Kerber, "The Republican Mother: Women and the Enlightenment—An American Perspective," *American Quarterly* 28 (Summer 1976): 187–205; Linda K. Kerber, *Women of the Republic: Intellect and Ideology in Revolutionary America* (Chapel Hill: University of North Carolina Press, 1980).

4. Catherine E. Rymph, *Republican Women: Feminism and Conservatism from Suffrage through the Rise of the New Right* (Chapel Hill: University of North Carolina Press, 2006), 1. For more on motherhood and conservatism in American politics during the decades following World War II, see Michelle M. Nickerson, *Mothers of Conservatism: Women and the Postwar Right* (Princeton, NJ: Princeton University Press, 2012); June Melby Benowitz, *Challenge and Change: Right-Wing Women, Grassroots Activism, and the Baby Boom Generation* (Gainesville: University Press of Florida, 2015); Erin M. Kempker, *Big Sister: Feminism, Conservatism, and Conspiracy in the Heartland* (Champaign: University of Illinois Press, 2018).

5. Fallin, interviewed by Finchum, 6.

6. Mary Fallin, interviewed by Rodger Harris, assisted by Bob Burke and Judith Mitchener, July 21, 1997, Oklahoma Historical Society.

7. Marianne Schnall, *What Will It Take to Make a Woman President? Conversations about Women, Leadership and Power* (Berkeley, CA: Seal, 2013), 68.

8. "Mary Fallin: 'Making a Difference,'" 10.

9. Fallin, interviewed by Harris.

10. Fallin, interview by Finchum, 6.

11. Fallin, interviewed by Harris.

12. Fallin, interviewed by Harris.

13. Fallin, interviewed by Harris.

14. Fallin, interviewed by Harris.

15. Mike Hunter was appointed Oklahoma's attorney general by Governor Mary Fallin in February 2017. In addition, he served as secretary of state for Oklahoma under two Republican governors, Frank Keating and Mary Fallin.

16. Fallin, interviewed by Finchum, 6–7.

17. Fallin, interviewed by Harris.

18. Fallin, interviewed by Finchum, 8–9.

19. Fallin, interviewed by Harris.

20. Mary Fallin, "The Lessons of Humility," in *Voices from the Heartland*, ed. Carolyn Anne Taylor, Emily Dial-Driver, Carole Burrage, and Sally Emmons-Featherston (Norman: University of Oklahoma Press, 2007), 205.

21. Fallin, quoted in Schnall, *What Will It Take*, 60–61.

22. Fallin, quoted in Schnall, *What Will It Take*, 60–61.

23. For more on pro-life activism, family values, and the rise of the Christian Right in the 1980s and 1990s in the American West, see Jennifer L. Holland, *Tiny You: A Western History of the Anti-Abortion Movement* (Oakland: University of California Press, 2020), esp. chap. 6, "Making Family Values."

24. "GOP Candidates, Democratic Loner Differ on Abortion," *Oklahoman*, August 3, 1990.

25. Fallin, interviewed by Harris.

26. Fallin, interviewed by Harris.

27. Fallin, "The Lessons of Humility," 205.

28. "Fallin Discovers Ways to Balance Family, Politics," *Oklahoman*, August 8, 2010.

29. Karen L. Adams, "Governors Debating: The Role of Situational, Discourse and Transportable Identities," in *Discourse, Politics and Women as Global Leaders*, ed. John Wilson and Diana Boxer (Amsterdam: John Benjamins, 2015), 225–26.

30. W. David Baird and Danney Goble, *Oklahoma: A History* (Norman: University of Oklahoma Press, 2008), 242; Cindy Simon Rosenthal, *When Women Lead: Integrative Leadership in State Legislatures* (New York: Oxford University Press, 1998), 101.

31. "State Fact Sheet—Oklahoma," Center for American Women and Politics, https://cawp.rutgers.edu/state_fact_sheets/ok. Twenty-five years later, in 2019, women's representation in the state house and state senate had increased to thirty-two women or 21.5 percent, yet Oklahoma remained the eighth-lowest state by percentage nationwide. See "Women in State Legislators for 2019," National Conference of State Legislatures, https://www.ncsl.org/legislators-staff/legislators/womens-legislative-network/women-in-state-legislatures-for-2019.aspx.

32. Fallin, interviewed by Finchum, 8.

33. Fallin, interviewed by Harris.

34. Fallin, interviewed by Harris.

35. "House Passes Bill to Outlaw 'Stalking,'" *Oklahoman*, February 19, 1992.

36. Fallin, interviewed by Harris.

37. Fallin, interviewed by Finchum, 15; "After Historic Win, Fallin to Become Lieutenant Governor," *Oklahoman*, November 9, 1994.

38. Fallin, interviewed by Finchum, 15.

39. "After Historic Win, Fallin to Become Lieutenant Governor."

40. Fallin, interviewed by Finchum, 15–16.

41. Fallin, interviewed by Finchum, 17–18; "Workers Comp Panel Given Recommendations," *Oklahoman*, September 26, 1996; "House Passes Alternative Workers Comp Reform Bill," *Oklahoman*, February 26, 1997; "Workers Comp Reforms Get Senate's Full Support," *Oklahoman*, February 27, 1997; "Politics Pays in Workers Comp," *Oklahoman*, April 6, 1997.

42. Fallin, interviewed by Finchum, 18; "Right-to-Work Vote Remains in Stalemate," *Oklahoman*, April 7, 2000.

43. "Taking a Stand for Fairness," *Oklahoman*, April 8, 2000.

44. "Fallin Divorce Hearing Heated," *Tulsa World*, December 6, 1998; "Allegations Fly at Fallin Hearing," *Tulsa World*, December 24, 1998.

45. Fallin, "The Lessons of Humility," 206.

46. "Police Called in Dispute over Fallin Children," *Oklahoman*, December 28, 1999.

47. Fallin, "The Lessons of Humility," 207.

48. "Largent Bids for Governor, Fallin Told," *Oklahoman*, February 22, 2001.

49. Fallin, interviewed by Finchum, 20.

50. "Fallin to Run for Seat Being Vacated by Istook," *Oklahoman*, October 5, 2005; "Fallin, Bode Set Pace for Congressional Race," *Oklahoman*, February 2, 2006; "Fallin Expects Difficult Race to Win 5th District Outright," *Oklahoman*, July 14, 2006; "Cornett, Fallin Head for Runoff," *Oklahoman*, July 26, 2006; "Candidates Trade Barbs over Experience," *Oklahoman*, July 29, 2006; "Campaign Finance Reports How Cornett

Lagging," *Oklahoman*, August 14, 2006; "Campaign Slogan Is Well-Traveled," *Oklahoman*, September 3, 2006; "Fallin Raises $1.5 Million in Campaign for Congress," *Oklahoman*, October 17, 2006.

51. Fallin, interviewed by Finchum, 21.

52. Fallin, interviewed by Finchum, 21; "Trailblazer Keeps Making History," *Oklahoman*, November 8, 2006; "Fallin Says Her Victory Paves Way for Women," *Oklahoman*, January 1, 2007; "Fallin Takes Office in Congress," *Oklahoman*, January 5, 2007.

53. "Positions Please Freshman," *Oklahoman*, January 11, 2007; "Fallin Joins Two Caucuses," *Oklahoman*, February 6, 2007; "Fallin's First Year in House Is Rewarding, Frustrating," *Oklahoman*, December 23, 2007.

54. Sean Murphy, "Motherhood an Issue in Okla. Governor's Race," NBC News, October 23, 2010, http://www.nbcnews.com/id/39812276/ns/politics-decision_2010/t/motherhood-issue-okla-governors-race/#.X38jSJNKjJw. See also Kenneth P. Kickham, "Oklahoma's Governor and Elected Executives," in *Oklahoma Government & Politics: An Introduction*, 7th ed., ed. Jan C. Hardt, John R. Wood, Brett S. Sharp, and Christopher L. Markwood (Dubuque, IA: Kendall Hunt, 2020), 111–24.

55. Christine Pappas and Kyle Foster, "What Not to Wear: Fashion and Female Candidates in Oklahoma," *Oklahoma Politics* (November 2011): 103.

56. Brittany L. Stalsburg and Mona S. Kleinberg, "'A Mom First and a Candidate Second': Gender Differences in Candidates' Self-Presentation of Family," *Journal of Political Marketing* 15, no. 4 (2016): 290–91.

57. Stalsburg and Kleinberg, 291; "Candidates for Governor Face Tough Race, Issues," *Oklahoman*, August 2, 2010; "Marriage, Family Become Issues in Governor's Race," *Oklahoman*, October 26, 2010; "Hopefuls for Governor Tout Successes, Goals," *Oklahoman*, October 29, 2010; "Historic Victory for Fallin, GOP," *Oklahoman*, November 3, 2010.

58. Adams, "Governors Debating," 219.

59. "Facts: History of Women Governors," Center for American Women and Politics, Eagleton Institute of Politics, Rutgers University, https://cawp.rutgers.edu/history-women-governors.

60. Kickham, "Oklahoma's Governor and Elected Executives," 120.

61. "Fallin Enjoys First-Time Win as Governor," *Oklahoman*, May 22, 2011. As John Wood's research indicates, executive power increased under Governor Fallin through a more centralized approach to state government. See John Wood, "Fallin's Formal Powers in Transition: From Weak Governor to CEO," *Oklahoma Politics* 26 (November 2016): 107–38.

62. "To Win Again, Fallin May Not Have to Break a Sweat," *Oklahoman*, October 20, 2013; "Fallin Has Earned Four More Years as Governor," *Oklahoman*, October 19, 2014; "'I Am . . . Thankful to Be Given the Opportunity for a Second Term,'" *Oklahoman*, November 5, 2014.

63. Fallin, interviewed by Finchum, 22.

CONCLUSION

For the past three centuries, women in Oklahoma have created a sort of "herland" through individual activism and commitment to improving their communities in the times and places in which they have lived. Many of the women examined here successfully crafted images that helped them further their agendas, but this was not the case for all of them. Moreover, even as many of the women accomplished significant change, it often came at a high price in terms of health and personal relationships.

Mattie Mallory, Alice Robertson, LaDonna Harris, and Mary Fallin successfully used maternalist politics to further their otherwise incongruent agendas. Mallory's use of religious imperative to care for orphans legitimized what otherwise might have been a rather troubling real estate empire. Harris's role in promoting Indigenous sovereignty and training next-generation leaders is remarkable, yet her rise to prominence contributed to tensions within her marriage, which ultimately ended in divorce. Robertson and Fallin both had successful political careers, but Robertson was largely considered an anomaly in her time while Fallin's conservative maternalist politics were more in keeping with other conservative women in the American West, especially by the time she was elected governor. Kate Barnard skillfully sidestepped the issue of voting rights for women with her a-suffrage approach to furthering the place of women in public and political decision making, but this, too, came at a personal cost. By the end of her life, she felt isolated and rejected. And her efforts to improve the state mental institution in Norman were long forgotten by the time Rosie Gilchrist took up forced occupancy there decades later.

Lilah Denton Lindsey and Rachel Caroline Eaton successfully used education and women's networks as ways to improve conditions for their tribes while maintaining a firm grounding in their Indigenous values, which is something that is apparent in LaDonna Harris's work more than a century later. Barbara "Wahru" Cleveland also recognized the importance of female networks, particularly to create a safe space for the LGBTQ+ community in the conservative political climate in Oklahoma City. She succeeded in many ways, but she encountered significant hardships, even as she looked to leaders like Clara Luper for inspiration.

California Taylor successfully carved out a space for herself in Boley through the construction of aspirational Black womanhood and by making advances in employment as a pharmacist and notary public among other things. But her final years in Boley were spent unsuccessfully trying to increase NAACP involvement in her community. Ada Lois Sipuel Fisher and Clara Luper played central roles in eradicating segregation, but their efforts put them in danger and took great physical and emotional tolls. Rosie Gilchrist successfully participated in civil rights demonstrations, but she paid an unthinkable price for trying to sell her home to a Black man. Her physical and mental pain went unaddressed even as she lived five of the last eight years of her life in a mental institution. Wanda Jo Peltier Stapleton had a long career of activism, but her effort to secure Oklahoma's ratification of the Equal Rights Amendment did not come to fruition.

This is not, then, a story of victorious women triumphing against all odds. Through the lives of the individual women studied here, we gain a glimpse into the complexities of women's activism as they sought to define the physical, social, and political spaces in which they lived. Wilma Mankiller, the first female chief of the Cherokee Nation and longtime advocate for Indigenous sovereignty and women's rights, often remarked that her election as chief led some people to incorrectly conclude that women had achieved full equality in the United

States. Following election to her final term as chief in 1991, in which she won with 82.5 percent of the vote, she explained the lack of equality, arguing that women have to be twice as qualified as men and that "only when mediocre women begin to get elected to high offices will equality truly be achieved."[1] Oklahoma is no closer to being a feminist utopia today than it was when Charlotte Perkins Gilman first wrote *Herland*. However, Oklahoma is a land that has been shaped by generations of determined women who skillfully—some more so than others—navigated gender role constructions, legal and political constraints, and racial and ethnic discrimination to create change. Oklahoma is the place they made.

NOTE

1. Sarah Eppler Janda, *Beloved Women: The Political Lives of LaDonna Harris and Wilma Mankiller* (DeKalb: Northern Illinois University Press, 2007), 110.

SELECTED BIBLIOGRAPHY

ARCHIVAL COLLECTIONS

Coleman Family Private Papers
    Central State (Griffin Memorial) Hospital
        Roslyn Coleman Gilchrist Medical File, 1963–1968
Manuscript Division, Library of Congress, Washington, DC
    Records of the National Association for the Advancement of Colored People
        NAACP Branch Files, Boley, OK
McFarlin Library Special Collections, Tulsa, OK
    Lilah D. Lindsey Papers
    Papers of the Robertson and Worcester families, 1815–1932
Northeastern State University Archives, Tahlequah, OK
    Isabel Cobb Correspondence
Oklahoma Historical Society Research Division, Oklahoma City
    Kate Barnard Collection
    Equal Rights Amendment Collection

Mary Fallin Oral History Interview
Clara Luper Collection
Wanda Jo Peltier Stapleton Collection
Oklahoma State University Archives, Edmon Low Library, Stillwater
    Women of the Oklahoma Legislature Oral History Project
        Mary Fallin Oral History Interview
        Wanda Jo Peltier Oral History Interview
State Archives of Oklahoma, Oklahoma City
    Charities and Corrections Collection
Western History Collections, University of Oklahoma Libraries, Norman
    Indian-Pioneer Papers
    Interview with Mrs. Lilah Denton Lindsey
Women's Research Center and BGLTQ+ Student Center, University of Central Oklahoma, Edmond
    Herland: Creating a Radical Lesbian Feminist Community. Directed by Jake Crystal and Mickayla Fisher (2019)
    Herland Voice Newsletter Archive

GOVERNMENT DOCUMENTS

Board of Education of Oklahoma v. National Gay Task Force, 470 US 903 (1985)
Gay Activists Alliance v. the Board of Regents of the University of Oklahoma, 638 P.2d 1116, 162 (1981)
Sipuel v. Board of Regents of the University of Oklahoma et al., 332 US 631 (1948)

NEWSPAPERS

Black Dispatch
Boley (OK) Beacon
Boley (OK) Dispatch
Boley (OK) Informer
Boley (OK) Progress
Chicago Defender
Daily Times-Journal (Oklahoma City)
The Guide (Oklahoma City, Oklahoma Territory)
Lawton (OK) Constitution
Los Angeles Sentinel
New York Times
Oklahoma City Times
Oklahoma Daily
Oklahoma Journal
Oklahoman
Tulsa Tribune

PUBLISHED PRIMARY SOURCES

Coleman. *Spoke: A Mother. A Son. Civil Rights. Vietnam.* Mineral Point, WI: Little Creek, 2013.
Eaton, Rachel Caroline. *John Ross and the Cherokee Indians.* Menasha, WI: George Banta, 1914.
———. "The Legend of the Battle of Claremore Mound." *Chronicles of Oklahoma* 8, no. 4 (December 1930): 369–77.
Fallin, Mary. "The Lessons of Humility." In *Voices from the Heartland*, edited by Carolyn Anne Taylor, Emily Dial-Driver, Carole Burrage, and Sally Emmons-Featherston, 204–7. Norman: University of Oklahoma Press, 2007.
Harris. LaDonna. *LaDonna Harris: A Comanche Life.* Edited by Henrietta Stockel. Lincoln: University of Nebraska Press, 2000.
Harris, LaDonna, and Jacqueline Wasilewski. *This Is What We Want to Share: Core Cultural Values.* Albuquerque, NM: Americans for Indian Opportunity, 1992.
Luper, Clara. *Behold the Walls.* Oklahoma City: Jim Wire, 1979.
Sipuel Fisher, Ada Lois. *A Matter of Black and White: The Autobiography of Ada Lois Sipuel Fisher.* Norman: University of Oklahoma Press, 1996.

SECONDARY SOURCES

Adams, David Wallace. *Education for Extinction: American Indians and the Boarding School Experience, 1875–1928.* Lawrence: University Press of Kansas, 1995.
Baird, W. David, and Danney Goble. *Oklahoma: A History.* Norman: University of Oklahoma Press, 2008.
Brown, Kirby. *Stoking the Fire: Nationhood in Cherokee Writing, 1907–1970.* Norman: University of Oklahoma Press, 2018.
Burbank, Garin. *When Farmers Voted Red: The Gospel of Socialism in the Oklahoma Countryside, 1910–1924.* Westport, CT: Greenwood, 1976.
Cahill, Cathleen D. *Federal Fathers and Mothers: A Social History of the United States Indian Service, 1869–1933.* Chapel Hill: University of North Carolina Press, 2011.
Chang, David. *The Color of the Land: Race, Nation, and the Politics of Landownership in Oklahoma, 1832–1929.* Chapel Hill: University of North Carolina Press, 2010.
Cobb, Amanda J. *Listening to Our Grandmothers' Stories: The Bloomfield Academy for Chickasaw Females, 1852–1949.* Lincoln: University of Nebraska Press, 2000.
———. "Powerful Medicine: The Rhetoric of Comanche Activist LaDonna Harris." *Studies in American Indian Literature* 18, no. 4 (Winter 2006): 63–87.
Collins, Reba Neighbors, and Bob Burke. *Alice Robertson: Congresswoman from Oklahoma.* Edmond: University of Central Oklahoma Press, 2001.
Dunbar-Ortiz, Roxanne. *Red Dirt: Growing Up Okie.* Norman: University of Oklahoma Press, 2006.
Eichenger-Swainston, Katja M. "Fox v. Fox, Redefining the Best Interest of the Child Standard for Lesbian Mothers and Their Families." *Tulsa Law Journal* 32, no. 1 (Fall 1996): 57–74.

Field, Kendra Taira. *Growing Up with the Country: Family, Race, and Nation after the Civil War.* New Haven, CT: Yale University Press, 2018.

Gaines, Kevin. *Uplifting the Race: Black Leadership, Politics and Culture in the Twentieth Century.* Chapel Hill: University of North Carolina Press, 1996.

Garrison, Tim Alan, and Greg O'Brien, eds. *The Native South: New Histories and Enduring Legacies.* Lincoln: University of Nebraska Press, 2017.

Houck, David W., and David E. Dixon, eds. *Women in the Civil Rights Movement, 1954–1965.* Jackson: University Press of Mississippi, 2009.

Jacobs, Margaret D. *White Mother to a Dark Race: Settler Colonialism, Maternalism, and the Removal of Indigenous Children in the American West and Australia, 1880–1940.* Lincoln: University of Nebraska Press, 2009.

Janda, Sarah Eppler. *Beloved Women: The Political Lives of LaDonna Harris and Wilma Mankiller.* DeKalb: Northern Illinois University Press, 2007.

———. *Prairie Power: Student Activism, Counterculture, and Backlash in Oklahoma, 1962–1972.* Norman: University of Oklahoma Press, 2018.

Koven, Seth, and Sonya Michel. *Mothers of a New World: Maternalist Politics and the Origins of Welfare States.* New York: Routledge, 2016.

Ladd-Taylor, Molly. *Mother-Work: Women, Child Welfare, and the State, 1890–1930.* Urbana: University of Illinois Press, 1995.

Loughlin, Patricia. *Hidden Treasures of the American West: Muriel H. Wright, Angie Debo, and Alice Marriott.* Albuquerque: University of New Mexico Press, 2005.

Mihesuah, Devon A. *Cultivating the Rosebuds: The Education of Women at the Cherokee Female Seminary, 1851–1909.* Urbana: University of Illinois Press, 1993.

———. *Indigenous American Women: Decolonization, Empowerment, Activism.* Lincoln: University of Nebraska Press, 2003.

Miles, Tiya. "The Long Arm of the South?" *Western Historical Quarterly* 43 (Autumn 2012): 274–81.

———. *Ties That Bind: The Story of an Afro-Cherokee Family in Slavery and Freedom.* Los Angeles: University of California Press, 2006.

Mitchell, Michele. *Righteous Propagation: African Americans and the Politics of Racial Destiny after Reconstruction.* Chapel Hill: University of North Carolina Press, 2004.

Musslewhite, Lynn, and Suzanne Crawford. *One Woman's Political Journey: Kate Barnard and Social Reform, 1875–1930.* Norman: University of Oklahoma Press, 2003.

Muzumdar, Maitreyi. "Alice's Restaurant: Expanding a Woman's Sphere." *Chronicles of Oklahoma* 70 (Fall 1992): 302–25.

Newman, Louise Michele. *White Women's Rights: The Racial Origins of Feminism in the United States.* New York: Oxford University Press, 1999.

Nickerson, Michelle M. *Mothers of Conservatism: Women and the Postwar Right.* Princeton, NJ: Princeton University Press, 2012.

Nielson, Kim E. *A Disability History of the United States.* Boston: Beacon, 2012.

———. *Un-American Womanhood: Antiradicalism, Antifeminism, and the First Red Scare.* Columbus: Ohio State University Press, 2001.

Reed, Julie L. *Serving the Cherokee Nation: Cherokee Sovereignty and Social Welfare, 1800–1907.* Norman: University of Oklahoma Press, 2016.

Reese, Linda Williams. *Women of Oklahoma, 1890–1920.* Norman: University of Oklahoma Press, 1997.

———. *Trail Sisters: Freedwomen in Indian Territory, 1850–1890.* Lubbock: Texas Tech University Press, 2013.

Reese, Linda W., and Patricia Loughlin, eds. *Main Street Oklahoma: Stories of Twentieth Century America.* Norman: University of Oklahoma Press, 2013.

Rhea, John M. *A Field of Their Own: Women and American Indian History, 1830–1941.* Norman: University of Oklahoma Press, 2016.

Rymph, Catherine E. *Republican Women: Feminism and Conservatism from Suffrage through the Rise of the New Right.* Chapel Hill: University of North Carolina Press, 2006.

Saunt, Claudio. *Black, White, and Indian: Race and the Unmaking of an American Family.* New York: Oxford University Press, 2005.

Schrems, Suzanne H. *Across the Political Spectrum: Oklahoma Women in Politics in the Early Twentieth Century, 1900–1930.* San Jose, CA: Writer's Club, 2001.

———. *Who's Rocking the Cradle? Women Pioneers of Oklahoma Politics from Socialism to the KKK, 1900–1930.* Norman, OK: Horse Creek, 2004.

Spruill, Marjorie J. *Divided We Stand: The Battle over Women's Rights and Family Values That Polarized American Politics.* New York: Bloomsbury, 2017.

Steineker, Rowan Faye. "'Fully Equal to That of Any Children': Experimental Creek Education in the Antebellum Era." *History of Education Quarterly* 56, no. 2 (May 2016): 273–300.

Stuckey, Melissa N. "'All Men Up': Race, Rights, and Power in the All Black Town of Boley, Oklahoma, 1903–1939." PhD diss., Yale University, 2009.

———. "Boley, Indian Territory: Exercising Freedom in the All-Black Town." *Journal of African American History* 102, no. 4 (Fall 2017): 492–516.

Taylor, Quintard, and Shirley Ann Wilson Moore, eds. *African American Women Confront the West, 1600–2000.* Norman: University of Oklahoma Press, 2008.

Threat, Charissa J. *Nursing Civil Rights: Gender and Race in the Army Nurse Corps.* Chicago: University of Illinois Press, 2015.

Wattley, Cheryl Elizabeth Brown. *A Step toward* Brown v. Board of Education: *Ada Lois Sipuel Fisher and Her Fight to End Segregation.* Norman: University of Oklahoma Press, 2014.

Weaver, Jace. *Other Words: American Indian Literature, Law, and Culture.* Norman: University of Oklahoma Press, 2001.

Weheliye, Alexander. *Habeas Viscus: Racializing Assemblages, Biopolitics, and Black Feminist Theories of the Human.* Durham, NC: Duke University Press, 2014.

Wynter, Sylvia. "Unsettling the Coloniality of Being/Power/Truth/Freedom: Towards the Human, after Man, Its Overrepresentation—An Argument." *CR: The New Centennial Review* 3, no. 3 (2003): 257–337.

CONTRIBUTORS

CHELSEA BALL is a doctoral candidate at the University of Oklahoma. She specializes in postwar gender and politics with an emphasis on Oklahoma and the West. She graduated with her MA from the University of Oklahoma in 2016 and earned her BA in History Education from the University of Central Oklahoma in 2014. Her forthcoming dissertation is tentatively titled "West of Feminism: Gender, Religion, and the Politics of the Equal Rights Amendment."

LINDSEY CHURCHILL is Associate Professor of History at the University of Central Oklahoma. She is the Creator and Director of the Women's Gender and Sexuality Studies Program. In 2015 she worked with the campus community to create the Center, which includes the Women's Research Center and the BGLTQ+ Student Center. She is author of *Becoming the Tupamaros: Solidarity and Transnational Revolutionaries in Uruguay and the United States* (Vanderbilt University Press, 2014). Churchill worked as a Fulbright Scholar Specialist in Latvia in 2016. She was recipient of the Oklahoma Human Rights Award from the Oklahoma Universal Human Rights Alliance and the United Nations Association Oklahoma City Chapter in 2016.

HEATHER CLEMMER is Professor and Chair of the History, Politics, and Law Department and General Education Director at Southern Nazarene University in Bethany, Oklahoma. She earned her PhD in History from the University of Oklahoma in 2008. She teaches Twentieth-Century American History, Oklahoma History, and Women's History. Clemmer served nine years as a member of the Oklahoma City Historic Preservation Commission and is author of "'We Can Fulfill Our Obligation as Women Citizens': San Francisco Women, Civic Identity, and the Great War," *California History* (Fall 2020).

AMANDA COBB-GREETHAM (Chickasaw) serves as Professor and Director of the Native Nations Center at the University of Oklahoma. From 2007 to 2012 she served the Chickasaw Nation as Administrator of the Division of History and Culture, where she was instrumental in launching the Chickasaw Cultural Center in Sulphur as well as the Chickasaw Press. Cobb-Greetham won the American Book Award for *Listening to Our Grandmothers' Stories: The Bloomfield Academy for Chickasaw Females, 1852–1949* (University of Nebraska Press, 2000; 2007). She is coeditor with Amy Lonetree of *The National Museum of the American Indian: Critical Conversations* (University of Nebraska Press, 2008). She serves as Vice Chair of the Board of Trustees of the Smithsonian National Museum of the American Indian.

SARAH EPPLER JANDA is Professor of History at Cameron University in Lawton, Oklahoma. She received a PhD in History in 2002 from the University of Oklahoma, where she focused on Twentieth-Century Oklahoma and Native American Women's History. She is the author of *Beloved Women: The Political Lives of LaDonna Harris and Wilma Mankiller* (Northern Illinois University Press, 2007); *Pride of the Wichitas: A History of Cameron University* (Oklahoma Heritage Association, 2010); and *Prairie Power: Student Activism, Counterculture, and Backlash in Oklahoma, 1962–1972* (University of Oklahoma Press, 2018). She is President of Cameron University's chapter of the American Association of University Professors (AAUP) and is an active member of the Coalition for Western Women's History, the Western History Association, and the Berkshire Conference of Women Historians.

FARINA KING (Diné) is Assistant Professor of History and Affiliated Faculty of Cherokee and Indigenous Studies at Northeastern State University in Tahlequah, Oklahoma. She received her PhD at Arizona State University in US History. King specializes in Twentieth-Century Native American Studies. She is author of *The Earth Memory Compass: Diné Landscapes and Education in the Twentieth Century* (University Press of Kansas, 2018). Learn more about her work at farinaking.com.

SUNU KODUMTHARA is Associate Professor of History at Southwestern Oklahoma State University in Weatherford. She graduated with her PhD in American History from the University of Oklahoma in 2011, specializing in the American West, Women's History, and Post-1865 American History. She is author of "'The Right of Suffrage Has Been Thrust on Me': The Reluctant Suffragists of the American West," *Journal of the Gilded Age and Progressive Era* (October 2020). She has served on the boards for the Western Association of Women Historians and the Coordinating Council of Women Historians.

PATRICIA LOUGHLIN is Professor of History at the University of Central Oklahoma. She specializes in History of the American West, American Indian History, and Women's and Gender History. Patricia serves on the Oklahoma Historical Society Board of Directors, has served on the editorial boards of the *Western Historical Quarterly* and the *Chronicles of Oklahoma*, and remains active in the Coalition for Western Women's History and the Western History Association. Her book *Hidden Treasures of the American West: Muriel H. Wright, Angie Debo and Alice Marriott* (University of New Mexico Press, 2005) received the distinction of Outstanding Book on Oklahoma History from the Oklahoma Historical Society, won the Director's Award, and was a Finalist in Nonfiction from the Oklahoma Center for the Book in 2006. She coauthored *Building Traditions, Educating Generations: A History of the University of Central Oklahoma* (Oklahoma Heritage Association, 2007) with Bob Burke and coedited *Main Street Oklahoma: An American Story* (Norman: University of Oklahoma Press, 2013) with Linda Reese. Her latest book, *Angie Debo, Daughter of the Prairie* (Oklahoma Hall of Fame, 2017), received the 2018 Oklahoma Book Award for Children/Young Adults from the Oklahoma Center for the Book.

AMY L. SCOTT is Associate Professor of History and the Director of Women's and Gender Studies at Bradley University. She is coeditor, with Kathleen Brosnan, of *City Dreams, Country Schemes: Community and Identity in the American West* (University of Nevada Press, 2011). She has authored several essays on post-1945 US urban history and social movements and edits the Urban West Series at the University of Nevada Press. Scott is currently revising her first monograph, *City Republic of Boulder: Lifestyle Liberalism and the Politics of the Good Life*, and is working on a short biography of Congresswoman Alice Robertson, Oklahoma's first and the nation's second congresswoman. Scott was a 2018 research fellow at the Gilcrease Museum's Helmerich Center for American Research in Tulsa, Oklahoma, and she presented at the Gilcrease Symposium on Gender and Identity in the American West in 2018.

ROWAN FAYE STEINEKER is National Academy of Education/Spencer Institute Postdoctoral Fellow and Assistant Professor of History at Florida Gulf Coast University. She received a PhD in History from the University of Oklahoma in 2016. Her areas of research include Education History, Native American History, and History of the American West.

MELISSA N. STUCKEY is Assistant Professor of African American History at Elizabeth City State University in northeastern North Carolina. Author of "Boley, Indian Territory: Exercising Freedom in the All-Black Town," *Journal of African American History* (2017), Stuckey is currently completing her first book, *"All Men Up": Race, Rights, and Power in the All-Black Town of Boley, Oklahoma, 1903–1939*, which unveils the Black freedom struggle in Oklahoma as it took shape in the state's more than two dozen all-Black towns. She also serves as Senior Historical Consultant to the Coltrane Group, a nonprofit organization in Oklahoma committed to helping these towns survive in the twenty-first century.

RACHEL E. WATSON (Citizen Band Potawatomi) completed her MSEd in Education, Culture, and Society at the University of Pennsylvania in December 2019 after receiving a BA in History from the University of Central Oklahoma. Watson's master's thesis, "The Product of Plantations: Teacher-Student Relationships and the Ghosts of Settler Colonialism," examines the way schooling can challenge or reinforce anti-Black and anti-Red racism. Watson's interests include the history of the intersections between Black and Indigenous activism, gender, and education.

CHERYL ELIZABETH BROWN WATTLEY is Professor of Law and Director of Experiential Learning at the University of North Texas, Dallas, College of Law. Wattley was formerly Professor and Director of Clinical Education at the University of Oklahoma College of Law. While at OU, Wattley was inspired by a painting of Thurgood Marshall and Ada Lois Sipuel Fisher to research Sipuel Fisher's fight to enter OU law school. Her research took her to state archives, where she uncovered original transcripts that had not before been accessed. Wattley's research has been presented in a full-length theatrical presentation, *A Step Forward*, and in her book *A Step toward* Brown v. Board of Education*: Ada Lois Sipuel Fisher and Her Fight to End Segregation* (University of Oklahoma Press, 2014). Her book received the Oklahoma Book Award in Nonfiction.

INDEX

References to illustrations appear in italic type.

abortion, 234, 236, 239, 252, 263, 267, 274
ACLU. *See* American Civil Liberties Union (ACLU)
Adair, Bluie, *104*, 109
Adams, Jan, 197–98
Adams, Ruth, 240
African Americans. *See* Black Americans
Agnew, Brad, 100
Alexander-Starr, Myra, 29n24
all-Black towns, 121, 122, 125–44, 231
Allotment Act of 1887. *See* Dawes Act
allotment of Native lands, 22, 99, 109, 110, 111, 130, 213
American Civil Liberties Union (ACLU), 234, 257
American Legislative Exchange Council, 269
Americans for Indian Opportunity (AIO), 207, 208–9, 211, 215, 216–17; Ambassadors Program, 221–25
Anderson, Hubert M., 184

Anti–Child Labor League, 83
anti-gay attitudes and activism. *See also* homophobia
antipoverty activism, 77, 78, 81, 82–83, 88
Argo, Henry, 145, 148
Askins, Jari, 271–72
assimilation: African American, 171; Native American, 17, 22, 57–59, 70, 111, 209–11, 219, 220, 224

Baker, Bill John, 113
Baldwin, Eliza, 13, 16, 18
Baptist Home Missionary Society, 33
Barnard, John P., 76
Barnard, Kate, 8, 27, 75–98, *79*
Bateman, Jodey, 186–87, 197
Battle of Claremore Mound. *See* Claremore Mound Massacre
Beckett, Nelson, 190
Behold the Walls (Luper), 171, 197
Bethany, Okla., 8, 32, *41*, 48
Bissett, Jim, 78, 96

Black Americans, 81, 82, 85, 121–23, 125–82; assimilation, 171; Cleveland, 246–61; Taylor, 122, 125–44; Luper, 122, 166–82, *170*, 186, 187–88, 197, 247; Gilchrist and, 184–93, *189*, 195–98, *198*; Sipuel Fisher, 122, 145–65, *147*, *162*, 203. *See also* all-Black towns; lynching; racial segregation and desegregation
Blackstock, Ben, 154
Blake, Louis and Elbert, 137
Boley, Okla., 121, 122, 125–44
Bonus Bill (1924), 68
Boren, David, 234
Bouziden, Deborah, 110
boycotts: Oklahoma City, 176–77; pro-ERA, 239, 241
Bradley, Oniel H., 126
Brock, California Minnie Taylor. *See* Taylor, California Minnie
Brock, Charles, 125–26, 132–33
Broken Arrow, Okla., 19
Brother President (Luper), 172
Brown, Charles P., 180
Brown, Della, 171
Brown, Kirby, 103, 108, 110
Brown, Ruth Murray, 234
Bryan, William Jennings, 81
Bryant, Anita, 3
Bullock, W. A. J., 146, 149, 150, 151, 153
Bureau of Indian Affairs (BIA), 54–55, 57, 58, 65, 209, 210, 218, 219
Burns, James Alexander, 109

Cahill, Cathleen, 57
Carlisle Indian School, 58
Carter, Jimmy, 216, 234
Central State College. *See* University of Central Oklahoma
Central State (Griffin Memorial) Hospital, 183, 186, 190–99
Chandler, M. L., 129
Chandler, William L., 129

Charities and Corrections Department. *See* Oklahoma Department of Charities and Corrections
Checote, Samuel, 58
Cherokee National Female Seminary, 100, 102, 103–5, 109, 113, 114
Cherokee National Male Seminary, 103, 109
Cherokee people, 12, 13, 55, 99–120
Chickasaw people, 1, 22, 33, 91
Chickasha, Okla., 122, 145, 146, 148, 154, 161, 179, 264
child labor laws, 83–84, 86, 92
child neglect, 93
Children's Center Rehabilitation Hospital (Children's Convalescent Center), Oklahoma City, 50
Christensen, Wade, 271, *273*
Christian fundamentalists. *See* fundamentalist Christians
Civil Rights Act of 1964, 178; Title VII, 230–31
Civil War, 12, 56, 148
Claremore, Okla., 99, 105, 107, 109, 112
Claremore Mound Massacre, 106, 107, 111
Clark, A. H., 89, 90
Clarke, Martha "Mattie" Cobb, 105
Cleveland, Barbara "Wahru," 204, 246–61, *249*
clubs, women's. *See* women's clubs and clubwomen
Cobb, Isabel "Belle," 100, 103, 105, 113
Cobb, Mattie. *See* Clarke, Martha "Mattie" Cobb
Cole, Willie, 179
Coleman (Joe Gilchrist), 184, 188, 190, 191, 193, 194, 195–96, 197; and *Spoke*, 184, 185–86, 188–89, 190, 195, 196
Coleman, Rosalyn. *See* Gilchrist, Rosalyn "Rosie" Coleman
colonization and colonialism, 210, 213, 217, 220, 226

Comanche women, 203–4, 207–27, *212*
Commercial Club (Oklahoma City), 46
Common Cause, 216, 234
Community Action Programs (CAPs), 218
compulsory education, 83, 84, 86
Congress, US. *See* US Congress
Congress of Racial Equality (CORE), 177
Constitutional Convention, 1906. *See* Oklahoma Constitutional Convention, 1906
Constitution of Oklahoma. *See* Oklahoma Constitution
Cornett, Mick, 271
Corrections Department, Oklahoma. *See* Oklahoma Department of Charities and Corrections
corruption, 93, 94, 95
Crawford, Suzanne, 76, 82, 94
Creek Nation. *See* Muscogee (Creek) Nation
Creek women. *See* Muscogee (Creek) women
Critz, Harry, 178, 180
Cross, George Lynn, 150–52
Cunningham, Agnes "Sis," 3
Curtis Act of 1898, 22, 60, 109

Daily Oklahoman, 77, 81, 82, 83, 87, 92
Daniel, Nancy "Nannie" Katherine. *See* Fite, Nancy "Nannie" Katherine Daniel
Davis, Junetta, 234
Dawes Academy, Berwyn, Indian Territory, 33, 34, 36
Dawes Act, 22, 99, 109, 213
Dawes Commission, 22, 57, 60
Daws, S. O., 86
Dawson, Patricia, 112
Deatherage, Cleta, 234
Debo, Angie, 111, 112

Democratic Party, 64, 70, 84, 85–86, 96, 268, 270; Barnard, 82; Eaton, 112, 113; ERA and, 232, 234; Fallin, 263–64; Nagle, 80
Denton, John, 12
Denton, Susan McKellop, 12, 13
Diamond, Nance, 269
disability activism, 193
disappearing Indian trope, 209, 210–11, 220
disenfranchisement of Black men, 134, 135
Dlugacz, Judy, 251
Doe Doe Amusement Park, Lawton, Okla., 178–80
draft resistance, 195–96, 197
Draper, Dan, 232
drugstore lunch counter sit-ins. *See* lunch counter sit-ins
Drury College, Springfield, Mo., 107
Dunbar-Ortiz, Roxanne, 3
Dunjee, Roscoe, 146, 149–54, 158; namesake high school, 172
Dunn, Garrell, 185, 190
Dunn, Kate, 48

Eagle Forum, 235
Eaton, Martha "Mattie." *See* York, Martha "Mattie" Pauline Eaton
Eaton, Rachel Caroline "Callie," 9, 99–120, *101*, *104*; *John Ross and the Cherokee Indians*, 9, 108, 110
Equal Employment Opportunity Commission, 230
Equal Rights Amendment (ERA) (proposed), 228, 231–32, 233–41, 263; Countdown Campaign, 240–41, 252

Fallin, Joe Price, II, 265, 270
Fallin, Mary, 205, 262–77, *273*, 278–79
Farmers' Union, 76, 92, 96n3, 104–5
feminist bookstores, 248–51

feminist organizations, 204–5, 246–61
Fisher, Ada Lois Sipuel. *See* Sipuel Fisher, Ada Lois
Fite, Nancy "Nannie" Katherine Daniel, 102, 103
Fite, Richard, 102
"Five Tribes," 11–12, 20–22, 25, 27, 60, 109; Minerva Boarding School, 59. *See also* Cherokee people; Chickasaw people; Muscogee (Creek) Nation
Fort Sill, 178, 180
Foster, Henry, Jr., 160
Foster, L. P., 133
Foster, Mariah, 133
Fourteenth Amendment, 122, 152, 156, 157
Fox, Donna Jeanne, 257
Fox v. Fox, 257
Friedan, Betty, 243
Friends of the Indians, 17, 59
Fry, Maggie Culver, 105
Fuller, Gwendolyn, 170–71
fundamentalist Christians, 234, 235–36

Gaines, Lloyd, 149
Gassaway, Percy L., 137, 138
gay student groups. *See* LGBTQ+ student groups
General Allotment Act of 1887. *See* Dawes Act
General Federation of Women's Clubs, 24, 110–11
Gilchrist, Joe. *See* Coleman (Joe Gilchrist)
Gilchrist, John, 184, 185
Gilchrist, Rosalyn "Rosie" Coleman, 122–23, 183–201, *189*, *198*
Girton, Clarence, 46
Girton, Susan Hershey, 34, 40, 42–43, 47
Goldman, Emma, 80
Governor's Commission on the Status of Women (Oklahoma), 232, 236, 238

graft. *See* corruption
Graham, Bob, 241
Graves, Bill, 253
Gray, Henry Clay, 132
Green, Henrietta "Hetty," 63–64
Green Corn Rebellion, 2
Green Peach War, 58
Griffin, D. W., 90
Griffin State Hospital. *See* Central State (Griffin Memorial) Hospital
Guernsey, Mamie and William, 45
The Guide (Oklahoma City), 33–38, 40, 42–48
Gulager, Nell Taylor, *104*
Guthrie, Okla., 132, 138

Hall, Amos, 152, 153, 158
Hall, David, 232
Hanraty, Peter, 83
Hanson, Fred, 153
Harding, Warren G., 64, 68, 69
Hargis, Billy James, 3
Harjo, Lochar, 13
Harrell, Mary Alice, 91
Harris, Colonel Johnson "C. J.," 100
Harris, Fred, 207, 215–16
Harris, LaDonna, 203–4, 207–27, *212*
Hart, Jeffrey, 236
Haskell, Charles N., 27, 76, 84–87, 89, 92
Hastings, W. W., 62
Haynes, Thomas M., 125, 126, 128, 132, 135
Hayworth, W. P., 19
Henry, Brad, 269
Henry Kendall College. *See* Kendall College
Herland Bookstore, 248–51
Herland Gender and Sexuality Studies Library, University of Central Oklahoma, 258n1
Herland Sister Resources, 204–5, 246–61
Hershey, Reuben, 34, 36, 38

Hershey, Susan. *See* Girton, Susan Hershey
Highland Institute, Hillsboro, Ohio, 16
Hilbert-Price, Shirley, 234
Hildreth, Marilyn Luper, 168, 186
Hill, Archibald, 178
Hinshaw, Justin, 161
Hochtritt, James, 20
Hodge, David, 15
Holiness movement, 33–48
Hollins, Jess, 137
homophobia, 239, 250, 253–54
Houston, Texas, and California Taylor, 127, 128, *136*, 138, 139–40
Hunter, David, 271
Hunter, Mike and Cheryl, 265
Hutchins, Ben, 178, 179–80
Hutchins, Ben, Jr., 178, 179–80

Indian Citizenship Act of 1924, 25
Indigenous Americans. *See* Native Americans
institutionalization, involuntary, 183, 186, 190–99
Ishii, Izumi, 21
Isparhecher, 58
Istook, Ernest, 271

Jacobs, Margaret, 57
Janda, Sarah Eppler, 208, 209
John A. Brown (Oklahoma City department store), 171
John Ross and the Cherokee Indians (Eaton), 9, 108, 110
Johnson, Lyndon B.: Great Society programs, 218, 219
Johnson, Peggy, 252
Johnston, Fannie, 34, 37, 42–43
Jones, Barbara Posey, 169, *170*, 171, 173
Jones, Fleming B., 133
Jones, Hallie Smith, 128
Jones, Lela, 193

Jones, Lynzetta, 171
juvenile delinquency, 78

Kansas: Green Peach War, 58; Barnard, 76; Mallory, 33, 42, 43; Oklahoma prisoner housing in, 88, 89
Katz Drug Store, Oklahoma City, 122, 166, 172, 173, 186
Keating, Frank, 269
Keeton, Paige, 160
Kendall College, 59, 60
Kerr, Robert, 215
King, Martin Luther, Jr., 187
Krebs, Okla., mine disaster, 1892, 77

labor unions. *See* unions
Ladies Industrial Club, Boley, Okla., 133, 135, 138
land allotment (Native lands). *See* allotment of Native lands
Langston, Okla., 121. *See also* Langston University
Langston University, 146, 149, 158, 159, 163, 168, 254; law school, 158–59, 160
Largent, Steve, 271
Lawrence, Bluie Adair. *See* Adair, Bluie
Lawson, Eldon, 190, 192
lawsuits: Peltier Stapleton, 230–31; Sipuel Fisher, 152–61
Lawton, Okla., 178–80, 215
League of Women Voters, 66, 230, 234
lesbian activism, 204–5, 246–61
LGBTQ+ student groups and services, 253, 258n1
Lincoln, Abraham, 139
Lindsey, Ben, 78
Lindsey, Lee W., 15, 18, 19, 24
Lindsey, Lilah Denton, 8, 11–31, *14*, *26*
Lowell, Elizabeth Putnam, 67
lunch counter sit-ins, 122, 166, 171, 173, 176, 186
Luper, Calvin, 168, 186

Luper, Clara Mae Shepard, 122, 166–82, *170*, 186, 187–88, 197, 247; *Behold the Walls*, 171, 197; *Brother President*, 172
Luper, Marilyn. *See* Hildreth, Marilyn Luper
lynching, 134, 137, 138, 145, 148

Mallory, Mattie. *See* Morgan, Maranda ("Mattie") Mallory
Mankiller, Wilma, 242, 279–80
March on Washington, 1963, 187–88, *189*
Marshall, Thurgood, 146, 149, 150, 151, 153, 154–55, 158, 160
maternalism, 278; and Robertson, 54–55, 57–58, 61, 63, 68, 69, 70, 278–79; of Fallin, 205, 267, 274, 278–79; and Harris, 205, 278
Maternity and Infancy Act. *See* Sheppard-Towner Maternity and Infancy Act
McBride, J. B., 48
McCain, John, 271
McClelland, Pink, 105
McKellop, Albert Pike, 17
McKellop, Susan. *See* Denton, Susan McKellop
McLaurin, George, 161
McNair, Cora, *104*
mental illness diagnoses for civil rights activists, 183, 186, 190–99
mentally ill people, advocacy for, 89–90
Merrill, Maurice, 153
Merriman, Carol Payne, 102
Mihesuah, Devon A., 100, 102–3
Mills, Rosalie, 105–6
miners and mining, 77
Minerva Boarding School for Girls, 59
Morgan, John, 48
Morgan, Maranda "Mattie" Mallory (1865–1938), 8, 32–52
Morgan, Mattie, 236

Murray, Donald, 149
Murray, William H. "Alfalfa Bill," 76, 84, 86, 91–93
Muscogee (Creek) Nation, 17, 56–60; African Creeks, 125, 130
Muscogee (Creek) women, 8, 11–31
music, women's. *See* women's music
Muskogee, Okla.: Alice Robertson, 60–64; Soldiers' Memorial Hospital, 68
Musslewhite, Lynn R., 76, 82, 94
Mvskoke (Creek) women. *See* Muskogee (Creek) women

NAACP. *See* National Association for the Advancement of Colored People (NAACP)
Nabokov, Peter, 111
Nagle, Patrick, 78, 80
Nanye'hi (Nancy Ward), 108
National American Woman Suffrage Association, 85
National Association for the Advancement of Colored People (NAACP), 122, 127, 135, 137–39; Chickasha, Okla., 146, 148, 154; Gilchrist, 186, 187–88, *189*, 192, 197; Phillips University, 159; Porter, 195; Sipuel, 146, 149, 151, 153–56, 159–61; Youth Council, 166–73, 175–80, 186, 187–88, *189*, 197
National Governors' Conference, 1981, 239
National Organization for Women (NOW), 240, 246, 250, 252
National Women's Political Caucus, 239, 241, 243, 248, 250
National Women's Relief Corps, 24–25
Native American Graves Protection and Repatriation Act (NAGPRA), 217
Native Americans: assimilation, 17, 22, 57–59, 70, 111, 209–11, 219,

220, 224; Barbara Posey on, 169; "disappearing," 209, 210–11, 220; federal policy, 22, 25, 60, 99, 109, 208–11, 217; forced removals, 55, 56; Kate Barnard and, 81, 93–94, 95; LaDonna Harris, 203–4, 207–27, *212*; land allotment, 22, 99, 109, 110, 111, 130, 213; Lilah Denton Lindsey, 8, 11–31, *14*, *26*; orphans, 93–94, 95; Peltier Stapleton and, 231; "termination," 209, 210, 221; Two Spirit Group, 257. *See also* Americans for Indian Opportunity (AIO); Bureau of Indian Affairs; "Five Tribes"; Oklahomans for Indian Opportunity (OIO); Osage people

Neese, Terry, 269

Nelson, Laura and L. D., 134

Newalla, Okla., 76

New Right, 229, 235, 236, 238, 242, 263

Nigh, George, 234, 239, 252

Nineteenth Amendment, 54, 61, 64, 130, 232, 235

Norman, Okla.: ERA Countdown Campaign, 240; Harris, 215; Oklahoma Sanitarium, 89–91; as sundown town, 152, 161; Women's Resource Center, 257. *See also* Central State (Griffin Memorial) Hospital; University of Oklahoma

Nuyaka Mission, 58–59

O'Donald, Kate, 105

Office of Economic Opportunity (OEO), 218–19, 220

OIO. *See* Oklahomans for Indian Opportunity (OIO)

Okemah Daily Leader, 139

OK-ERA, 234, 237, 238

Oklahoma Association Opposed to Woman Suffrage, 53, 62

Oklahoma Baptist University (OBU), 230–31, 264

Oklahoma City: Anna Maude Cafeteria, 169, *198*; Baptist Hospital, 184–85; Barnard, 76–77; *Black Dispatch*, 146; boycotts, 176–77; Calvary Baptist Church, 185; Christensen, 271; Commercial Club, 46; desegregation, 122, 163, 166, 169, 173–74; E. Melvin Porter, 195; ERA Countdown Campaign, 240, 252; Fallin, 264–65; Gilchrist, 184–85; Herland Sister Resources, 204–5, 246–61; John A. Brown store, 176l; Katz Drug Store, 122, 166, 172, 173, 186; Luper, 167, 168–79; Mallory, 32–40, 42–48, *49*, 50; Mick Cornett, 271; Northwest Classen High, 168–69; Peltier Stapleton, 242–43; Roscoe Dunjee High, 172; Ruth Meyers store, 237; sanitation workers, 174–77; Wedgewood Amusement Park, 187; Women's Educational Equity Act, 231. *See also Daily Oklahoman*

Oklahoma Constitution, 22, 25, 82–83, 86, 87, 131

Oklahoma Constitutional Convention, 1906, 8, 25, 76, 81–85, 91

Oklahoma County Fair, 1898, 36

Oklahoma Department of Charities and Corrections, 84, 87–95

Oklahoma Federation of Labor, 92

Oklahoma Federation of Women's Clubs, 82

Oklahoma legislature: Barnard and, 84, 89, 90, 91–92, 94, 95; E. Melvin Porter, 195; ERA, 232, 238, 241, 252; Fallin, 262, 265–69, 270, 273; Fred Harris, 215; LGBTQ+ people and, 253; Peltier Stapleton, 232, 242–43; Reagan address, 252; Sipuel Fisher and, 161; women's representation, 268, 276n31

Oklahoman. See *Daily Oklahoman*

Oklahomans for Indian Opportunity (OIO), 207, 208–9, 211, 215–21, 223, 225
Oklahoma Orphanage, 32, 33, 39–48, 50
Oklahoma Sanitarium, 89–91
Oklahoma Socialist Party. *See* Socialist Party of Oklahoma
Oklahoma statehood, 22, 23, 81, 131, 134
Oklahoma State Hospital. *See* Central State (Griffin Memorial) Hospital
Oklahoma State Penitentiary, 89
Oklahoma State University, 264, 265
Oklahoma Supreme Court, 153, 154, 157–58, 161, 253, 257
Oklahoma territorial legislature, 76
Oklahoma Universal Human Rights Alliance, 243
Oklahoma Women's Political Caucus (OKWPC), 204, 234, 237, 238, 241
Okmulgee, Okla., 18, 19, 59
OK STOP ERA, 235, 236
Oldland, Robert, 174–76
Olivia Records, 251
orphanages, 32, 33, 34, 39–48, 50
orphans, Native American, 93–94, 95
Osage people, 106, 107
Owen, Narcissa Chisholm, 113
Owen, Robert Latham, Jr., 113

Page, J. F., 48
Palin, Sarah, 268
Park Hill, Okla., 103
Pascoe, Peggy, 77
Peltier Stapleton, Wanda Jo, 204, 228–45, 233, 242
penitentiaries. *See* prisons
Perryman, Alice, 20
Pevehouse, Edna, 199n12
Phelps, Edna Mae, 234
Phillips University, 159
Porter, E. Melvin, 176, 178, 179, 187, 195–96, 197

Porter, Mabel, 46
Porter, Pleasant, 15, 18, 57
Posey, Alma. *See* Washington, Alma Posey
Posey, Barbara. *See* Jones, Barbara Posey
poverty, activism against. *See* antipoverty activism
Pratt, Richard Henry, 58
Presbyterian Board of Foreign Missions, 18
Presbyterian Board of Home Missions, 59
prisons, 88–91, 238
Provident Association of Oklahoma City. *See* United Provident Association of Oklahoma City
psychiatric institutionalization, involuntary. *See* institutionalization, involuntary
public libraries, Black-established, 133, 138
Putnam, I. M., 46, 47

racial segregation and desegregation, 134, 139, 146, 148–61, 163; Lawton, Okla., 178–80; Oklahoma City, 166–73; Tulsa, 177–78. *See also* sundown towns
Rahe, Paul, 195–96
Reagan, Ronald, 234, 252, 263, 265
Red Scare, 67
rematriation, 213, 217–18, 224, 225, 226
Republican Party, 82, 84, 86; Robertson, 53, 54, 55, 61–70; ERA and, 232, 234; Fallin, 263, 265–74
Rhea, John, 112
Robertson, Alice Mary, 8, 53–74, 65, 271, 278–79
Robertson, Ann Eliza Worcester, 13, 15, 18, 55–56, 58
Robertson, Clara, 176
Robertson, William, 13, 18, 55–56, 58

Roosevelt, Theodore, 59, 60
Ross, Ioney, 111
Ross, John, 110
Ross, Mary Golda, 113
Ross, Nellie, 99–100
Rymph, Catherine E., 263

Sawokla Cafeteria, Muscogee, Okla., 61, 62
Sawyer, G. W., 48
Schlafly, Phyllis, 235, 239
Schmidt, Kathy, 197–98
Schnall, Marianne, *What Will It Take to Make a Woman President?* 266–67
schooling, compulsory. *See* compulsory education
Scoggins, Shirley Williams, 177
Sequoyah Historical Society, 99, 109
Shadid, Ernest G., 196
Shaw, Laura, 34, 42–43
Shawnee, Okla., 82, 264, 269
Shepard, Clara. *See* Luper, Clara Mae Shepard
Shepard, Ezell, 167
Sheppard-Towner Maternity and Infancy Act, 66, 67–68
Simpson, Audra, 210
Simpson, Leanne Betasamosake, 106
Sipuel, Lemuel, 146
Sipuel, Martha Bell, 148
Sipuel, Travis B., 148, 153
Sipuel Fisher, Ada Lois, 122, 145–65, *147*, *162*, 203
Sisemore, Janice J., 102
sit-ins, lunch counter. *See* lunch counter sit-ins
Smeal, Eleanor, 240, 252
Socialist Party of Oklahoma, 2, 78, 85, 96
Spradling, Okla., 104
Stanislaus, Dorothy, 234
Stapleton, Wanda Jo Peltier. *See* Peltier Stapleton, Wanda Jo
Stark, Donna Hopper, 212

State Hospital for the Insane. *See* Central State (Griffin Memorial) Hospital
Steinem, Gloria, 242, 252
stereotypes: Native people, 16, 21; women, 50, 64, 229, 266
Stolper, J. H., 93
STOP ERA (Oklahoma). *See* OK STOP ERA
Storm, W. W., 45–46
Strawberry Moon, Battle of. *See* Claremore Mound Massacre
strikes: Oklahoma City sanitation workers, 175–77
Students for a Democratic Society (SDS), 186
Sturgis, Susanna, 255
suffrage, Black men's. *See* disenfranchisement of Black men
suffrage, women's. *See* women's suffrage
sundown towns, 148, 152, 161
Supreme Court of Oklahoma. *See* Oklahoma Supreme Court
Supreme Court, US. *See* US Supreme Court
Synodical Female College, Fulton, Mo., 15

Tabbytite, John, 213
Tabbytite, Wick-kie, *212*, 213, 214
Tahlequah, Okla., 9, 103, 112
Tatge, Clara, 192–93, *194–95*
Taylor, A. D., 176
Taylor, California Minnie, 122, 125–44
Taylor, Hilliard, 125–26, 127–28, 133
Taylor, Nell, *104*
Tecumseh, Okla., 264
temperance movement, 16–17, 21–23, 81–82. *See also* Woman's Christian Temperance Union (WCTU)
Temple, Earl, 169
Theus, Harold, 190
Thompson, Eugenia, *104*

Trinity University, 107
Tullahassee Manual Labor School, 12–13, 18, 55
Tullahassee Mission, 55, 56, 58. *See also* Tullahassee Manual Labor School
Tulsa, Okla.: Amos Hall, 152; Borden's Cafeteria, 177–78; desegregation, 177–78; ERA Countdown Campaign, 240, 241; Kendall College (University of Tulsa), 59; Lindsey, 19–26; Race Massacre (1921), 122, 145, 148, 177; Sipuel family, 148; Tulsa Indian Women's Club, 109, 114
Turner, Dale, 210
Turner, David J., 132, 133–34
Turner, Minnie, 132, 133, 134
Tuttle, Okla., 179
Twin Territories Suffrage Association, 82
Tyrell, Ian, 30n49

unions, 77, 92–93. *See also* Farmers' Union
United Provident Association of Oklahoma City, 77
University of Central Oklahoma, 247–48, 258n1, 259n4
University of Oklahoma: Fred Harris, 215; Gay Activists Alliance, 253; gay film fest, 254; Junetta Davis, 234; Luper, 168; Peltier Stapleton, 230, 231; Sipuel and desegregation lawsuit, 146, 149–61, 163; Southwest Center for Human Relations Studies, 218; Women's Studies Program, 253
University of Oklahoma Press, 112
University of Tulsa, 59
US Congress: and Alice Robertson, 61–70, *65*; and Mary Fallin, 262, 271, 274
US Supreme Court, 153, 155–57, 159–60, 161, 234

Vogt, Jana, 243n2
voting rights of Black American men, 134, 135
voting rights of women. *See* women's suffrage

Walsh, Joseph, *65*
Ward, Nancy. *See* Nanye'hi (Nancy Ward)
Wardell, Morris, 112
Warr Acres, Okla., 185–86, 188–89
Washington, Alma Posey, 170
Washington, George, 139
WCTU. *See* Woman's Christian Temperance Union (WCTU)
Wealaka Mission School, 18
Weaver, Jace, 223
Welfare League of Oklahoma, 32
Wesley, John, 35, 43
West, James, 188, 192, 193
Wharton, Joe, 175
White Citizens' Councils, 177
white civil rights activists, 183–201
white supremacy, 168, 169, 170, 171, 172, 173, 193; women's suffrage and, 25–26
Williams, Ben, 152, 153
Williams, Cecil L., 174
Williams, Lucy Ward, 107, 108, 109
Williams, Penny, 237
Williams, R. L., 25
Williamson, Mac, 153
Wilson, Ann Florence, 103–4, *104*, 105, 109
Wilson, William, 229, 230
womanist organizations, 204–5, 246–61
Woman's Christian Temperance Union (WCTU), 17, 21–23, 26, 30n49, 81–82, 85
women's bookstores, 248–51
Women's Civic League of Tulsa, 24
women's clubs and clubwomen, 24, 55, 66, 67, 82; Boley, Okla., 129, 130, 133, 135, 137; Eaton, 109, 110–11, 114

Women's Educational Equity Act, 231
Women's Home Missionary Society, 129, 137
Women's International Union Label League, 83–84
women's music, 251, 257
women's rights amendment (proposed). *See* Equal Rights Amendment (ERA) (proposed)
women's spaces, 255–56
women's suffrage, 25–27, 55, 76, 80–81, 85, 87–88, 113, 232; anti-suffragism, 62–63, 80, 85; Nineteenth Amendment, 54, 70, 100, 130
Woodrow, O. C., 47

Woodworth, Julia, 82
Worcester, Ann Eliza. *See* Robertson, Ann Eliza Worcester
Worcester, Samuel, 13, 55
World War I, 2, 24–25, 61, 134
World War Adjusted Compensation Act. *See* Bonus Bill (1924)
Wright, Herbert, 172
Wright, Muriel, 106

York, Grady, 112
York, Martha "Mattie" Pauline Eaton, 108
Young Women's Christian Association (YWCA), 109, 152

www.ingramcontent.com/pod-product-compliance
Lightning Source LLC
Chambersburg PA
CBHW022104150426
43195CB00008B/268